Postconflict Development

Postconflict Development

Meeting New Challenges

edited by
Gerd Junne
Willemijn Verkoren

LYNNE
RIENNER
PUBLISHERS

BOULDER
LONDON

Published in the United States of America in 2005 by
Lynne Rienner Publishers, Inc.
1800 30th Street, Boulder, Colorado 80301
www.rienner.com

and in the United Kingdom by
Lynne Rienner Publishers, Inc.
3 Henrietta Street, Covent Garden, London WC2E 8LU

Library of Congress Cataloging-in-Publication Data
Postconflict development : meeting new challenges / Gerd Junne,
Willemijn Verkoren, editors.
     p.   cm.
  Includes bibliographical references and index.
  ISBN 1-58826-327-4 (hardcover : alk. paper) — ISBN 1-58826-303-7
(pbk. : alk. paper) 1. War relief. 2. Postwar reconstruction.
3. Peace-building. 4. Economic assistance. 5. Economic development.
I. Junne, Gerd. II. Verkoren, Willemijn.
  HV639.P66 2004
  338.9—dc22

                                       2004014977

British Cataloguing in Publication Data
A Cataloguing in Publication record for this book
is available from the British Library.

Printed and bound in the United States of America

5 4 3 2 1

Contents

Editors' Note

We invite readers to respond to the content of this book on the website www.netuni.nl/postconflict, which offers a short summary of each chapter, additional information about the authors, and details of the project research agenda. We hope that the bulletin-board format of the site will encourage postings of alternative hypotheses, references to potentially useful literature, and suggestions for further research, as well as reactions to specific material within the book.

The Challenges of Postconflict Development

Gerd Junne
Willemijn Verkoren

This book deals with the many countries that have gone through a period of violent civil strife. Its focus is on the period immediately following such unrest. The term "postconflict development" can be misleading in this context. There are few truly postconflict situations. Conflicts become more or less violent, more or less manifest or latent, but they seldom stop altogether. "Postconflict" in this book is shorthand for conflict situations, in which open warfare has come to an end. Such situations remain tense for years or decades and can easily relapse into large-scale violence. In 44 percent of all postconflict situations, war resumes in the first five years after the violence has stopped (World Bank 2004, 8), and about 50 percent of postconflict countries revert back to war in the first decade of peace (Collier et al. 2003, 7). Recent violent conflict, therefore, is the best predictor of future large-scale violence.

One of the crucial determinants of whether the shooting and looting will start again may be the degree of economic and social development that has been achieved in the meantime and the fair distribution of its fruits to different groups of the population. The World Bank notes that "countries affected by conflict face a two-way relationship between conflict and poverty—pervasive poverty makes societies more vulnerable to violent conflict, while conflict itself creates more poverty" (World Bank 2004, 14).

Economic development gives different groups something to work on together. Orientation may change from looking at the past to focusing on the future. An interesting job is not only an alternative to fighting but could also give rise to a new professional identity. If people see another perspective than continuous fighting, they may be more resistant to renewing conflict. One could argue that there will be fewer fighters to pick up their arms as well as stronger efforts to stop those who will.

There may be cases, however, when some economic development could be the precondition for the resumption of fighting. If the decline of military activity is due mainly to the exhaustion of the conflicting parties and a lack of means to continue, then development may take these constraints away, and with a culture of conflict unabated, violent conflict may resume. Therefore, it is not just economic growth that is important but a specific economic development that addresses the grievances of different groups, allows compromise between contending factions, and offers sufficiently attractive alternatives to the main opponents.

Economic development itself is certainly no guarantee against violent conflict. But a lack of development can be a guarantee for the resumption of violence. If a large number of young males remain unemployed, if conflicts about scarce resources remain intense, if there is no perspective for some way out of the present misery and a normal life, then chances are high that conflicts will become violent again.

The label "postconflict development" may have originally been inspired by the wish to return to normal development strategies after the interruption of development by civil wars. The World Bank, particularly, has been accused of wanting to apply the usual development strategies (market orientation, liberalization, privatization, etc.) too quickly after violent conflicts (cf. Moore 2000), though its creation of a "Post-Conflict Unit" in 1997 demonstrated the acknowledgment that countries emerging out of such a situation may need a special approach.[1] In line with international initiatives to use development assistance for conflict prevention, the World Bank in 2001 broadened its approach from one focusing on rebuilding infrastructure to one that "seeks to understand the root causes of conflict, to integrate a sensitivity to conflict in Bank activities and to promote assistance that minimizes the potential causes of conflict" (World Bank 2004, 8). In accordance with this, the Post-Conflict Unit changed its name to "Conflict Prevention and Reconstruction Unit."

Despite recognition by the World Bank (and others)[2] that development strategies may have to differ in postconflict situations, "there is no consensus, let alone best practices, on how to integrate the conflict nexus or the key elements of conflict-affected PRSP [Poverty Reduction Strategy Paper] processes" (World Bank 2004, 14).

However, the number of developing countries that have recently been the scene of civil strife is such that postconflict development has become the norm rather than the exception. The pursuance of traditional development strategies may have even contributed to the increase rather than prevention of violent conflicts. With a large share in state income in the poorest countries, development aid given to governments can incite opposition groups to fight for their share. "Structural adjustment" reduces the capacity of states to respond to the needs of their population, increases general dissatisfaction with the government, and intensifies the struggle for the remaining sources of income.

Having explained what is meant by "postconflict," we will complete this section by adding a few words about what we mean by "development." More than referring simply to economic growth, development is about improving the standard of living for all people in poor countries. As such, development includes improvements in areas as diverse as health, environment, education, and political participation. The United Nations Development Program's (UNDP's) Human Development Index represents a good tool to measure progress in this respect.

Peace Versus Development in Postconflict Situations

Violent conflicts at the end of the twentieth century devastated many developing countries and thwarted development efforts in which vast amounts of human energy and money were invested. Many countries are actually worse off than they had been when they became independent. With every violent conflict, a society loses part of its capacity to handle future conflicts in a peaceful way (Miall 2001, 15).

Organizations involved in conflict resolution and peacebuilding, therefore, argue for a shift in emphasis (and financial means) from development projects to peacebuilding and conflict prevention. These organizations contend that a relatively small effort to avoid violent conflict could save large investments in development and prevent enormous expenditures for peacemaking, peacekeeping, and the alleviation of humanitarian problems that result from large-scale violent conflict. To some extent, this competition for means pits development organizations and peace builders against each other.

A close look reveals that the cleavage is not just between these two groups but rather between three groups: organizations involved in conflict prevention and resolution, organizations that offer humanitarian help in emergency situations, and organizations concentrating on long-term capacity development and institution building. They may have different priorities, different experience, and their involvement implies specific risks (see Table 1.1).

Table 1.1   Differences Between Conflict Resolution, Humanitarian, and Development Agencies

	Organizations' Focus		
	Peacebuilding	Emergency Help	Long-term Development
Example	Search for Common Ground	Médecins Sans Frontières	Oxfam
Priorities	End and prevent violence; stimulate better understanding between different groups of the population	Satisfy basic human needs (water, food, shelter, health)	Create structures that promote long-term sustainable growth and social stability
Experience	Mediation, dialogue, mass communication, and education	Technical, medical, logistical, and organizational	Agricultural, economic, and technical; institution building
Blind spots	Economic underpinnings of reconciliation processes; immediate needs of victims	Long-term effect of humanitarian aid on future government activity and legitimacy	Security risks to development projects; possible contribution of aid to conflict dynamics
Risks	Locks parties into conflicting identities and can perpetuate cleavages	Undermines build-up of government activities and institution building	Can create contended assets in future conflicts

Recognition of the need to reconcile the fields of development and peacebuilding is growing. In a report written for the UNDP, for example, Bernard Wood concludes that "development cooperation itself needs to apply the lessons of experience, and improve its own flexibility and practices to maximise its contributions . . . in helping build peace and prevent violent conflict" (Wood 2001, 10). From a more theoretical perspective, Mark Duffield notes that "development concerns have become increasingly important in relation to how security is understood." The growing use of the concept of "human security" by UN and other international planners also testifies to this. Duffield even goes so far as to say that it is "now generally accepted that international organisations should be aware of conflict and, where possible, gear their work towards conflict resolution and helping to rebuild war-torn societies in a way that will avert future violence" (Duffield 2001, 1).[3] Little has been written, however, about how that should be done. Duffield writes, "[T]he new development-security terrain remains underresearched and its study has yet to establish its own conceptual language" (Duffield 2001, 9). This book aims to contribute to that understanding by identifying *how* international organizations, and other actors designing and implementing development strategies in postconflict settings, should go about doing this.

Different organizations have had different reasons to give relatively little attention to the problem of postconflict development. Organizations that specialize in conflict prevention and conflict resolution have seen their hopes shattered by war and may find it too early to work with a highly traumatized population. Humanitarian organizations rush in but are neither interested in the causes of the conflict nor in long-term development. Development organizations see these situations as an exception and may find the situation too unstable to resume their work.

Scholars (and politicians) interested in conflict transformation and conflict resolution often pay attention to a conflict as long as it is "hot." Once the violent phase is over and the situation starts to stabilize, there are always enough other hotspots on earth to shift attention to those areas deemed more in need. Those who stay behind, then, suddenly find that their funds dry up and that their work cannot be continued.

Organizations concentrating on emergency relief are structurally pressed for time. Dealing with emergencies, they cannot devote too much attention either to the root causes of conflict nor to the long-term development perspectives of the region. The root causes often are of little concern to them. In most cases, they are contested anyway, and the organizations want to stay as impartial as possible in order to maintain access to the victims of violent conflicts. They are neither equipped nor willing to handle long-term development issues.

Scholars specializing in development questions also tend to neglect the topic. Development theory itself has been questioned from all sides. It is already difficult enough to devise development strategies for a "normal" country, let alone for a country torn apart by civil conflicts. In such a situation, some of the established knowledge about development processes (e.g., spend less money on military and police and liberalize capital flows) seems less applicable. Development economists often do not have much feeling for politics, although the recent "aid effectiveness debate" has prompted development scholars and practitioners to look more closely at the role of political and legal structures in stimulating or inhibiting development. The growing attention for the role of the state in development is also related to the increasingly pressing issues of postconflict development, which obviously is burdened with heavy political problems.[4] Aid agencies "began to seek broader strategies that would strengthen citizens' capacities and reduce their vulnerability so that they would be more resilient against adverse shocks: The trick of aid delivery in these cases is to secure more stable livelihoods and—ultimately—more stable polities" (Munro 2001, 8–9). Still, development economists' unease with political issues remains, and many continue to avoid a thorough analysis of conflict altogether.

The different types of organizations form part of different "epistemic communities," which all center on their own discourses, with relatively little overlap and discussions between these different groups. With this book, we should like to make a contribution to the integration of these three fields. We are convinced that the activities of the three groups do not just complement each other, but that—in order to do their own work properly—they will have to integrate each others' perspectives into their own work and act accordingly.

Conflict resolution and peacebuilding efforts can only be fruitful in the long run if they consist of activities involving all other kinds of policy development as well as permeate all development projects and policy issues. Emergency help should contribute to peacebuilding instead of prolonging conflicts, and it should not stand in the way of long-term development efforts. And future-oriented development planning has to take the realities of a conflict-torn society into account and conceive development strategies that help to overcome existing cleavages rather than perpetuate or aggravate them.

Existing development strategies and plans, therefore, have to be reevaluated. The reasons that have led to large-scale violence have to be analyzed and taken into account in order to avoid having the development efforts again thwarted by large-scale conflicts.

Thus, the primordial task of postconflict development is not just rebuilding or reconstruction, because this may lead to the rebuilding of the very structures that have given rise to the devastating conflicts (see Chapter 17 in this volume). What the situation demands is another type of development that addresses these structures and helps to avoid violent conflict. The immediate aftermath of such conflicts can create a political window of opportunity in which all parties agree that basic structures of society have to be changed to avoid a repetition of disastrous destruction. A new social contract may have to be forged.

Conflict-Conscious Development

Development efforts thus have to take the conflicts explicitly into account. Planners not only have to acknowledge the existence of conflicts, they must address the very causes of conflicts in order to avoid aggravating them. Much of development thinking has been influenced by the World Bank, which often pursued a development strategy that knew little variation from country to country. But development strategies for conflict-torn societies do have to differ, depending on the causes of conflict.

One of the basic assumptions of this book is that the challenges of postconflict development vary with the causes of conflict. Four clusters of causes can be distinguished, depending on the level of social organization at which the root causes are situated: external/international, characteristics of the state, characteristics of society, or individual orientations.

1. *External/international:* The root causes may be found outside the country in question. The remnants of colonial rule may have left social cleavages that are not yet overcome. Different groups of the population may be set up against each other by external intervention. Or social frictions may be caused by the process of globalization, which exposes the whole fabric of society to harsher external competition, thereby aggravating the internal competition for resources.

2. *Characteristics of the state:* The state may be too strong or too weak. A weak state cannot protect its citizens, who may then turn to subnational organizations (militia, gangs, etc.) for protection. Or the state can be oppressive, giving rise to resistance and separatist movements. If the state is a main (or even the only) source of income (e.g., from mineral resources or from development aid), then conflict about access to these resources can be expected.

3. *Characteristics of society:* Specific characteristics of society can make conflicts more probable. Great economic inequalities lead to class struggle. Ethnic cleavages are a fertile feeding ground for rival nationalisms. Or the prominent forms of economic activity may lead to an overuse of natural resources (land, water) that could cause conflicts about the ever scarcer means to earn a living. However, an abundance of natural resources may also lead to conflict (Renner 2002; Smillie 2002).

4. *Individual orientations:* The root causes could also, finally, be situated in the heads of people. They may be divided by different political ideologies, as was the case during the Cold War. They may adhere to different religions. Or they may speak different languages, which may also imply different cultures, images, customs, and worldviews.

The different root causes cannot always be clearly distinguished. They normally interact. Colonial rule may have given rise to a weak state, and the weak state in turn cannot resist the forces of globalization. International competition can increase tensions between different ethnicities, which often overlap with class affiliation and language spoken. Nevertheless, different conflicts have different dominant causes that may pose different challenges for postconflict development.

Let us illustrate this idea on the basis of the relatively technical task of rebuilding infrastructure after the destruction of roads, railways, bridges, air fields, electricity production and distribution, water installations, and the like. Rebuilding may not be a good idea altogether. All too often, the infrastructure was inherited from the colonial period, when it mainly gave access to raw materials and facilitated their transport to the nearest harbor. This has led in many countries to a kind of feudal structure of roads and railroads: They connect the periphery to the capital but do not connect the different parts of the country to one another. If the different parts of the country were to acquire an interest in each others' well-being, they should get better connected to deepen the internal division of labor.

If the state obtains large funds to build a new infrastructure but is itself firmly in the hands of a specific group, then this group can enrich itself by putting an infrastructure in place that primarily serves its own needs—by passing on important orders to affiliated construction companies or by receiving large bribes from foreign companies that get the orders. Conflicts may result also from investment patterns of former governments that may have given advantages to regions in which their own constituency is situated while disadvantaging others. This can spur resistance or separatist movements. The process of rebuilding can fuel these rivalries anew. Even a fair distribution of infrastructure projects, which explicitly takes the existing cleavages into account, can perpetuate these cleavages, because it strengthens the thinking in terms of conflicting political constituencies, rather than in terms of optimal public services.

Construction projects for infrastructure provide an important source of employment not only for the duration of construction. The sites themselves determine very much the distribution of future life chances for different groups of the population. Decisions about construction sites are, therefore, even less than in other cases the result of neutral, technical evaluation.

There is an additional aspect that has to be taken into account. In a society torn apart by serious conflicts, infrastructure projects have to be located and structured in such a way that they do not give one party a strategic advantage over another, such as the opportunity to cut off water or electricity or to deny access to a harbor. The location of infrastructure projects can have an immediate impact on the power structure in a country. Sometimes, a technically suboptimal solution may have to be chosen so that one group does not get an unfair advantage over another.

Large parts of infrastructure development also have an intrinsically political character: Better roads are not merely a precondition for access to markets. They can also have a predominantly military character and lay open the vast hinterland. They provide opportunities for a quick relocation of troops and thus give central government an advantage, while reducing the opportunity for guerrilla movements to hide in regions that are difficult to access.

To avoid the politicization of decisions about the future infrastructure, it may be tempting for state authorities and international organizations to opt for the privatization of parts of the infrastructure (electricity, water), which—at least for a while—used to correspond to the preference of many international donors anyway. This, however, is more problematic, too, in a conflict-ridden society than elsewhere (see Chapter 11 by Bertine Kamphuis). The business community may be organized along ethnic lines, and increased prices for privatized services may intensify existing social cleavages.

Another dilemma that has less to do with the different root causes of conflict is the tension between the objectives of peace and development. To achieve peace and a quick normalization of daily life, fast (re)construction of infrastructure can be desirable, if necessary by foreign firms. From a development point of view, it would be more desirable to put local constructors to work that make more use of local manpower and create more local employment. But construction may take longer, and sometimes quality criteria may not be met. From the political view, much public discussion may be desirable. Especially in a community that is deeply divided, this would take much time before results are reached and stands in the way of short-term reconstruction and economic growth.

Culture in Postconflict Development

Most of the chapters in this book deal with economic and political structures and developments. They concentrate on an increase in material welfare; on personal security from military threats, criminal acts, and human rights violations; and on equal participation in political decisionmaking. Some critics have mentioned that such an approach misses the crucial point—that it looks at development too much through a Western lens in which welfare ranks quite high on the list of priorities. If culture does not receive enough attention, it will not be possible to understand how formal political structures and institutions work.[5]

Other cultures have different priorities. David Pinto (2000b, 32) distinguishes two different pyramids of needs (see Figure 1.1) in which "self-fulfillment" stands at the top of a Western pyramid and "honor" at the top of an alternative pyramid that is more representative for societies in which the group plays a central role.

Conflicting parties may not necessarily be interested in more income and welfare. Any improvements in living standards will remain overshadowed by the immense differences if compared to Western countries, which still keeps them in a kind of underdog position. They want, foremost, to uphold their honor.[6] They want to be recognized as equals. They want to overcome the humiliation that they have experienced at the hands of their adversary, at the hands of former colonial powers, or as a result of their inferior position in the international division of labor and world politics. Recognition is at the top of their agenda. This obviously poses quite different problems and challenges for postconflict development. Development itself may have to be defined in different terms.

In spite of the importance of these aspects, we have not included any contribution on cultural facets of postconflict development in this volume. There are at least three reasons for that, among them:

Figure 1.1   Different Priorities

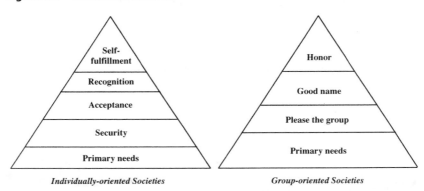

Individually-oriented Societies   Group-oriented Societies

Source: David Pinto, *Een nieuw perspectief. Herziening van beleid, onderwijs, communicatie, maslowpiramide dringend nodig* (Amsterdam: Vossiuspers AUP, 2000b), 32.

1. Culture is defined as those characteristics that only change slowly. While cultural change is needed, this obviously is a kind of long-term development, difficult to achieve in a few years after large-scale violence stopped. It also usually changes as a result of other developments, not through conscious design. Cultural changes follow other changes (e.g., when a democratic system brings satisfactory results, democratic culture may grow).

2. Culture is specific to a region or population. Because it is specific, it is difficult to generalize how culture affects the prospects of postconflict development.

3. "Culture" itself is an umbrella term for quite different phenomena, ranging from religion to language to customs and value systems. It is linked to—and may change as a result of—changes in everything from the mode of production (nomadic versus sedentary) to the degree of urbanization and the geographical relationship to the rest of the world (urban versus rural, capital versus province, cosmopolitan versus parochial) to work ethics (Calvinist versus Catholic) and value systems (masculine versus feminine).

These issues are complex enough to warrant another volume or series of volumes.

A Holistic View of Postconflict Development

It sounds perhaps strange to explain first why an important factor has been left out and then formulate claims with regard to a holistic view on postconflict development. What we aim at is to bring the different issues analyzed together. Individual people/professionals/civil servants or staffs of nongovernmental organizations (NGOs) will often have to deal with one specific sector or institution. That is why this volume follows a sectoral approach. But at the same time, we are, of course, aware that the development in the different sectors is highly dependent on what happens in the other sectors touched upon. Therefore, all chapter authors have been encouraged to point out as explicitly as possible the links between their issue or sector and the societal context. In addition, we have added three chapters that try to bring the different aspects together in a country study on postconflict development. El Salvador seems to be an example of a success story, relatively speaking, whereas Cambodia is not. Mozambique, often praised for its success, might be somewhere in between. However, a closer analysis may reveal that it is quite problematic (see Chapter 15 by Joseph Hanlon).

Structure of the Book

At the very basis of postconflict development is the security dilemma. Only if security can be guaranteed to some degree can any kind of development take off. Nobody will invest in the future without a minimum of stability. Security is a central issue in any postconflict situation, affecting the prospects for development and peacebuilding. In Chapter 2, Dirk Salomons notes that the successful disarmament, demobilization, and reintegration (DDR) of former combatants represent "the touchstone, the moment of truth" for any peacebuilding process. Salomons's chapter addresses the conditions that support or threaten the successful reintegration of former combatants into society. It describes the component elements of such a process and provides illustrations of activities that have been effective, as well as of initiatives that have failed. The "seductive tenacity of war economies" constitutes an important barrier to the success of DDR and of postconflict development as a whole, and no strategy of DDR can succeed without taking this aspect into account. What, then, can the international community do to help to shape a secure environment after conflict by supporting DDR? The basic formula, writes Salomons, is simple: Where strong political will, effective military enforcement capacity, and sufficient economic resources converge, the transition from a war economy to a peaceful society has a fair chance of succeeding.

In Chapter 3, Jose Luis Herrero addresses the (re)building of state institutions in the immediate aftermath of violent conflict, which is a unique undertaking that has little resemblance to standard institution-building efforts or development work. The main differences lie in the order of priorities; in the aftermath of violent conflict, there is one obvious priority: avoiding renewed violence. Introducing a fully democratic system does not guarantee the preservation of peace in a situation such as the one in Kosovo, which was characterized by a collapse of previously existing official administrative structures; a withdrawal of previously existing security and law enforcement structures; and the prevalence of the ethnic, political, and social tensions that originated the conflict. In such a situation, democratization may have to proceed gradually. Thus, as in Kosovo, allocating fixed numbers of parliamentary seats to minority groups may be a useful tool to prevent violence and discrimination during the early stages of institution building and postconflict development. In addition, contrary to what is being done in Afghanistan and Iraq, the UN administration in Kosovo did not grant formal independent authority to local representatives for as long as they were not democratically elected. Because local authorities appointed by a third party lack legitimacy, this intermediary step is a crucial one.

Chapter 4 deals with the development of local institutions in the postconflict phase. There is a general trend toward decentralization and devolution in developing countries as a way to increase good governance. Tanja Hohe illuminates some of the pitfalls of these processes in postconflict countries, drawing lessons from the Community Empowerment and Local Governance Project (CEP) launched in East Timor by the World Bank and the UN. To engage in social engineering exercises seems very tempting in a postconflict scenario. Yet without full knowledge of local dynamics, the empowerment of new leaders will fail as local realities are stronger; traditional leaders and power structures will continue to exist parallel to the new institutions. The same constraint counts for democratization and the promotion of gender equality and raises the question of when and how far to buy into local power structures.

In Chapter 5 Mark Plunkett addresses the issues that arise when attempts are made to restore or create the rule of law in the aftermath of violent conflict. In peace operations the (re)establishment of the rule of law must take priority over, and take place irrespective of, constitutional settlement. The task of a peace operation is to restore the rule of law first and foremost before re-creating the state. This restoration of the rule of law is achieved through the delivery of specific peace operation justice packages using a combination of the enforcement model and the negotiated model. The enforcement model entails legitimate, minimal, and lawfully sanctioned coercion such as arrest, prosecution, detention, and trial by war crimes tribunals and transitional peace operations courts. It also includes public shaming and office disqualification by peace operation criminal justice commissions and resourcing and training local judges, police, prosecutors, defenders, and custodial officers. The negotiated model is an important complementary package of measures that contribute to the public internalization and acceptance of the rule of law, including securing voluntary compliance by negotiating fundamental shifts in population consciousness at the three levels of the elite leadership, functionary, and village level to replace the culture of violence with negotiated management systems. The negotiated model ensures that the establishment of the rule of law is shaped by the desires and needs of the population.

Chapter 6 looks at the seemingly neutral (re)building of infrastructure. In fact, as Richard H. Brown shows, the reconstruction and development of infrastructure after war is not a mere technical task but requires a deep understanding of socioeconomic and physical elements as they relate to the long-term needs of a country and its communities. Planners should be sensitive to the fact that infrastructure can serve to connect as well as divide communities. Wherever conflict has divided communities, the connecting potential of infrastructure should be an integral part of any strategic plan for reconstruction. Interaction with the communities concerned is a prerequisite for a successful rebuilding strategy. The importance of getting it right the first time cannot be over-stated. The (re)establishment of infrastructure, particularly electricity, water, and telecommunications networks, is for the long term; prescribing dividing networks is likely to reinforce political/ethnic divisions for a lengthy time, while establishing connecting networks, delivered with sensitivity, can contribute very positively to long-term political/ethnic harmony.

The role of the news media in contributing to peacebuilding after conflict is discussed in Chapter 7 by Ross Howard. In the past the media have functioned as a weapon for war as well as an instrument of conflict resolution. Particularly in democratizing environments, there is a window of opportunity to help the media to steer the right course. But what does this right course entail? There is a healthy debate over journalistic objectivity versus intent and responsibility in shaping people's perceptions toward understanding and reconciliation. In fact, journalists mediate conflicts whether they intend to or not. Even free media in a democratic environment can exacerbate conflicts: Bad news has a higher news value, and a concentration on such news can have a negative impact on the perception of "the other." But even with no intent beyond doing the job according to accepted standards, the news media can deliver an essential requisite of conflict resolution, which is communication. The media educates, corrects misperceptions, identifies underlying interests, and humanizes the parties to the dispute. It also provides an emotional outlet, enables consensus building, and can offer solutions and build confidence. In the 1990s, the media's peacebuilding potential became integrated into the foreign aid and intervention policies of a number of major donors. The purpose of most of the interventions remains the support of conventional, reliable journalism. However, there is also a new trend to foster media activities that go well beyond conventional journalism, aiming to produce information specifically designed to influence attitudes toward conflict resolution.

In postconflict situations that involve issues directly related to education—such as the recognition of identity, cultural development, community survival, the distribution of resources, and access to political power—usually little attention is paid to educational reform. Wondem Asres Degu makes a plea in Chapter 8 for more attention to education in the postconflict phase. The content of curricula significantly affects attitudes and ideas of communities, contributing either to conflict or to peacebuilding. In addition, seemingly technical decisions, such as in which language to teach, can also affect the fragile peace that has been established. Another issue is that in many cases the education system does not match the demands of the labor market. Degu addresses these and other issues prevalent in the education sector in postconflict situations, drawing mainly on experiences in Ethiopia.

The health system is discussed in Chapter 9 of the book. In postconflict situations, health facilities are often damaged or destroyed, and there is a shortage of health personnel, both because many fled the country during the conflict and because of limited training opportunities. At the same time, the health situation is often alarming. Many have been injured in the war. In refugee camps there are often risks of epidemics. Many people experience mental health problems such as traumas. Building on the East Timorese experience, which in many respects offered the ideal circumstances for a rapid reconstruction of the health system, Vanessa van Schoor discusses the right and wrong ways of dealing with such a situation. How can available funds best be used? Has the establishment of health services helped to move the East Timorese away from future violence?

Environmental concerns, writes Martijn Bijlsma in Chapter 10, should not be left out of postconflict development planning. Not only can a conflict have environmental causes and consequences, which need to be addressed, but the postconflict phase also presents opportunities for incorporating environmental concerns into policy. When addressing environmental issues in a postconflict situation, decisionmakers will have to be highly aware of the remaining conflict potential, as well as the general limitations posed by the situation. Among the specific dilemmas that decisionmakers might be confronted with are the politicization of environmental policy, bias in the selection of beneficiaries, hostility between institutions involved in environmental operations, and a lack of resources. Citing examples from El Salvador and elsewhere, Bijlsma expands on these issues and makes a case for the incorporation of environmental concerns to achieve more sustainable postconflict development.

Central to this book's attempt to combine the development and peacebuilding schools is a conflict-sensitive economic strategy. In Chapter 11, Bertine Kamphuis sketches some of the main concerns that economic policymakers should consider in postconflict contexts. Protracted violent conflicts change the economic structures of national economies profoundly and create a "conflict economy," one not quickly altered by a peace agreement. Such an economy perpetuates the very structures that have given rise to the conflict and can easily lead to new violence. A conflict economy consists of four different subeconomies: the "international aid economy," the "criminal economy," the "informal economy," and the remaining "formal economy," which covers only a small fraction of the total economic activity. Rebel groups, violent and criminal entrepreneurs, and aid agencies create new structures of access to resources and power. These alternative structures produce new winners and losers. Economic winners and losers of the conflict economy can be found at both sides of the conflict, independent of who won or lost the civil war. Kamphuis assesses the impact of economic policy on the conflict economy for the policy fields of employment, taxation, privatization, and export. Her chapter discusses which economic policy is a stumbling block or a stepping stone to peacebuilding.

In Chapter 12, Tony Addison, Abdur R. Chowdhury, and S. Mansoob Murshed address the role of finance in postconflict development. How to pay for reconstruction? How to build a conflict-sensitive financial system? The chapter looks at the financial effects of conflict as well as the effects of financial policy on peacebuilding, paying special attention to the tax system, currency reform, banking, and poverty reduction. The authors argue that notwithstanding the political challenges, countries should aim for a *broad-based* recovery that benefits the majority of people and not just a narrow elite. An overarching priority for the poor should be central in postconflict reconstruction strategies. To achieve this, currency reform should be directed toward ensuring a rapid resumption of normal economic activity, and every effort must be made to ensure that banks engage in sound lending, as financial problems invariably become fiscal problems.

Chapter 13 deals with the role of international donor assistance in postconflict development. Rex Brynen looks at donor assistance to two of the largest programs of peacebuilding in the post–Cold War period, drawing on a number of lessons from the program in Palestine and analyzing the role of the donors in the reconstruction of Afghanistan. Both Palestine and Afghanistan represent cases of peacebuilding and reconstruction amid uncertainty, tension, violence, and the danger of a return to war. Four issues of donor assistance are explored in particular detail: pledging gaps and disbursement delays, aid coordination, host-country ownership, and the political usages of aid.

Three case studies have been included in the book to illuminate the interactions between the various policy areas discussed in the preceding chapters and to provide concrete examples of more and less successful postconflict development practices. The first case study, in Chapter 14, deals with El Salvador. Chris van der Borgh pays particular attention to the dynamics of local capacity building by international donors and organizations, looking at rural development programs in Chalatenango, a province in El Salvador that was heavily affected by the civil war. Numerous international donors started working in this province to support the process of reconstruction. As political tensions are still considerable, the choice to work with particular actors and to bypass others is crucial. Do external agents choose to work with government agents, groups from civil society, or political parties (or a combination of them)? How do external agents and local counterparts establish their agenda? What are the consequences of development programs for political processes at both the village level and the provincial level?

In Chapter 15, Joseph Hanlon takes a closer look at developments in Mozambique, a country often cited as a success story of postconflict development. Hanlon stresses the necessity to qualify this success, however. Over a decade after the peace accord, there are growing concerns about the stability of the country on two grounds: Growth has been sharply unequal because of the failure to permit a special postconflict development strategy, while the transition from one government to another has become locked in what is called "democratic minimalism." Narrow donor obsessions and short-term demands have played into the hands of an increasingly corrupt elite.

The third case study, in Chapter 16, examines the case of Cambodia. Cambodian postconflict development is no success story. Willemijn Verkoren identifies a number of cross-cutting issues that affect development strategies in the various sectors of society: the failure of demobilization and the reintegration of combatants, the troublesome depoliticization of structures and institutions, the lack of trust and reconciliation, and the fact that many of the causes of the conflict have yet to be addressed. The underlying causes of the Cambodian conflict were strengthened, not solved, by armed warfare, and are still present in Cambodian society today.

In Chapter 17, our concluding chapter, a number of central and returning themes are identified and a list of dilemmas, open questions, and topics for further research is provided.

Although this book does not give a complete and comprehensive account of postconflict development strategies in all sectors of society, nor prescribe detailed recipes for postconflict planning, it contributes to policy formulation by providing a broad and thorough overview of the main considerations that have to be taken into account when designing and applying development policies in countries recovering from violent conflict. It will serve to make the reader more conscious of the dangers and opportunities inherent in postconflict situations and the ways in which development can contribute to building peace.

Notes

1. See Collier et al. (2003, 6), regarding the World Bank policy research report *Breaking the Conflict Trap:*

> Economic development is central to reducing the global incidence of conflict; however, this does not mean that the standard elements of development strategy—market access policy reform, and aid—are sufficient, or even appropriate, to address the problem. At the most basic level, development has to reach countries that it has so far missed. Beyond this, development strategies should look different in countries facing a high risk of conflict, where the problems and priorities are distinctive. In addition, some policies that are not normally part of development strategy affect the risk of conflict, such as the presence of external peacekeeping forces, the tendency toward domestic military expenditures, and the design of political institutions.

The World Bank's 2004 report *The Role of the World Bank in Conflict and Development* adds that "countries facing a high risk of conflict must also look at the development challenge through a different lens, paying particular attention to their vulnerability to conflict and the impact that strategies and policies may have in mitigating or aggravating the risk of conflict" (14).

2. Already in 1995, the Development Assistance Committee of the Organization for Economic Cooperation and Development established a task force to focus on the linkages between conflict, peace, and development cooperation. The U.S. Agency for International Development hosted an international conference on postconflict development in 1997. The UN Development Program started to address postconflict situations explicitly in the second half of the 1990s (UNDP 2002a).

3. Duffield adds that this new commitment to "the reconstruction of societies in such a way as to prevent war" represents a marked radicalization of the politics of development. "Societies must be changed so that past problems do not arise, as happened with development in the past; moreover, this process cannot be left to chance but requires direct and concerted action." See Duffield (2001, 15).

4. The World Bank's 2004 report *The Role of the World Bank in Conflict and Development,* for example, explicitly mentions the aid effectiveness debate and growing recognition of the special needs of conflict-ridden countries as reasons to reassess standard economic development policy, at least in postconflict countries.

5. See Robert Putnam's *Making Democracy Work* (1993).

6. Michael Ignatieff (1998) found this aspect important enough to give his book on civil wars the title *The Warrior's Honour.*

2

Security:
An Absolute Prerequisite

Dirk Salomons

ecurity—that is, freedom from violence and coercion—is the one absolute prerequisite to any effective recovery process after the intensity of armed conflict subsides. Without the prospect of security, there is no hope; without hope, there is no commitment to a common future. Security is a human right. Security-sector reform, therefore, should be at the heart of any postconflict development debate.

Threats to security in a region emerging from conflict can come from many sources: military forces, be they under a central command or dispersed among ragtag units; militias and organized gangs working for the powerful actors of war economies; ideological extremists; religious zealots; rogue police forces; or armed civilians acting individually. The response to such threats, therefore, has to be flexible and broad, using political, military, and economic tools. Time is not on the side of those who seek to bring stability: Lack of action aggravates the problem exponentially. Institutions are not created overnight. Building a new, disciplined army under state control takes years, and creating a competent police force functioning in a context of law and order takes even longer. Thus, just getting the random violence under control is usually the first step.

From this perspective, the successful disarmament, demobilization, and reintegration (DDR) of former combatants after violent conflict represents the touchstone, the moment of truth, for any peacebuilding process. When combatants are asked to give up their arms, they face a point of no return. They, and their leaders, must have faith in a future where the advantages of peace outweigh those of war. Without a vision of that future, they will not make the choice for peace—and if they remain a threat, no one else will be able to make that choice either. A country or a region without peace and security is doomed to a marginal

existence. Neither its inhabitants nor its neighbors will risk an investment in its development, and thus the vicious circle of instability and
poverty will tighten its grip. However, DDR is no substitute for a comprehensive peace process. In no case has DDR succeeded when the
peace process was flawed. Yet no peace process has ever come to
fruition unless the former combatants were effectively reintegrated.

If the international community wants to restore hope in a country or
region emerging from violent conflict by supporting and nurturing a
peaceful resolution, it will have to pay special attention to the long-term
prospects of the military and the warlords who are about to lose their
livelihoods. Supporting a demobilization process is not just a technical
military issue. It is a complex operation that has political, security,
humanitarian, and development dimensions as well. If one aspect of this
pentagram is neglected, the entire fragile peace process may unravel.
While the violence may have abated, the underlying sources of conflict
may take years, if not generations, to overcome. Moreover, if support to
the demobilization process is not matched by the efforts required to
facilitate the entire peacebuilding and recovery process, failure is again
likely. Thus, the response of the international community cannot be
halfhearted or piecemeal—yet it usually is.

This chapter addresses the conditions that can support or threaten
the successful reintegration of former combatants into society. It
describes the component elements of such a process and provides illustrations of activities that have been effective, as well as initiatives that
have failed. It focuses in particular on the question: What can the international community do to support DDR and thus help to shape a secure
environment after conflict? In the final analysis, the formula is simple:
Where strong political will, effective military enforcement capacity, and
sufficient economic resources converge, the transition from a war economy to a peaceful society has a fair chance to succeed.

The Seductive Tenacity of War Economies

Many demobilization efforts have failed in recent years. The aborted
ventures in Angola during the 1990s, the ongoing series of mishaps in
Liberia (voiding fourteen peace accords since 1990), the stagnating disarmament in Djibouti, and the bungled stabs at disarmament during the
United Nations 1992 humanitarian mission in Somalia were completely
predictable.[1] They were based on unrealistic assumptions about the
combatants' motivation to play by the rules, and they made the fatal
mistake of granting a political role to lowlifes and thugs, such as Jonas

Savimbi and Charles Taylor, who should have been put behind bars early on as common criminals, instead of being courted at far too many international conferences when it was too late to control them. Too little attention was often paid in the past to the importance of understanding the political economies of conflict (see Chapter 17), and it is only fairly recently that scholars such as the team assembled by Mats Berdal and David Malone have analyzed the lucrative lure of perpetual violence.[2] A turning point has been the UN Security Council's interest in exploring the scope of the "dirty diamonds" trade that financed the war in Angola, leading to the "Fowler report," which in turn spawned a relatively effective sanctions regime and led to a closer look at the financial interests behind the Congo crisis.[3]

Too much time is often wasted in trying to probe for the underlying motives and ideology of spoilers who have only one thing in mind: exerting power and plundering their environment. At the same time, too little time is spent seeking out the international enablers of such renegades: the shady banks, trading companies, shipping firms, and the ignorant or addicted consumers that make these war economies possible. We also still do not quite understand how these criminal economies can survive the end of conflict and begin to lead a life of their own in the murky anomaly that characterizes many countries coming out of conflict, such as Serbia, the Central Asian states, or Afghanistan.

To illustrate the strength of such spoilers, one can sketch the influence of the warlords in Afghanistan. The most powerful one, Ismail Khan, a longtime northern militia commander, strongly supported the United States' intervention against the Taliban and Al-Qaida and was made governor of Herat after the Bonn accords were signed. He controls the flow of cars, trucks, television sets, and other goods across the borders with Iran and Tajikistan, raking in some $500,000 to $1 million a day in taxes.[4] He is not accountable to the central government and maintains his own standing army of 40,000 well-equipped fighters. Human Rights Watch has blasted his restrictions on women, his political repression, and his violent ways with opponents.[5]

At the same time, drug trafficking of Afghan opiates across the border with Tajikistan into Central Asia generated some $2.2 billion in 2002 alone.[6] The total output may have an annual value of some $5 billion, and Afghanistan's capacity to process opium into heroin (more compact and easier to transport) is increasing exponentially. All this again generates profits that keep the warlords in power, that finance the purchase of arms, and that reinforce Afghanistan's intricate network of fiefdoms and patronage ties.

It goes without saying that the incentive for the warlords to dismantle their militias is nil. The new national Afghan army, consisting of less than 10,000 men under the command of yet another warlord (serving as minister of defense), is no threat. Yet at the time this chapter was written, in April 2004, there were major plans to initiate a DDR program in Afghanistan, with $50 million in funding from the Japanese government pledged one year earlier. Implementation, however, has been deferred several times. In the absence of any credible solution to the warlord problem, the futility of such plans is evident.[7]

Equally graphic illustrations of commercial interests trumping any peace initiative could be drawn from the ongoing conflicts, fueled by vast illegal financial undertakings in the Democratic Republic of Congo and Liberia (with timber dealings expanding into China). Any thought of a DDR program in such settings would be absolute folly.

To Intervene or Not to Intervene?

At the beginning of any DDR process, the question should be raised: Are there parties one can work with? Not only thugs and criminals can frustrate peacebuilding efforts, but terrorists and religious extremists can be equally impervious to logic or incentives. Sometimes we may have to accept that military might should be an essential element in the international community's toolkit. Unfortunately, international law at present has no tools to reconcile respect for national sovereignty with the need to intervene when that sovereignty is mocked by persistent human rights violations.[8] In retrospect, Tanzania's intervention to remove Idi Amin in Uganda and Vietnam's incursion into Cambodia in order to isolate Pol Pot were exemplary models of a judicious use of force where reason or politics had no chance of succeeding. If a DDR program becomes a tepid substitute for such robust peace enforcement, if there is no assurance that the problems to be solved fall within the political and economic realm of possibility, any investment of time and effort is a waste.

A successful DDR process starts with a realistic political scenario. When the government of Mozambique and the rebel movement Renamo reached an agreement in the early 1990s, their access to external resources had been resolutely cut off through an agreement between Russia, the United States, and South Africa. Military aid had ceased for both parties, and revenues from arms smuggling or timber exports dwindled as the international community began to put up hurdles. In this climate, and with a robust peacekeeping force in place, the UN Operation in Mozambique (ONUMOZ), 1992–1994, managed to plan and implement an effective DDR program involving some 50,000 combatants and 150,000 family members. It took longer than planned, but it went well and it appears that the long-term integration of these former fighters has been largely successful.[9] At the same time, it has taken nearly a decade for the next success story to unfold, Sierra Leone in 2002–2003, where again the political will of the international community, the military force of the United Kingdom (UK), and the prospect of building a viable economy on a legitimate basis all converged to provide a credible scenario for the participants.

Should DDR Indeed Be a Priority?

Typically, hostilities will decrease and demobilization of combatants will be contemplated when a country's crisis has reached such magnitude that even war has become unprofitable and unsustainable and when all resources have been exhausted. At this stage, the need for humanitarian assistance in the area usually reaches its apex. True, combatants, ex-combatants and their dependants, child soldiers, and others are key actors in the peace process. Nonetheless, for humanitarian agencies and national/local authorities, their requirements represent only a minor concern in the context of overall needs. For example, in Mozambique there were approximately 200,000 demobilized soldiers and dependants, compared to 3 million members of the general population who were directly affected—and often devastated—by the war (such as the internally displaced, returning refugees, and people whose livelihoods had been destroyed).

Hence, a dilemma arises. On the one hand, former combatants can be a threat to their societies, and unless exceptional efforts are made to get them and their guns off the scene, they can destabilize any peace effort. On the other hand, an objective difficulty exists when attempting to plan and establish DDR priorities with government authorities, including the Ministry of Health, donors, and NGOs. There can be a perceived sense that there is an excessive focus on the needs of a few, while daunting global needs for relief and reconstruction loom on a national scale. The civilian population is likely to have suffered most during the conflict, and former soldiers are easily perceived as those responsible for violence. Therefore, structures and systems that produce the impression that the worst offenders receive the most generous privileges must be avoided. How can the international community best contribute? What tools are at its disposal?

As a peace accord is signed after civil conflict, the international community is usually asked to foot the bill for peace. Multilateral or regional institutions are invited to oversee the accord's implementation, and major economic aid is required. What are the indicators of success as the peace process unfolds that will allow the international community to assess the validity of its investment? When is it time to step up aid, and when is it time to cut one's losses and run?[10] How can violence be curtailed and security be restored?

The Tasks at Hand:
The Holistic Nature of the DDR Process

When it comes to supporting countries in their efforts to disarm, demobilize, and reintegrate former combatants, particularly after violent conflict, the international community has been on a steep learning curve. Numerous reports and studies have analyzed every DDR effort from the early days in Zimbabwe and Namibia to recent events in Liberia and Sierra Leone.[11] By now there is an impressive body of policy recommendations and lessons learned. Yet many practitioners in the field of postconflict recovery are concerned that these cumulative insights have not led to a more informed and harmonized international response capacity.[12]

One could speculate that this may be due to a lack of coordination rather than to willful blindness. There still is no internationally accepted institutional focal point for postconflict recovery comparable to the UN's Office for the Coordination of Humanitarian Affairs (OCHA), and every time reconstruction efforts are needed, the wheel is reinvented— often seeming crooked rather than round.[13] However this may be, the key lesson to be put into practice may be this: The disarmament, demobilization, and reintegration of former combatants must be components of a holistic process, and every element needs to be integrated closely into the whole. In fact, there are five key interconnected processes:

• *Political:* consisting of ongoing negotiations and power shifts well beyond the conclusion of a peace accord, leading to the integration of the former combatants into a new power structure (and possibly into a new military framework, such as a consolidated army);
• *Military/technical:* leading from a cease-fire and cantonment to disarmament and discharge while peacekeeping mechanisms are employed to prevent conflicts from recurring;
• *Security:* linking reductions in the threat posed by combatants with guns to broader disarmament and weapons-collection efforts intended to create a climate less prone to violence, as well as to general conflict prevention and reductions in the arms trade;

• *Humanitarian:* linking the well-being of the former combatants to that of vulnerable groups within and on the fringe of their ranks (e.g., child soldiers, female combatants, disabled soldiers, chronically ill soldiers), as well as to the well-being of other vulnerable groups in the population at large (while maintaining a balance among the various interests), leading to their (re)insertion into society as healthy and stable citizens; and

• *Socioeconomic:* cutting off resources for the "business of war" and linking the prospects of the various skill-based subgroups within the demobilizing population to the potential opportunity structure (e.g., employment, land, credit, training) created by the peace process, thus leading to the former combatants' (re)integration into the economic activities of their communities.

As a matter of principle, the main responsibility for the planning and execution of a DDR process should rest with the parties and should involve local communities, not only official institutions. In some instances, such as the peace process in Somaliland, large groups of soldiers have been demobilized with little or no support from the international community; more often than not, however, international support is sought. At that stage, it is essential that the planning and preparations for each of these five processes begin simultaneously and in a concerted fashion; if one strain is neglected, the others will by necessity suffer.

It should also be borne in mind that DDR can be a sterile exercise if the overall needs of the country are not addressed. DDR is only a part of the peacebuilding process, and it needs to be planned in strict coordination with other activities (e.g., institutional reinforcement, restoration of law and order, administrative reorganization, and rehabilitation of social services such as health and education). Therefore, it makes sense to establish strong linkages from the very onset of the DDR process with other ongoing or planned initiatives by various actors, with the aim of identifying and bridging gaps. If this is not done, or done poorly, as was initially the case in Sierra Leone in the 1990s (where the implementation of the Lomé Peace Accord met with serious logistic delays and where the underlying economic issues were neglected), one can predict with certainty that the peace process is doomed.

A Framework for DDR Planning and Evaluation

Although each conflict is unique, requiring that each will have to be resolved in a manner that reflects its particular circumstances, there are several core activities that all successful DDR programs share.

These tasks can be grouped into seven major areas: (1) building political and popular support for peace and reconciliation; (2) negotiating military/DDR aspects of the conflict settlement; (3) military oversight of the demobilization process; (4) civilian support for the demobilization process; (5) reinsertion: short-term, into a new consolidated army; (6) reinsertion: short-term, into civilian life; and (7) reintegration: long-term. Each of these sets of tasks has to be developed with an eye to its impact on the five key areas described earlier; each of these activities has potential implications for the others on the list. Military oversight, for example, has political ramifications, and it needs to have humanitarian dimensions, connections to broader security concerns, and so on.

This checklist, while possibly sequential in its execution, should not be sequential for planning purposes. Some activities have a long lead time. Procurement, for example, to establish cantonment areas may take months, and often it cannot start until budgets have been approved and funds have been obligated. Other activities, such as food aid, may play a vital role during the entire process, beginning with the cantonment of troops and ending only with the successful reinsertion and reintegration of demobilized militaries and their dependants. Ensuring that each of the tasks sets described above is carefully managed—taking into account the fivefold range of potential implications—may be the most daunting challenge to the implementing actors. The planning for long-term reintegration, for example, is crucial at the early stages of the peace process in order to build confidence among the combatants that there are concrete opportunities beyond the confines of their barracks; the political, humanitarian, security-related, and socioeconomic implications are self-evident.

From the nature and the complexity of the work to be done, then, certain specifications emerge for the competencies required from the actors who contribute to this process. These competencies should match the challenges posed by the key areas of possible intervention. Political, military/technical, security, humanitarian, and socioeconomic expertise are all called for in equal measure to provide meaningful support. Above all, there is a clear need for the capacity to provide guidance and leadership to the entire international DDR support process so that the individual capacities and competencies of the participating actors are best integrated into a concerted effort where the whole becomes more than the sum of its parts. This poses a particular challenge to the UN Resident Coordinator in the country, as well as the interagency team that provides backup, for these players are usually at the heart of the planning process for DDR.

A Step-By-Step Planning Tool

The following "checklist" could possibly serve as a planning and evaluation tool, as the required competencies and indicators of success are clearly evident from the tasks described. The implementation partners, however, will by necessity vary from conflict to conflict.[14]

Building political and popular support for peace and reconciliation. Major components include:

- advocacy of peace, reconciliation, and disarmament;
- economic analysis of viable alternatives to war;
- mobilization of resources for specific aspects of DDR; and
- advice and guidance to parties in conflict.

Building political and popular support must be tackled well before a peace accord is even contemplated. Here, things most frequently go wrong. At the early stages of peace negotiations, little attention is paid to the details of the DDR process, and politically inspired timetables are established that have no basis in reality.

Negotiating military/DDR aspects of the conflict settlement. Key activities include:

- establishing a coherent management and coordination structure;
- establishing cease-fire provisions;
- defining and identifying eligible combatants;
- defining and identifying combatants' arms;
- surveying combatants' expectations and skills;
- implementing disarmament or arms registration provisions;
- designing a program for material assistance in cantonment areas;
- identifying cantonment areas and designing specifications;
- identifying the needs and concerns of surrounding population;
- defining specifics and phased timing of cantonment and release process;
- designing special measures for vulnerable groups, including female and child combatants, disabled and chronically ill soldiers;
- starting public health education and information among combatants and dependants;
- providing immediate and short-term demobilization incentives;
- clarifying reintegration options within successor military structure, if any; and

- adjusting veterans' benefits to perceived fair levels in comparison to demobilization incentives.

It is essential that all these considerations be reflected in any peace accord that is drawn up, specifying exactly who will do what and how possible differences of interpretation will be adjudicated. Here, the UN can play a vital role. Its institutional knowledge, its ability to integrate past experience into new settings, its technical expertise, and its reputation of impartiality all make it an ideal broker or facilitator.

Special attention also has to be paid to the gathering of information about troop strength and levels of armament; the parties usually are not a reliable source in this respect, but independent military observers and intelligence agencies may be consulted. A clear and concise timetable for each step needs to be developed, as delays invariably lead to a loss of morale and to backsliding on commitments made.

The cease-fire can only be effective if there is a sufficient number of neutral military observers available. If violations or allegations of violations are not verified immediately, hostilities are likely to resume in earnest (as happened repeatedly in Angola during the 1990s). Having a few robust contingents of peacekeeping troops in the area is no luxury either; often their presence provides the assurance that a power vacuum will not be abused.

Furthermore, when one is dealing with militias, it becomes particularly difficult to define who is eligible for demobilization benefits—far more people tend to show up than foreseen, and their status is hard to determine. During the most recent demobilization efforts in Angola, the number of combatants who were identified to be returned to their places of origin nearly doubled from 65,000 in August 2002 to 105,000 in 2003, as the World Bank began to provide the promised incentives.[15] Giving each party a fixed cap for the number of soldiers who may show up in the cantonment areas prevents clashes (and last-minute recruitment) later on.

The time in the cantonment areas must be used productively. Plans must be drawn up to make this an appealing phase of the process, and adequate resources have to be mobilized well in advance. Sports programs, literacy and numeracy training, health education (including HIV/AIDS prevention), and medical as well as dental care can all help to keep the ex-combatants occupied and out of trouble. However, it is essential to keep the period of cantonment as short as possible, as boredom easily leads to loss of discipline and banditry.

Military oversight of the demobilization process.   Key activities include:

- collection and destruction/disposal (or registration and licensing) of arms;
- establishing secure weapon armoires;
- ensuring security of access to cantonment areas through emergency road repair and demining;
- supporting broad-based disarmament programs, including those held by paramilitaries or civilians; and
- supporting internal security, including handovers to police forces.

Disarmament is often an illusion. The parties to the conflict rarely give an accurate picture of their weapons strength, and even if each combatant who registers for demobilization hands in a weapon, it may not be the latest model. The UN Angola Verification Mission's (UNAVEM's) experience (1991–1992) showed how easily the rules are circumvented: The weapons brought in by União Nacional para a Independência Total de Angola (UNITA, or National Union for the Total Independence of Angola) were antiques and did not correspond to independent assessments of UNITA's capacity. When UNITA was not called on its bluff, the peace process was essentially dead. Anyhow, when the area is flooded with guns, so that they are found in every home, the military weapons handed in are easily replaced from the civilians' supply.

If a decision is taken to disarm the ex-combatants, it must be done in the context of a national disarmament program, otherwise the demobilized soldiers would be the only unarmed players in the game and they would soon get new weapons in the open market. Buy-back schemes have proven to be no match to the inventiveness of the arms dealers, who can resupply faster and cheaper than the international community can buy up old weapons. Tracking the flow of illicit arms, supporting public awareness campaigns, linking voluntary disarmament to community development, and job creation are all helpful strategies, but they require a robust state or donor capacity.[16]

If total disarmament is not possible, it makes sense to focus initially on the removal of heavy gear, such as tanks, armed personnel carriers, long-range artillery, and rocket launchers, and deal with small arms as a secondary issue, collecting what can be found, but accepting that this represents only the tip of the iceberg. The question should also be raised whether full disarmament is culturally appropriate. In Afghanistan's tribal areas, for example, the carrying of a personal weapon is a sign of manhood and independence. Registration and licensing may in such cases be a better way to gain control.

The international community's role in providing independent military expertise is crucial, as independent oversight by definition cannot come from any of the parties involved in the conflict—even "joined observer teams" need impartial arbiters. Often, also, an international military observer presence, fortified by peacekeeping troops, is required to enable the combatants to relinquish strategically valuable positions without running the danger that their opponents will play foul and grab those holdings.

As Bernd Hoffmann and Colin Gleichmann have argued, the military function of any demobilization process should not be overlooked either. There is a need to restructure the security sector—army and police—in tandem with the discharge of combatants, both to ensure that there is no security vacuum and to facilitate the redeployment of combatants who want to be absorbed in the new structures.[17]

Civilian support for the demobilization process. Key activities include:

- preparation and construction of cantonment sites;
- registration and issue of identification documents;
- provision of food, water, and sanitation;
- support to families;
- support and psychosocial care for child soldiers and female combatants;
- support and psychosocial care for combatants with stress disorders;
- medical and nutritional screening on registration;
- socioeconomic surveys and skills inventories of ex-combatants;
- documenting and monitoring case histories of combatants in vulnerable groups;
- immunization;
- health care and epidemiological surveillance in cantonment area;
- provision of HIV/AIDS control and reproductive health services;
- recreational activities;
- weapons collection programs, buy-back schemes, or "arms for development" initiatives; and
- mine clearing in areas of cantonment and areas of return.

Again, the international community has numerous opportunities here to contribute. A well-coordinated assistance program, with a major role for UN specialized agencies, funds, and programs; the humanitarian NGOs; and specialized international actors, such as the International Organization for Migration (IOM), the bilateral German Gesellschaft für Technische Zusammenarbeit (GTZ, or Society for Technical Cooperation), or the United Kingdom's Department for International Development (DFID), can make all the difference. Coordination among the donors is crucial and has to be linked to the economic and political support framework for the process (e.g., to support the achievement of deadlines, to link ex-combatants' skills to employment opportunities, or to build morale and confidence among the parties to the conflict).

Women and children are not marginal in the demobilization process. In Eritrea's war for independence, for example, around 30 percent of the guerrilla force consisted of women, and when these female combatants were demobilized, special programs were set up, offering skills training, workshops and market facilities, and day care centers.[18] Women and girls may also be forced to follow groups of armed combatants, providing domestic services or being used as sexual slaves.[19] In designing special demobilization programs, one should keep in mind that women and children are disproportionately targeted in armed conflict and constitute the majority of war's victims; special programs, therefore, have to be anchored in broader plans to support women and children in entire communities, without singling out those who were active participants in the fighting. Addressing the psychosocial aspects of war trauma is particularly important in this context.[20]

The plight of children in armed conflict should be an issue of primary concern. In some conflicts, child soldiers constitute up to one-third of the combatants. The demobilization and reintegration of children need not wait until a formal DDR process is in place—for children, it is always the right moment to demobilize. Moreover, the demobilization of children should be separated from that of adults. At the time a peace accord is being considered, specific provisions should be made for child soldiers; agency field reports should refer to their status; and planning for reintegration should clarify what options are available for children. Communities should be sensitized to the children's return, and every effort should be made that they are not stigmatized.[21] The Security Council's agreement to include a child protection officer in the 2000–2001 UN Mission in Sierra Leone (UNAMSIL) is an important precedent and has led to a very effective program: Between May 2001 and February 2003, some 7,000 children were demobilized, and nearly all were reunited with their families or their communities and absorbed in community-based education and counseling activities.[22]

Reinsertion: Short-term, into a new consolidated army. Often, the remnants of the various fighting factions will be joined together into a new, consolidated national defense force. It requires a major psychological tour de force to build a common spirit among former enemies, but it has been done successfully in Mozambique, where UK forces provided technical support. Key is intensive joint training to build bonding and esprit de corps.[23] One might ask, however, whether the nearly automatic response of creating a "new" army serves any purpose. Far too often, these armies, reconstituted with considerable support from the international community, do not serve any purpose of national defense, but, as was the case in Rwanda, Uganda, and Zimbabwe, are used for regional troublemaking or internal repression.

During the first half of 2003, the international community had begun major efforts to create a national army in Afghanistan, meant to fill a power vacuum created by the projected demilitarization of militia groups. One year later, that nascent national army still had no authority outside of Kabul, and the irregular militias of the warlords had only gained in strength. This assumption of a power shift by itself is unrealistic, for reasons set out earlier, but in addition, one could question the effectiveness in terms of national security of a process that might take ten years until full force strength of 70,000 men is achieved. In addition, the selection of recruits for the new army appears to be ethnically unbalanced, and half of those trained by U.S. forces leading the venture have already defected, possibly to rejoin local militias.[24]

The experiment in Kosovo to regroup the ethnically Albanian fighters of the Kosovo Liberation Army (KLA) into a civil protection corps (CPC) with no military role has also backfired. They were given, among other tasks, the responsibility to manage the national mine clearing program. Missing was the appropriate training, while some 800 Kosovars who had been trained by NGOs and commercial firms were dismissed. Politically, this was a stunted decision. No Kosovar Serb who suspects that his land is mined will ever call in the former KLA, and the CPC has now been implicated in various drug and trafficking schemes, so that the security threat of an uncontrollable band of thugs has returned.[25]

In the short term, having plans for a new army may seem like a useful strategy to absorb a large number of former combatants into a familiar environment and to establish some level of control over their activities. From a long-term perspective, however, it commits the state to high recurrent expenses with little social or economic value, and it creates the threat of a "state within the state" that may devour the society that built it.

Reinsertion: Short-term, into civilian life. Preparing the former combatants and communities necessitates:

- job counseling and referral;
- health counseling;
- medical and dental care;
- family reunion and/or services;
- specific measures for vulnerable groups;
- transportation;
- departure packages (e.g., tools);
- cash;
- clothing;
- food and food coupons; and
- housing and housing materials.

This stage of the DDR program is another touchstone of the peace process's viability. Preparing the former combatants for their return and inserting them into the civilian population requires an extraordinary amount of preparation, not only for the aid agencies involved but also for the receiving communities. If there is no element of overall community development in the broader peace process, the sudden return of former combatants will wreak havoc.

With the prevalence of HIV/AIDS in societies destabilized by conflict, it becomes ever more important to link the planning for the demobilization of ex-combatants to the national AIDS prevention and healthcare plans. Soldiers and former soldiers tend to be a primary source of the epidemic's spread, but at the same time, the demobilization process provides for teachable moments, opportunities for diagnosis, and facilities for counseling.

When it comes to managing the return of demobilized soldiers to their communities, the IOM is by far the best equipped and the most experienced agency to provide technical support, as it did, for example, in Mozambique after the civil war. It has the mobile technology to register combatants and their families, extensive survey models to support reintegration planning, and a remarkable track record in working with refugees, internally displaced people, and migrants (most recently in orchestrating the return of Afghan refugees).[26]

There is a certain risk in providing lump sums of cash to demobilizing soldiers: It is often wasted on impulse purchases, and it distorts the power relations between the soldiers and the communities to which they return. Better results have been achieved with vouchers for building materials, agricultural tools and seeds (honored by local traders), or by allocations of funds to communities, enabling them to fund the employment and integration of the returnees.

Reintegration: Long-term. Major components include:

- programs to integrate and balance programs for demobilized soldiers, returning refugees, and the internally displaced;
- public health education;
- credit;
- land (and land reform);
- professional and vocational training;
- public works job creation;
- income-generation programs;
- microenterprises;
- participation of the private sector, including hiring incentives;
- business and legal advice; and
- veterans' programs and outreach.

At this stage, the reintegration program for demobilized combatants should, if all is well, begin to blend in with the overall postconflict recovery program for the region. There should be general efforts to rebuild the infrastructure, rehabilitate agriculture, meet educational and health needs, and build a new framework for governance and civil society.[27]

Unity in Diversity: The Need for Common Values and Policies Among Donors

It follows from the detailed inventory of activities set out above that numerous considerations come into play, requiring a coordinated response with political, economic, social, cultural, and security components. In discussions among donors, governmental or nongovernmental, on whether (and if so, how) to support a potential peace process, certain criteria should figure prominently:

- ensuring that humanitarian values and concerns—including the rights of children—are fully integrated into the design and execution of DDR activities;
- taking a holistic approach to DDR support, linking it closely to other elements of the peace process;

- approaching the DDR process as an opportunity to build national capacity;
- simplifying and clarifying the complex funding mechanisms affecting the DDR process;
- building on the specific competencies and capacities of a broad range of partners: the UN system, regional, and subregional organizations; other intergovernmental bodies; NGOs; bilateral donor programs; civil society institutions; academics; and the private sector;
- ensuring that the experience gained is transformed into lessons learned through effective contemporary documentation, analysis, and above all, cross-organizational learning; and
- establishing broad, participatory coordination mechanisms across sectoral divides.

Values and Concerns

There is a danger that DDR plans are totally shaped by the parties around the negotiation table and their immediate advisers. There are, however, broader values and concerns that should be reflected in DDR planning and design. First of all, there are principles enshrined in international humanitarian law, such as neutrality, impartiality, and the right of noncombatants to protection. Human rights and the concept of dignity are also of great importance to all organizations; in this respect, the UN High Commissioner for Refugees (UNHCR) has often emphasized that ex-combatants should be able to return to their communities without being subjected to discrimination—the "sustainability of return" is not just an issue for refugees and internationally displaced persons (IDPs).

Advocates of peaceful conflict-resolution attach special importance to the disarmament of both ex-combatants and the civilian population who may be in possession of weapons in a postconflict situation. To be successful, weapons-recovery programs as well as programs to develop civilian support for disarmament should involve local and national authorities, civil society, and the international community. These plans should include specific guidelines for safeguarding and disposal of weapons, including their destruction. As argued earlier in this chapter, it may sometimes be more prudent to let people keep their personal weapons. In some cultures, where arms are part of a traditional value system, it may be more realistic to register and license personal weapons so that they can be traced. UN experience has proven that civil society can play an integral role in the development of a culture of peace, thereby reducing the likelihood of large amounts of unauthorized weapons circulating within society.

Holistic Approach

Bringing all the potential actors together at the earliest possible stage, to ensure that all aspects of the multisectoral DDR process are duly considered, is essential in the eyes of most development practitioners. Obtaining the "buy-in" of all the parties involved in the conflict, to the point that the merits of a postconflict scenario have been fully internalized by all the players, is crucial. If the combatants around the table do not truly believe that their long-term concerns and expectations have fully been taken into account, the DDR process remains an option, not a commitment, and the parties will slide back into violence the moment the opportunity presents itself.

The holistic approach supported in this chapter places special demands on the start-up phase of a DDR support operation, as the establishment of a multisectoral task force of the key donors, the identification of implementation partners, and the mobilization of resources would all have to be undertaken simultaneously in a very short time frame. UN field coordination structures offer the best organizational framework for such tasks.

Capacity Building

Many of the governmental and nongovernmental organizations called upon to provide support cannot resist the temptation to plan DDR operations as external interventions, rather than as programs in support of national institutions. This makes it even more important for the international community to develop rapidly a robust analytical and planning capacity at the country level, preferably through the Resident Coordinator System of the United Nations. Only by working closely with the factions and institutions on the ground—not just during formal negotiations but before, after, and instead—can support be structured and tailored to meet the real needs and match the real capacities of the main protagonists of the peace process.[28]

Civil society institutions, such as religious organizations, should not be neglected in this capacity-building process, and often the NGOs and the diplomatic community working in a country have better contacts and insights in this respect than the organizations brought in specifically to support the peace process. Establishing effective partnerships is thus best done very early on as a peace initiative takes hold.

Funding Mechanisms

Financial support for DDR activities comes from a wide range of sources. In a peacekeeping environment with a mandate from the UN Security Council, there will normally be funds from assessed contributions under the peacekeeping account. Humanitarian activities will partly be covered by funds raised in special UN appeals. There may be trust funds, parallel funding by bilateral donors, or national/regional resources, often in kind, that are essential to the overall operation.[29]

It is well beyond the current capacity of the international community to program all these different inputs in a coherent manner. Even to keep track of them is a major task. The gaps between pledges and disbursements, the inefficiencies of bureaucratic procedures, the lack of transparency, and the long lead time of some budgetary processes are infuriating for the practitioners at the country level and make effective integration of the actors' respective strengths even more of a challenge. Any discussion about an effective distribution of labor, according to the practitioners consulted for this chapter, needs also to focus on an effective and timely distribution of resources. Additionally, it should be noted that some crises are more "popular" than others and that especially the DDR process is difficult to "sell," given the sometimes unsavory image of its primary beneficiaries. This makes resource mobilization more difficult.

Support for the DDR process, therefore, has to be patched together from a plethora of separate funding sources, and this makes coordination, let alone collaboration, particularly complex. Different donors have different procurement and reporting standards, and most agencies have to maintain their separate identity, making the pooling of resources nearly impossible. Eventually, these operational problems may need to be addressed at the level of the Organization for Economic Cooperation and Development's (OECD's) Development Assistance Committee, at a dedicated donor roundtable, or in special sessions of the UN's General Assembly, similar to the ones held about the landmark Brahimi Report on UN peacekeeping operations.

Partner Capacities

Although the organizations of the UN system, including the World Bank, contribute greatly to countries emerging from conflict and seeking support in the disarmament, demobilization, and reintegration of former combatants, they do not by themselves have sufficient capacities or resources. In all of the DDR operations that were successful thus far, other intergovernmental, regional, bilateral, and nongovernmental actors have played a major role and have occasionally even taken the lead.

Particularly the IOM, the German GTZ, and the UK's DFID have considerable experience in the actual demobilization phase of the DDR process. The International Committee of the Red Cross (ICRC) and the International Federation of Red Cross and Red Crescent Societies can provide effective links between DDR programs and broader measures to alleviate the suffering of vulnerable groups. The effective reintegration of ex-combatants can be best supported in close collaboration with major NGOs such as Save the Children, Oxfam, or CARE. The participation in the UN Interagency Standing Committee (IASC) by Interaction (a consortium of U.S.-based NGOs) and the International Council on Voluntary Agencies (its European equivalent) provides an opportunity for more systematic standby arrangements whereby the capacities of their various members are mapped out and "prepackaged" as potential components of a DDR program. Here, the UN, through its Resident Coordinator field coordination mechanism, can take the lead as "honest broker."

Another aspect of potential partnerships is the role of the private sector. Reintegration and private sector development are closely linked, and the experience gained in Mozambique, for example, shows how private investors are very agile when they sense that incipient peace can be transformed into economic activity. Unfortunately, countries emerging from conflict often do not meet the conditions that will enable the World Bank and the International Monetary Fund (IMF) to provide assistance and pave the way for investors. However, the Bank has other tools at its disposal (technical assistance, postconflict fund, etc.) that allow it to be active even immediately after war ends, avoiding thus a gap in the Bank's involvement (e.g., Bosnia, Kosovo, East Timor, Sierra Leone). The UNDP has also focused its mandate on the immediate postconflict reconstruction phase, which may last some two to three years and requires special support from the donor community. Its newly established Bureau for Conflict Prevention and Recovery is rapidly becoming the focal point for programs bridging the gap between relief and development, and it has established direct links with the private sector. As the question of incentives and disincentives normally is high up on the agenda of any peace process, and often is at the heart of DDR negotiations, early consultations on private sector involvement—often through the diplomatic community in-country—may well be profitable.

Economic and Social Analysis

As argued earlier in this chapter, many of the international community's efforts to stem violence and to disarm combatants with a view to integrate them into a peaceful society are doomed to fail because they do not dovetail with the economic interests of the combatants. The close links among armed conflict, the drug trade, smuggling, the illegal exploitation of natural resources, and trafficking in women and children are well documented. Goons with guns who use violence to make money are not easily persuaded to take a bag of seeds and go home. It is, therefore, important to analyze the economic aspects of armed conflict: How is money made? How does it flow? Who are the main beneficiaries?

This then allows for a detached analysis. Ultimately, one will have to convince the warlords that there is a better business model in their future: safer, sustainable, and acceptably lucrative. The costs of doing business in a lawless environment can be calculated. Security is extremely expensive, as numerous people have to be kept on the payroll purely for protection or as a patronage payoff. Equipment has to be bought with cash and cannot be written off over time, for nobody knows how long the business will continue. Market access can require various middlemen, again adding to the cost. The absence of law and order also vastly increases the risk that the franchise can be captured by a competitor with bigger guns.

It may, therefore, be useful to carry out some scenario planning with armed leaders. What would it take to integrate them into a peaceful economy? Title to some of the resources they control anyway? Government jobs? Investment in a new kind of enterprise? What will give them hope for a better future? How can they gain the respect of their communities while renouncing violence?

Coordination: Form Follows Function

It would be desirable, in principle, to have a firm international model for the distribution of labor in support of DDR among the various components of the international community. In practice, however, one is better off when there are very few hard-and-fast rules in this area, given the large variety in circumstances under which a DDR process might be conducted. In some situations, there is a clear victor and a clear loser—in others, a stalemate. Here, there are two factions, there six or more. One conflict can be contained within state borders, another can cross several international borders simultaneously. In one conflict, donor interest is vivid and generous—another is mostly neglected by the donor community. In one situation, there is a functioning government able to call for World Bank support; in another, there remains no more than the shell of a failed state, unable to function even at the most basic level. It is not always certain that there will be a robust peacekeeping operation, authorized by the Security Council—possibly there would just be a few military observers on the ground.

Sometimes, individual donor countries or even NGOs will have taken on a major role in the peacebuilding process well before the UN or the international community as a whole becomes involved, as was the case with Italy and the Community of Sant'Egidio in Mozambique; in other situations, the international community will just stay away, as was the case in Somaliland. In Afghanistan, ample resources were pledged at the 2002 Tokyo conference but not delivered, and by June 2003 donor interest was rapidly fading. At the same time, renewed efforts were under way to address the crisis in the Democratic Republic of Congo and the Great Lakes region in Africa, with the Europeans emerging as the main protagonists. Thus, there should be considerable flexibility in the international community's approach to DDR support, depending on the context, the level of international commitment, and the capacities of the players already on the ground. Ad hoc alliances of the willing and the able provide the best opportunities.

Conclusion

The international community has sunk vast resources into the bottomless pit of failed peace accords—often falling into the same trap repeatedly, as was the case in Angola, Liberia, and Sierra Leone. Yet much can be learned from failure, and successful precedents for peacebuilding do exist. A solid touchstone to assess the viability of any peace agreement after civil conflict is the quality of the disarmament, demobilization, and reintegration programs embedded in the peace accord. When they are integral components of a carefully calibrated plan with clear political, military, security, humanitarian, and socioeconomic dimensions, the entire peace process is off to a good start.

Notes

1. For a detailed account of the Liberian fiasco, see Adebajo (2002).
2. See Berdal and Malone (2000).

3. Security Council document S/2001/357, April 2001. See also Smillie (2002).

4. Marc Kaufman, "Karzai's Taxing Problem," *Washington Post,* March 19, 2003.

5. "Hamid Karzai's Ragtime Infantry," *The Economist*, May 3, 2003.

6. "Deadly Traffic," *The Economist,* March 29, 2003.

7. See also Carlotta Gall, "Letter from Asia," *New York Times,* June 11, 2003, making the case that the lack of credible donor support to the reconstruction process, the lack of internationally guaranteed security, and the fragility of the 2002 Bonn accord all make it likely that the country "could end up being ruled by a mixture of drug lords and mujahedeen—in other words, people not much different from the Taliban."

8. International Development Research Center (2001).

9. See also Salomons (2003).

10. This chapter is based on a study conducted in 2000 by the author's consulting firm, the Praxis Group, Ltd., for the Executive Committee on Humanitarian Affairs of the United Nations; related materials were presented at a workshop on DDR in Afghanistan, held in May 2003 under the auspices of the Liechtenstein Institute on Self-Determination in Princeton, New Jersey.

11. Of particular interest are Berdal (1996); Colletta, Kostner, and Wiederhofer (1996); and Hoffmann and Gleichmann (2000).

12. The best, most authoritative and comprehensive policies in this respect can be found in OECD (1997). Another core document is United Nations (2000c).

13. See, inter alia, the discussion on the frail international architecture for postconflict reconstruction in Forman, Patrick, and Salomons (2000).

14. Much of this checklist is derived from my experience as executive director of the UN's peace operation in Mozambique (ONUMOZ, 1992–1994), where I was directly involved in the planning and preparations for the DDR process. As far as peace accords go, the General Peace Agreement of Mozambique, in its Protocols IV and VI on military questions, provides one of the best game plans for demobilization (see the translation from the Portuguese contained as Document 12 in the United Nations Blue Book Series, vol. 5, *The United Nations and Mozambique, 1992–1995* [New York: United Nations Publications, 1995]).

15. "Peacebuilding in Postconflict Angola," address by Professor Ibrahim Gambari, Undersecretary General and Special Adviser on Africa, United Nations, at the International Peace Academy Forum on Angola, New York, June 6, 2003.

16. See also the UNDP's website on small arms, www.undp.org/erd/smallarms/index.htm.

17. Hoffmann and Gleichmann (1999).

18. Hoffmann and Gleichmann (1999).

19. Report of the UN Secretary-General on women, peace, and security, S/2002/11154, October 16, 2002.

20. Rehn and Sirleaf (2002).

21. www.un.org/special-rep/children-in-armed-conflict/.

22. United Nations Press Release OSRSG/PR03/11, February 28, 2003.

23. See, inter alia, Synge (1997).

24. "Hamid Karzai's Ragtime Infantry," *The Economist,* May 3, 2003.

25. The Praxis Group, Ltd.: "Willing to Listen: An Evaluation of the Mine Action Programme in Kosovo." Report commissioned by the United Nations Mine Action Service, December 2002, www.mineaction.org/misc/resultdisplay.cfm?doc_ID=848.

26. See www.iom.int.

27. Forman, Patrick, and Salomons (2000).

28. See also Anderson (1999).

29. Salomons and Dijkzeul (2001).

3

Building State Institutions

Jose Luis Herrero

C reating, transforming, or rebuilding state institutions in the immediate aftermath of violent conflict is a unique undertaking that has little resemblance to standard institution-building efforts or development work. The main differences lie in the order of priorities—in the aftermath of violent conflict, there is only one priority: avoiding renewed violence.

Efforts toward bureaucratic and administrative efficiency and effectiveness and economic rationality would be in vain if violent conflict reemerges. Serious inefficiencies in government and public administration as well as in the functioning of the economy are preferable, in an initial phase, to a political impasse leading back to open conflict.

Efforts to establish democratic institutions or democratize existing ones may have to be timed to the capacity of a postconflict society to absorb democratic change. This requires a change in political culture or, very often, a whole cultural change. It is wrong to assume that democracy, defined narrowly by free electoral competition among potential collective decisionmakers, is an antidote to civil conflict.[1]

Despite common elements, postconflict situations differ significantly from one another. Most of the existing literature does not address the immediate aftermath of the conflict—the emergency phase. There is considerable knowledge and accumulated experience on how to deal with the humanitarian consequences of conflict and an emerging corpus on transitioning from the humanitarian to the development phase. Most of it, however, addresses the role of the international entities playing a humanitarian assistance role or assisting in economic development. The security, political, and administrative vacuum resulting from conflict, as important as it is, is often neglected. This chapter will concentrate on the very first postconflict stages, emphasizing the importance of looking ahead during these phases and, therefore, introducing elements of sustainability and anticipation in the policies to be applied.

Institution Building in Kosovo

The Kosovo case is one of postconflict institution building piloted by a third party with full authority and almost unlimited resources. When it comes to postconflict reconstruction and development, resources are never enough, but it is difficult to imagine a situation where the expenditure per capita of the international community, when including military expenditure, can surpass the one in Kosovo.

The main facts that defined the situation on the ground in the aftermath of Operation Allied Force, when the North Atlantic Treaty Organization (NATO) and the United Nations took full control over Kosovo, were the following:

- collapse of previously existing official administrative structures;
- withdrawal of previously existing security and law enforcement structures;
- prevalence of the ethnic, political, and social tensions that originated the conflict; and
- existence of local parallel structures with some degree of control over the population, administrative capacity, and/or perceived legitimacy.

The mandate of the military and security presence in Kosovo, contained in UN Security Council Resolution 1244, was broad enough to allow this presence to fill the void left by the withdrawal and collapse of the previous regime. The mandate contained a general instruction to the civilian presence to "perform basic civilian functions" and to "organize and oversee the development of provisional institutions for democratic and autonomous self-government."[2] How this was to be done was left entirely in the hands of a Special Representative of the Secretary-General (SRSG) and head of the Kosovo International Administration.

The strategy that was followed, with respect to the development of provisional institutions, was partly planned and partly reactive. Despite the many advantages of planning ahead, a process of institution building led by a third party requires consultation and the sharing of decisions with the local parties. Flexibility to accommodate the views of local parties is key to gaining their acceptance, and it generates a feeling of ownership in local stakeholders and population. The third party's capacity to plan is, therefore, conditioned by the acceptance of those plans by local actors.

In Kosovo, the shaping of local and central institutions was conducted in permanent consultation between representatives of the UN Interim Administration Mission in Kosovo (UNMIK) and local representatives. Consultations sometimes resulted in agreement and sometimes in disagreement, with subsequent delays in the inception of political and administrative bodies. Unforeseen events such as the fall of Slobodan Milosevic and the outbreak of violence in the Former Yugoslav Republic of Macedonia (FYROM) affected the pace of the political process and institution building. Altogether, the strategy has proved moderately successful in creating a framework of quasi-democratic institutions in a context of extreme ethnic and political tensions. How the institution-building process may have affected the political process that will eventually lead to determining the final status of Kosovo through predetermining or conditioning its potential outcome is a different matter that will not be addressed in this chapter.

Three phases—emergency, joint administration, and provisional democratic institutions under third-party authority—can be identified in the building of institutions. Taking into account that Kosovo is still under interim arrangements, the third phase does not yet bring the institutional setting to its final state, which would allow international disengagement.

Phase One: Emergency

Immediate priorities emerging after the end of hostilities—ensuring a minimally secure environment and vital public services as well as delivering humanitarian aid—do not relate directly to the building of government institutions. Nevertheless, the activities and the mechanisms used to respond to those priorities can facilitate or delay the building of permanent structures. In particular, they can help set up the embryo of a basic administration, the skeleton of an administration of justice, and interim consultation mechanisms for political participation. How they are conceived at the outset will determine how smooth the transition from the emergency phase to the development phase will be.

Basic Administrative Instruments

Three key administrative elements were introduced in Kosovo at a very early stage: a fully transparent public budget, the Central Fiscal Authority (CFA), and the Banking and Payments Authority of Kosovo

(BPK). The withdrawal of the previous regime had left thousands of families formerly living on a public sector wage without income or alternative means of survival. An initial system of stipends was put in place, whereby some categories of public sector employees would receive a minimal income at irregular intervals, regardless of whether they were still performing any work. This system originally responded to a humanitarian concern and was not necessarily meant to become—as it eventually did—the public sector payroll.

As can be expected in a postconflict scenario, generating resources for the public sector through organized taxation was not possible right after the end of hostilities: The tax base was almost nonexistent, and while some economic activity rapidly increased—mainly trade and the provision of services to international organizations—no accounting and enforcement procedures could be introduced overnight. The only source of income for a broad segment of the population, the stipends system, depended on the goodwill of foreign donors who were extremely reluctant to transform these ad hoc donations into a permanent liability on a public budget. To obtain longer-term commitments from donors and build the embryo of a public sector budget, UNMIK had to make the commitment to develop a fiscal system and try to make the public budget self-sustainable as soon as conditions permitted. Donors accepted the risk, and a first Kosovo Consolidated Budget was established on November 8, 1999, totaling 125 million German marks for 1999, 70 percent of which was funded by international donors.

With donors' funding came an obligation of transparency and accountability leading to the establishment of the Central Fiscal Authority and the Banking and Payments Authority of Kosovo. The CFA and the BPK ensured a transparent management of the Kosovo Consolidated Budget, implemented accounting standards, and set up payment facilities for public sector payments.

Civil Service

The impact of the Kosovo budget went well beyond the economy and provided a basis for some political stability, especially at the municipal level. One of the main causes of instability was the struggle among factions to control municipal administrations left vacant by the Milosevic regime. Self-appointed authorities from the different factions that had participated in the civil conflict were taking over offices and functions throughout Kosovo's municipalities, making it difficult for UNMIK to exert its administrative authority on the ground.

The Kosovo budget, which contained municipal budgets for salaries and recurrent expenditures, permitted UNMIK to negotiate the inclusion in the municipal payrolls of former Kosovo Albanian civil servants and individuals supported by the various political factions. The recruitment process was highly politicized and often did not respond to criteria of merits and efficiency. UN municipal administrators had to negotiate with different factions in an environment of threats and intimidation. The resulting labor force was oversized and did not always contain the skills required for municipal administration. Some political factions managed to take a predominant position in the municipalities, not always corresponding to the population's preferences. This embryonic and ineffective system, however, contributed to diminishing social and political tensions and to creating a unified municipal structure of basic services under international authority.

At the central level, the inclusion of local structures into UNMIK proceeded at a slower pace. The main Kosovo Albanian political organizations—the Democratic League of Kosovo (LDK) and the Kosovo Democratic Progressive Party (PPDK)—had a long history of confrontation (resulting from the different strategies adopted during the 1990s to oppose Serbian rule) and had no intention of cooperating with each other. In addition, the PPDK—the political branch of the former armed resistance movement Kosovo Liberation Army/Ushtria Çlirimtare E Kosoves (KLA/UCK)—was not readily accepting the authority of UNMIK. Faced with these circumstances, the UN began building central administrative structures on its own, staffing the different departments exclusively with international staff. It was clear, however, that, as administrative functions would grow in scope and complexity, the participation of local manpower would become a necessity.

Mechanisms for Political Consultation

Ensuring local participation in building state institutions is the key to the acceptance of those institutions by the local population. This is particularly so in a postconflict environment, where the previous institutional setting has failed and the parties are not willing to give up shares of their de facto power to institutions that do not guarantee what they see as their legitimate political aspirations. It could be argued that as pieces of the institutional setting can be replicated from other places—an electoral system, for instance—the same could apply to the overall political system—in effect creating a model democratic system. In practice, it doesn't work.

When the institution-building process is led by a third party, consultation becomes necessary to avoid the perception of a colonial presence. The third party may benefit from varying degrees of acceptance by the different constituencies. In the Kosovo case, initially NATO and the UN were generally welcomed by the Kosovo Albanian population, though not so by the Kosovo Serb population. But the level of acceptance changes over time as one or the other faction sees its aspirations fulfilled or frustrated. In general, local political structures and leaders have a stronger capacity than the foreign presence to acknowledge what the different social groups think and feel. The cooperation of those structures and leaders is necessary.

The satisfaction of the different factions with the political process also has potential security consequences: Former armed groups have the capacity to hold the political process hostage by threatening to resume violence until demobilization and reintegration is complete, which can take many years. In general, no foreign security presence, as strong as it may be, can ensure a relatively safe environment unless it benefits from the support of the overwhelming majority of the population.

In a complex political environment and in the absence of democratically elected representatives, the difficulties of ensuring consultation with local parties begin with the identification of suitable interlocutors. Interlocutors should be those who the community itself has adopted as its leaders, not those who are most sympathetic to the third party. In Kosovo, the main political representatives of the bigger Kosovo Albanian political factions, the LDK and KLA, were clearly identified but were not willing to cooperate with each other. In the case of the KLA, it was not clear either whether they were willing to cooperate with UNMIK. Non-Albanian ethnic groups were not structured or, in the case of Kosovo Serbs, still aligned with Milosevic's positions.

In the very first days of its presence in Kosovo, UNMIK set up a consultative mechanism, the Kosovo Transitional Council (KTC). Originally composed of about twelve members, the KTC included representatives of the two main Kosovo Albanian structures, a number of notables, and a representative of the Bosniac minority community. Representatives of the Kosovo Serbs were invited as well. Only representatives of the Orthodox Church based in the center of Kosovo took up the invitation and participated in a number of sessions, whereas Kosovo Serbs from the municipalities bordering Serbia proper continued their allegiance to Milosevic and ignored UNMIK. The KTC had no formal powers or competencies. It was mainly a forum for the exchange of ideas between local leaders and the international administration. From June to December 1999, the KTC met at irregular intervals. Walkouts and internal disputes were frequent. Despite its exclusively consultative role, the KTC sent the signal to the people of Kosovo that the international administration was willing to listen to them. More important, it facilitated a rapprochement between the two major Kosovo Albanian factions and formed the first platform for dialogue between Kosovo Albanians and Kosovo Serbs.

Phase Two: Joint Administration

During the last weeks of 1999, a landmark agreement setting the Joint Interim Administrative Structure (JIAS) was brokered by the SRSG. The agreement was signed on December 15, 1999, by the three Kosovo Albanian organizations that had participated in the failed Rambouillet negotiations prior to the NATO campaign. These organizations were the LDK, the PPDK, and the United Democratic Movement (LBD—a less important political party with limited popular support).

The agreement's main achievement was political. It brought together the two Kosovo Albanian factions that had until then refused to cooperate. By signing the agreement, the PDK (successor to the PPDK) and the LDK also explicitly accepted the UN's authority and agreed to dismantle all parallel administrative and representative structures. This was a major step forward in obtaining acceptance of the international administration by the local parties and establishing a relatively orderly framework for cooperation. The extreme pressure under which the agreement was negotiated did not allow for careful consideration of the administrative arrangements it contained from the perspective of administrative effectiveness or organizational rationality. Rather, the organizational chart of the JIAS that resulted from the agreement was meant to accommodate all the parties concerned, in an exercise of formal power sharing, and to satisfy their aspirations to be included in quasi-governmental structures.

Political Bodies

The JIAS contained two main political bodies: the Kosovo Transitional Council and the Interim Administrative Council (IAC). The original KTC was expanded to about thirty members. They included most Kosovo Albanian parties, representatives of civil society (NGOs, media, and the chamber of commerce), representatives of minority communities, and representatives of the Catholic, Muslim, and Orthodox faiths. Representation of the Kosovo Serb population was never complete because Serbs from the northern municipalities refused to send their representatives and generally boycotted the JIAS institutions.

The KTC met weekly under the UN Special Representative's chairmanship. It had no formal powers except that of discussing any matter it considered appropriate and conveying the members' views to the Special Representative and other senior international officials. The KTC was often underestimated because of its exclusively consultative role. Members complained about their lack of executive power and were not interested in participating in the different thematic committees that were set up to discuss specific issues. Its impact, however, was significant. First, it allowed local political leaders from all political and ethnic groups to debate among themselves in a relatively orderly framework—something close to parliamentary procedures. These leaders lacked democratic experience and had never before engaged in constructive dialogue among themselves. Some of them were enemies, and it was feared that they would resort to violence, not dialogue. Having them meet weekly and express their differences with international facilitation was a significant advance. Second, it contributed to the perception that UNMIK listened and responded to the questions of the people it was overseeing. The most senior international official, the Special Representative, faced the questions and complaints of KTC members each week, a procedure comparable to a prime minister's parliamentary questioning. Perhaps as a consequence of the lack of democratic tradition, this remarkable feature was not given the value it deserved by local political representatives. But it contributed considerably to bringing UNMIK closer to the people of Kosovo and to making it more responsive to their concerns.

The IAC was the top executive and legislative body, under the authority of the Special Representative. Its eight members were the top four international officials (the heads of the four international administration "pillars"), the leaders of the three Kosovo Albanian parties having signed the JIAS Agreement, and a representative of a newly created Kosovo Serb political platform (the Serb National Council, SNC).

The JIAS Agreement established that the IAC would review legislation to be enacted by the Special Representative and amend it subject to the Special Representative's final review. The main legislative instrument was regulations that the IAC would discuss prior to the Special Representative's signature. The IAC would also direct the policies of the administrative departments established under it to carry out all the functions of a public administration. In practice, the local members of the IAC lacked the capacity to scrutinize legislation, often of a very technical nature, and referred it to their experts. At the technical level, the input of international experts determined the contents of the legislation. On many occasions, though, concerns of the local IAC members were taken into account when enacting new legislation, as a result of the IAC mechanism. These concerns were more related to the political consequences of the regulations than to their administrative impact.

Administrative Bodies

Under the IAC, twenty administrative departments were established to deal with all the areas of public administration (these departments were considered as the equivalent to ministries).[3] The number was exaggerated for the size and the population of the territory to be administered. It was determined in order to accommodate several political factions into the governmental structures, giving each a number of administrative departments approximately in accordance with their political weight. The LDK, the PDK, and the LBD received five departments each, and the remaining five were given to the SNC, the representative of the Bosniac community, and an independent. The five departments granted to the LBD were an exception to the approximate representation principle because, as municipal elections later showed, this party had almost no popular support.

Two co-heads were at the top of each administrative department: one international official and one from the local parties. Formally, both co-heads had equal competencies and powers over the administrative departments. This system was meant to make the local co-head develop a sense of ownership and responsibility over the department. In practice, it worked very unevenly across departments. While some local co-heads tried to make a significant contribution, others left most of the decisionmaking to the international official. The obstacles to full local ownership over the departments were mostly technical: Local co-heads and their staffs did not posses the necessary skills, internal documents were in English, and the modus operandi of the departments was inspired by the workings of international organizations and difficult to understand. But there was also the perception that in case of disagreement between the international and the local official, the views of the former would prevail because the international official would call on the final authority of the Special Representative to rule in his or her favor. This acted as a disincentive to full local engagement.

The departments faced very different challenges. Generally, those building structures from scratch were more successful than those having to work with existing structures or parts of the previous system. Thus, the CFA introduced a new fiscal system and rapidly brought it close to international standards. The departments of education, health, and public utilities, by contrast, had to work on the basis of preexisting structures and faced more difficulties in bringing them up to international standards.

Ethnic tensions also made the work of the departments unevenly difficult. While every administrative function can be tainted with ethnic bias, some are more likely to be controversial than others. Education and health were particularly bound to generate problems, with Albanians and Serbs refusing to attend the same schools and medical personnel refusing to work together. Even patients distrusted medical personnel from the other ethnic group and refused to be treated by them.

Phase Three: Provisional Democratic Institutions Under Third-Party Authority

The success of the municipal elections in October 2000 and the fall of Slobodan Milosevic paved the way for general elections. The almost complete absence of violence during the municipal elections campaign and polling day and the acceptance of results by the parties contending the elections indicated that Kosovo's people and political structures were ready for free general elections. The critical factor was the political maturity shown by the political parties that had emerged from the Kosovo Liberation Army (the PDK and the newly created Alliance for the Future of Kosovo, or AAK), which accepted without contestation the victory of the LDK in most municipalities. Milosevic's fall gave rise to the hope that Serbs from the northern municipalities would finally decide to participate in the political process led by the international administration and contend in general elections.

During the first months of 2001, UNMIK opened a negotiating process aimed at defining what institutions would result from elections, how they would function, and what their relationship with the international authority would be. Some voices in the international community and in Kosovo were of the opinion that elections for an assembly should be called and the resulting assembly be left to decide on its own on the remaining institutional arrangements for Kosovo. UNMIK, however, was convinced that providing an institutional framework *prior* to the elections would best guarantee an orderly process. In particular, the limits to the powers of the elected institutions would have to be established to guarantee that they would not trespass on areas (such as defense) that were not foreseen in UN Security Council Resolution 1244.

Constitutional Framework

The resulting institutional arrangements are contained in the Constitutional Framework for Provisional Self-Government in Kosovo (the CF).[4] Its name reflects the compromise reached between the Kosovo Albanian side, which wanted a full constitution, symbolically closer to their goal of an independent Kosovo, and the international side, which wanted to avoid prejudging the final status for Kosovo, in accordance with Resolution 1244, and which originally proposed a "legal framework."

The Constitutional Framework provides for an assembly, a president of Kosovo, and a government with a prime minister and ministers. The overall setting and procedures are reminiscent of a standard model of central administration with legislative and executive branches.[5] What makes the Constitutional Framework unique and a model case or post-conflict institutions is a set of features built in with the objectives of safeguarding the authority of the Special Representative, keeping internal security and law enforcement in international hands (through, inter alia, special provisions for the judiciary), guaranteeing to the extent possible minorities' rights, and avoiding granting all the attributes of sovereignty to the new institutions. Additional mechanisms were introduced as well to foster consensus within the institutions, which was considered instrumental in forcing cooperation among parties and the emergence of a sense of shared responsibility among elected authorities.

Special Features to Preserve UN Authority

Chapter 8 of the CF is dedicated to the powers and responsibilities reserved for the Special Representative.[6] The Special Representative keeps an overall prerogative to *dissolve the Assembly and call for new elections* "in circumstances where the Provisional Institutions are deemed to act in a manner which is not in conformity with [Security Council Resolution] 1244."[7] The CF, however, does not specify who will assess whether these circumstances occur. It would appear that the Security Council and the Special Representative are the entities judging whether the provisional institutions are acting in conformity with Resolution 1244. This prerogative clearly puts the provisional institutions under international control, inasmuch as their respect for Resolution 1244 is concerned.

In the economic area, the Special Representative keeps final authority over the Kosovo budget and monetary policy. However, the provisional institutions have full competencies in preparing and executing the budget. As the Kosovo budget has come closer to being fully funded by locally generated resources, this clause could come into question. The rationale behind final international control in the economic area is to ensure an efficient use of resources as well as equitable distribution of public expenditure across ethnic groups. This second reason remains valid regardless of the origin of public resources. The administration of socially and state-owned property also remains in the hands of international administrators, though there is an obligation to cooperate with the provisional institutions in this area.

Attributes of state sovereignty such as concluding agreements with states and international organizations remain a reserved power of the Special Representative.[8] The CF, however, accords the provisional institutions the capacity to reach and finalize agreements.[9]

Internal security and law enforcement are the areas in which the powers of the provisional institutions are more restricted. The international police (UNMIK Police) supervise the local police (the Kosovo Police Service) and have primacy over them. The CF, nevertheless, foresees that the Kosovo Police Service will "gradually assume additional responsibilities for the maintenance of law and order."[10] The Special Representative exercises authority over law enforcement institutions and the correctional service. While most functions of the administration of justice are developed by local judicial personnel, the Special Representative decides on the assignment of international judges and prosecutors to specific judicial cases. This competence, initially resisted by local judicial personnel, has proved to be instrumental in facilitating the prosecution of Kosovo Albanians accused of war and other serious crimes. But it also puts the local judiciary in a situation of subordination to the international judges and prosecutors and blurs the independence of the judiciary vis-à-vis the de facto executive embodied in the Special Representative.

The Special Representative exercises "control over the management of the administration and financing of civil security and emergency preparedness."[11] This provision guarantees international control of the Kosovo Protection Corps (KPC), a civil protection body set up within the process of demilitarization of the KLA and whose members are mainly former combatants. While the creation of the KPC helped considerably in that process (and generally in keeping former combatants under some form of international control), it also postponed a final resolution of the issue of former combatants. The KPC is ambiguous with respect to its functions: Whereas the CF defines those as "rapid disaster response tasks," many KPC members consider themselves soldiers of the future army of Kosovo. In addition to controlling the administration and financing of the KPC, the CF further states that the Special Representative exercises an overall prerogative of "control over the Kosovo Protection Corps" to ensure that the future of the KPC is determined by the UN authority.

Common Elements for Postconflict Institution Building

What can be extrapolated from the Kosovo experience to other postconflict institution-building scenarios? It could have been expected that the lack of clarity regarding the future status of Kosovo would have seriously hampered the institution-building process because it was not clear what the final institutional setting would be—an independent state or a unit within a bigger state. This did not happen. Despite the ambiguity with respect to Kosovo's future status, UNMIK has made massive and rapid progress in building a relatively sophisticated institutional framework. This framework benefits from a relatively high degree of acceptance, as proved by the participation of all major political forces in several elections. This acceptance, however, does not mean acceptance of a final status that would not please the Albanian majority. It means only acceptance of the provisional arrangements pending a final settlement. It does not mean either that true reconciliation is taking place. As riots in the spring of 2004 showed, hatred persists and radical groups still believe that violent means are the best way to achieve their political goals. These riots also showed that multiethnicity, while probably accepted to different degrees by most of the people, is still rejected by some.

Formally, the framework is democratic, it respects minorities' rights, and is close to international standards of public administration. In practice, a lot remains to be done to ensure full implementation of the rule of law, full realization of minorities' rights, and efficient, transparent, and accountable public sector management practices. The lessons are many and impinge upon all domains of postconflict governance. But two lessons are especially clear and relate to situations found recurrently in postconflict scenarios in which a third party is given authority: (1) Devolution of power needs to be phased and offer a clear sense of direction to the local population and political elites, while being flexible enough to accommodate their preferences (within democratic parameters) and be timed to the capacity of local institutions to assume new powers; and (2) consultation with and inclusion of representatives of all political, ethnic, and social groups at all levels in the political process is key to avoiding a feeling of alienation of the local

population and to gain their support for the process of institution building led by the third party.

Phasing the Process

The Kosovo experience yields the following model sequence:

1. full third-party administration in consultation with appointed
   local representatives;
2. joint administration with appointed local representatives under
   third-party authority at municipal and central levels;
3. municipal administration by local democratically elected authorities under third-party supervision as well as joint central administration under third-party authority; and
4. municipal and central administration by local democratically
   elected authorities under third-party supervision.

A fifth and final step of the postconflict period, not yet reached in
Kosovo, would be municipal and central administration by local democratically elected authorities with third-party technical assistance.
Third-party authority over limited areas, such as defense or border control, can still apply.

The originality of this sequence lies in step 2. Contrary to what the
U.S.-led coalition is doing in Iraq or to the arrangements that the Bonn
process established for Afghanistan, the UN Interim Administration in
Kosovo did not grant formal independent authority to local representatives while those were not democratically elected. During the JIAS
phase, locals appointed by the UN to the KTC, the IAC, the administrative departments, and the municipal administrations had very limited
authority. Whenever they had direct executive authority, they were
paired with an international official and under the final authority of the
Special Representative. International supervision was effective on a
daily basis and not only a final safeguard. This fact was consolidated
with the establishment of consultative mechanisms at all levels in which
the international authority listened and tried to accommodate the views
of *all* the social groups.

Local authorities appointed by a third party lack legitimacy. The
third party may try to estimate the popular support of one or the other
local faction or organization and appoint authorities accordingly, but
this is not equivalent to democratic legitimacy. The risks are high. First,
large segments of the population may feel alienated from the very outset of the postconflict period and abandon the process proposed by the

third party. Second, the arbitrariness of appointments creates a window of opportunity for fortune seekers and an incentive to further fragmentation of political structures. Finally, the third party's recourse to appointments based on ethnic or religious allegiance creates an incentive for ethnic and religious alignment and acts against interethnic and interreligious integration.

In Kosovo, the international community perceived the public opinion wrongly at the beginning by overestimating popular support to the political parties emerging from the KLA, to the detriment of the LDK. During step 2, the LDK accepted a share of power in the interim structures that, as elections later showed, was well below its share of popular support. This did not create major problems because, in addition to the generally cooperative attitude of the LDK, the positions offered by UNMIK were always within an international structure and of a clearly temporary character. The LDK waited patiently until elections gave it the share of power it deserved according to the people's preference.

Extending the period of third-party formal executive authority also helps local parties build their capacity for the future without exhausting their political credit. During this period, they can participate in governmental structures without being responsible for their performance in the eyes of the public. The third party acts as a buffer in protecting the local parties—and future democratic leaders—by taking the blame for the public services that do not work and for the many sacrifices that the population goes through in the postconflict period.

Consultation and Cooperation at All Levels

Extending third-party executive authority to all administrative areas does not mean third-party isolation from the administered people. On the contrary, it obliges the third party to undertake close cooperation with local parties at all levels. Dividing functions between locals and third-party representatives is what may lead to the third party being isolated. The crucial point is that third-party representatives have to work *together* with locals and not divide up functions and work separately.

Groundwork at the community level by the third-party representatives is crucial to generating a cooperative attitude from the local population. The importance of dialogue with community representatives cannot be overestimated. This is particularly so at the very beginning of the third party's presence in the territory. The impression created during the first few weeks of the presence of the third party on the ground will be long-lasting and will determine the attitude of the population toward it, beyond relations of senior third-party officials with top local leaders at the central level. The process of identifying interlocutors must be thorough and go beyond dialogue with de facto local power holders to establish consultation mechanisms with representatives of vulnerable groups and nonpolitically affiliated people whose voice is often silenced but who make up important segments of the population and will be the strongest supporters of nonextremist options.

Notes

1. For an operational definition of democracy, see Huntington (1991, 7).
2. UN S/RES/1244 (1999), June 10, 1999.
3. The number of departments was not part of the original JIAS Agreement. It was determined after the agreement was signed in consultation with the parties to the agreement.
4. The Constitutional Framework was promulgated in UNMIK/REG/2001/9 of May 15, 2001.
5. See UNMIK/REG/2001/9, Chapter 9, which establishes the competencies and functioning of Provisional Institutions of Self-Government.
6. The Constitutional Framework lists twenty-six powers and responsibilities reserved to the SRSG. This chapter addresses only those considered more relevant for the purpose characterizing the model institutional framework established in Kosovo.
7. UNMIK/REG/2001/9, paragraph 8.1.b.
8. The Constitutional Framework specifies the reserved powers of the Special Representative including "concluding agreements with states and international organizations in all matters within the scope of UNSCR 1244"; UNMIK/REG/2001/9, paragraph. 8.1.m.
9. UNMIK/REG/2001/9, paragraph 5.6.
10. UNMIK/REG/2001/9, Chapter 6.
11. UNMIK/REG/2001/9, paragraph 8.1.l.

4

Developing Local Governance

Tanja Hohe

A s a result of the brutal rampage that followed the "popular consultation" for independence in 1999 and during the withdrawal of Indonesia, the occupying power, the entire official administration of East Timor was eliminated. For the first time in history the international community assumed political administration and sovereign authority over a country. The UN Transitional Administration in East Timor (UNTAET) was mandated to rebuild the public administration and govern the country at the same time. Within two and a half years it established some basic institutions for governance and administration. The transitional administrator twice appointed transitional cabinets. Eighty-eight Constituent Assembly members were elected, who drafted a new constitution in five months time. The assembly was eventually transformed into a parliament. On May 20, 2002, the country's administration was transferred from international supervision to Timorese control.

This most comprehensive attempt of state building by the international community mainly focused on national-level institution building and on elections as an exit strategy. As in other postconflict scenarios with UN governance operations, such as the UN Transitional Authority in Cambodia (UNTAC) or the UN Interim Administration Mission in Kosovo (UNMIK), the establishment of local governance was low on the agenda. While decentralization and devolution have become the main international objectives to enhance good governance in developing countries, they are not yet commonly integrated in state building after conflict. The problem of the involvement of national leaders in the state-building exercise has been pointed out (Chopra 2000, 31ff.), but the local population is still left out of the equation. Though UNTAET paid lip service to decentralization, it embodied a fundamentally centralized administration that was transmitted to the Timorese leadership with the transfer of sovereignty. The result is a young nation with national democratic institutions that have an unstable grassroots foundation.

One of the few attempts to decentralize and to create local participation was the Community Empowerment and Local Governance Project. In an unprecedented exercise of interorganizational collaboration between the UN and the World Bank, the CEP was to support the establishment of local bodies of authority to guarantee local participation in the reconstruction of the country. The intention was to formalize and integrate these bodies into the local governance structure. At the same time, the CEP aimed at poverty reduction and hence put forth an approach that combined development, democratization, and state building during the emergency phase of a postconflict setting.

The CEP can teach many lessons for state builders. It provides an example for designing development projects to support the setup of local governance structures. It raises the question about how far local governance structures can and should be established shortly after conflict when there is no national government to support it. The CEP also showed the practical problems of interinstitutional cooperation, falling victim to UNTAET's lack of decentralization. The project design itself illustrates the importance of working with local knowledge and raises the question of the degree of social engineering that can or cannot be conducted after a conflict has taken place.

State Building at the Grassroots

For the establishment of a subnational administration, UNTAET created thirteen district administrations throughout the country. They were initially staffed by international personnel and then handed over step-by-step to Timorese counterparts. From these centers, district field officers (DFOs) were responsible for subdistrict activities. The villages and hamlets were entirely in the hands of the National Council for Timorese Resistance (CNRT) throughout the process. The CNRT had been established a year prior to the popular consultation as an umbrella organization for all resistance parties. Immediately after the destruction of East Timor in September 1999, the CNRT appointed representatives at every level: in the hamlets, villages, subdistricts, districts, and at the national level.

Whereas UNTAET was mandated by the international community as the sole authority of the country, the local population saw the CNRT as the legitimate power. The UN decided to avoid recognition of the CNRT as an official partner (Conflict, Security, and Development Group 2003, paragraphs 293, 294) and considered it only as a factor to be dealt with. This constituted a difficult task for the district administrations that had to deal with the CNRT, which was everywhere present at the grassroots. While the two were often competing at the district level, in the subdistricts and villages UNTAET depended on the CNRT support to govern. Here CNRT representatives delivered data on the population to UNTAET and acted as the main link and messenger between the administration and the people.

On the hamlet and village level, the CNRT appointees enjoyed unchallenged power during the first half of the international administration. Their position became questioned when the CNRT dissolved in June 2001 in preparation for the Constituent Assembly elections. Fretilin, the main resistance party, had left the CNRT a year prior. Its strength had been underestimated in the early period. It had now started to win back the grassroots and had put Fretilin representatives in place at all levels, from hamlet to the national level. In some of the hamlets and villages, the Fretilin representatives now started challenging the position of the CNRT hamlet and village chief.

An additional dilemma was the UN's employment of Timorese in subnational administrative positions. People expected that the positions of Timorese district and subdistrict administrators would be filled with regard to the indigenous and resistance power structure. According to local social and authority structures, specific families are designated as "holding political authority." Only their senior members can act as legitimate leaders and fulfill the functions of a political ruler. They are appointed by the ritual leaders of the community. Yet when the new administrative staff under UNTAET was chosen, their appointments were based on their educational background and not indigenous criteria. The "modern" concept of the purely technical appointment in the administration was new to the population. The discrepancy between the modern way of selecting administration staff and the local ideas about legitimate leaders in these positions led to the rejection of personnel by local populations. The result was that UNTAET-selected staff lacked local legitimacy.

Presently, the local level is still plagued by confusion, caused by an unclear local governance structure that was left behind by the international administration.[1] The idea of neutral, nonpoliticized, technical administrative personnel as introduced by UNTAET fails to find any support, as it is such a strange idea in local concepts. In addition, the former CNRT structure and many of the UNTAET recruits are in opposition to the ruling party Fretilin and lack its recognition. The government has gradually politicized the administration and tried to put in place the party faithful. This has created a situation in which "the national government has only a roof but no roots."[2]

UNTAET also handed over a structure in which subnational administrators were not given any real powers. An important indigenous concept is that of the "center," which is combined with a rigid hierarchical power structure. Transferred to a governmental level, a centralized and authoritarian rule seems culturally legitimate. UNTAET gave only insignificant power to the district administrations, and the capital Dili evolved as the power center. The government that came to power after UNTAET did not have to make an effort to reverse decentralized structures because such structures simply did not exist. Although the constitution is committed to decentralization,[3] that goal is far from being achieved (UNDP 2002c). In addition there has been a general lack of ensuring local participation in the administration. Not only is participation a main pillar of democracy, but it is a crucial component of state building. Otherwise no downward accountability can be guaranteed.

Timorese actors—at the receiving end of the UN's democratization—were well aware of the lack of democratic features within UNTAET itself. In a general UN fashion, decisions were taken top down from the Special Representative of the Secretary-General. Moreover, in the case of UNTAET the SRSG at the same time acted as the transitional administrator, or head of state. Therefore, authoritarian-style decisionmaking was not only conducted internally within the mission but also in the administration of the country. Technically, the transitional administrator had the final say in any matter. While in most democratic countries there is a separation between legislative, judicial, and executive powers, under UNTAET all powers were combined in a single individual. The transitional administrator's extreme powers, which have been referred to as "benevolent despotism" (Beauvais 2001), might be the fastest way to rule after conflict—given that he makes the right decisions. It certainly did not teach a lesson in democracy, however, but stimulated the acceptance of a dictatorship—in this case internationally legitimized. One dictator might be benevolent, but his successor might have a different agenda and democracy could fall victim.

Empowering the Community

Shortly after the destruction of East Timor, the Asian Development Bank, bilateral donor countries, UN agencies, and regional specialists undertook a Joint Assessment Mission (JAM) under the leadership of the World Bank (Joint Assessment Mission 1999a). The JAM described that the "two indigenous key institutions," the CNRT and the church, had severely lost their capacities due to the destruction. Traditional powers such as the *liurais* (kings) had been constrained during Indonesian rule and had lost influence. In addition, there was now an urgent need for reconciliation between ex-militias and pro-independence fighters, which, if not dealt with would result in long-term social problems. Hence, the three main issues in the postconflict country were the rebuilding of the administrative structure, reconciliation, and strengthening of civil society (Joint Assessment Mission 1999b). The logic of the JAM was that the end of the Indonesian system resulted in a power vacuum. This seemed to provide an opportunity for social engineering to create grassroots institutions and reformed governance. The JAM called for "immediate action in order to fill the existing vacuum and ensure that communities have an effective vehicle for participating in and guiding the rebuilding of their nation" (Joint Assessment Mission 1999b, 12). The need of local participation was emphasized because it promised to overcome problematic issues through "rapid involvement of the population in positive rehabilitation and re-construction operations" (Joint Assessment Mission 1999b, 11).

The result of the mission was taken as the basis for the establishment of the World Bank's Community Empowerment and Local Governance Project. The CEP was a successor of the Kecamatan Development Program (KDP) in Indonesia, of which East Timor had been part. Therefore, the funding for an altered KDP in East Timor was readily available at the beginning of UNTAET's deployment. This enabled the CEP, which was to be conducted in most villages in East Timor (only Dili District was excluded), to play a crucial role in the early stages of local governance building during the emergency phase.

The program intended to enable villagers to make their own development choices, via mediation and accountability, through village development councils. These councils were designed as channels for development rather than traditional government agencies. They would receive support from other community institutions in their key tasks: the preparation and execution of developmental plans, dispute resolution, management of village funds, liaison with subdistrict and district levels for greater cooperation, and training of participation and democratic practices (Joint Assessment Mission 1999b, 13–14).

During the first emergency cycle, grants were to be given in equal amounts to each village once the election of council members and the formal establishment of the village development council were achieved. Grants were to be used for rehabilitation and reconstruction of social infrastructure and for economic recovery. For the second cycle of grants, subdistrict councils were to decide how to use the money by prioritizing proposals submitted by villages. Money was allocated through a competitive selection process between villages and between the hamlets within a village.

The program intended to access and promote ideas from the grassroots to strengthen local populations, to give them ownership, reduce corruption, and implement projects of relevance to the recipients. At the same time the program intended to change local power structures. Opposed to local mechanisms of decisionmaking, it sought to train and introduce a democratic sense of equality by giving each community member an equal voice to be represented in the village council. Village chiefs and traditional leaders were excluded from the councils. Gender equality was to be introduced by radically constructing the councils with 50 percent women. New parallel powers could challenge old ways and finally be turned into a local governance structure based on the will of the community rather then being implemented from the top. At the beginning of the project, it was not clearly defined how the new structure would be converted into official local governance and assume the place of the local leadership positions left vacant by UNTAET.[4]

Collaborating Institutions

The creation of the village councils was established under UNTAET Regulation 2000/13. It provided the legal framework, thus creating an entity at the community level, legally entitled to receive and disperse funds from CEP or other potential donors. The actual agreement on the regulation happened with great delay after UNTAET had rejected the project twice in negotiations and signed on to it only after intervention from the UN and World Bank leadership, as UNTAET was not in favor of decentralizing their power (Chopra 2002, 992–994; *La'o Hamutuk Bulletin* 2000, 8; Beauvais 2001, 1126).

The negotiations between UNTAET, the World Bank, and the Timorese leadership about the establishment of the CEP were influenced by Timorese politics at the time. The Internal Political Front (FPI) of the main resistance party Fretilin had started to conduct elections for village chiefs. The role of the FPI within the CNRT was unclear because the latter appeared as a rather monolithic entity to the international community. To integrate these ongoing elections into the structure of the CEP, it was decided to exclude the freshly elected village chief from the CEP village development councils and hence create a separation of powers on the very ground level: the village chief as executive, the CEP council as a quasi-legislative body, and the council of elders as a quasi-judicial body. The Timorese leadership agreed on the modified plans, and the FPI was promised a joint socialization campaign for the project and their own village chief elections.[5] During the CEP socialization campaign, conducted in the first months of 2000, a partnership was established between the CNRT subdistrict chiefs and the CEP subdistrict facilitators. Together they undertook the major task of informing the local populations about the CEP and its electoral process for the establishment of village councils.

The initial interorganizational differences between the World Bank and UNTAET resulted in a lack of cooperation between the CEP structure and the official administration. Although the CEP was officially a governmental project, during its first cycle it had not been integrated into the UNTAET administrative structure and functioned rather independently. Despite an international official in the district administration who acted as a CEP focal point, in charge of guaranteeing the coordination between CEP project staff and UNTAET, information dissemination was often poor. Some UN field officers and most of the population did not realize CEP was not an UNTAET program but a World Bank project. This often led to duplication of initiatives and lack of joint planning at the local level. The relationship between UNTAET and the CEP varied across the districts. Among the international staff, the idea of a bottom-up approach was not well appreciated and the sustainability of the projects, chosen by the communities, questioned.

One of the main ideas about the village development councils was that they could function as a main agency for development at the village level and, therefore, become the focal point for other donors or NGOs (Cliffe, Guggenheim, and Kostner 2003, 4). The latter could avoid the upper levels of authority and work directly with the villages. This was a strange approach for local NGOs, as it excluded the usual expression of respect to higher authorities, which can undermine or paralyze an undertaking. International agencies arrived with their own concepts and strategies of how to conduct development and were not willing to use creations of other organizations. In some subdistricts international NGOs started to make use of the village council as advisers on developmental issues in the villages. Council members also wrote proposals and handed them to other agencies. UNTAET was supposed to raise awareness among NGOs to involve the councils in their work, but UNTAET struggled to develop its own relationship with the CEP.

Subdistrict, village, and hamlet chiefs were the respected power holders at the local level. Therefore, they had the capacity to mobilize community involvement in the assessment, design, and implementation of projects promoted by village development councils. In their position as main interlocutors, they had privileged information regarding the development projects to be undertaken by the government and other potential donors. Yet they were excluded from being eligible for the councils.

This exclusion met resistance of the local leadership of some areas. It was felt that the councils with their new power, which was more official than the village chiefs' position, were not interested in a working relationship. The CNRT representatives ideologically relied on unity, based on a hierarchical structure of command, and saw themselves as sole authority; if "everybody starts giving their own orders the system cannot work." They claimed that if the councils did not start working with the CNRT, they would lose their legitimacy. "CNRT is the face. The CEP has to work with the local authorities, and then things can work. The local leadership has to be behind it."[6]

However, the council members had more financial means than the local power holders, who were regarding themselves as superior. This was not considered appropriate for their social position, and the situation created a gap between village chiefs and councils. The village chiefs traditionally were supposed to be in charge of public issues and relationships with the external world. Their responsibility for distributing shelter and food aid from international NGOs and their involvement with UNTAET provided them with legitimate power from another source.

Establishing Community Councils

One of the main features of the CEP was the introduction of democratic elections for the council members. Democratic elections of village chiefs had taken place under the Indonesian system, but this had not challenged the selection of the "appropriate" individual confirmed by the indigenous order. The leader of a community traditionally has to stem from a specific family, which is designated as the entity to hold "political authority" (Traube 1986, 98–124). This order is ancestor given and, therefore, not to be questioned. In the democratic elections under the Indonesian government, Western democratic means were applied to confirm and express indigenous ideas. The person from the "right" family was usually elected (Hohe 2002, 569–589). Elections for the CEP village development council confirmed the fact that just by introducing democratic means, one does not necessarily introduce democracy.

The elections for village council members at the hamlet level were conducted during the first half of 2000 in more than 400 villages. Clear instructions provided the framework of how elections were to be held.[7] Candidates had to be over eighteen years old, be a resident of the hamlet, not be a traditional or local leader, and have time to work in the council. Eligible voters were every hamlet resident, male and female, and older than seventeen years of age or married. At least 50 percent of the hamlet residents had to participate in the election.

In reality, the way to choose candidates mostly involved local means of decisionmaking. Traditionally, candidates for important positions are never selected by secret vote; potential candidates are chosen by village elders through discussion (as in the election of the village or hamlet chiefs), because only they know of people's ancestral heritage. Afterward the constituency is invited to vote.

Significantly, the council member elections were not accompanied by ritual activities. This differed from the previously held village chief elections, which were conducted with significant ceremonial support. It indicated that the village chief was considered as an important authority, which had to be ancestrally legitimized. The election of council members was perceived as profane. A look at who was elected into the councils tells a lot about communities' perception of their functions.

The most important criterion mentioned by the voters about the election of the council members was their capacity to "do the job." Further, literacy and age (literacy is higher among young people) were the overall striking features of the council members. Thus, it seemed that no political power was associated with their position. Voters denied that being a descendant from a specific family was of importance. Indeed, council members did not stem from the usual political authority families, which would traditionally supply the village chief. They were purely seen to be implementers of projects and not in a leading position to take decisions for the community. The CEP was perceived as an outside institution; it had no important meaning for the inside community. Therefore, the people elected had experiences with the outside and the governmental world.

The social setup of the council indicates that actual decisionmaking powers would not be transferred to the council members. Although most people described the decisionmaking process as driven by the people with the facilitation of council members, in reality council members hardly ever actively took part in or facilitated the discussions. They adopted ideas agreed to by consensus once the more vocal people in the meetings advocated for them. The counselors themselves perceived their role as facilitators or a bridge between community members and decisionmakers.

In many cases, the real power holders of the village played a dominant role in the process. Local powers, such as village chiefs, teachers (mostly the older and educated people in the village), and church representatives, discussed project proposals on behalf of the people. The results were passed to the traditional elders to legitimize them. People were seen as free to make suggestions for the program, but traditional elders had to ensure that the program worked in accordance with the ancestral order.

Discussion seemed a very important part of the process, confirming an indigenous idea about decisionmaking. Through discussion a consensus can be reached and every member of the group can be convinced of a specific proposal. This contradicts the concept of Western democracy, where a number of alternatives are identified and each member of society decides, with an equally valued vote, on his favorite choice. The local way excludes the notion of opposition. Everybody ought to agree on the final proposal. Local authorities and concepts, even in the CEP process, were still in place and were not challenged by the councils as new institutions.

The CEP was also an attempt to challenge traditional gender relations. The technical requirements of the program, to have 50 percent of women elected into the councils, was perceived as strange by a large part of the population, but it was easily achieved. However, there were constraints that prevented the women from taking a more proactive role. To achieve the status of equal partners with men in the decisionmaking process, a long process involving change of mentality in both men and women was needed, particularly in rural areas. Female council members were sidelined, and their knowledge about the program was often insufficient. During the CEP village meetings, female council members were mostly taking care of food and drinks for the people who attended the meeting.

Challenging Local Authorities

The crucial component of the project was the establishment of the village development councils to promote a more horizontal and democratic system of governance, breaking through traditional systems of power and former corruptive top-down decisionmaking processes. A Western democratic system was to be established at the grassroots, in a setting where the separation of powers does not run between the lines of the executive, legislative, and judiciary but between political and ritual authorities. This was not only an attempt to change the remains of the Indonesian system but also to challenge local structures that had provided stability in the past.

The assumption of a "power vacuum" on the ground opened the doors for social engineering at the grassroots level. It appeared to be the right moment to introduce democratic structures. This was a misperception. Even under the most difficult circumstances, local power concepts had survived in the past. East Timor had seen many changes in its administrative systems throughout history. Local stability was based on indigenous power structures that always served as a framework to absorb external influences. In fact, especially in times of crisis, traditional structures were relied on most; they provided a commonly understood basis for action when everything else had vanished. It is important to realize that as soon as a community exists, its members always have a concept of who should be in power and why. In East Timor it had taken the CNRT only days after the destruction to reestablish a complete structure from the hamlet to the national level that had local legitimacy. What the JAM had perceived as a power vacuum was essentially only a lack of an official administrative-governmental system.

Social engineering on the ground was attempted in an environment where strong ideas about leadership existed. The changes were to be introduced through the exclusion of the village chiefs from the councils and the empowerment of the council members through financial means, while the village chiefs and traditional leaders lacked financial capacity. The councils were set up to develop into new power centers in the community. Yet as new creations, they had no resemblances to the local structures (*La'o Hamutuk Bulletin* 2000, 7). It proved difficult to enforce a separation of powers that was not an integral part of the local system. One system had to lose in favor of the other.

On the side of the international staff, the introduction of the separation of powers was understood to empower a new part of the community and challenge hierarchical traditional structures. On the side of the Timorese, the noneligibility of the traditional powers was understood as an attempt to undermine the power of the village chief and not as democracy. The village councils were not perceived as part of the political sphere of the world, nor of ritual life. Anybody could be elected to the councils. As the council members turned out to be young people from random families, they remained powerless. They were not expected to be responsible for the traditional political tasks of conflict resolution and political decisionmaking. They were only seen as implementers of projects and, therefore, their position in the local socio-cosmos did not collide with the traditional powers and in turn could not challenge them. Decisionmaking remained with the traditional power holder, namely, the hamlet or village chief.

As a result, the quality of the projects conducted under the CEP suffered from the CEP's attempt to conduct social engineering and introduce grassroots democracy. The CEP would have shown better short-term results if it had relied on local power structures. The village chief and his monopoly of knowledge of village issues could have proven useful for the council.

Only long-term education in development issues could have turned the council members into an acknowledged power whereby the indigenous power concept could have changed. To have this impact on the sociopolitical structure of Timorese societies, the CEP should have been planned for a longer period. Social engineering seems very tempting in a postconflict scenario, yet without full knowledge of local dynamics, attempted empowerment of new leaders will fail as local realities are stronger. The same constraint applies to democratization and promotion of gender equality and raises the question when and how far to include local power structures, especially in a postconflict scenario where society has to recover (Chopra and Hohe 2004).

Conclusion

The establishment of a central government that is legitimate in the eyes of the population is undoubtedly crucial in state-building exercises. In addition, a strong local governance system that is within reach of the population and is acknowledged by it is of great relevance to overcome a vast number of problematic issues in postconflict reconstruction. "The emphasis in state building should be on the local level, as this is where the peace settlement happens" (Jackson 2002, 1–2). So far the relevance of this level in the creation of a well-working state has been dramatically underestimated. The international focus has been on the establishment of national institutions, based on the mispresumption that a stable national democratic government will necessarily promote a peaceful nation. Yet it is ill-fated logic that the national level can exist without stable grassroots. The need for stability and clear official structures is extremely high in postconflict scenarios. The neglect of the subnational level weakens the population in its efforts to reestablish their normal life.

In East Timor, two years after independence and five years after the destruction of the former system, there is still no definite local governance structure in place. Timorese leaders have understood the importance of the lower levels, and a political competition to win them has swept through the country. Only recently a team of international consultants in cooperation with a Timorese technical working group designed possible models for a local governance system, under the auspices of the Timorese Ministry of Internal Affairs.[8] However, the final selection of the new system will be made by the present government in a much more politically charged environment than right after the destruction of the country. It now provides the opportunity for a single party to determine subnational administration in its favor. Early development of local governance structures by a sensitive international community in cooperation with local stakeholders could have set the stage before political oppositions started to play out.

The use of developmental funds and initiatives or even the delivery of humanitarian aid to support early development of local governance is a positive innovation. It has been attempted in a few examples, such as East Timor and Rwanda (Cliffe, Guggenheim, and Kostner 2003) and should be further elaborated in the future. However, the main hurdles to overcome are interinstitutional differences. Lack of collaboration between the CEP and UNTAET put additional constraints on the success of the program in East Timor. Important knowledge from either side could have helped the quality and choice of projects. Even the best plans for development and local governance cannot take root if simple disagreements between international institutions prevail.

Development projects that support local governance as well as the establishment of local administration both have to operate with sufficient local knowledge. A conscious decision on the degree of social engineering has to be taken. Indigenous structures are often prevailing and have the trust of the population. Established leaders have the monopoly on knowledge, as they are the main representatives dealing with the external world. To make economic development and the rebuilding of the country more efficient in the short term, the involvement of traditional authorities and the appreciation of local understanding can ease the process. What was thought to become a new parallel power, the East Timorese village councils, could have been turned into development focal points to work alongside the traditional powers. This could have guaranteed more efficient poverty alleviation and the smooth development of local governance with full recognition and understanding from the side of the local population.

Notes

1. See, for example, "Chefi Aldeia protes kebijakan UNTAET," *Suara Timor Lorosae*, June 22, 2001.

2. Interview with a district administrator, East Timor, November 2002.

3. Constitution of the Democratic Republic of East Timor, Part I, Section 5.

4. At the end of 2002, the CEP structures were finally integrated into the local administration. CEP subdistrict council heads became part of the newly created District Community Development Committees.

5. Personal communication with Jarat Chopra, Dili, September 2001.

6. Interview with CNRT representative, Bobonaro, 2001.

7. UNTAET Regulation 2000/13.

8. Since April 2003. The project was funded by Ireland Aid and implemented by UNDP.

Reestablishing the Rule of Law

Mark Plunkett

The engine that has driven most United Nations missions has to conduct an election of a Constituent Assembly, criticized as the "vote and forget" approach of the UN to international crises. A preoccupation with formal state building has predominated most peace operations to the neglect of the reestablishment of the rule of law (ROL). Since the early 1990s, lawyers from all over the world involved in the UN missions have lamented this fundamental failure. True and enduring peace only occurs when there is a genuine return of the rule of law, which is the guarantee for a proper functioning of any emerging or restored state.

Following the disasters of UN missions in the mid-1990s, including the failures to prevent the 1994 massacre in Rwanda and the 1995 massacre in Srebrenica, Bosnia and Herzegovina, the UN embarked upon a high-level review of the shortcomings of its previous peace operations (Dursch 2000, 1). The result of the review, the Brahimi Report, released in September 2000, recommended a "doctrinal shift" in the use of civilian police and other judicial and human rights specialists in peace operations to reflect an increasing focus on strengthening the rule of law and respect for human rights in postconflict environments (United Nations 2000b).

Most peace operations take place in an operational climate where there is substantially reduced or a complete absence of a ROL. International military peacekeepers usually enter a ROL vacuum. The effectiveness of all aspects of a peace operation—such as cantonment, safe havens, humanitarian relief, and electoral enrollment for the Constituent Assembly—is seriously hampered until a ROL is established. Banditry, revenge killing, and general violence will threaten not just the local populace but also NGO workers, civilian peacekeepers, and even armed military peacekeepers.

Systematic organized theft of peace operation resources severely hampers delivery of materials and services to needy people and undermines the entire peace operation. Repression and systematic human rights abuses against the people by factional elites and their functionaries will protract the conflict and prevent postconflict reconciliation necessary for peace. Institutionalized official corruption, nepotism, criminalized economies (i.e., the illegal sale of natural and cultural resources, narcotics, and arms), racketeering, and black markets will retard economic recovery and development. The expense and effort of nation rebuilding and elections by peacekeepers will be rendered nugatory if the emerging government maintains order by lawless means and in breach of fundamental human rights.

The motivations for armed conflict are varied and changing. The emergence of shadow states with blurred lines between war and peace and war and crime hamper the reestablishment of the ROL. Political motivations that drove war activity are mixed with and give way to financial opportunism that involves crime. Peace operations have to recognize that many of the local players while purporting to be political factions are also sophisticated criminal organizations or crude criminal gangs that the international community has had to deal with to broker a peace agreement taking place in a domestic legal void.

Peacekeepers work in dangerous operational environments where there is:

1. horizontal violence between the major feuding factions (continuing or returning to war, cease-fire violations) and between people themselves (mainly domestic crimes—murder, rape, arson, theft);
2. vertical violence by factions against the people (extortion, political intimidation, oppression, human rights abuses, corruption, genocide, murder, rape); and
3. horizontal violence against the peacekeepers from factions (attacks on peace processes, killing of peacekeepers) and from people (killing, robbery of peacekeepers, theft of equipment).

Unless there is an adequate mandate, a strategically planned program, and adequate resources for the restoration of the ROL, peacekeeping operations will fail to achieve the ultimate objective to bring peace to people formerly deadlocked in armed conflict. True and enduring peace only occurs when there is a genuine return of the ROL, which is the foundation for a proper functioning and legitimate state. The peacekeepers will not be able to eliminate all criminal behavior. What they must do is to strive to replace a culture of violence and impunity with systems of rule observance without using violence for the management of conflicts.

All armed conflicts finish some day. The objective of the peace operation is to bring that end date forward in time. Peace operations are exercises in shrinking conflict time by condensing and terminating coercion activity. This is achieved by focusing on the restoration of the ROL as the primary objective of every peace operation.

All conflicts are managed in one (or more) of three ways, namely by: (1) force and coercion (war is the ultimate expression of this genre); (2) merit review umpires (including judges, juries, and elections); or (3) negotiated agreements (peacemaking and peacekeeping). The use of force to manage conflict has a very high cost but a very low utility return. Criminal and civil litigation involves a medium to high cost with medium utility return. Negotiations involve a low cost but can deliver a very high utility return. The reestablishment of the ROL in peace operations requires the use of all three management techniques with the ease, economy, efficiency, and effectiveness exponentially rising in later order. In peace operations ROL restoration must take priority over constitutional settlements. Peace operations take place where there is no ROL. The task of a peace operation is to restore the ROL first and foremost before re-creating the state. This is achieved through the delivery of specific planned and implemented peace operation justice packages using the two combined models:

1. *Enforcement model:* legitimate, minimal, and lawfully sanctioned coercion such as arrest, prosecution, detention, and trial by war crimes tribunals and transitional peace operations courts; public shaming and office disqualification by peace operation criminal justice commissions; rebuilding, resourcing, and training local judges, police, prosecutors, defenders, and custodial officers; and

2. *Negotiated model:* securing voluntary compliance by negotiating mass community psychology to bring about fundamental shifts in population consciousness at the three levels of the elite leadership, functionary, and village level to replace the culture of violence with negotiated management systems.

What Is a Rule of Law, and Why Is It Important?

The continued existence of the state is dependent on the primacy and strength of its ROL. The existence of the state and the ROL are mutually inclusive and dependent upon each other. Levels of coercive conflict management rise with the withering away of the ROL first and ultimately the state. The degree to which the state exists is measured by the extent of functioning of the three branches of the state in service of the people. To what extent is there an effective working utility of the legislature (lawmakers), executive (law administrators), and judiciary (law deciders)?

The ROL is a precondition for the existence of a community of people who live together in a reciprocal relationship between each other and between themselves and the state. A ROL exists where both the ruler and the ruled respect the legal rules that govern the relationships. The ROL is the glue that holds together the web of legal relationships that forms the state. The ROL is a notional social contract by people who consent to regulate their behavior by rules that have the force of law, usually deriving their authority from the state.

An essential feature of the rule of law is that it constrains those with the most power in a group of people from doing what they would otherwise do if there was no rule of law. A rule of law asserts the supremacy of law over all people, including the government. As summarized by F. A. Hayek: "Stripped of all its technicalities this means that government in all its actions is bound by rules fixed and announced beforehand—rules which make it possible to foresee with fair certainty how the authority will use its coercive powers in given circumstances, and to plan one's individual affairs on the basis of knowledge" (Raz 1979, 210). However, the concept goes further than rule *by* law but is also about *justice:* "The rule of law does not merely mean formal legality which assures regularity and consistency in the achievement and enforcement of democratic order, but justice based on the recognition and full acceptance of the supreme value of the human personality providing a framework for its fullest expression" (OSCE 1990).

To measure the degree to which the rule of law exists, the following questions are to be answered:

- Are the relationships between people regulated by rules?
- Are the rules commonly accepted as legitimate?
- Are the rules observed by ruler and ruled alike?
- Is force used to manage conflict?
- If force is used, is it authorized by the rules?
- Where a dispute exists about the rules, is there a rule that the dispute is determined by an independent umpire whose decision is accepted by all parties? Do the state elites and functionaries (government and police) observe the rule to submit themselves

to the determination of the independent umpire and abide the decision of the independent umpire?

The state has a monopoly on the legitimate use of force, which can only be exercised subject to the strict requirements of the ROL. Under the ROL an independent judiciary is the neutral arbiter of disputes between people themselves and between people and the state. It determines the lawfulness of the exercise of force by a person (e.g., self-defense) or by the state (e.g., arrests, detention, and imprisonment in the execution of the law).

The authority of the state is weakened when force is used against the ROL whether by the state against its own people, by the state against another state, or by people within the state against the state or each other. If the state or its people continue to use illegitimate force in breach of the ROL, the ROL is eroded and may collapse completely. This will undermine the authority of the state. If unabated this will result in the collapse of the state itself. As the ROL and, as a consequence, the state wither away, the degree of coercive conflict management through the use of illegitimate force against people rises exponentially.

Peace operations occur when a state is disrupted, fractured, or has collapsed. They usually occur when there is no functioning ROL but mostly where there is neither a state nor a ROL. The objective of peace is to restore the ROL and the state. The first and fundamental objective of a peace operation is to restore the ROL thereby achieving the second objective of re-creating the existence of a state that enables people affected by an armed conflict to live together in an enduring peace. Peace operations for people without a state or ROL that attempt to re-create the state (e.g., through internationally supervised elections), without first re-creating the ROL, go backward and run the risk of slipping back to a collapsed state (e.g., post–peace operation coups), which will prolong the conflict and fail to achieve the objective to bring about enduring peace. Where there is a collapsed state, peacekeepers should concentrate on the reestablishment of the ROL before trying to establish a state.

Officials of the UN and foreign offices of nations in the planning of past missions have falsely assumed that the rule of law automatically follows the conduct of a democratic election. The defect of this approach is the mistaken belief that the only source of authority for a rule of law derives from the social compact of a democratic election. The problem with this approach is to ignore the sociocognitive reality that people are regulated by many lesser social compacts built around relationships based on Abraham Maslow's hierarchy principles relating to survival, identity, and fulfillment that involve alliances based on region, family, religion, work, and so forth. These compacts, or systems, are sufficient to support a rule of law even in the absence of a functioning state. This is so in small communities and especially in traditional communities. These informal systems may not be visible to, or may be little understood by, the outside interveners who give ascendancy to often comparatively recent artificially imposed colonial systems of European laws using an imported Westminster-style constitutional system, which may be largely irrelevant in village societies (Brown 1986; 1999). The formal law system and traditional systems exist side by side, constituting a social pluralism and a peculiarly legal dualism (Fraser 1999). All missions are likely to suffer from a lack of insight into these social, if not legal, relations with much mutual cultural bafflement impeding the objective to reestablish the rule of law. Without overidealizing traditional law systems, these micro ROL systems are as important in the negotiated model for the rule of law as will be the resourcing of the institutional model for the rule of law.

The primary objective of a peace operation is the creation of the ROL. The ROL will only finally be reestablished when most of the people are prepared to accept and freely submit themselves to it at the level of: the great mass of the population; the military commanders, police, and local warlords (functionaries); and ultimately the central leadership (ruling factional elites). What cannot be underestimated is the difficulty of the task. It is easier to lose the rule of law than it is to restore it. The time and effort required to resuscitate the rule of law is longer and harder than the time and effort involved in its demise. The initial establishment of security is an easier objective than establishing a long-term durable peace that must persist after the withdrawal of the mission. The challenge for the mission is to engineer major social changes by eradicating an entrenched culture of impunity for violence and kleptocracy using both the formal and informal legal systems.

War and People's Search for Alternative Rule of Law Systems

The rise of war and the demise of the ROL are an inverse ratio. But the restoration of the ROL is not an inverse ratio to the end of war. Peace operations planners should not assume that the ROL automatically resumes with a formal peace. Continuing and residual conflict, enmity, and anger may persist between people for generations after the end of fighting. The cause of this is that in modern wars members of the general population are not only deliberate military targets but also suffer the bulk of the casualties of war. After civilians have been attacked in war, they are loath to accept legitimacy of any authority. Violent coercion is continued by former war players against civilian populations who respond in kind and use weapons indiscriminately. The cessation of hostilities does not herald the resumption of the ROL happening hard on the heels of a peace agreement, however comprehensive the agreement is stated to be. Peace operations planners in the past have erroneously assumed otherwise. The return of the ROL occurs gradually and hesitatingly long after a formal peace treaty and the end of warfare. Peacekeepers must identify what social preconditions are necessary to bring about the restoration of the ROL.

The ROL is usually described in the context of the relationship of the broader community (usually the state) to an individual within it. Irrespective of war and peace, some people living traditional lifestyles may not recognize or even be aware of the primacy of a state but nevertheless have strong but small ROL systems. In situations variously described as stateless societies or alternatively village-states, people follow a sophisticated ROL system derived from ancient legal systems (usually oral) that regulate the distribution of all resources—material, human, and spiritual. Peacekeepers need to constantly question their own assumptions about what really motivates people and what rules have ascendancy over others. In peace operations the reestablishment of the ROL focuses on individual people and their relationship to others and to an emerging state. Where there is a micro ROL without a state, the units of compliance consist of very small groups of people. The point is to bring these cohesive units of people with micro ROLs together into a larger efficient one-unit organization of a state whose one ROL is compatible with the many micro ROLs. The art of reestablishing the state is to understand how to harmonize all of the micro ROL systems into one large ROL. In questioning assumptions about the priority given to laws and rules and the motivation for compliance, it is important to compare the differing perspectives of the leadership elite and functionaries with the perspectives of the mass of ordinary people during war.

The priority given by an individual to a rule system may be radically altered in times of war, particularly where the state is fractured, frustrated, or collapsed. While the official will assert allegiance to the authority of the state or to "his group," an individual is likely to have a complete reverse of priority of rule observance, especially when the state is weakening or has collapsed. War will alter and even reverse the priority of rule observance of an individual.

Motivation plays an important part of a person's decisionmaking processes, which are activated when a gap is recognized between an ideal and actual state of affairs. Dissatisfaction with a malfunctioning ROL system will motivate a person to search for alternatives—for example, protection and ROL systems offered by warlords.

The Enforcement Model for the Reestablishment of the Rule of Law

As there is no law without a sanction, the first objective of the enforcement model is to build legal mechanisms to redress wrongdoing. Under the enforcement model for a ROL, a peace operation reintroduces a domestic criminal justice system to prosecute offenders for crimes committed during the currency of a peace operation. Most major human rights breaches are straightforward acts of criminal culpability, such as murder, grievous bodily harm, abduction, rape, arson, and theft, which are often committed to hamper the peace process, including the creation of a neutral political environment necessary for a free and fair election and formation of a government of national reconciliation. The primary focus of the ROL enforcement model is to prevent or stop such acts and to ensure the safe and effective conduct of all other aspects of the peace operation. The objective is to create a fair, impartial, and independent judicial mechanism to provide accountability for criminal misconduct, which must replace the persisting culture of impunity. Under the enforcement model, a peace operation also assists any international war crimes tribunal staff in apprehending past human rights violators under international conventions as crimes against humanity, torture, or genocide—but this is incidental and subsidiary to the ROL enforcement model.

The enforcement model for the restoration of the ROL is achieved by the establishment of two major justice institutions. The first is a functioning criminal justice system consisting of police, custodial officers, correctional officers, prosecutors, defenders, and judges to:

- detect and investigate major crimes involving serious breaches of human rights such as war crimes, genocide, murder, arson, and rape;
- arrest and detain accused persons;
- bring accused persons to justice by prosecuting them;

- provide a fair trial by an independent, competent, and credible court (where none exists, then provide transitional trial and appeal courts composed of cross-factional judges chaired by distinguished international jurists until local courts can be established);
- observe the verdict of the court; and
- carry out the sentence imposed (if convicted) including community service, fines, imprisonment, correctional supervision (probation and parole), and paying of criminal compensation to victims.

The second justice institution consists of a criminal justice commission or truth and reconciliation commission (where no local independent, competent, and credible equivalent exists, then a transitional commission composed of cross-factional judges chaired by a distinguished international jurist should be assembled until a local independent, competent, and credible judge is found). Its purpose is to inquire into and report on: genocide and war crimes; official misconduct including corruption, abuse of office, lack of impartiality, and electoral misconduct; and reform of the criminal justice system. The commission educates the people on human rights, ethics, and norms and allows victims and perpetrators an opportunity to testify on record. It oversees: the granting of amnesties from prosecution and civil suit; the initiation of prosecutions; removals from public office; the prohibition of electoral candidature; public exposure, censure, and shaming; reminders of past atrocities; payments of compensation; and participation in the reconciliation processes.

Prior to a peace operation, field survey missions assess the existing justice assets. Some countries can be seen as likely candidates for peace operation intervention well in advance of a peace operation. The remnants of existing justice assets are built on, developed, and improved to standards set by UN conventions. Where there is an absence of the ROL, peace operations have to be prepared to bring their own laws and to establish their own transitional criminal courts and transitional criminal justice commissions and detention centers in the short term. However, the objective is to help the local people to re-create their own justice institutions composed of their own people using their own laws, language, and culture, adjusted and improved to international standards.

In peace operations there will always be a gap in ROL resources available to peacekeepers. This will manifest itself in an absence of: legal resources (adequate laws to cover the peace operation and to empower the peacekeepers if necessary to enforce a ROL); human resources (independent and competent judges, court administrators, prosecutors, defense lawyers, police and prison administrators, and salaries); and physical resources (court houses, law libraries, police stations, and detention centers).

Notwithstanding, what is often a daunting task can be achieved with basic resources. Courts can be convened under trees and people called to tell their stories. Often the process of investigation and having an open and fair hearing—so long as security can be guaranteed—can have a significantly beneficial social effect to show that even in strained circumstances the law will (or should) prevail. It demonstrates that a reckoning for impunity will eventually have to be accounted for.

The starting point for peacekeepers is to be unambiguous about their own source of legitimacy and legal authority. While each contributing country brings with them a body of internal legal authority governing its personnel, when in the host country, the legal authority for enforcing a ROL will derive from: international law; domestic law of both the peacekeeper's country and the host country; and consent through negotiated agreement from the host country's feuding factions and the peace operation members.

Often there will not be any law in the host country because the state and the ROL will have collapsed. Where there is an intrastate war, each faction will assert the ascendancy of their own "laws" over any others. To use the laws of one group over the other will imperil the neutrality of the peace operation. Another issue is that a peace operation can only use existing local laws and local courts to enforce the laws when those laws and courts reasonably meet international standards. Usually there will be no domestic substantive or procedural law that is competent, credible, and independently administered. Even if there were an adequate local law, it will not be universally accepted. Peacekeepers cannot seek to enforce the ROL under only one faction's legal system unless the offense is intrafactional only (i.e., offender, victim, and witnesses all from the same faction). Because most crimes will be cross-factional, justice will not be seen to have been done in the courts of any one faction. Where more than one faction is involved in the offense, there is risk of the perception, if not the reality, of bias if peacekeepers use laws and courts rejected by other faction(s). As a result, peacekeepers find themselves entering into a legal emptiness, legal chaos, or at the very least considerable legal ambiguity.

Treaty makers usually fail to make sensible or adequate provision for the ROL. When peacemakers negotiate agreement for the intervention of a peace operation, they must secure agreement from the factions for comprehensive measures for the reestablishment of the ROL. This should include full authority for the establishment and operation of transitional peace operation trial courts. Where the head agreement omits reference to enforcement mechanisms for the reestablishment of the ROL, the peacekeepers will need to renegotiate its provision with the factions, but this will prove difficult in most cases.

In northwest Cambodia, the UN Civil Police was able to secure the endorsement of a local faction to adhere to the terms of the peace agreement, for all operational purposes, by separate negotiations conducted on the ground after the arrival of the UN Transitional Authority in Cambodia. In the Solomon Islands an antigovernment rebel faction led by Andrew Keke on the Weather Coast agreed to cooperate with the regional intervention peace force after separate on-the-ground negotiations notwithstanding the fact that hitherto the faction had remained outside the peace process and was opposed to the government that had invited the outside peace operation.

Hence, a proper legal basis must be provided for the creation of the criminal justice system during the immediate and transitional phase. Ultimately it is necessary to develop off-the-shelf international criminal laws, practices, and procedures to enable peacekeepers automatic recourse for the establishment and conduct of transitional peace operation courts. The Yugoslav and Rwanda war crimes tribunals offer some precedents, especially on laws of evidence and rules procedures. With the establishment of the International Court of Justice, an authoritative jurisprudence is beginning to emerge. Soon it will be necessary for international law to recognize a peace operations criminal code setting out criminal offenses and defenses, practices, procedures, and evidence. An essential feature of the ROL enforcement model is the need for a wide public dissemination of simple statements of the requirements of the law. Public education and media must campaign to inform people of their obligations, responsibilities, and rights under the laws of the peace operation.

Consequently, in the absence of the existence of competent, credible, and independent courts, peace operations will be required to establish transitional courts until the people of the host country are able to do so. Soon it will be necessary for international law to recognize the authority of peace operations to establish their own courts to administer the peace operations criminal code. To this end peacekeepers will bring with them a panel of distinguished international jurists, either retired or serving judges, to chair transitional courts during the peace operation. The peace operation judges may constitute the only judicial forum for the conduct of trials where either the local courts are inadequate or will not act or where the accused, victims, and witnesses are from different factions. The peace operations courts might also hear complaints and actions against the peacekeepers themselves. The distinguished international jurists will be required to sit alone, or more desirably, as a chair of a bench composed of judges from each of the factions. An appeals court must also be established to hear appeals from the peace operations courts, again composed of distinguished international jurists sitting with judges from each of the factions. These courts will require proper resources such as premises, hearing rooms, clerks, transcription services, and other administrative support.

The former local judges and clerks may have grown up under authoritarian systems and have little understanding about the proper role of courts in society. The peace operation judges provide on-the-job training and mentoring of acceptable former and new local judges who take over the criminal justice system as local courts are resumed or when the work of the peace operations transitional courts is over. The distinguished international jurists, international prosecutors, and defenders phase themselves out with the reestablishment of a local competent, independent, and resourced judiciary. The peace operation undertakes judicial training designed to provide on-site training and assistance to judges in the implementation of human rights and criminal law with a view to improving the judicial system.

After prolonged war, the courthouses will be destroyed or in a run-down state. Along with police stations, courthouses are often the first structures to be burned to the ground. Postwar reconstruction and maintenance of courthouses greatly enhance the community prestige of the judiciary and working conditions of judges. The local courthouse should not only be a focal point for the administration of justice but also serve as a visible architectural symbol of the reestablishment of the ROL.

After a long war, there is often a complete absence of legal texts, right down to a shortage of clerical materials such as filing cabinets, desks, pens, and paper necessary for running a court. Courts require copies of the existing laws that are to be interpreted and applied. Basic legal materials and texts will be required. The provision of textbooks, even if they are outdated and discarded, can be valuable for local jurists and law enforcement officials in seeking assistance from the models and precedents of other jurisdictions as a solution to domestic legal problems. The courts require adequate administrative support. The standard of education of most clerks may be very basic. Modest assistance to the conditions of the clerks and filing facilities goes a long way to improving the functioning of the courts. Transcripting staff and local script word processors are also an essential need of the courts.

In the early stages of the peace operation—where there is no effective local independent judiciary or police—the peacekeepers will be required to take on the task of arrest, prosecution, and trial of serious offenders where the existing officials are unwilling to act or where the local officials are, in fact, the perpetrator of offenses themselves. This will be essential where major human rights breaches are being perpetrated by the leadership of the existing factions and functionaries, which threaten the neutral political environment, imperiling the free and fair elections.

Peace operations special prosecutors will be required to conduct the initial prosecutions. They must be independent from the peace operation hierarchy. A peace operations prosecution policy should be established to guide the prosecution criteria, especially where it is decided not to prosecute. Political considerations and expediency on the part of the peacekeepers can play no part in these considerations. The peace operation special prosecutors should be answerable to the courts for their conduct and not to any administrative hierarchy. As a lawyer, a prosecutor not only has a professional obligation but also an ethical duty to see that the law is respected and upheld to the best of his capability and to prevent and rigorously oppose any violation. The peace operation should ensure that prosecutors are able to perform their professional functions without intimidation, hindrance, harassment, improper interference, or unjustified exposure to civil, penal, or other liability. In the performance of their duties, special prosecutors must carry out their functions impartially and avoid all political, social, religious, racial, cultural, sexual, or any other kind of discrimination and to protect the public interest, act with objectivity, take proper account of the position of the suspect and the victim, and pay attention to all relevant circumstances, despite whether they are to the advantage or disadvantage of the suspect. A prosecutor has a heavy duty to ensure that an accused person receives a fair trial. The peacekeepers and international trained personnel must be model litigants. In the performance of their professional duties and obligations in determining whether a prosecution is to be commenced, the prosecutors have to be independent of political considerations or directions from legislative and executive functionaries. In the final analysis the prosecutors are not servants of the government or individuals—they are servants of justice.

In the transitional phase, the peace operations will be required to provide competent defense counsel for accused persons. Local prosecutors and defenders obtain on-the-job training by working alongside the special prosecutors and defenders who will phase out their role as the local courts are established. In many peace operation theaters, there is a complete absence of a legal culture and legal profession. Law schools and bar associations also need to be established to educate and nurture a corps of professional legal practitioners, including local prosecutors and defenders.

In the transitional phase of a peace operation, international civilian police will be required to take complaints, investigate crimes, and apprehend offenders as the members of existing local police forces are often human rights violators themselves. Like the special prosecutor, the peace operations police require independence from the peace operation hierarchy in the exercise of their arrest and prosecuting discretion. A police officer is required to exercise individual discretion. In the discharge of duties in a dispute between offender and victim, a constable is not subject to the direction of a superior. In the decision to arrest or not to arrest, to prosecute or not to prosecute, a constable is answerable not to his immediate superior but to the court. This accountability is to an independent court and not up the chain of command. Police are trained to use minimum force in the discharge of their duties, whereas the military are trained to use maximum force—another reason why this task is performed by civilian police and not the military in peace operations. Yet the arrest of accused offenders is a dangerous undertaking, especially in a postwar setting where there are likely to be heavily armed bandits and criminal gangs, many of whom may have remained aloof from the warring factions and have taken no part in the peace process. In some circumstances armed factions may live in terror of these heavily armed criminal organizations who live in hard-to-access isolated locations. The question posed is whether the peace operation civilian police are prepared to be shot at and to shoot back in endeavoring to make an arrest.

A more significant and low-risk role of the civilian police is to use community policing techniques, which can do much to slow down rates of crime without making actual arrests. This involves having a highly visible presence in the community and forming relationships with local people. When an offense is committed, the peacekeeping civilian police can conduct a proper investigation. Going about asking questions of the community and warning and interviewing suspects can have a significant deterrent impact. This community policing signals the unacceptability of tolerance for continuing unaccountable violence. This work also involves questioning the existing factional police and military functionaries about what they propose doing about criminal violations and helping them with on-the-job-training. By treating the commission of criminal offenses seriously in this way, major advances can be made to eradicate the culture of impunity. Hence, major inroads against crime and a measurable slowing down of offenses can be achieved without making a single arrest.

A vital task for peace operation civilian police will be the training of a local responsible constabulary in the practices and policies of community policing. What the ROL requires foremost is good community police and, second, trained investigators who understand the apprehension of offenders, the collection of evidence, and the preparation of prosecutions. Training should take the form of joint training of all faction personnel for induction into a new police force.

The construction of jails and detention centers that are consistent with the UN Minimum Standards for Prisons and are environmentally and culturally simpatico for the inmates is a priority of the peace operation. Prison custody diversion programs, bail procedures, and alternatives to imprisonment (e.g., fines, community service, probation, and parole, where appropriate, to reduce prison populations) are essential. A dilemma involved in the construction of detention centers is that convicted criminals may be better housed and fed than nearby villagers; this may breed resentment of the peacekeepers, or worse still, provide an incentive to be taken into custody. Along with the release of political prisoners in Cambodia—and people lost in the system without papers or evidence as to their crimes—there was public outcry at the danger posed to the community along with great resentment at the much-improved conditions of the criminals in local jails. This is yet another bottomless dilemma and conundrum of peace operations.

Physical security for judges, prosecutors, defenders, police, and correctional and custodial officers must be provided by the peacekeepers. This is especially so for the local judges who will be most at risk in the early stages and especially after the departure of the peacekeepers. Therefore, the peace operation will need to make provisions for the training of local police to protect judges or be prepared to provide a reliable protection during and perhaps long after the peace operation has been completed.

The peace operations must provide a proper witness-protection program to ensure the safety of informants and their families in order to bring about successful prosecutions. This may require the permanent relocation of victims and witnesses. This is a high-cost undertaking, which in some instances will involve ongoing protection for entire villages that witnessed atrocities. The offering of rewards and indemnities are also useful tools.

The peace operation must make provisions for the secure salaries for the judges, court staff, prosecutors, defenders, police, and correctional and custodial officers. In third world countries this may be reasonably inexpensive. Justice budgets are usually minuscule when compared to military budgets. The security of tenure of an entire judiciary can usually be inexpensively resourced. The cost of a justice system in these circumstances is cheap and attainable. It is certainly cheaper than the extremely high cost of the use of military hardware. The budget of the new nation must be geared to make adequate provision for sustaining the costs of the ROL and its strengthening. Postmission audits of the performance of local staff following the transfer of functions from the UN personnel to local staff are an essential feature. Continued funding after the peacekeeping exercise may be used to ensure the continued observance of judicial decisions made during the transitional authority peacekeeping period. Postpeacekeeping enforcement of judicial decisions must be secured and monitored.

Working parallel with the courts is a transitional criminal justice commission or truth and reconciliation commission. In addition to presiding over trials, distinguished international jurists are required to sit on criminal justice commissions. The commissions act as commissions of inquiry. Given lower standards of proof, such inquiries may be used to stop human rights abusers by publishing the names and misdeeds of transgressions as a deterrent or administratively disqualifying them from existing office or election to office. A purpose of such inquiries is to air public concerns, bring transgressors to account, and to embarrass wrongdoers without the need for prosecution through the courts. The relatives of the victims have an opportunity to hear what happened to their loved ones and reconcile their loss, and the perpetrators are required to publicly account before an amnesty is granted by the commission. This device may be a more powerful tool for lasting and durable community reconciliation than protracted and costly prosecutions and imprisonment for offenders.

The criminal justice commission is given full powers to investigate allegations of official misconduct. The commission is given investigative power, using sophisticated fraud and audit-detection mechanisms, especially for inquiry into allegations of abuse by officials. Antiracketeering measures to trace money trails and inquire into criminal organizations are also required. As important are ethics integrity training, financial and conflict of interest disclosure, and the development of codes of conduct for public officials.

The Negotiation Model for the Reestablishment of the Rule of Law

As pointed out above, peace planners often erroneously assume that the creation of the organs of justice alone can bring about a return to the rule of law. More than paper institutions is required. Competent people need to be vested with responsibility and accountable to that responsibility. In addition to the design of organizational structures, deep reconciliation and personal redemption are essential for a ROL. While the enforcement model for ROL compliance involves the use of legitimate minimal and lawfully sanctioned force by arrest, prosecution, detention, and trial, the negotiated model secures voluntary compliance by negotiating with the local people to bring about fundamental shifts in population consciousness against tolerance for impunity for violence. The effectiveness of force and merit review umpires (such as courts and commissions) is uncertain, risky, and costly. Negotiations give greater control of outcomes and enable the parties to make their own future. Peacekeepers show people how to create a better future for themselves. People locked in intractable conflict rarely, if ever, pause, maturely reflecting on possible future scenarios for enduring resolutions. The job of the peacekeeper is to road map the conflict, draw up menus of navigable and safe pathways, and if necessary act as a guide, walking the parties through these pathways. Getting the local people to think of molding their own future through negotiation is a powerful concept.

The negotiation model for the reestablishment of the ROL is a high-intensity, people-centered activity. Nevertheless, it is low cost and low risk. Importantly, it gives a considerably higher yield for compliance with the ROL than the enforcement model does. It involves a process of direct and continuous negotiation and ROL training by peacekeepers at the levels of the (1) great mass of the population; (2) military commanders, police, and local warlords (functionaries); and (3) central leadership (ruling factional elites). The negotiation model for the restoration of the ROL is achieved by negotiating agreements with the host people using community consultation, public participation, stakeholder representation, mutual gains negotiation, alternative dispute resolution, and the techniques called Rapid Participatory ROL Appraisal (RRA) and ROL Participatory, Assessment, Monitoring, and Evaluation (RPAME).

It is worth remembering that there may be no immediate solutions to many postwar problems. The legacy of violence will persist into future unborn generations. For example, the demand to deal with land disputes arising from successive dispossession caused by war is usually beyond the capacity of any peace mission because the claims will be so innumerable and resource consuming, requiring years before proper determinations can be made. Rather than trying to impose specific solutions in the short term, therefore, peacekeepers should aim to impart good processes for coping with conflict generally in the long term.

Elegant outcomes are more likely to result from concentrating on providing fair negotiation processes rather than on substance. The job of the peacekeeper is to teach people to manage conflict rather than impose rapid quick-fix resolutions. This task involves negotiation training (preferably cross-factional), the provision of communication facilities, relationship building, confidence building, and reconciliation processes.

Peacekeepers themselves must be properly trained negotiators to negotiate effectively. The objectives of the peacekeepers' negotiations are to persuade and secure agreements from the factional elites, military and police functionaries, and the ordinary people to:

- cease using violence, force, coercion, and intimidation as a means for managing conflicts;
- accept the legitimacy and operation of a criminal justice system to umpire disputes about the use of force and the rules that govern it;
- submit disputes to the criminal justice system when they are victims and/or accused and abide by the result; and
- negotiate internally within themselves and externally with each other.

The negotiated compliance approach for the ROL focuses on the formation of working relationships at a grassroots level that serves the locals. It is commonly recognized in the setting of a peace operation that one day the peacekeepers will leave. Thus, in order for their efforts to have long-term sustainability, peacekeepers must achieve self-reliance in preparation for their withdrawal. Peacekeepers with an abundance of resources and expertise may be enthusiastic to *teach* the ROL to the local people and keen to show them how to make and keep the peace. However, as "outsiders," peacekeepers must try to avoid *talking at* the local people but rather instead *listen and learn from them*. The members of the host community, as "insiders," know a great deal. The aim is to ensure that the peacekeepers—the temporary outsiders—are not attempting to impose awkward solutions.

The community—the permanent insiders—with the support and resources of the peacekeepers must be full and active participants in all peacekeeping ROL decisionmaking. Because the intervention will change the lives of the host people, they have a basic right to participate in the decisions that will affect them. True participation is possible only when the local people are able to determine their own goals in the negotiations about ROL planning.

The point of entry for peacekeepers may be the moment of maximum influence as expectations then will always be unattainably high. Hence, this is a time to use moral authority to persuade people to comply with sensible ROL measures. But by helping the locals set high goals, the peacekeepers must avoid raising undue expectations.

Peacekeepers help the insiders identify their own ROL issues and problems to arrive at solutions crafted by them. With the help and guidance of the peacekeepers, the locals are encouraged to set the objectives, design the activities, and monitor and evaluate progress toward the reestablishment of the ROL. The locals must be allowed to develop greater ROL self-determination with the facilitation of the peacekeepers. This participatory approach is based primarily on understanding the ROL needs, wants, concerns, and fears of insiders, which provide a means of creating adaptive feedback to peacekeepers. These needs may be abundantly obvious to the outside peacekeepers and even starkly apparent to the community itself. The process is about getting the insiders to decide for themselves and exercise authority as a self-determining people, so as to give genuine legitimacy to rule making and rule enforcement. There is a time for the outside peacekeepers to intervene and a time to leave the insiders alone in this process. Peacekeepers assist as facilitators, as providers of new ideas, and as stimuli to discussion. If the host people have such an input into the ROL projects and program, the results become community property and thus more likely to be accepted and become a reality. Unless the locals own the outcome by designing it themselves, they are unlikely to observe the ROL measures agreed upon.

More specifically, the host people (at the three levels), with the assistance of the peacekeepers:

- define their ROL problems;
- identify their own ROL wants, needs, fears, concerns, and criteria;
- rank these;
- brainstorm and generate doable options and alternatives for reestablishment of the ROL;
- measure, weigh, and rate the options and alternatives;
- give achievable commitments to the ROL; and
- make and carry out the optimal ROL planning decisions.

The Rapid Participatory ROL Appraisal

In the past peacekeepers have been woefully ignorant about local communities and social processes. As a result, some peace proposals were inappropriate (well meaning but misguided) ROL measures, and they misfired. Before going into the field, peacekeepers need accurate information of the ROL realities in order to plan. There is a need to understand the social, economic, and cultural context of the intervention. Many social mechanisms and complex systems of patronage are not apparent to outsiders. Cultural conundrums often lead to mutual bafflement between the peacekeepers and the host people. Field survey missions are necessary to conduct a RRA to measure the extent of existence of the ROL and determine existing justice assets. This information is necessary to plan, and execute the extent of the peacekeeping ROL intervention. This is first and foremost an exercise in anthropology and sociology. In planning for the field survey mission the key questions to ask are:

- What is not known about the area for which ROL negotiations and target groups are planned?
- What information is already available about past and present ROL assets, social dynamics, and community practices for conflict management and dealing with violence?
- How do you find out what is not known?
- How much is it going to cost?
- How long is it going to take?

The purpose of the RRA is to learn as much as possible as quickly as possible by collecting primary data from insiders through a process of participation by local people in the field, which leads to bottom-up planning. It is worthwhile bringing in developmental workers proficient in participatory techniques to train peacekeepers and to be part of the appraisal teams. The RRA should be conducted by multidisciplinary teams collecting information directly from the people in the field in order to understand as much as possible on the ground from the perspectives of different professional fields. A mix of institutions such as military, police, human rights lawyers, anthropologists, and other members from different institutions is helpful. By using this approach the peacekeepers engage in an exploratory analysis of on-the-ground conditions to assist both the locals and the peacekeepers in project identification that actually addresses the real needs and priorities of the locals as end users.

The first stage of the RRA is to obtain insight into and understand how the local people currently manage conflict and how they relate to the ROL. The peacekeepers need to learn as quickly as possible about current circumstances at various locations in the host country. The peacekeepers need a balanced view of the fears, needs, wants, concerns, and priorities of the local people. In the RRA exercise, they need to avoid risks of bias and avoid raising unrealistic expectations of the locals only to later disappoint them. Because the bulk of most peace operations are made up predominantly of men, there is a high need to avoid gender bias by having women adequately represented on the team as well as taking gender debiasing measures in the analysis. Special attention is required to talk to "invisible" people (e.g., a small, marginalized ethnic minority group) who may be difficult to talk to or readily discerned. While key community figures and obvious information gatekeepers will be readily identifiable, the vast majority of the ordinary people may have no organizational structure to represent their interests. They will usually be impoverished, isolated, illiterate, undereducated, excluded from power, and dependent on and intimidated by factional elites and their functionaries. Hence, the members of the field survey mission need to speak directly to the ordinary people in addition to functionaries (military and police) and factional elites.

The second stage of the RRA is to obtain information about the state of existing ROL assets of operating laws, personnel, and structures. What remnants of the ROL exist? Are there laws and justice institutions that can be resuscitated? Would these laws receive the respect of the people? Do they meet international standards? What can be done to bring them up to international standards? Are there existing judges, court staff, lawyers, police, and correctional and custodial officers available that would hold the respect of the people? Are they resourced? Are there courthouses, police stations, and detention centers? Are there alternatives to imprisonment? What material and training resources are needed to put in place a functioning criminal justice system? The field survey mission can gather information about how this might be best effected. Most important, where there is no independent, competent, and credible criminal justice system, the field survey mission must assess the viability, variants, and impacts of the transitional peace operations courts and transitional criminal justice commission.

The third stage of the RRA is to provide planning pointers and guidelines for the ROL intervention and to design appropriate ROL programs, projects, and training. While operation of the transitional peace operations courts and criminal justice commission is for the peacekeepers to plan and implement, local input would greatly facilitate their effectiveness. To enhance effectiveness the peacekeeping training needs to be tailored for local and cultural conditions. The final ROL programs and projects are jointly designed and committed to by the peacekeepers and the factional elite, functionaries, and ordinary people.

Peacekeepers are dealing with complex human catastrophes that are incomprehensible and inexplicable to the traumatized victims as well as the peacekeepers. The peacekeepers need to constantly update their information and question their assumptions about the host people. Outside "experts" undertaking quick visits using superficial knowledge and having limited contact run the real risk that they will reach conclusions biased by their areas of expertise, backgrounds, prejudices, and priorities. The data-collection tools should be flexible and creative enough to be reworked for each different country context and rethought in response to field reality. Choosing and redesigning appropriate tools involves:

- careful listening and watching how local people think and communicate information among themselves (e.g., greater or lesser emphasis on oral, written, or visual traditions);
- observing what media they like to communicate in (ceremony, rallies, rituals, social events, marketplace talk, leaflets, posters, books, newspapers, radios, television, or the Internet);
- asking how information is passed on (bush telegraphs, village meetings, at the bazaar, at the washing pump, social chit-chat, religious meetings, or posters);
- discovering and assessing what information-gathering and problem-solving techniques are already used;
- pondering what ROL programs have worked and not worked in the past; and
- preparing a menu of means of communication and asking the community to decide which medium they want or prefer.

Although questionnaires are a useful tool, peacekeepers need to be careful about using detailed surveys that are too structured, time-consuming, prone to bias (validating outsiders' preconceptions), and that generate masses of valuable information that are never collated, analyzed, or used. Semistructured interview techniques will allow local people to communicate their own priorities for the ROL. In the interviews, as with police informants, peacekeepers need to strictly respect confidences of the people (usually their identity). Peacekeepers should be alert to the high probability that some people in existing institutions such as the factional elites and their functionaries may be hostile to participatory approaches. Therefore, the interviews should be conducted in private, and some meetings may have to exclude some officials and others in whose presence the informants are fearful of speaking frankly. There may be social taboos, fear of retribution, or a learned behavior of telling authority figures what they want to hear. In many social and cultural settings, the imparting of information depends on the building of personal relationships. This takes time and in some cultures only happens after the formation of genuine friendships. Building relationships with trust between the peacekeepers and the local people is at the heart of the negotiated compliance model. The time frame of the peace operation will be short. Local people generally will not understand or be responsive to this constraint. Moreover they may have cultural constraints that do not permit individualized representation of few speaking on behalf of all. Some cultures require complex internal consultation rituals to be observed before a corporate community response can be given to outsiders, especially when it involves significant lifestyle decisionmaking.

Useful information-gathering tools may include semistructured interviews involving free-flowing discussion, classification and ranking interviews to ask local people to list important priorities, key informant interviews with community leaders or similar figures, individual household interviews, community meetings, workshops, focus group discussions, historical maps, daily activity charts, and perspective maps.

The ROL Participatory, Assessment, Monitoring, and Evaluation

Under the RPAME model, the first step is for the local people and peacekeepers to assess the current ROL situation. Both need to understand the nature and extent of the problem. A diagnosis of the causes of the current ROL situation is undertaken. Some general directions are determined and strategies outlined. Finally a plan of action can be devised. Facilitated by the peacekeepers, the local people identify the conditions necessary for the restoration of the ROL and whether, when, and how these conditions can be met. Participatory assessment provides the framework for the insiders and outsiders to determine whether they want, need, and can support the ROL activities proposed. The insiders and outsiders should establish and recognize their objectives, identify the necessary conditions, draw an assessment framework, rank necessary conditions, and gather and analyze relevant information.

Under the RPAME, the peacekeepers negotiate with host people to set baselines for crime incidents (or civil conflict) and management, the number of police and amount of judicial resources, and the extent of human rights training and public education. The baselines are measured against prewar circumstances, current circumstances, and some future desirable goals. It is important to establish criteria to measure change so that the peacekeepers, factional elites, functionaries, and local people can readily observe progress or regression. The steps in establishing the participatory baselines involve:

- discussing the purpose of the baseline;
- reviewing objectives and activities;
- establishing baseline questions;
- choosing key indicators, both direct (e.g., measurable statistics) and indirect (e.g., anecdotal);
- identifying information sources and tools for baseline questions;
- deciding on the resources in terms of skills, time, and labor; and
- deciding when information gathering can be done, who will gather it, and what to do with it.

The baseline measurements are more than a mere gathering of crime or other statistics but are used as a means of assessing the success or failure of responses for an adjustment to ROL plans.

Once the peacekeepers have arrived and have fanned out throughout the host country, incident reports will soon be generated that will begin to systematically record significant events involving violence, such as cease-fire violations, massacres of civilians, large-scale criminal activity, and attacks on peacekeepers. These events will trigger a demand for action by the peacekeepers for appropriate responses. While the peacekeepers can take active measures by using their own peace operation courts and criminal justice commission, the objective is to remove the culture of impunity by negotiating with the local people to take proper nonviolent responsibility for the criminal acts of their own people.

The incident reports prepared by the peacekeeping military observers, civilian police, civil administration, NGOs, and the media provide outsider observation of degrees of lawlessness. The receipt of information and investigation of these incidents should be done as a part of on-the-job training with local military and police. Independent of the peacekeepers, the locals are also asked to report and record the same and/or other additional incidents. The second step of participatory monitoring is undertaken by peacekeepers and locals by broadly examining progress toward objectives and activities during the life of the peace operation. The monitoring provides information for decisionmakers so that adjustments can be made to ROL plans if necessary. An ongoing picture—where problems, challenges, and opportunities are identified and solutions sought early—is built up over time. Encouraging that good standards be maintained and resources be used effectively will help produce a complete picture of the project and provide information for future evaluations.

The third step in RPAME is the joint undertaking of the evaluation of the data collected from the monitoring. Insiders take the lead and the responsibility for the ROL in their own community with the outside peacekeepers facilitating the participatory evaluations using information to guide managerial decisions. Community and peacekeeper relationships are strengthened in this joint enterprise. In the participatory evaluation the community is able to make better decisions with developing evaluation skills as the peacekeepers learn from their perspectives. The community can develop culturally sympathetic options and make achievable commitments.

The fourth step of RPAME is the presentation of the results to the community by the peacekeepers in an interesting, understandable, convincing, and timely manner using written formats (reports, case studies, community newsletters, newspapers, graphics, and posters), oral formats (drama, puppet shows, tape recordings, video, story telling, community and commercial radio, teaching lectures, public addresses, and debates), and visual formats (photographs, drawings, video, slides, cartoons and graphics, community and commercial radio, and television).

The peacekeeping negotiations at the three local levels have to be transparent and open. Every step should be carefully taken without surprise and in full consultation by collaborative design of all persons concerned so that the locals own the process and the outcomes as much as possible. RPAME does not reduce peacekeepers to performing artists, popular theater, actors, or puppeteers. For peacekeepers, these activities are an important part of building working and trustworthy relationships with the population, as are sport and languages classes. Any change toward the adoption of the ROL will be gradual and incremental. The ROL proposals must address the grassroot needs of the host people at the three levels. The ROL measures, while needing to be culturally appropriate, must also aspire to and be consistent with international standards. The negotiated model for the ROL when used in conjunction with the enforcement model for the ROL can deliver the foundations for the creation of a new state and ultimate peace.

Conclusion

After the immediate priorities of protecting people from violence, providing emergency medical care, food, water, and shelter, the operational mechanics of peace operations require the intelligent application of justice logistics to establish the rule of law. This task is fundamental and comes before the reestablishment or maintenance of the apparatus of the state. Elections for a Constituent Assembly to write elaborate constitutions are often impossible and meaningless unless a living rule of law system is established. Over a decade of accumulated experience from the baptism of trial and error in such diverse theaters as Namibia, Cambodia, Somalia, Rwanda, Zimbabwe, Uganda, Haiti, Bosnia, Kosovo, East Timor, and the Solomon Islands has given peacekeepers a strategic insight into the so-called lessons learned in the establishment of functioning justice institutions at the elite, functional, and village level.

6

Reconstructing Infrastructure

Richard H. Brown

The reconstruction and development of infrastructure after war is a complex science requiring a deep understanding of socioeconomic and physical elements as they relate to the long-term needs of a country and its communities and their constituents.

This chapter defines infrastructure and describes the possible outcomes as a result of war; it then profiles strategic options for reconstruction with the emphasis on process more than product. With sustainability as a principal objective, policies for implementation are outlined; these include the powerful concepts of community empowerment and community enablement. Also explained is how well-designed infrastructure programs can be useful devices for peacebuilding. The chapter concludes with a set of generic principles for the development of postwar infrastructure.

Infrastructure Defined

The term "infrastructure" incorporates a wide range of engineering systems. However, in this context, infrastructure will be considered as part of the community's contribution to a sustainable economy. As such, the following categories are perceived as forming the essential backbone toward recovery:

- water supply
- storm drainage
- sanitary drainage
- wastewater treatment
- waste disposal facilities

- electricity supply
- fuel supply
- highways
- railways
- seaports
- airports
- telecommunications systems
- medical facilities
- educational facilities
- administrative facilities

Shelter and housing are not included as part of community infrastructure, as they are often privately owned and subject to a rather different set of reconstruction criteria.

Infrastructure in War

Violent conflict is a sudden and catastrophic interruption in the natural development of society, with infrastructure one of its main victims. The outcomes from attacks on physical infrastructure during armed conflict are perhaps some of the most vivid and tangible results of war and, alongside human suffering, are used to portray the degree of severity of the conflict in question. However, these outcomes take several forms, and an understanding of not just the root causes of the conflict but also what is driving its various manifestations can be vital in considering strategies for reconstruction and development.

Conflicts generally derive out of greed or grievance. While economic factors may be the root cause, the conflict may manifest itself in the form of social/ethnic grievances. Misinterpretation or confusion in relation to root and proximate causes can lead to the wrong solution in terms of infrastructure provision with the possible result that livelihoods are not restored and peace is not sustainable. Thus, strategies for infrastructure development should be constructed on a case-by-case basis, although they should follow a set of generic principles.

Civil infrastructure can be damaged, looted, neglected, or unaffected during armed conflict. For damaged infrastructure, the nature of the conflict will determine whether it is specifically targeted by category or ownership. Specific targeting is now just as possible in high-tech interstate wars as it is in intrastate civil conflicts. The development of precision munitions now makes aerial bombardment very selective; increasingly, selection will be based on strategic considerations for gaining tactical advantage and also longer-term postconflict reconstruction. In ground conflicts, ownership may be the key factor for selection, especially in ethnically driven wars. The degree of damage will determine its propensity for repair.

The degree of destruction may indicate whether there is an intent by those causing the damage to take control of the particular items of infrastructure after their assumed victory. Efficient infrastructure forms the backbone to a viable economy, and an astute commander will be acutely aware of this in formulating his strategic objectives. Conversely, a commander facing defeat may seek to maximize damage to civil infrastructure from which he is withdrawing so as to limit economic recovery, especially if he sees little prospect in regaining the initiative.

Looting can be a spontaneous and opportunistic act by groups and individuals. It can also be a deliberate conspiracy from warlords and others who make a criminal industry out of conflict, with stolen equipment being sold onward, thus feeding and prolonging the black economy.

An often-overlooked manifestation of conflict on infrastructure is that of neglect. Wars redirect state funds and administrative attention, leaving infrastructure facilities undermanaged, undermaintained, and sometimes overused, such that in long conflicts they become unserviceable before armed conflict ceases. In short conflicts, it is more likely to be the breakdown in organizational structure that leads to dysfunctionality.

The demise of adequate administration may arise out of the untimely migration of skilled managers and support staff. This inherited situation is likely to be a particular problem for a new postwar government because of the need to build new organizations as well as rehabilitate physical structures. However, before embarking on any rapid assessment of the causes of neglect, an understanding of the status quo before the conflict is essential. It may be that evidence of neglect is in fact evidence of a failing state such that failing infrastructure becomes a contributory cause of the conflict itself. And so, in certain circumstances, evidence of failing infrastructure can be a warning sign of impending conflict.

Infrastructure After War

The recovery process after war has two extra dimensions after a natural or other man-made disaster. First, whereas with natural disasters prior physical defensive measures (such as good design) will mitigate the effects of the hazards on the vulnerable, this is much less true with wars where deliberate human actions drive the outcomes. Second, after natural disasters the cohesive nature of communities will often hasten the reconstruction process, whereas after wars there will be the additional task of repairing social, political, and cultural divisions. The type, degree, and length of healing required depend largely on the character of the conflict (interstate or intrastate, economic, ethnic, religious, etc.) and will have an impact on policies and strategies for infrastructure provision. Care must be taken to ensure that in the rush to reconstruct after conflict, long-term sustainability is not compromised.

There is a delicate balance to be effected between the urgency to reconstruct and the opportunity to develop. Reconstruction implicitly has a certain finality associated with it, whereas development denotes betterment. Both can be undermined if vulnerability is retained, but for both the key links are people and sustainability. If one assumes that the reestablishment of cohesive communities is a key component to constructing a durable peace, then it is logical to design a recovery strategy based on policies and plans built up from community data and built around community requirements.

There are two key objectives to be met in devising strategies for reconstructing infrastructure after war: (1) an assurance that its provision is an investment in the process for building peace, and (2) the creation of a legacy for sustainability. The former can be met through an understanding of the concept of "connectors and dividers," and the latter can be achieved through an interpretation of the meaning of sustainable infrastructure in a postwar context.

Connectors and Dividers

The concept of connectors and dividers, as described in Anderson's *Do No Harm* (1999), can be applied to any aspect of conflict and postconflict reconstruction. However, it has particular relevance to physical infrastructure because of a generally linear symbolism associated with many types of service infrastructure. In the right circumstances infrastructure can reconnect divided communities and become the catalyst for gradual reconciliation (effectively a peace tool). Infrastructure links that conform to real or notional boundaries can, of course, have quite the opposite effect. Arguably, wherever conflict has divided communities (principally intrastate conflicts), the concept should be applied as an integral part of any strategic plan for reconstruction. Insensitive application that fails to interact with the communities concerned is likely to fail. The wishes of each community may fall outside what is considered to be for the overall strategic good—hence the need for gaining consensus.

The importance of getting it right the first time cannot be overstated. The (re)establishment of infrastructure, particularly its networks, is for the long term. Prescribing dividing networks is likely to reenforce political/ethnic divisions for a lengthy time, while establishing connecting networks, delivered with sensitivity, can contribute very positively to long-term political/ethnic harmony. Some examples from the Balkans follow to illustrate the application of this concept.

1. In Bosnia and Herzegovina, the electrical grid system was severely damaged around the lines of confrontation. Under the 1995 General Framework Agreement for Peace (GFAP), the territory of Bosnia and Herzegovina was divided into two entities, and the resulting inter-entity boundary line often coincided with lines of confrontation. In the reconstruction phase, the communities preferred single-entity grid systems, a policy that if pursued would embed political and ethnic division within infrastructure for the long term.

2. In Bosnia and Herzegovina, as part of GFAP, a special road was built in 1996 linking the Muslim enclave of Gorazde and the divided city of Sarajevo (the "Gorazde Access Track"); this amounted to parallel infrastructure and reinforced ethnically separated vehicle movement. In contrast, in 1998, agreement between the two entity governments was achieved in respect of the introduction of the "common license plate." The concept was to have neutral plates for all vehicles in Bosnia and Herzegovina (previously, ethnic allegiance was apparent from any of the three specific plate symbols, preventing unharassed movement in more than one entity). The solution was ingenious, if somewhat contrived—a central letter is used (among numbers), one of the five other than "O" that are common to both Roman and Cyrillic alphabets.

3. In Kosovo, part of the urgent relief program instigated immediately after NATO's land entry in 1999 was the recommissioning of Kosovo A & B Power Stations, located just outside Pristina. They were the major generators of electricity for Kosovo and also were linked into the Yugoslavian/Serbian grid system. Because Yugoslavia's electricity supply system was built as a national network, any fragmentation would disadvantage all the new states, not just the fragmenting state. This was recognized by all parties; consequently, in the power sector a high level of cooperation was maintained between Serbia and Kosovo in the difficult year after the NATO bombings, with power flowing freely either way depending on surge requirements. Ironically, in the rush to restore

power generation in Kosovo, Serbs became excluded from employment within the power company, a factor that has had a detrimental effect on the general long-term policy of ethnic inclusion (or more realistically coexistence)—a case of third-party impartiality perceived as being compromised in the interests of expediency. There was also some mischievous redirection of power away from the Serb minority communities by the Albanian management team.

4. In Kosovo, after the events of 1999, the reestablishment of the rail system became important for those minorities who otherwise would have been isolated from the outside world. Multiethnic transport systems were the only safe way of traveling for these groups, thus preempting ethnically targeted attacks. Passenger trains were restored to link Serb, Roma, and Albanian communities on the main north-south line. In effect the railway system became the linchpin in the goal to establish and maintain freedom of movement for all.

5. In Kosovo, the now divided city of Mitrovica has entrenched Serb and Albanian communities on either side of the Ibar River. The road bridge linking the two parts of the city had become a symbol for standoffs between extremist elements of the two ethnic communities. An opportunity was taken to reconstruct the decaying bridge with the specific aim of using skilled and unskilled labor from both communities, thus transforming—at least temporarily—a "divider" into a "connector."

Sustainable Infrastructure

Sustainable infrastructure, in the context of the postwar environment, may be defined as follows: physical assets that provide net benefits to a community, its neighbors, and the environment on a long-term basis. Sustainable infrastructure forms part of a larger socioeconomic model and is a critical function in facilitating the development of other basic structures in society such as business, education, and health. There are some major administrative functions that contribute to its sustainability, and these can be summarized into three generic elements (Özerdem 1998):

1. *An appropriate specification and level of technology.* The design of the system must take account of available materials and technologies as well as available or potential expertise for operation and maintenance. A trade-off must be struck between using modern technology to best advantage and simplicity of operation and maintenance. A strong focus should be applied to the involvement of local people as much as possible.

2. *An environmentally positive (or at least neutral) physical portfolio.* The system must not produce environmental benefits in one community at the expense of negative outcomes in a neighboring community. Thus, a holistic approach must be taken for planning, specification, and design.

3. *An appropriate organization to plan and manage infrastructure design, construction, operation, and maintenance.* This requires the early selection of local people with the potential to master the skills necessary to undertake these activities. Mentoring from external or higher agencies will be necessary for some considerable time. There must be sensitive human resource management and development plans that are impartial to all groups and facilitate focused training to the job in hand. There must be robust financial arrangements that project toward sustainability. The capital expenditure profile must reflect the ability of local enabled teams to manage the schemes. Therefore, because of the training and mentoring processes, it is likely to start later, be flatter, and last longer than past programs. In consequence, donors will need to be educated and persuaded accordingly.

These principles can be applied universally. However, programs need to be designed according to the particular postwar situation. They will be particularly demanding where settled people have suffered repression over a protracted period but less onerous with more technologically advanced states.

The end of the Cold War precipitated a large increase in subregional conflicts, and consequently there has been an associated rise in the demand for postwar reconstruction. Yet the emphasis has been on pure reconstruction rather than reconstruction through development. For infrastructure, much of this reconstruction has been project based rather than people based, characterized by funding focused on achieving early physical outputs rather than sustainable solutions harnessed through vocational development of local people. This policy has put serious doubt into the long-term sustainability of reconstructed infrastructure, especially in less developed territories where there is a dearth of indigenous management and technical expertise.

Community Enablement:
Key to Sustainable Infrastructure

A strategy for postwar reconstruction requires an approach that is tailored to the particular context of the area and its people. For example, it could be expected that reconstruction in the Balkans might require a different approach to that required somewhere in the Indonesian archipelago.

Wars bring opportunities after destruction. Wars highlight the inherent weaknesses within societies and facilitate opportunities to solve long-standing problems. However, in designing recovery programs, great care must be applied in understanding the culture and organization of prewar communities and in ensuring that development plans reduce rather than increase individual and community vulnerabilities such that a strong platform for sustainable development is firmly established.

A full understanding must be gained of not only where the country/area has come from in terms of conflict but also where it is to go in terms of development. Two principles concerning the latter are vital. General consensus with the population must be achieved, and a suitable transition policy must be established. The particular emphasis within infrastructure development for a technologically advanced society is likely to be different than for a low-technology society; nevertheless, the two principles stand for both.

The pivotal factor that will transform infrastructure from being a short-term to long-term utility is securing ownership by the community (or set of communities where network infrastructure is involved). To achieve this, a change of culture from central dependency to community responsibility will be necessary by establishing local organizational structures, a pool of local expertise, and appropriate charging mechanisms. This can be particularly difficult for countries in transition from centralized oligarchies to participatory democracies. Initially, this will need to be driven by a change agent who could be an imported, experienced manager working with a local counterpart under a mentoring arrangement. The dividend for the community is reliable infrastructure and additional employment. Safe and reliable infrastructure provides access and services and so improves the performances of enterprise, education, and health, and these in turn contribute to more sustainable communities.

Part of the process involves understanding changes to the capacities and vulnerabilities of each community, as described by Anderson and Woodrow (1989), an activity that needs to happen very early in the postwar reconstruction phase and preferably while the armed conflict is still in progress. This knowledge will allow strategies to be devised that focus on the human input to sustainable development; good development practices can reduce vulnerabilities and increase people's capacities to cope, thus reducing the need for relief.

Community responsibility can only be developed through community participation. As Goulet describes, participation performs three vital functions: It instills dignity, mobilizes people as problem solvers in their own social environments, and facilitates access to higher arenas of decisionmaking (Goulet 1995, 98–101). However, he recognizes the need for government to take some nonparticipatory decisions concerned with national infrastructure and international exports. Successful development is, therefore, dependent on successful participation. But Goulet depicts the resulting dilemma as follows:

> The most difficult form of participation to elicit and sustain is also the most indispensable to genuine development. This is participation that starts at the bottom and reaches progressively upward into ever-widening arenas of decision-making. It matures into a social force which may form a critical mass of participating communities progressively empowered to enter into spheres of decision or action beyond their immediate problem-solving arenas. The itinerary followed moves from micro- to macro-arenas. Numerous successful micro-operations never expand beyond their initial small scale. Many others, although they may grow to achieve "critical mass," do not successfully resist being repressed, co-opted or marginalized. The supremely difficult transition is precisely that which takes a movement from the micro-arena to the macro-arena without dilution or destruction. (Goulet 1995, 96–97)

These difficulties indicate that much attention needs to be given to making participation effective. The key to bridging the gap between effective community participation (part of the empowerment process) and sustainable development is the much underrated and understated concept of "community enablement." Community enablement involves encouraging resourcefulness, increasing vocational abilities, and removing obstacles, and it is often facilitated by an outside agent. It provides a separate dimension to empowerment, because it enhances personal security and community esteem—through employment and ability recognition—without necessarily advertising a new empowered status in relative terms, thereby adding to the inevitable postwar "power tensions." Participation and enablement within communities are the precursors to self-actualization—the opportunity to take control of one's own life. A perceived (but probably unreal) threat is that political activism may follow.

Development of infrastructure can be seen as an instrument toward conflict resolution. In the case of linear infrastructure, such as roads and power lines, the development can be symbolic as well as utilitarian. Revitalized infrastructure helps restore livelihoods by facilitating trade and providing employment, reversing the combination (lots of time and no money) upon which conflict breeds. The corollary is that the lack of development of infrastructure can be restraining on the peacebuilding process. The revitalization of infrastructure can become an object of negotiation, thus providing a space for more general dialogue involving intellectuals and professionals rather than just warlords.

Implementation

The sense of urgency created by the manifestations of war has often led to short-term decisionmaking. Rightly, the emphasis has been on relief, that is, saving and preserving lives by donations of material aid. However, reconstruction and development require a strong strategic framework to ensure that sustainable programs are devised. Because these processes should start as early as possible—and in parallel with relief programs—the strategic planning process may need to commence early in the conflict. The plan can then be tweaked or reshaped as the conflict matures and peace becomes a possibility.

A widely held view is that it may be possible to design targeted relief programs that contribute directly to development programs, thereby transforming consumption subsidies into investment subsidies. Yet for infrastructure, it is appropriate that planning for development should start as early as possible and that actions should run in tandem to those for relief. Running the two as one operation would dilute, if not extinguish, the effectiveness of the early entry approach to community enablement as the urgency of relief subsumed resources otherwise allocated for development. So, although most modern theory points toward the concept of developmental relief, it is not, in the way it is generally interpreted, appropriate here. Better suited is the "continuum approach," where relief and development are not sequential or overlapping but coexisting (Zeeuw 2001, 7).

The tendency with imported administrations, and indeed many national governments, has been to overcentralize decisionmaking, leaving outlying districts as pariahs with economic and social peripherality. Barakat finds that "total decentralization is almost impossible, particularly in places where centralization is a strong culture" (Barakat 1993, 102–103). He recognizes the importance of communal decisionmaking and outlines the concept of controlled decentralization as a halfway solution but suggests that ideally a communal administrative structure should be established "especially fit to deal with the problems of reconstruction." For decentralization to work, it has to be accompanied by enablement at all levels—in community and in local government.

The framework for establishing community-led infrastructure will come through strong rather than bureaucratic governance. This is where "facilitating" government can play its part. Collating all these elements together successfully will go some way toward creating a stable and sustainable economy. The interrelationship is displayed in Figure 6.1.

The concept is founded on government providing the right framework for communities to take ownership of most categories of infrastructure and thus contribute to their sustainability. The challenge for a new (or old) postwar government, whether interim or permanent, is to

ling structures quickly—
at the same time ensuring
management of essential

le reconstruction is entire-
l leadership. As Goulet
following attributes: (1)
) ability to reconcile mul-
urage, (4) ability to com-
els of motivation, and (5)
ly from mistakes (Goulet
al, they require very high
. The resulting communi-

ent to facilitate the provi-
s to flourish. Initially, the
majority of donor funding.
ropriate international ele-
ollapse of a failed state.

The implementation of the plan will ideally commence at the end of an armed conflict (or even before—in the deescalation phase—as a

Figure 6.1   Framework for Establishing Community-Led Infrastructure

Stable and Sustainable Economy

Good
Governance

Sustainable Communities   Sustainable Infrastructure

Figure 6.2   Inspirational Leadership and the Virtuous Rectangle

mechanism toward achieving peace); it should not wait for the peace process to mature, because by then much time will have been lost and a dependency culture will have developed. Early entry in selected areas where the level of conflict is subdued may refocus fragile communities away from conflict and toward reconstruction.

The empowerment process must be simple if it is to be efficient and effective, with delegated authorities no more than two steps up from the empowered. This process will determine what the communities want, whereas the enabling process will determine how the agreed outcomes of this process are to be achieved; the enabling process will gradually come under the control of local people. As some of them whose potential abilities are technically aligned gain the necessary expertise to manage, operate, and maintain local infrastructure, so the community will become a stakeholder in this infrastructure. Both empowerment and enabling processes will engender ownership; yet it is the enabling process (which arguably has more depth) that will, in the long run, contribute most to sustainability.

In short, while an empowerment process should be used to encourage community participation in the political process of deciding what needs to be done, an enablement process should be used to facilitate the training of suitable people to determine how things can be done. This process should be carried out with the aim of creating multiskilled technical teams that should aspire to meet the objectives outlined within the three administrative elements for sustainable infrastructure described earlier, such that they became enabled teams. Figure 6.3 shows the major inputs necessary to achieve a sustainable infrastructure.

A proper understanding of the strengths and challenges of community enablement as applied to infrastructure development is essential by

Figure 6.3 Major Inputs Necessary to Achieve Sustainable Infrastructure

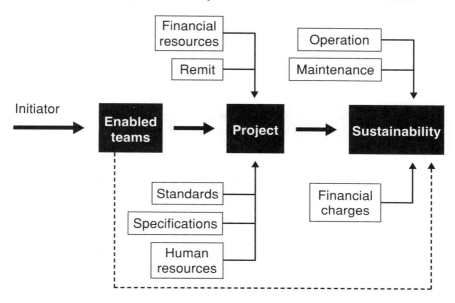

all interested parties. Community enablement should be an integral element within the strategic plan. A summary of the strengths and challenges in using it is set out in Table 6.1.

Infrastructure Networks

As a nation develops it will tend to merge localized networks of linear infrastructure, such as water and electricity, into national networks in order to optimize efficiencies. There may also be disguised political objectives. However, local operation and maintenance will still be essential even though they are likely to be less locally empowered. Networks can provide socioeconomic reinforcement and enhancement to the state and its communities provided they embrace the needs of societal groups.

Summary

The primary objective of sustainable infrastructure is to support communities and economies in the long term. A sustainable economy requires sustainable infrastructure. During armed conflict, civil infra-

Table 6.1   Strengths and Challenges of Community Enablement

Element	Strengths	Challenges
Policy	Robust in the long term	High-quality dedicated facilitators necessary to manage enablement process
Community	Actions centered around local people; local economy stimulated; additional local employment; less rural-urban migration	Specialized education and training required
Infrastructure	Locally managed projects, sustainable in the long term; ownership of infrastructure by the community; good aftercare	Long learning curves for local teams—therefore, slow progress initially (need for external assistance until full competencies acquired)
Authority and Accountability	Dispersed from center—risks controlled locally and of relatively low value; also, accountable to local community	Possibility of local corruption; also potential for manipulation by warlords
Donors	Investment in long-term stability; good returns overall	New funding profiles required; few early results; need to escape from short-termist approach

structure can be damaged, looted, neglected, or unaffected. The end of war brings the opportunity to develop infrastructure in line with the needs of a state and its communities.

The development of infrastructure has the potential to bring communities together, stimulate markets, sustain livelihoods, and thus aid the consolidation of peace. This can only be achieved comprehensively if people-led initiatives take precedence over project-led ones or, in other words, by facilitating resourcefulness through the development of people rather than by just transferring resources; for without local people gaining the ability to manage, operate, and maintain local infrastructure, new facilities will not be sustainable in the long term. The mechanism for achieving this is through a process known as community enablement; this is an essential element of development and should feature strongly in strategic plans for the reconstruction of a war-torn country. Such development programs should be separate but concurrent processes to relief programs.

Box 6.1   The Special Case of Ethnic/Religious Division

Although not usually root causes of conflict, ethnic and religious divisions are often symptoms and sustaining characteristics that have strong influences on potential healing mechanisms. As a result, the principles for achieving sustainable infrastructure as so far described must be applied sensitively. In postconflict East Timor, for example, there was initial concern that existing local political structures should be avoided because, as yet, there was no democratic process. However, the UN was perhaps too over-cautious, for the conflict was never an ethnic nor religious one, and the population was almost entirely Catholic. Consequently, decisionmaking was, in the early days of reconstruction, centrally driven with little local involvement. However, in postconflict Bosnia and Herzegovina and Kosovo, the situations were more complex. The portrayal of the conflicts as acutely ethnic in character became, by default, a reality. Equitable processes leading to long-term solutions inevitably were going to be difficult to devise.

The challenges of delivering development dispassionately in divided societies can be summarized as follows: (1) local empowerment may reinforce divisions; (2) the enabling process may be targeted (innocently) in favor of majorities or minorities; and (3) locally controlled infrastructure may be used against minorities.

The dangers are multiplied exponentially if infrastructure is centrally controlled and unsupervised by intervening third parties. Minorities, already under extreme pressures, can become overwhelmed politically, and misuse of infrastructure can be the means to isolate them socially and economically.

An example of this is Kosovo, where the Serb minority had been reduced to about 5 percent of the population after the 1999 conflict. Some of the minority villages had become trapped geographically, socially, and economically. The Albanian majority took every chance to use their extreme numerical advantage such that it became difficult for the UN to secure effective Serb representation in any of the institutions. The UN seemingly became complicit to Albanian influence, which further alienated Serb participation (for example, the passive acceptance of the Albanian language without enforcing parallel use of the Serbian language

continues

Box 6.1   continued

on some official buildings, notices, and documents relating to infrastructure). In contrast, in Bosnia and Herzegovina the ethnic groups were more balanced as a whole numerically, which may be one reason that the healing process has progressed and hatred has dissipated to an extent.

In situations of intense ethnic or religious conflict, strong third-party influence will be essential to maintaining an aura of fairness to all. Otherwise, there is a distinct danger that in seeking to encourage local participation, equitable treatment will be squandered in favor of achieving early tangible progress. The inevitable long-term outcome will be permanent social separation reinforced by ethnically engineered infrastructure.

The principles can be applied universally, although the programs need to be designed according to the specific postwar situation. They will be particularly demanding where indigenous and settled peoples have suffered repression over a protracted period or where communities are divided through long-term mistrust or externally induced hatred. Where technical and managerial skills have been retained to a sufficient level on an equitable basis, proactive participation in the reconstruction process alone may be sufficient.

In forming policies for rebuilding war-torn societies, achieving sustainable infrastructure is all about developing a sustainable community. The two closely interact and neither is more or less dependent on the other. If this mutual enhancement can be achieved, then sustainable development will follow. The nation or territory will grow in stature from the bottom up and gradually obviate the need for international assistance, ultimately achieving the status of a wholly sustainable society.

Community enablement leads to strengthened economic security, one of the four broad categories of human security (others are personal, political, and community) that can be threatened at times of internal conflict (Cockell 2000, 24–26). Community enablement and the development of infrastructure are therefore a powerful combination in mitigating the likelihood of renewed conflict.

In the words of Kofi Annan, UN Secretary-General: "The prevention of war begins and ends with the promotion of human security and human development" (Annan 1998).

Box 6.2 Generic Principles for the Development of Postwar Infrastructure

1. Sustainability is the core value of a shared development vision. Sustainable infrastructure is a key component of a stable and sustainable economy.
2. Postwar policy planning should set priorities for building sustainable communities at the top, alongside those for ensuring human security. The demand for infrastructure projects should be initiated through the community empowerment process. This should be supported at the government level by an overall strategic vision for reconstruction and development.
3. Community enablement as a component of development can be a crucial element in effecting a peaceful transition and is the key to achieving sustainability in infrastructure; initially, it requires substantial external input in the form of facilitation/mentoring. However, proactive participation alone may be sufficient where technical and managerial skills have been retained.
4. Most aspects of sustainable infrastructure are a community responsibility, although central coordination of networks, standards, and funding is essential. The central administrations should set overall technical and environmental *standards,* while the enabling groups should set particular technical and environmental *specifications* for each project.
5. Achieving sustainable infrastructure in a postwar environment may require adjusting funding profiles over a longer time frame.
6. For infrastructure, relief and development should be separate but concurrent processes, assuming the concept of community enablement is a key component of its development.
7. As an example of sustainable development, sustainable infrastructure can mitigate the likelihood of renewed armed conflict.
8. The conversion of current central administrations and future policymakers to these principles can only be achieved through education and winning influence.

7

The Media's Role in
War and Peacebuilding

Ross Howard

The news media is a curious instrument. It can be a weapon of war, or it can uphold prospects for peace. In the hands of totalitarian interests it can be a terrible device when it spreads messages of intolerance and disinformation that manipulate public sentiment. The use of government-controlled Radio Television Libre de Mille Collines to foment genocidal impulses in Rwanda in 1994 is one appalling contemporary example. The ethnic hatred propagated by the Serbian state on its broadcasting system in Bosnia is another recent case.

The news media is also capable of causing considerable damage when no one is intentionally doing so at all. Under ideal conditions the news media is supposed to have a mind of its own and operate according to professional codes of conduct. But its culture of professional and financial instincts can drive the media to practices that obsess with violence and influence opinion in socially destabilizing ways. In conflict-stressed or undemocratic states, media bias, inaccuracy, and sensationalism can generate xenophobia and violent conflict. The anti-Thai violence in Cambodia on January 29–30, 2003, is one example.

There is, however, another side to this sword called the media. It can be an instrument of conflict resolution. When it responds well to its own professional strictures such as accuracy, impartiality, and independence, the media can have an influence on peacebuilding. It can present alternatives to stereotypes and conflict, and it can enable citizens to make well-informed decisions in their own best interests. This potential of the media has been less examined in the research into democratization than other factors. Although there is substantial academic and popular analysis of the media's role in conflict, there is surprisingly little concerning the media in peacebuilding (Wolfsfeld 2001a).

Nonetheless, the influence of the media has caught the eye of international agencies and NGOs closely involved in peacebuilding since the early 1990s (Howard 2002). Since then, an estimated U.S.$1 billion has been invested in interventions relating to the media in conflict-stressed societies. There is an emerging belief that the media may well be the most effective means of conflict resolution and preventing new wars. However, the paucity of research into media intervention hampers democratization, as analysts Dusan Reljik in the *Berghof Handbook for Conflict Transformation* and Christopher Spurk, writing for SwissPeace, have commented (Reljik 2002; Spurk 2002). There are too few impact assessments based on accepted yardsticks or indicators, and no literature on lessons learned. This has led to substantially flawed media initiatives such as the post–Dayton Peace Agreement media interventions in Bosnia.

The following considerations may contribute to a much-needed overall framework on media and peacebuilding:

1. The undeniably deadly side to the news media, when it is used by totalitarian regimes as in instrument of repressions or conflict instigation, is the least accessible. It can hardly be called news media and should not be treated as such.

2. It is a contradiction but true that in the singularly most accessible democracies, where the media has complete freedom, the strongest impulses of the news media may still lead it to play a destructive role. Sensationalism and partisanship can deliver profit but at the price of peacebuilding. This needs to be better recognized. There is an emerging debate within the journalistic profession now about the role of the independent media.

3. There is much that can be done, and is being done, at the in-between stage, in states emerging from totalitarian regimes toward democracy. This should be of interest to anyone dedicated to the study and the pursuit of peacebuilding.

The Media Defined

The term "the media" needs some narrowing for the purposes of this discussion. The media here refers to the several mediums or channels used in an organized fashion to communicate information to groups of people as a service to the public. Newspapers and magazines, radio and television, and the Internet are the main channels. The gathering and dissemination process is called journalism. Journalism includes reporting, commentary, opinion, and analysis. The process is distinguished by at least three central principles: accuracy, impartiality, and responsibility in the public interest, sometimes collectively known as reliable journalism.

Most succinctly, the benefit of reliable journalism, under ideal conditions that include a diversity of independent media outlets, is that it enables citizens to make well-informed decisions. Well-informed decisionmaking includes the right to free expression and debate—reflecting Article 19 of the International Declaration of Human Rights—and it includes the right to vote freely, which substantially represents the practice of democracy.

Media Influences on Conflict

The influences of the conventional media on the way war is conducted are well known. One example is that the media, as a witness, can be an instrument of restraint. The sudden arrival of cameras and journalists on a local scene that averted, or at least forestalled, indiscriminate slaughter of persons in the Balkan conflicts, has been reported innumerable times. The presence of the international media was most significant, reflecting that while local norms of humane conduct had broken down, there were international standards to be reckoned with and potential consequences to be avoided.

At the macro level there is or was briefly a period of the so-called CNN effect, referring to the media's role in defining state or international policy. It was argued that the end of the Cold War had created a vacuum in policy formulation that was filled by media-specified crisis management. Round-the-clock images of a U.S. soldier's body dragged through the streets of Mogadishu in 1993 were credited with prompting a U.S. withdrawal from peacekeeping in Somalia. However, such significance may be exaggerated and operate only on occasions where leadership is weak and policy unclear (Stroebel 1998). Also, governments around the world have become more adept at using the media and maintaining their own course. Yet the traditional influence of the media in igniting and fueling conflict is far less debatable. It ranges from exhibiting patriotic ethnocultural bias to disseminating propaganda and directly advocating and encouraging violence, as occurred in Rwanda and more recently in the former Yugoslavia.

This latter phenomenon, known as hate media, bears little relationship to professional journalism. There is nothing accurate, impartial, or responsible about it. And responses to it have been beyond the subject of journalism, as in the NATO destruction of Radio Television of Serbia transmitters in Bosnia and Herzegovina in 1995 and the bombing of Serb radio and television facilities during the 1999 Kosovo conflict. Less controversial, largely because it is less violent, is the electronic jamming of the transmissions. Either kind of intervention raises concerns about whether it represents an abuse of the right of free speech— no matter how odious. But the extent of concern may be circumscribed now by the successful prosecution of so-called journalists for their involvement in the hate radio in Rwanda. The International Criminal Tribunal has judged the broadcasters' message to be beyond the limits of anything that could be considered journalism or free speech. The tribunal has identified it as public incitement of hatred and genocide, which makes it a crime against humanity. And the tribunal has held some individuals guilty for their personal participation.

Current Conditions Affecting the Media's Role

As Terzis and many others have pointed out, the current post–Cold War landscape is a different, more volatile environment for the kind of conflict in which the media can be most influential (Terzis and Melone 2002). Interethnic clashes are the central characteristics of the violent conflicts being waged today around the globe, as groups cite ethnicity as the answer to their dilemmas of identity and security. The media in these conflict-ridden societies often create and facilitate arguments for conflict, such as oppositional metaphors of "us versus them" linked to internal or external issues. The media often become the mouthpiece for ethnic power circles. A deliberate distortion of news reporting for particular interests exacerbates the tension between opposed factions and becomes the main trigger for violent conflict. For example, the twenty-year conflict in Sri Lanka and the fragility of the current peace process there are partially due to sensationalist, partisanized, and ethnically divided media.

A second factor in the significance of the media for modern conflict is the virtual ubiquity of the media, which has been achieved since the mid-1980s. Thanks to technology, the media—and most particularly the electronic sector—is able to reach even the most remote corners of any state. Inexpensive radio broadcasting and the inconsequential cost of radio receivers have eliminated the barrier that illiteracy posed to spreading news, information, or propaganda. Television, to a lesser extent but with greater influence, has enjoyed a similar rise in accessibility. Even printed material has achieved a wider circulation based on modern production and distribution technologies and increased literacy rates. For example, Sri Lanka has an exceptionally high literacy rate, and attitudes are significantly influenced by the plethora of newspapers appealing to citizens on the basis of their separate ethnic identity.

Given such vulnerable societies and such capacity for pervasive presence, the news media is now a pivotal influence in either peacebuilding or conflict. Ideally, with its professional objectives of accuracy, impartiality, and public responsibility, the media should be a contributor foremost to peacebuilding. But for much of the past two decades, this has been doubted because even under the most ideal conditions, it appears the media most often gravitate toward a destructive role. As argued by Gadi Wolfsfeld and many others, the media sensationalizes conflicts with simplistic reporting, which reinforces stereotypes (Wolfsfeld 2001a). The media also tends to reflect and reinforce elite consensus, as well as to reflect its own environment of shared or isolated context. Moreover, this is driven by commercial imperatives that accelerate that gravitation toward a destructive role. As Robert Manoff of the Center for War, Peace, and the News Media, put it, journalism is the handmaiden of conflict (Carnegie Commission on Preventing Deadly Conflict 1999).

Within many less-than-ideal environments, such as barely emerging democracies and conflict-stressed states, conditions and practices are worse. In many cases journalists have low social status, meager pay, and no professional training but only on-the-job mentoring by equally untrained individuals. The journalists are, or have been, intimidated or endangered; they have no legal protection nor any media-supportive infrastructure of courts, legislation, and regulation; and they work for intensely partisanized gatekeepers—editors and owners—who survive on financial support from powerful interests in an otherwise unsustainable uneconomic market. The journalists quite possibly have never seen the concept of a reliable, diverse, and independent media at work in their country. The journalists have to take bribes in order to continue to do their job and feed their families.

In such environments, where governments or powerful interests exercise complete control over the media, the news is simply another form of propaganda or partisanship and compelled to aggravate societal pressures through biased and manipulative reporting.

Objectivity Versus Intent in Reporting

The downward spiral toward a violence-enhancing media culture within full democracies, and the immense weight of unprofessional, penurious, perilous, and highly partisanized conditions in emerging democracies and failed states, has inspired new debate among journalists and some academic circles about the media and conflict and the media's professional practices. The debate became particularly vigorous among Western correspondents over their coverage of the 1990s conflict in the Balkans, which British Broadcasting Corporation correspondent Martin Bell and some others seriously questioned. Bell was distressed by the early stages of the ethnic cleansing in 1993–1995. In his view the West stood idly by because the media reported the slaughter with all the objectivity of reporting on a football match (Bell 1997). The enormity of the tragedy never reached western Europeans because of journalism's professional disinterest in outcomes. Bell argued for a more engaged journalism that would cause Western audiences to more seriously consider acting to resolve the conflict.

Bell's argument struck a chord with some researchers and particularly with advocates of conflict prevention. Encouraged by the success in the previous decade of using the media as a powerful new tool for assisting in the provision of immediate humanitarian relief (such as in broadcasting advisories on locations of food depots and clinics and in aiding longer-term development strategies such as AIDS awareness, agricultural practices, or child health), they suggest the media can play a critical role in defusing tensions.[1] Many journalists and some researchers (Spurk 2002) reject Bell's modest call—for a shift in tone and for an empathy for humanity—as an affront to classic journalistic objective neutrality.[2] Others, however, have taken it considerably further. Jake Lynch may be the most articulate proponent, presenting a new "ethics of responsibility" for reporting, which utilizes concepts of conflict resolution to seek alternative news and outcomes (Lynch and McGoldrick 2001). Jannie Botes describes media outlets in South Africa that consciously seek to mediate (Botes 2000). Sandra Melone and George Terzis put it bluntly, arguing that the media should ensure balanced reporting but "cannot be neutral towards peace."[3]

This debate over journalistic objectivity versus intent and responsibility in an ideal setting is healthy.[4] The debate is widening journalists' understanding of their profession, prompting new interest in the role of media, particularly in conflict-stressed societies moving toward democratization. This brings the most positive developments concerning journalism and conflict to the fore.

Journalism as Mediator

As Manoff and others have pointed out, professional journalism in its normal pursuits has innate potential for contributing to conflict resolution (Carnegie Commission on Preventing Deadly Conflict 1999). The similarities of function, position, and even attitudes between reporters and mediators who assist disputants to resolve their differences are considerable, though largely unrecognized by journalists (Botes 2000). Even with no intent beyond doing its job according to accepted standards, the news media can deliver an essential requisite of conflict resolution, which is communication. The media educates, corrects misperceptions, identifies underlying interests, and humanizes the parties to the dispute. It also provides an emotional outlet, enables consensus building, can offer solutions and build confidence, and so on. As Bauman and Siebert put it, "[J]ournalists mediate conflict whether they intend to or not" (Bauman and Siebert 2001).

As a profession, journalists are in constant search of conflict, as news, and they have rudimentary to highly sophisticated skills in reporting it in conventional terms. But worldwide, journalism training and development contains almost no reference to the discipline of conflict analysis. Little of the wisdom of nearly five decades of academic and professional study of conflict is included in journalism training, and certainly not at the basic level. This is unfortunate because such knowledge can better inform journalists in their work, especially in their analysis of conflict, its sources, and its alternative responses, as well as in their reporting of efforts to defuse conflict. As U.S. journalist Jay Rosen argued to his colleagues at the Carnegie Commission's inquiry into conflict news reporting, "[W]e make an error if we assume that the price of an interest in conflict resolution is giving up commitment to truth and professional objectivity. It is in fact quite the opposite: conflict sensitivity is a journalist's pass into a deeper understanding of what it means to seek the truth in journalism" (Rosen 1999).

Journalism and Peacebuilding

Recognition of these inherent benefits of reliable journalism provides much of the impetus for a greatly accelerated program of professional journalism development in emerging democracies (Howard 2003). These are the areas of opportunity. On the one hand, the freewheeling and intensely competitive media of many Westernized democracies has not resolved, or has resigned itself to, its obsession with commercialized conflict. On the other hand, in many autocratic states the media has virtually no freedom and there is no debate for it to represent. However, in between, there are several dozen countries at various stages of democratization where the role of the media can be critical. And international donor and intervener attention has turned to them. Whereas the extent of an independent and reliable media industry was once seen as an indicator of democracy, it is now viewed as an actor in its own right in the process of democratization.

Since the early 1990s, media and peacebuilding have become integrated into the foreign aid and intervention policies of a number of major donors including members of the European Community, the United States, the United Nations Educational, Scientific, and Cultural Organization (UNESCO), the World Bank, and many international foundations, plus a significant number of individual countries. A survey of these in mid-2002 identified well over 115 million euros budgeted in that year for specific projects related to media and peacebuilding, and it was by no means a complete survey (Spurk 2002).

The purpose of most of the interventions remains the support of conventional, reliable journalism. Reliable means journalism practices that meet international standards of accuracy, impartiality, and social responsibility. There also is support for creating diversity within the media industry to reflect competing opinions and to ensure the industry enjoys independence.

There is also a new trend to foster media activities that go well beyond conventional journalism. Here, the definition of media is extended to include unconventional channels of communication such as street theater, posters, radio dramas and comedy, and other entertainment. The purpose is to produce information specifically designed to influence attitudes toward conflict resolution. The media becomes a facilitator of positive social change rather than a professional disinterested observer. This kind of initiative, called intended outcome programming, is not journalism as we know it, although it adheres to values such as accuracy, fairness, and responsibility. It is attracting audiences and donor support.

The proponents of intended outcome programming, such as Francis Rolt of the NGO Search for Common Ground, argue that organizations and individuals working in conflict zones have been blinded too long by the debate over whether journalism techniques should be used to make the media an element of conflict resolution (European Center for Conflict Prevention 2003). Going beyond news journalism through a variety of forms of media can contribute to peacebuilding in many ways and has enormous attractiveness. Residents and refugees in conflict zones hunger for alternatives to propaganda as news and alarmist coverage of conflict. More attractive (and entertaining and informative) are broadcasts such as soap operas, comedies, music shows, and call-in shows crafted to break down stereotypes, exchange viewpoints dispassionately, seek commonalities, dispel myths, and achieve other nonadversarial images.

Opportunities for Media in Postconflict Development

The opportunities for intervention are extensive in societies that are emerging out from under regimes that practiced violence, ignored human rights, suppressed civil society, and neglected the legal infrastructure. Under such regimes, the media were largely limited to serving as a propaganda agency, and professional journalism training was largely nonexistent. There was also no system of independent regulators and often no privately owned media outlets at all.

The climate for media-related peacebuilding in such post-totalitarian environments is challenging. State censorship often continues in a less predictable manner, sometimes favoring media outlets that support the state or powerful interests. In the absence of an independent regulator or impartial courts to appeal to, the media intentionally or unconsciously adopt self-censorship to avoid transgressions. Accuracy and impartiality are sacrificed for safety's sake. News reporting lacks diversity of opinions and is uncritical of the state or powerful interests. Particularly lacking is a diversity of news media outlets as the state controls licensing of media outlets in its own interest or at the behest of powerful interests operating competing media. Much of the permitted reporting is superficial but highly sensationalized, and the influence on public opinion can be highly destabilizing.

The most prevalent media and peacebuilding initiatives to respond to these conditions have focused on basic training of professional reporting and editing skills, the provision of technical resources, and direct financial support. Training increasingly includes specific skills such as financial reporting, health reporting, or investigative reporting. Responding to common flash points in emerging democracies, journalism training increasingly includes human rights reporting, diversity reporting, and techniques of conflict analysis. Particularly to accelerate the development of independent and diverse media outlets, training has also focused on business practices including advertising and financial management.

In environments where the challenges to such traditional journalism interventions are daunting, or insurmountable at the time, the above-mentioned use of journalism techniques in media for intended outcomes may provide an initial entrance. Professional journalism seeking to play a watchdog role over the government or powerful interests may face accusations of being inflammatory, irresponsible, or threatening security—and in turn be suppressed. Intended outcome media programming, however—which is more calming and seeks consensus, and offers to entertain and educate—may prove popular while posing no specific threat of exposure to any one side in the conflict. Such programming may encourage dialogue and reconciliation among the citizenry, which may lead to reduced tension and reduced repression of traditional professional journalism as the next stage.

Media interventions in support of conflict reduction and democratization have suffered their shortcomings, as was revealed after five years of unprecedented media-related interventions in Bosnia by numerous donors, following the Dayton Agreement. Tens of millions of dollars were assigned to training, journalist protection, equipment, and direct subsidies to newly emerged media outlets. The intention was to create diversity and independence within the Bosnian media to counter state broadcasters who continued to foment ethnic hatred. What was produced was a saturated and artificial media market almost wholly dependent upon donor aid, with minimal responsiveness to the Bosnian public, and practicing highly unreliable and partisanized journalism. In addition to extremely overenthusiastic funding, there had been a serious mistaking of self-declared opposition media outlets for independent, professional journalism. The widely documented failures of the Bosnian interventions,[5] including the lack of donor coordination and unfounded expectations, illustrate a major shortcoming of the field of media and peacebuilding, as mentioned earlier, namely, its lack of well-researched methodology.

A Holistic Approach to Media Intervention

The Bosnian intervention experience illustrates another essential point about enthusiasm for media and peacebuilding. It is increasingly clear that journalism development in the absence of a media-supportive infrastructure cannot function very well or likely very long. Media development initiatives must take a larger approach to a state's democratization (Krug and Price 2002). A media-supportive infrastructure includes a system of legislation, courts, and tribunals that complement, defend, and discipline a reliable news media. Without this, there is no access-to-information legislation to enable well-informed journalism, no courts to protect journalists from intimidation and to address media malfeasance such as libel and slander, and no independent regulators to fairly allocate publishing and broadcasting rights. It requires a multisectoral approach to enable the media to contribute to a society's resolution of its conflicts. It may be called something else, such as legal and administrative reforms or civil service modernization, and may be funded separately, but these sectors are essential for media security and professionalism.

The holistic approach to media interventions for peacebuilding must also reflect upon economic conditions. Professional journalism and the presence of a media-enabling infrastructure will have little effect if a local economy is too impoverished to support companies buying advertising in the media. Media managers unable to finance their operations in the open market will remain vulnerable to subsidization by political interests who seek to dictate news judgment. In addition, journalists—regardless of advanced training—remain liable to corruption, bribery, and intimidation on the job if they obtain very low pay and low status in reflection of the national economy. While democratization initiatives often encourage the formation of private outlets to foster media diversity and independence, those new players may not be economically self-supporting. A donor-dependent media may be a starting point but media outlets must achieve sustainability or fail. State-owned broadcasters in numerous Western democracies should not be overlooked as an acceptable model in emerging democracies where other essential elements such as independent regulators are in place.

Conclusion

There is at this time a cacophony of media-related initiatives in support of democratization and development around the world. Most of the initiatives focus on basic and increasingly sophisticated journalism. Others are exploring redefinitions of conventional journalism to include a conscious ethic of conflict resolution. A third momentum is expanding the concept of intended outcome programming for conflict resolution.

The number of interveners is growing, and even within bilateral donors or international agencies such as UNESCO there can be complementary or competing programs that unwittingly operate in isolation. There are initiatives being pursued, upon which a reliable media greatly depends, such as legislative and legal and regulatory reforms, although these initiatives are supported under the name of good governance or human rights or civil society support. There is a need for much greater coordination of the work being done.

In addition, acknowledged wisdom about what works and what does not is only beginning to be identified and shared. Although the processes and the immediate outcomes have in many cases been recorded, particularly for funders' purposes, the effect of media interventions is not well documented. It is not a question of how many journalists were trained or how many laws were changed but how the standard of reliable journalist was raised or how much the fairness of regulatory decisions was enhanced. It is a slow and expensive process, but evaluation and scholarship need to be built into media interventions from the point of inception. The extensively documented success of media-based human development initiatives, such as educational programs relating to HIV/AIDS development, offers some insight. But for media and peacebuilding, new yardsticks, indicators, and frameworks will be needed.

Notes

This is an adaptation of an article to be published in *Media and Security Governance: The Role of the News Media in Security Oversight and Accountability* by Nomos Verlagsgesellschaft in Baden-Baden, Germany, in 2004.

1. See Botes (1994); Media and Conflict (1998); and Havermans (1998).

2. See Journalists Covering Conflict: Norms of Conduct, a conference supported by the Carnegie Commission on Preventing Deadly Conflict (1999) at www.ccpdc.org/events/journalist/report.htm.

3. Terzis and Melone (2002); European Center for Conflict Prevention (2003).

4. Much of the strongest objection to the debate comes from U.S. journalists and media owners. It is argued that there is no place for novelties like peace journalism in the coverage of U.S. foreign policy, for example. And yet for more than a decade, U.S. journalists and editors have been exploring a domestic version, called civic journalism, that argues there is more to journalism than being a professional spectator. Civic journalism, which engages the media directly in the search for solutions for troubled communities, is now widespread in the United States.

5. See Stalnaker (2001); Price (2000); Taylor (1999); and Curtis (2000).

8

Reforming Education

Wondem Asres Degu

n the world we live in, conflict of some sort is a constitutive part of society. The nature of most conflicts and their respective solutions depend largely on the causes that triggered the conflicts and the factors and actors involved. The root causes of a conflict and the factors and actors involved also determine whether the attempted solutions eliminate the root causes or generate a new type of conflict. Especially, if the attempted solutions are somehow imposed and are not accepted by the various parties to the conflict, and/or the actors responsible for implementing the solution are not recognized as legitimate actors by the society at large, the old conflict may continue or new types of conflict may develop. This means that the end of one type of conflict may be the beginning of another, sometimes more severe and devastating. The frequency with which such a cycle has occurred in the past makes it difficult to talk about postconflict development.

Educational reform as part of postconflict development can contribute to break the cycle of conflict or fuel the old conflict or trigger a new one. This is mainly because education is strongly connected with many of the root causes of conflict:

- recognition of identity, cultural development, and community survival;
- distribution of resources;
- access to political power; and
- ideological orientation.

This makes educational reform difficult and often more political than pedagogical, which is what it should be. If a decision on educational reform is made only with political considerations in mind, the result can

129

be conflict rather than peace and stability. Special attention should thus be given to educational reform if such reform is to contribute to any postconflict development. A number of questions should be raised here: What is the role of educational reform in postconflict development? Why is no proper attention given to educational reform in most post-conflict situations? How should educational reform be tackled? Which reforms are important? What can we learn from past experiences? This chapter attempts to provide some answers to these questions.

What Makes Education Reform Difficult?

Educational expansion has been considered part of the modernization process by the newly independent countries in Africa and elsewhere. Many governments proclaimed that education was given high priority. The achievements of the immediate postcolonial period were significant. The number of schools, teachers, and students increased notably in the 1970s and 1980s. If we look at the 1990s and beyond, however, it seems that education as a sector has not been given the necessary attention. The introduction of the World Bank and International Monetary Fund's structural adjustment programs forced many developing countries to cut their public sector budgets, education included. As a result, the achievements of the previous decades were largely lost. According to UNESCO data, the increase in educational expenditure was far more substantial in the 1970s and 1980s than in the 1990s.

In postconflict situations, usually little attention is paid to educational reform. Much more attention has been paid to political and economic reforms in these situations. Whenever educational reform as part of postconflict development is considered, major decisions are taken for political and economic reasons. Education on its own merit has rarely been taken seriously. A number of reasons may be offered. First, even though education is an important sector for every society, the impact of a specific education system is not immediately recognized. It may take years or sometimes decades to recognize its failure or success, whereas leaders seeking support tend to prioritize measures that yield immediate results. Second, political leaders may not recognize the failure or success of an education system because they spend most of their time struggling to maintain their power. Third, it is not only the failure or success of an educational policy that takes time to be recognized but also the failure or success of its implementation. Fourth, the implementation of a new educational policy as part of postconflict development often needs much more human, financial, and material resources than political leaders are willing or able to invest. Priority is mostly given to political and economic reforms that give results within a short period and may be used as evidence that postconflict development is on the right track.

Educational Reform in Conflict and Postconflict Development

It is important to understand what role education plays in conflict and postconflict development before talking about educational reform. There are three fundamental issues: language as a medium of instruction; disparities of educational opportunities; and the connection between educational expansion, economic developments, and job opportunity. These issues will be examined here to show how and why educational policy can play a major role in either triggering conflict or breaking the cycle of conflict.

Language as a Medium of Instruction

In multiethnic countries, the language policy has proved to be crucial. One important aspect of the language policy is the decision on which languages will be used as a medium of instruction in the school system. Such a policy is strongly connected with wider political issues: state building, socioeconomic mobility, the distribution of resources, and political power. It is also connected with the issues of cultural integration versus autonomy, political integration versus political separation, and modernity versus tradition.

Let us take only the cultural aspect for now. There are three important assumptions to be considered. First, every language indexes (records) its associated culture more fully than others do. Second, every language symbolizes its associated culture more fully than others do. In this respect, the use of minority languages as media of instruction in educational institutions is a symbolic statement in itself. The speakers of such languages will say, "[W]e are here, we exist" (UNESCO 1984, 51). Third, every language enacts its associated culture more fully than others do. Language not only indexes and symbolizes its associated culture, but it is part and parcel of that culture. In this respect, according to UNESCO, "it is crucial that schools teach the language and teach through the language, thereby becoming an active agent in securing the continuity of the culture" (UNESCO 1984, 54–55). Furthermore, at the most general level the indexical, symbolic, and active links between any language and its associated culture always make that language a prime factor in the formation of corresponding cultural identity.

Politically, language has been a very strong element in the formation of ethnic identity. Ethnic politics has also been an important means for organizing and mobilizing specific communities for political gain (be it autonomy or wider participation within the central political arena). More important, the right to use one's own mother tongue (first language) is one of the fundamental human rights that should apply equally to all children and parents. It is for these reasons, among others, that language policy, that is, language as a medium of instruction, is a very sensitive cultural and political issue.

Pedagogically, in multilinguistic countries where a single language is used in schools, children from the minority linguistic groups do not communicate at home in the same language they use at school. Realization of this may come as a shock to them when they start school. Children who do not use their first language in their school may find it more difficult than others to join and compete in their scholastic work, acquire reading and writing skills, and take part in verbal communication with teachers and fellow students. Such circumstances have a negative impact not only on academic achievement but also on socioeconomic development. Therefore, UNESCO recommends, "In the initial phase of schooling the actual linguistic variant used by children must be treated with the greatest respect" (UNESCO 1984, 69). It is also very true that "there is no reason why children should not learn to read and write the linguistic variant they use at home. The transition from this to the standard form will be far easier than having to learn to read and write in an alien standard" (UNESCO 1984, 70).

Thus, in many multiethnic countries choosing any one or more languages as a medium of instruction gives the groups speaking those languages an obvious advantage. As a result, other linguistic groups will identify themselves as disadvantaged. This may induce them to apply serious pressure on their government, which may result in political instability. This has been one of the causes of ethnic conflict. For this reason an appropriate language policy should be part of any postconflict development, especially when ethnic cleavages are part of the conflict. To solve this problem different countries adopted different language policies. Let us briefly look at some examples.

In the former Soviet Union, Article 34 of the constitution stated that citizens were equal before the law, without distinction of language. One of the major guarantees of this equality as stipulated in Article 36 was "the possibility to use their native language and the language of other peoples of the USSR" (*The Soviet Constitution* 1986, 154–155). It was further stipulated:

> The goal the CPSU [Communist Party of the Soviet Union] has set is to ensure the freedom of the . . . languages of the peoples living in the USSR, the freedom of each citizen to speak, bring up and educate his children in whatever language he chooses without privileges, restrictions or compulsion in the use of any particular language. (*The Soviet Constitution* 1986, 153)

This means that officially the Soviet Union's educational policy was multilingual and that all citizens had the right to educate in their mother tongue. In reality, however, every language was not used as a medium of instruction at every level. Some languages were used as media of instruction unlimitedly while others were used only up to certain levels (Lowe, Grant, and Williams 1971, 186–187). This problem created friction between the central government and many minority linguistic groups.

In October 1961, the French Cameroon and the Southern (British) Cameroon merged to form the Federal Republic of Cameroon, which in 1972 became the United Republic of Cameroon. As a result, Cameroon is a country where English and French are widely used. Its first constitution stipulated that "the official languages of the federation shall be English and French" (Tadadjeu 1975, 56). At first, however, the medium of instruction was often one, not both, of the official languages: English in schools of West Cameroon and French in schools of East Cameroon (Chumbow 1980, 290). Later on, as Chumbow pointed out, in recognition of the status of English and French, schools were encouraged to offer or intensify the study of the other official language as a subject in the curriculum and achieve a respectable degree of proficiency in it by graduation (Chumbow 1980, 290). This policy appears to be dictated by pragmatism and by considerations of national unity.

The language policy of apartheid South Africa is an interesting example. The apartheid government in the Republic of South Africa consistently demoted English. "This was not only to promote Afrikaans, the language of the ruling minority, but also to encourage the use of so-called tribal languages such as Setswana, Sesotho, Khosa, and Zulu in pursuit of a divide-and-rule policy" (Bloor and Tamrat 1996, 53). This shows that the introduction of the mother tongue in education is not always intended to develop local cultures and to respect the rights of the communities to use their languages. It can also be used to divide the society into smaller units. The commitment to the introduction of English as an official language by the African National Congress and other antiapartheid organizations during the struggle was, as Bloor and Tamrat put it, "an outcome of their clear recognition of the reactionary nature of the government's language policy and its potential detrimental effect on African unity in the battle against apartheid" (Bloor and Tamrat 1996, 53).

Let us now consider two cases, Tanzania and Ethiopia. There is a clear difference between those countries with regard to the use of ethnic community languages and the development of one national language as a medium of instruction. Tanzania has been highly praised for having solved the national language problem with the Swahilization policy of 1967. This policy adopted Swahili as the country's national and official language. Yet English has continued to be the language of education. There is, however, a growing demand for the use of Swahili. There is a strong feeling of dependency that follows from the use of an alien language—English. In addition, most, if not all, Tanzanians widely use Swahili and other ethnic community languages in everyday activities.

In 1969, the Ministry of National Education sent a circular to all secondary schools outlining the plan for the gradual introduction of Kiswahili as a medium of instruction (Brock-Utne 2002, 26). In 1980, the Presidential Commission on Education recommended the change from English to Kiswahili and even set a date: January 1985 for secondary schools and 1991 for the universities. However, this recommendation was deleted from the official publication of the report of the commission in 1984 (Brock-Utne 2002, 26; see also Rubanza 1996, 92).

The 1995 Education and Training Policy stated that the medium of instruction for pre-primary and primary education shall be Kiswahili and that English shall be a compulsory subject. The medium of instruction for secondary education shall continue to be English, and Kiswahili shall be a compulsory subject (Brock-Utne 2002, 28). In August 1997, the Ministry of Education and Culture issued another policy document in which it was stated: "A special plan to enable the use of Kiswahili as a medium of instruction in education and training at all levels shall be designed and implemented" (Brock-Utne 2002, 28). The same document also explicitly stated that "English will be a compulsory subject at pre-primary, primary and secondary levels and it shall be encouraged in higher education. The teaching of English shall be strengthened" (Brock-Utne 2002, 28). It is important to note that the government avoided making any statement on the status and role of the approximately 120 ethnic community languages (Rubanza 1996, 83).

Two problems are still unsolved in Tanzania. The policy of changing English with Swahili as a medium of instruction as it was intended has not been materialized. And there is no clear policy on the introduction of ethnic community languages as media of instruction. Even though a three-tier policy was proposed by scholars (see Rubanza 1996, for instance) for pedagogical and politico-cultural reasons, there has been no sign that the country is moving in that direction.

The three successive regimes that ruled Ethiopia for over half a century—the imperial government, the Marxist-Socialist Derg regime, and the current government led by the Ethiopian People's Revolutionary Democratic Front (EPRDF)—claimed to be giving education high priority. Each of these regimes developed education policies and institutions and tried to build educational systems that could serve many of their respective political objectives. Let us consider the Ethiopian experience in relatively more detail, for it has played a major role in creating conflicts between the government and the citizens as well as between different linguistic groups.[1]

Language policy, especially language as a medium of instruction, has been an important issue in Ethiopian politics. For instance, according to Article 31 of the Eritrean Constitution, during the federation period (1952–1962), Tigrigna and Arabic had been official languages in Eritrea (Wagaw 1979, 97–98). This was adopted as a postwar solution. However, later on the federation was dissolved and the two languages were replaced by the Amharic language. This measure became one of the root causes of the war in northern Ethiopia.

The right to use one's own mother tongue together with other political issues has also been behind the emergence of many ethnic liberation fronts in other parts of the country. Even though there have been demands for the introduction of ethnic languages as media of instruction, only Amharic and English were used in schools.[2]

The Transitional Government of Ethiopia, which came to power in 1991, redrew the country's internal boundaries on the basis of linguistic identity and ethnic settlement of groups in certain areas. Ethnic regionalization did not stop at redefining regions but ended in complete federalization of the country's political system and administration. The new regions are now responsible for the management and administration of basic social services, including education.

According to the new ethnic federal system, primary and secondary education, which used to be under the central government, became the responsibility of individual administrative regions (states). A new "Education and Training Policy" to guide the education sector under the federal system was declared in 1994. As a result, many far-reaching changes and reforms have been introduced, which include, among other things, decentralization of the school system, curriculum reform, and the use of nationality languages.

Every ethnic state, according to the federal constitution and the new educational policy, was encouraged to choose not only its medium of instruction but also the type of alphabet to be used. As a result, currently Ethiopia uses twelve languages and three different alphabets: the Ethiopian (Ge'ez), the Latin, and the Arabic. In addition, the government tried even to create a new language based on shared elements of four related Omotic language-speaking groups in southern Ethiopia (the Wolayta, Gamo, Gofa, and Dauro) called "Wogagoda" as a medium of instruction, which locally resulted in strong public protest in 1999 and 2000. The program was later dropped, making the educational materials produced for the schools useless.

Some critical remarks should be made here with regard to the new Ethiopian language and educational policy. First, there was no meaningful attempt to study which languages were ready to be used as a medium of instruction and what kind of program would be suitable to help the development of other languages. It seems that the choice of languages was made for purely political reasons.[3]

Second, there was no effective plan for the training of teachers and other supporting personnel in the different languages.

Third, students who had one or more years of education were forced to continue their education in another language and a different alphabet. It seems that the translation started before the provision of any guidelines regulating the transition from Amharic to other national languages was adopted. There appears to have been no study available on how those students who were in grade four and above in 1993–1994 would cope with the transition and with the national final examination (Negash 1996, 82).

Fourth, the existing content of education was translated into many languages in spite of the fact that it had been criticized, among other things, for producing school leavers who had very little chance of getting employed in the modern sector. The chances of the school leavers going back to the villages were even smaller, as most of them were from urban areas and their training was mainly theoretical.

In Ethiopia ethnicity is not only used for the political restructuring of the country and the educational system but also of civil organizations. The two major examples are the Ethiopian Trade Union and the Ethiopian Teachers Association, which were forced to reorganize themselves along ethnic lines. The objective in this regard is to minimize the power of these organizations in challenging the policies of the government by fragmenting them into smaller and weaker ethnic organizations. The Ethiopian Trade Union has been strongly challenging the policy of the government on structural adjustment programs while the Ethiopian Teachers Association opposed the ethnically based educational policy, which was not based on relevant research and did not involve any popular participation (Degu 2002, 223).

A number of questions should be raised here: How much of these reforms are motivated by political and/or pedagogical objectives? What are the opposing views on—and ideals for—education among the various players in the field, among them the still independent Ethiopian Teachers Union? What are the political objectives behind these educational reforms? What will be the short- and long-term policy implications of the announced reforms on Ethiopia's educational and training system? Will there be a political effect on people's identification with Ethiopia as a nation-state or as members of one national political community? These are some of the questions that need answers.

For the reasons I have indicated above, there has been and still is strong opposition to the new language and education policies. More important, there is a growing feeling among many Ethiopians that ethnically based political and educational policy may destroy the national unity and territorial integrity of the country. There is also a growing suspicion that the ruling party initially organized to liberate one specific region—Tigray (the Tigregna-speaking people of Ethiopia)—cannot be the legitimate political force that will develop a genuine education policy for the country at large. It is strongly believed that the ruling party is playing the ethnic card to maintain its power and favor its specific ethnic group. To give one example, Professor Andargachew Tesfaye of the Addis Ababa University points out:

> What is more disheartening is the fact that education is used as a political tool to favour or disfavour regions under the pretext that education at the first and second level is a regional affair. One only wishes that those responsible will realise, soon enough, that this is a dangerous game and speedy amends are needed. It is also high time for the people, particularly [those] who can see the unfair game being played and understand the long run consequences, to start speaking up and speak loud. (Support Group to the Ethiopian Human Rights Council 2000, 18)

As a result of the introduction of ethnic federalism, the country's political groups are divided between supporters (mainly ethnic political groups allied with the ruling party) and opponents of ethnic politics (nonethnic and ethnic groups that reject ethnic federalism). The introduction of three different alphabets in the school system also created strong public opposition, especially from the teachers and other trade union members. There has been conflict—at times violent—between linguistic groups whose languages are used as media of instruction and linguistic groups whose languages are not. There is also a growing demand from linguistic groups whose languages are not used as media of instruction for their right to use their own languages in the school system. If these demands are not met, they may develop into wider political movements. Therefore, language and educational policies, which are supposed to be part of postconflict development, can push the country into another cycle of conflict.

Regional Disparities of Educational Opportunities

Education is an area in which there have been many fights for equal opportunities. The expansion of education, especially primary and secondary education, at the national level has proven not to be a sufficient condition for equalizing educational opportunities to the various regions or ethnic or religious communities. In most cases, the expansion of education is concentrated in and around urban areas. It is also true that educational expansion has been relatively visible in the center when compared to the periphery of a country. In this regard the central issue is how the expansion affected the disparities in educational participation (Shebeshi 1989, 26).

Thus, the central plan of any infrastructure of social services, including education, should apply the principle of proportional development, which implies an equitable distribution of these services. Then–vice minister of education Tekle-Haimanot Haile Selassie asserted: "It should be borne in mind that unequal measure or differential steps are required to be taken in order to move towards equality. This is an important strategic aspect of securing equitable distribution of resources that should result in equal opportunity to services of education or otherwise" (Selassie 1983, 1).

The failure to do so could lead to a situation in which distributional inequality or disparity might result in spatial discrimination. This in turn will give rise to complaints by the disadvantaged groups—especially by disadvantaged minority groups if the country is multiethnic or multireligious—that may have serious political implications.

Educational disparity may result from the control of political and economic power by specific groups. This is based on two important assumptions. First, those who control political and economic power tend to allocate priority of educational opportunities first and foremost to their own children and then to those who are next in line in maintaining the power holder's position of interest (ethnic, religious/regional communities). Second, those who control political and economic power will control and guide the educational curriculum to reflect their own cultural perception vis-à-vis the peripheral segments of the society (Tuso 1982, 276). In other words, the issue is not only the allocation of educational opportunities in favor of specific groups by the people in power but also the control of the content of education to make it reflect their own culture at the cost of other cultures. It is, therefore, crucial to understand that conflict over education is also conflict over political and economic power as well as over cultural development and identity.

Inequality in educational opportunities is also strongly related to socioeconomic development. Educational disparities usually coincide with disparities between the socioeconomic development of different regions. Economically poor regions usually have less and poorer educational facilities. Less educational opportunities may also result in poor economic development. However, rectifying the disparities in educational provisions can help remedy the whole range of social and economic inequalities (Shebeshi 1989, 27). It is also believed that better economic development will help improve the provision of educational opportunities. It is, therefore, imperative that educational policies should be part and parcel of the political and socioeconomic policies of a country.

Disparity in educational participation has also serious political implications. First, in a heterogeneous political community, schools can play an important role in the process of socialization. For schools to play an effective role in political socialization of the youth from every part of a country and enhance national integration, every child should be given equal opportunity for education.

Second, in every society education is a means for upward mobility, because the chances of getting employed and building a career are heavily dependent on educational qualifications. Hence, distributing educational opportunities is the same as allocating a future status in a society (Shebeshi 1989, 29–30). "Ignoring this problem could lead to political vulnerability of the leaders or even threaten the nation-hood of the given country, especially when the setup of regions coincides with ethnic division" (Shebeshi 1989, 29–30).

Third, educational disparity is also reflected in the sharing of power. In a situation where certain ethnic/religious/regional groups identify themselves as disadvantaged as a result of the unequal distribution of educational opportunities, members of these groups feel they do not have their fair share of power. Members of such groups, especially educated elites, count the number of people (from the different groups) who are included in the top echelon of their country. If the number or the proportion seems to be in favor of other groups, they are likely to demand their fair share. This can be a demand for more participation in the country's leadership and for more resources to correct the imbalance. If these demands are not reasonably satisfied, the problem may develop into dangerous conflict, such as demand for more autonomy or separation, which can threaten national integrity. The Ethiopian case is a good example. In the pre-1991 years it was assumed that the Amhara linguistic groups dominated the government and the civil society. Following 1991 it has been repeatedly argued that the Tigray linguistic groups have dominated the political and socioeconomic arena of the country. In both cases there were and still are strong demands from different linguistic groups who believed that they were denied their fare share of power. This has been one of the country's unsolved problems.

Educational Expansion, Economic Development, and Job Opportunity

A related issue is the need for the harmonization of education, economic development, and job opportunity, which has its own political and economic repercussions. In many developing countries the increasing gap between the expansion of education and the lagging behind of economic development and job opportunities has been a critical problem resulting in the creation of political instability.

The expansion of education in many developing counties has been strongly influenced by the widely accepted idea that "education is one of the main prerequisites to the movement forward into sustained growth" (Gray-Cowan 1966, 22). There is truth in this assumption, but it should be noted that:

> There is no evidence that education will lead automatically to economic development. Only if education becomes part of a closely integrated and comprehensive plan for development, involving both governmental and private sectors of the economy and including all levels of society, can it play its full part. (Gray-Cowan 1996, 27)

In other words, as Gray-Cowan asserts, "if education is pursued as an end in itself, it may well retard development, since political instability may result from the failure of the national economy to provide the reward expected by its educated citizens" (Gray-Cowan 1996, 27). The problem may be worse if the majority of unemployed educated citizens belong to disadvantaged (minority) communities.

Michael Carton has clearly pointed out the effect of the disparity between educational expansion and job opportunities as follows:

> Those who leave school without a job find themselves in a vague state in which they are neither children nor adult workers. This experience can make them cynical and bitter, with a feeling of having been aban-

doned by the society which had promised them much but given them very little. As a result, they become alienated from the world around them, gradually losing all confidences in themselves and without any hope of finding work. (Carton 1984, 92)

There may be far more serious political effects. The failure of a country to provide jobs for its educated citizens will undoubtedly frustrate the young. It may also lead to the deterioration of national feeling and belongingness. It may force the young to question what their country has given them and will give them in the future. What does citizenship mean for them? Such young people who feel they are victims of the status quo may be used as a literate reserve army for antigovernment forces who are fighting against the existing regime for various objectives. Thus, it is reasonable to argue that the expansion of education without the corresponding economic development has and will have negative political repercussions rather than help national development. Especially in developing countries with high political instability, many separatist movements, interethnic conflicts, and antigovernment groups, the existence of such a huge literate and dissatisfied population will contribute to the worsening of the situation. And in postconflict situations, such young unemployed people may be easily tempted to again take up arms, even if only as a way of making a living.

Educational Reform as Part of Postconflict Development

I have argued that education can be an important factor in contributing to the creation of conflict or to the intensification of existing conflict or positively to breaking the cycle of conflict. This is so especially if the society is heterogeneous. Furthermore, if education is one of the causes of conflict, educational reform should be part and parcel of the postconflict development process. If there exists a problem of language as a medium of instruction—such as regional disparities of educational opportunities, a disparity between educational expansion and economic development, or that the content of education does not reflect the society at large—there will be the need to rectify these shortcomings to avoid new conflict and to create a lasting postconflict development. The specific steps that need to be taken depend on the specific situation of the countries concerned and on the nature and intensity of the problem. However, it is possible to formulate some general ideas.

The very process of rectifying the weaknesses and reorienting and reorganizing the existing curriculum content of a country's educational system should depend on the precise and clear redefinition of a country's national goals: political, economic, social, and cultural policies accepted by the different sociopolitical groups. It is important that, especially in a heterogeneous society, a country's national goals are the result of a negotiated consensus between the various sociopolitical groups. It will be in reference to attaining such national goals that the country's educational goals, which will guide the overall educational activities, should be articulated. If, for instance, there is a problem of national unity—a serious problem in heterogeneous societies—the education system should be developed to contribute to the consolidation of national unity. Appropriate emphasis must be put on developing a state of mind that will accept the country's diversity as the source of future strength and development. Education should be reorganized to help cultivate deep and lasting national consciousness, national pride, and a sense of national belonging in the minds of the youth. In general the new education system and its content must be designed to produce a generation of people who think and act as equal citizens of a country.

In a situation where the attitude of preferring violence and war as a means of solving problems and differences has been strong, education can play a crucial role to change such an attitude, especially the attitude of the youth. In such a situation, a country's education system needs to be redesigned and developed so that it can contribute to this end. As Professor Mesfin Wolde-Mariam points out, education should contribute to the development of an attitude in which:

> Peace must not be and must not mean the defeat and humiliation of one group and the victory and jubilation of another . . . peace can only mean the substitution of violent and destructive conflict by a positive and a constructive one, the substitution of fighting with the bullet by fighting with words and ideas. . . .
>
> Violence as a means of resolving differences or as a means of acquiring power over any section or the whole society is both morally and intellectually unacceptable. The resort to violence is not only a concrete demonstration of rejecting the sovereignty of the people, it is also a violation of one's own stand against oppression and arbitrary rule by force. (Wolde-Mariam 1991, 5)

The development of such an attitude in the minds of the society and especially in the youth must be taken as the responsibility of the structured education system.

Regional disparities of educational opportunities and the disparity between educational expansion and economic development should also be addressed as part of postconflict development. To rectify the regional disparities, unequal measures or differential steps will be required to move toward equality. Such steps should be taken as a crucial strategic aspect of securing equitable distribution of resources that will result in equal opportunity of education services at all levels. Unequal measures or differential steps mean directing or allocating a significant proportion of financial, material, and human resources to areas that are identified to be disadvantaged in the old system. In short, more attention should be given to areas or social groups where there are few or no schools and other educational facilities.

Building educational facilities by itself might not solve the problem. Other steps to improve the political, economic, social, and cultural development of the disadvantaged areas should also be considered. This is due to the fact that effective utilization of educational facilities has been proved unthinkable in socioeconomically and culturally backward societies. To solve the problem of regional disparities of educational opportunities and reverse their sociopolitical and economic impact, an effective and efficient comprehensive development program must be launched.

Other related issues that need to be tackled are the disparity between educational expansion and economic development, the integration of education and the country's trained workforce needs, and the ever-increasing number of educated unemployed. These are interrelated problems that need serious consideration. To tackle these problems and reverse their adverse effect, a comprehensive and integrated educational and training policy should be developed based on the workforce needs of a country. The education sector must fundamentally be reorganized and redirected toward a country's socioeconomic and political development, especially toward the dominant economic sectors. It should be, above all, oriented toward facilitating a country's economic development by enhancing labor productivity—especially because economic development can help a country reorient itself away from conflict and achieve lasting peace. Some serious measures should also be taken to increase the absorptive capacity not only of the modern economic sectors but also of the traditional rural sector. This can be done by developing a socioeconomic program taking into account the needs of the people and the country on the one hand and a country's national resources, experience, culture, local knowledge, and international development on the other hand.

As discussed above, one of the root causes of violent conflict in multiethnic countries has been the language policy of a country. The demand for mother-tongue education and the use of one's own native language has been a growing problem in many countries. The world has witnessed many circumstances when such demands were not satisfied where the result has been conflict and sometimes violent conflict. It is, therefore, imperative to undertake educational reform as part of the postconflict development process. The reform should consider, among other things: (1) the rights of every citizen to use their native languages in education and other public arenas; (2) the socioeconomic and political impacts that are attached to the uses of one's own language; and (3) the economic capacity and trained workforce needs of the country.

Postconflict education policy should in principle be multilingual. However, the policy should be based on the results of a thorough research on which languages are suitable to be used as a medium of education, at what level of education, and when to be used. Different measures should also be taken to help some languages develop to be used as a medium of instruction.

Postconflict educational policy should also give special attention to improving the professional and moral qualities of teachers, who are the central actors in education. Special attention should be paid to the recruitment, quality of training, job satisfaction, social prestige, and the spiritual and material incentives of teachers. For teachers to devote their knowledge, energy, and time in producing young productive citizens with confidence and purpose, teachers must be motivated.

For all of the points discussed above to be effective in developing a new educational policy, there should be attitudinal changes among the political leaders and educators on the one hand and in the society at large on the other. A system should be devised that makes it possible to have effective popular participation in the major educational activities, namely decisionmaking, implementing, evaluating, and controlling. Political leaders and educators must develop the will to consider the views and opinions in society. They should have the will to have effective dialogue with different groups in society. Dialogue requires an intense faith in the human being, "faith in his power to make and remake, to create or recreate, faith in his vocation to be more man, which is not the privilege of an elite, but the birth right of all men" (Freire 1973, 77–79).

Political leaders and educators should change their attitude on what education is all about by revising past experiences, mistakes, and successes. Furthermore, educators should take into account that "authentic education is not carried on by 'A' for 'B' or by 'A' about 'B,' rather by 'A' with 'B'" (Freire 1973, 82–83). As Freire correctly puts it, "we simply can not go to the laborer-urban or peasant in the banking style, to give them 'knowledge' or to impose upon them the model of the 'good man' contained in a program whose content we have ourselves organized." The society should have a say in organizing the educational system. "Many political and educational plans have failed because their authors designed them according to their personal views of reality, never once taking into account—except as mere objects of their action—the men in a solution to whom their program was ostensibly directed" (Freire 1973, 82–83).

If politicians and educators are determined to launch genuine educational reform that can contribute to avoiding conflict and/or to breaking a cycle of conflict, there should be no reason to fear the people, their expressions, and their effective participation. Initiators of genuine mass-based educational reform must also be accountable to the people; they must speak frankly to the society of their achievements, shortcomings, miscalculations, and difficulties and, of course, invite the people to submit their views and opinions. In short, they must make continuous effort to enhance the role of the society and develop the will to seriously consider public opinion.

However, for such reform to be meaningful and lasting, the members of the society must be aware that they are and should be the real sources of the articulation of, and the decisive actors in, the practicality of the educational reform. They must be prepared to consciously contribute to the decisonmaking, implementing, and evaluating processes of the educational reform and the effectiveness of the educational system in general.

Notes

1. I worked under the Ethiopian Ministry of Education for a long time and was involved in the process of the reform.

2. Amharic is one of the Ethiopian languages widely used in the country. Amharic was used in elementary schools while English was used in secondary and tertiary education as a medium of instruction. Yet in the late 1970s, when the national literacy campaign was launched, fifteen different languages were used as media of instruction in the campaign. This multilingual language policy, which was appreciated by many linguistic groups, was not implemented in the formal education system of the country.

3. A significant majority of the political parties that formed the transitional government in 1991 and later the federal government were ethnically based and favored the adoption of such a policy. The major nonethnic parties were excluded even to work as legal opposition.

9

Reviving Health Care

Vanessa van Schoor

Trauma and disease draw attention. The crisis in East Timor in the last months of the twentieth century brought together a large number of international experts and resources. Poor health and human rights conditions had been exacerbated by violence and intimidation. Most Indonesian medical personnel had left before the ballot on independence, leaving urgent cases to a handful of local doctors and nurses supported by a small corps of internationals. As the Timorese officially rejected the Indonesian offer of autonomy in a referendum on August 30, 1999, the systematic destruction of the infrastructure began. With expectations that emergency relief would be brief and that longer-term development initiatives would take time to be organized, there was a need and an opportunity to develop a middle ground for postconflict development.

East Timor: Historical Background

The island of Timor is located at the eastern end of the Indonesian archipelago a few hundred kilometers north of Australia. Originally colonized by the Portuguese in the early 1500s, East Timor was finally given a chance at independence in 1974. Unfortunately, the U.S. and Australian governments, reeling from Vietnam, fearing the establishment of another communist stronghold, and seeking to secure the deep-sea submarine channel north of the island, thwarted plans by encouraging Indonesia to annex East Timor.[1] According to the governor of East Timor, 60,000 East Timorese died in the first wave of Indonesian military operations.

Over the next quarter century, Indonesia made significant investments in infrastructure and services but was unable to maintain order without a significant troop presence. Military operations and draconian population control measures resulted in 140,000 deaths and an even longer list of human rights violations.

History of the East Timorese Medical System

Traditional healers were the first to provide care to the Timorese. They were followed by Catholic missionaries who set up clinics and schools in hopes of winning converts. The Portuguese government invested in a central hospital and some district clinics but was not able to adequately support the structures.[2]

After their invasion, the Indonesians sought to win popular support by increasing East Timorese health staff and facilities. The new clinics struggled with staff absenteeism and supply shortages. Indonesian doctors and interns were not trusted due to inexperience, lack of motivation, or their limited understanding of the local culture and languages. Family planning programs were plagued by accounts of forced contraception and sterilization (Sissons 1997). Indonesian health workers were accused of complicity in military crackdowns. Many villagers opted for Catholic clinics or returned to traditional healers.

Decades of sustained intervention by the Indonesian government did not bring health standards up to national, let alone international, standards. Trauma and malnutrition were complicated by malaria, tuberculosis, diarrheal diseases, and respiratory infections. Infant and maternal mortality rates were among the highest in the world. (See Table 9.1.)

History of the Crisis

The international community was slow to respond to East Timor's early calls for help. Intensive lobbying since 1975, a student massacre in

Table 9.1 Mortality Rates and Life Expectancy

	East Timor	Indonesia	Australia
Infant mortality per 1,000	70–90	35-41	5
Under-age-five mortality per 1,000	99–124	75	7
Maternal mortality per 100,000	450–850	373–470	15
Life expectancy	57–61	64.25	78.8

Source: World Health Organization, *Health System Inputs (HSI) Index 2002,* http://www.who.int.

1991, and a Nobel Peace Prize for Timorese activists in 1996 were not enough to mobilize action. It was not until the Asian economic crisis and the fall of Indonesian president Suharto that U.S. and Australian foreign policy began to shift. The Indonesian military begrudgingly allowed for a referendum, confident that the Timorese would choose to remain within Indonesia and that the process would quell separatist interests elsewhere.

On August 30, 1999, the UN-sponsored referendum in East Timor resulted in 78.5 percent of the population voting against autonomy status within Indonesia.[3] In response, the Indonesian military together with the militias began systematically destroying the infrastructure,[4] killing upward of 2,000 people (UNDP 2002c) and deporting more than 200,000 others. Buildings were burned, clinics looted, and ambulances confiscated or destroyed. International medical workers, including nuns, were expelled at gunpoint, and national staff either escaped to neighboring countries or fled into the mountains.

As the violence peaked, the Australian government lobbied the UN for permission to lead an international force into East Timor. By October 1999, with international troops in place and formal Indonesian recognition of the referendum results, political obstacles had been neutralized, significant international finances were available, and experienced personnel were ready to respond.

The Medical System in Crisis

Almost 35 percent of clinics were completely destroyed and up to 70 percent of buildings in many towns had been razed (World Bank 1999). Reaching patients depended on securing the areas in which they were hiding. Clinics swelled as internally displaced persons and almost 40 percent of the refugees returned within the first months. After locating patients, the next challenge was finding staff to help treat them. Of the nearly 3,000 former health workers, only twenty doctors and 600 nurses/midwives were actually East Timorese. Once found, they would be needed to form the backbone of a new health system.

From Emergency to Development

The conflict was over, the belligerents were out of the country, and the local population was appealing for international assistance. With formal government departments in chaos, the humanitarian agencies had no bureaucratic systems to hinder them from launching broad-based support programs. The resources, experience, and expertise were available to not only establish emergency medical services but to also set the foundations for an effective new system. Following on years of experience working under harsh conditions with limited supply networks and difficulties negotiating with authorities, East Timor would prove to be one of the most straightforward operations in the careers of many aid veterans.

Emergency specialists knew that international attention and support would only be available until a new crisis came along. If efforts could be coordinated, East Timor had a good chance of making it into the new millennium with more than adequate resources. A proper diagnosis and treatment could lead to a successful recovery. In this context it was going to mean asking the right questions about personnel, financing, transport, equipment, supplies, and communications networks.

Coordination

On the international side, staff assigned to the humanitarian intervention in East Timor was of an unprecedented caliber and professionalism. The operation was coordinated, not controlled, by top staff from the OCHA. Other UN agencies sent personnel from headquarters and key field operations. This ensured that the expertise and authority needed to take operational decisions was immediately present on the ground. The international NGOs that responded were among the most experienced agencies or smaller groups with long-standing links to East Timor. Donor representatives came in early and worked alongside the humanitarian agencies to make funds readily available. Even the armed forces had pretrained for civil-military cooperation and were prepared to collaborate with humanitarian aid workers. Respect for the expertise of other partners and the enormous amount of work ahead stopped personal agendas from getting in the way.

Daily meetings were held on security, health, water, shelter, food, and general coordination. With a relatively small territory to cover, problems were put on the table, gaps were identified quickly, and all agencies collaborated or shared assets where needed.

Health

The health sector was one of the first to establish a forum with local counterparts. Working directly with the Timorese from the outset meant that assistance targeted the needs of the population rather than simply meeting the predetermined priorities of international agendas.

Information was shared, responsibilities were divided, and basic operational protocols were established. Mentoring Timorese counterparts also increased the odds of establishing sustainable programs.

An East Timorese Health Professionals Working Group was established. Working together with the international organizations, it helped to choose priority sites for health facilities and to confirm the credentials of medical workers who had lost documents during the violence. Timorese health workers were flexible in their initial deployments and worked long hours helping to reestablish their medical services.

In the early stages, international NGOs provided daily incentives to medical staff rather than contracts, allowing the flexibility to reassign staff once needs were more clearly defined. The salary scale accounted for previous wages, minimized disruption to local markets, limited "shopping around" by national staff, and acknowledged the spending limits a new government was sure to face.

The medical forum quickly developed into an Interim Health Authority with a majority of Timorese members, then a Division of Health Services, and finally a Ministry of Health. They assumed responsibility for coordinating health services and for developing national health policies, systems, and legislation.

Challenges

Most Timorese were overwhelmed by the magnitude of the international operations. Despite an early emphasis on community consultation and developing a new strategy appropriate to the Timorese context, time restrictions on the UN mandate and the limited span of donor interest often resulted in operational plans being simply translated from those used in other countries rather than being written explicitly for East Timor.

As the UN set up a Transitional Administration in East Timor and expanded operations, standard UN policies were introduced. The humanitarian salary scale was ignored as the UN maintained its precedent of offering inflated salaries to attract the best people. While this policy may have merit in countries where UN operations are small, it had drastic consequences in a struggling postconflict society where the UN was to be the main employer. For the burgeoning East Timorese civil service, it also meant that many of the most experienced people were not available when recruitment was done for government positions.

Job descriptions were drafted by the East Timorese health professionals, assisted by the World Health Organization (WHO) and NGOs, but recruitment was managed by a newly formed East Timorese Civil Service and Public Employment department. This was a body of individuals with mixed capacities struggling to meet the hiring needs of not just health but all government departments. Political affiliation and seniority reemerged as criteria in hiring. In health, there were no skilled administrators, so staff were drawn from the small base of practicing doctors and nurses. The recruitment process needed more skill, depth, and support if people were to be placed correctly.

Gender equity is difficult to implement. NGOs often go beyond traditional biases, and in East Timor the leadership officially supported the promotion of women. Despite the rhetoric and claims that female nurses and health workers were to form the core of the health service, the reality of government hiring was that men continued to dominate nursing and only a handful of women were brought into management and policy development.

Training is essential. Initial upgrading was done by foreign doctors and nurses through on-the-job coaching and small seminars. Three years into postconflict development, a National Center for Health Education and Training was established for nurses, sanitarians, and nutritionists to allow for learning to continue. A number of foreign scholarships were established to ensure that advanced training continued.

International NGO assistance was phased out too quickly in East Timor. As the World Bank became increasingly involved in reestablishing the health sector, international NGOs were reclassified as "contractors" and asked to submit district health plans to tender. Not accustomed to competing for the right to provide assistance, the NGOs submitted plans for districts where they were already present. Only once the plans were in were the NGOs informed about UN/World Bank/Timorese government decisions to further restrict budgets and personnel. NGOs were dismissed by the World Bank as overstretched and underfunded. The number of health workers was further reduced to less than 50 percent of what it had been in Indonesian times. The reduction raised concerns among NGOs about whether minimum health standards and services could be assured. Only a small number of international advisers remained throughout the emergency and postconflict period to ensure continuity and support for the new East Timorese health system.

Five years on, East Timor is shifting out of postconflict and into a development period. There is a functioning health-care service and staff and clinic numbers have been reincreased to meet community needs. East Timor has become an accredited member of the WHO, and while health planning moves more slowly than international advisers would like, the health sector is moving forward and remains one of the most active and committed East Timorese government departments.

Financing

After security, health is one of the early sectors to receive funding. In East Timor this was provided through a range of sources: NGOs, private funds, a UN Consolidated Appeal, trust funds, bilateral government donations, Quick Impact Projects, the budget of the UN Department of Peacekeeping Operations, the Catholic Church, and eventually government revenues.

Most medical NGOs were able to launch operations quickly by using independent resources raised through private donations and core funding. This allowed for prepositioning and rapid deployment of materials and personnel. Once teams were on the ground and needs were clarified, formal project proposals were submitted to donors. With the nonprofit ethos of NGOs, the majority of funds went directly into operations. In an operation like East Timor, the priorities were clear and the millions spent by the NGOs remained a fraction of what was dispersed through UN or military budgets.

The OCHA organized a Consolidated Appeal Process (CAP) while agencies waited to get back into East Timor. A CAP is a tool for coordination and strategic planning used by the UN to outline funding needs during emergencies.[5] This mechanism has advantages as programs and expenditures can be mapped out. The drawback is that participating organizations need to have the resources ready to prefinance their activities. There are also no guarantees that the funds requested will be granted. For the sake of consistency and identifying gaps, many of the larger NGOs submitted program information to the CAP without requesting funds. Some smaller organizations saw the CAP as easy access to big money but then found themselves facing community leaders trying to explain why administrative delays hundreds of thousands of miles away were hindering the delivery of promised aid. Independent diversified nongovernmental funding was again shown to be key to maintaining flexibility and meeting the most urgent needs in emergency and postconflict operations.

Some military contingents sent medical teams to East Timor. While their primary role was assisting their own troops, a number of them became involved in civilian care. They provided life-saving but nonsustainable and costly services. As contingents rotated out, staff and equipment were taken away, and luxuries like air ambulance evacuations were clearly services the Timorese government could not afford.

Based on the needs identified in the CAP and a 1999 World Bank Joint Assessment Mission, governments were invited to a series of biannual donor conferences on East Timor. The NGOs worked to mentor East Timorese counterparts to participate in these meetings and establish their own direct lines of communications with donors and governments. The World Bank, the Asian Development Bank, and the UN helped the East Timorese government establish a budget, a fiscal authority, a treasury, and currency exchange. To the credit of the new government, health and education were identified as priorities, with 45 percent of the budget allocated to social services.

In health, the World Bank and the WHO planned for $38 million to be spent over four years. They targeted staffing, rehabilitation, and medical supplies—also the main items in NGO budgets. By taking these budget lines away from the NGOs, their funding options became limited and many of the smaller support programs were not enough to draw donor interest. This did not pose a problem for the government, as it had a growing interest in taking over the management of the health sector funds. A formal request was made from the government to the international NGOs to finish their interventions by the end of 2001.

The World Bank's Community Empowerment and Local Governance Project (see Chapter 4 in this volume), launched prior to the ballot, also worked at cross purposes to the new government agenda. Community clinics were built in areas that met local needs but that fell outside of the scope of the government plans. The building was there, but there were no health staff or medicines available to supply them.

East Timorese became increasingly concerned about financial transparency and the large amounts of money that did not seem to be translating into tangible assistance. There was mistrust with the planning and spending being done outside the country. There were concerns about information reaching donors and external governments before it was shared with the local population. People were unhappy about the disparity between what was spent on international versus local staff salaries and the high overhead costs of the foreign partners. There were fears that the international assistance was harboring dependency.

In postconflict financing, there are basic principles to be considered (see Oxfam 1999; and Chapter 12 in this volume). One of the key points was to ensure that East Timor did not go into debt after the intervention. Participation and leadership from the local population are essential to defining the real needs. Donations and donor assistance need to be coordinated so that development strengthens civil society by supporting local initiatives, including gender equity and incorporating human rights and reconciliation.

Facilities

In the initial period of the crisis, there was a huge influx of refugees and displaced persons into the capital. Emergency services had to be set up quickly. Tent clinics were thrown up at ports, airports, and in football stadiums. Surgical cases were referred to the central hospital where the Red Cross had resumed emergency services. Responsibilities across the capital and then out to the districts were divided up between the medical NGOs. Buildings were quickly rehabilitated using local labor and materials.

The World Bank then did its own assessment of medical facilities and drew up plans for rehabilitation, construction, and maintenance. More than $11 million was requested over four years. World Bank plans fell short in not including factors like population shifts due to newfound security or prior NGO work done on rehabilitating health facilities. Rather than taking the time to reassess and identify locations most appropriate to the newly liberated population, the World Bank focused on locations formerly used by Indonesian authorities. The World Bank international building standards and contracting procedures eliminated most new East Timorese companies from the bidding process. Australian contractors had the edge on experience and proposal writing, plus their ability to get materials in from Australia before labor and import regulations were established. National capacity building was traded away for rapid reconstruction.

The transitional government was unclear about how to deal with the twenty-three clinics run by the Catholic Church. While many of the nuns running these clinics were deported in 1999, the majority of their orders returned. Even though they charged for services and drugs, they were trusted by the population and their services remained in demand. Protestant-run clinics were also reestablished. A small clinic in central Dili (the Bairo Pite Clinic) treated 200 persons daily and hosted international academics and staff, as well as maintained an up-to-date website on the health conditions in East Timor.

The privatized Timor Coffee Cooperative set itself up to run three clinics and planned for an additional fourteen facilities for its workers and their families—approximately 70,000 people, or almost 10 percent of the national population.

Under the Indonesian administration, most East Timorese villages had a clinic with a nurse and/or midwife. The population expected these services to continue or be expanded. With the financial restrictions on the new government, this was not possible. In reestablishing services, despite the best of intentions, the population was rarely consulted on their needs or priorities, and new funding mechanisms allowed for very limited flexibility.

Transport

There is an incredible range of elements that need to be considered in dealing with population movements. To get to the scattered East Timorese population, the Indonesians had established an extensive road network, ports, and two airports. Most of this infrastructure was located along the northern coast, leaving access to the south hampered by rough seas and a mountain ridge running down the middle of the island. The entire system needs regular maintenance and repair due to the unsettled nature of the young Timorese soil. The onset of tropical rains causes flash flooding and road closures that affect not only remote villages but also major centers.

On the evening of October 29, 1999, there were 600 refugees due to arrive by ferry from Indonesia. This was the first group to come out of one of the most heavily guarded militia strongholds. The first rains of the season triggered flash flooding. City streets could not be distinguished from rivers. The football stadium that was being used as a transit center was under two feet of water with those already present struggling to find high ground and shelter. With water running down toward the port, it was impossible to land the ferry and safely disembark the passengers. While the UN and military officials argued about logistics, night was falling. Permission was obtained to get a medical team on board for emergency treatment and triage. People stood by astounded as an Australian army captain defended humanitarian principles to a UN protection officer who wanted to leave the refugees out on the water overnight. Eventually an alternate landing site and accommodations were found for the hungry and terrified group. The emergency cases were taken away in an ambulance.

Air, sea, and land transportation networks had to be reestablished. As most vehicles had been either looted or destroyed in September, new imports had to be arranged. The military brought in excellent vehicles, but these would leave with their troops. Humanitarian organizations were divided on using military support due to the hidden costs.[6] NGOs did not want to add to Ministry of Defense arsenals by increased funding due to "military-humanitarian support activities," knowing these funds would be drawn from foreign aid and development budgets. Humanitarian organizations sought to establish independent means and local options.

Even before regaining access to East Timor, NGOs coordinated with donors to discuss the appropriate size and numbers of vehicles that had to be brought in. These cars and trucks were not only for emergency operations but would eventually be handed over to the new government, so most NGOs purchased heavy-duty four-wheel-drive vehicles. The UN, however, brought in a combination of brake-sensitive Land Rovers and Indian-made Tatas that were in disrepair by the time of the handover. Timorese government departments did not coordinate when they received funds to buy vehicles, resulting in a mixed fleet not always appropriate for use outside of major city centers and requiring a wide range of mechanic skills and spare parts.

Transport of staff, patients, supplies, and reports also depend on fuel. Diesel, gasoline, and oil had to be imported. The best-quality fuel came from Australia, and the cheapest source remained Indonesia. The combination of large tankers negotiating narrow mountain roads, insecure storage sites, and the dramatic price increase after the removal of the Indonesian government subsidy led to a host of challenges.

Public transport was difficult to reestablish with only a few older taxis and trucks reclaimed after the violence. After some months, East Timor was overwhelmed by the sleek city cars imported from Singapore where the cars no longer passed emissions tests. Road signs and licensing took a long time to be established, and road fatalities were one of the major causes of injury and death.

Ambulance and hearse services were also among the most contentious community issues. With ambulances restricted to the heavy demands of carrying patients, few vehicle owners were willing to assist in transporting dead bodies. This in turn caused patients to hesitate about taking sick relatives to health facilities. The responsibility of bringing bodies back to villages passed begrudgingly to the police and then to UN government staff. Funerary cars were finally donated in 2001 and now operate on a fee of $1 per kilometer.

Supplies and Equipment

NGOs coming into East Timor brought basic medicines to replace stocks destroyed in the conflict. With prior experience in the region and in other developing countries, the NGOs were able to quickly identify appropriate materials and suppliers. NGO staff worked with local counterparts and the WHO to establish an essential drug list, a central pharmacy, and legislation on rational drug use.

In addition to drugs for treating the main infectious diseases, diagnostic equipment had to be imported. To counter malaria and dengue fever, bed net and drainage programs had to be launched. Vaccination cold chains (the means by which to transport and store vaccines at the proper temperature) had to be completely reestablished. HIV/AIDS, while not prevalent, needed to be addressed quickly due to the risk factors arising from poverty and the significant presence of foreign troops.

Health awareness programs had to address not only local health needs but to respect traditional Catholic values and beliefs. One of the biggest drawbacks in the awareness programs has been the simple translation of materials used in other countries and their lack of cultural acceptance. Few qualitative community studies were undertaken to develop materials appropriate to the range of experiences, language, and literacy levels in East Timor.

With supplies and equipment, it is not so much a case of mistakes as opportunities missed. Some new generators and labs have been provided, but medical teams busy with clinical programs were too busy to submit proposals for upgrading oxygen compressors, X-ray machines, operating theater equipment, or importing solar cells when the larger budgets were available. The shift to a reduced drug list was done without socialization to explain the reduction or shift away from injectables to pills. Appropriate and sustainable technologies were rarely criteria for new orders.

Communications and Reporting

Prior to independence, most records and reports on East Timor were produced in Indonesian or Portuguese. Overviews were available on trade, political, and human rights issues, but there was very little on the history of disease and health care. Indonesian government restrictions had limited foreign access to local sources, and official state records were either incomplete or of questionable validity. The groups preparing to intervene were predominantly English speakers, even though English is understood by only 2 percent of the East Timorese population.

International organizations did not have problems communicating among each other. Information from all sides was regularly posted and circulated. NGOs in the districts coordinated with OCHA representatives and local counterparts to identify needs and resources. The greatest shortcoming of the international intervention has been in producing data not easily accessible or understandable to the local population.

Epidemiological surveillance was established from the onset to follow the main conditions and ensure a rapid response to epidemics. NGOs provided weekly district data to the WHO as they produced national surveillance bulletins.

Radios, satellite telephones, mobile phones, and high-speed Internet systems were all introduced across the country. Unfortunately, the plugs were pulled as many of the larger organizations pulled out and the Timorese found themselves dependent on systems they could no longer afford. The switch to the Portuguese-run telecommunication system has left most districts without reliable phone systems, let alone Internet access. Mobile phone and Internet users in the capital were shocked as telephone bills tripled. Only the police and health services have remained with independent radio communications to deal with emergencies.

Final Remarks on East Timor

Could early investment in medical services help steer a population toward development and create conditions that people would not want to risk losing in renewed fighting?

In East Timor, low-level violence simmered for twenty-four years, with the peak of the conflict lasting only a few weeks between the announcement of the ballot results and the arrival of international forces. Medical teams were allowed to intervene quickly. The goodwill of international organizations was matched by the experience of teams who worked together using high international standards and key relationships built during interventions elsewhere. International organizations moved out from the capital as quickly as security would allow in order to work with the local populations to rebuild.

The international community was aware of the risks East Timor took in its bid for independence and came through with promised support. As much as the international community wanted to believe that it was helping to deliver a new baby, East Timor was already an adolescent with its own ideas. It took time for those assisting to understand that the postconflict development process needed to be slowed down so that the East Timorese could grasp the basics in setting up and running a country.

Even with the provision of free health-care services, a review of the local response indicates that people in East Timor were not altogether happy with prepackaged programs and felt that more could have been done. On the national level, the UN admitted that it had mistakenly tried to manage problems rather than mentoring East Timorese to develop their own solutions. The UN SRSG confirmed, "In some areas we have been too ambitious and have moved at a speed that may not have allowed for the establishment of sufficiently resilient foundations."[7]

The challenge in East Timor was to see whether a population could be given the means to rebuild and move away from violence into development. Significant and coordinated investments were made in the health sector, contributing to a sense of stability and stimulating the local economy. The inclusion of Timorese counterparts from the outset allowed for both mentoring and establishing longer-term relationships for them with donors and technical experts. There is a functioning health service with sustained funding coming from the national budget and outside donors. But has establishing health services helped to move the East Timorese away from violence?

East Timor is an exceptional case due to the extraordinary political circumstances involved in gaining its independence. Political will and funds were mobilized to make amends for a twenty-four-year absence. The belligerents pulled out leaving a population wearied but united in their defiance and determination to rebuild. East Timor is still struggling with unemployment, poverty, land disputes, court legitimacy, and an insecure border. New trauma is being held to a minimum, but the emotions and anger have not yet been fully dispelled. Time will tell how the Timorese will manage when law and order come fully under their own responsibility.

Conclusion

East Timor was a chance to get it right. It was an opportunity to take the experiences since the 1980s and pull together some of the most experienced actors and resources that could work with local communities to define postconflict needs and development. It is a model for future interventions.

The Timorese foreign minister has called East Timor a UN success story. But while the UN deserved praise, he also noted that work had been done collectively by member states, civil society, NGOs, and the solidarity movements. When considering whether the same prescription could be used in other areas, the foreign minister warned to look out for the realities specific to each country and to take care about getting involved or using resources in places where the local population had not yet come to terms with their situation and made a clear commitment to ending violence.

There is no single prescription for all postconflict conditions, but rather there are basic questions to be asked for the best diagnosis, treatment, and chances of survival.

How can the funds available best be used? Donors do not simply act out of charity but invest in peace, prosperity, and future markets.

While aid funds are often limited during fighting,[8] once peace is declared military expenditures can be redirected toward infrastructure building and social programs. Attention has to be given to the fact that health is an essential service and a basic human right, so it needs special financial consideration that goes beyond the cost-effectiveness of the intervention. A mechanism needs to be developed to allow money from the emergency period to be carried over to development phase and prevention activities.

Who is the target of the intervention? Before providing assistance, it is important to know the patient—their history, culture, economic status, health beliefs, and so on. Information needs to be gathered from multiple sources: government records and statistics, NGO and human rights reports, newspaper articles, political analyses, economic forecasts, social science reports, and literature. With the Internet, access to and sharing of documents has been revolutionized. Once on the ground, reports have to be checked against data gathered directly from the local leaders, health workers, and patients. Health care is a balance between individual needs, community concerns, and government capacities. Final accountability must be to the patients and their families.

Who are the stakeholders? The quality and success of any intervention often depends on the skills of the people involved and their abilities to work together in teams. International staff may be needed in large numbers during the emergency phase, but they should be replaced with qualified local personnel as early as possible. Knowledge of the administrative system is needed for both hiring local personnel and countering corruption from prior systems. A transparent hiring system needs to be followed up with clear job descriptions and job security. Efforts need to be made to include the recipients at all levels and stages of the intervention. Once people are freed from violence, they are very likely to become mobile. The new system will have to be set up with the flexibility to adapt to such changes.

How will resources be procured and maintained? A portion of the early funds can be used to replace or repair looted materials, secure storage facilities, ensure regular supply networks, and to arrange maintenance and repair contracts. Procurement networks have to be established quickly, but ethical decisions need to be made when the best supplier may also be the former occupier or belligerent. Care has to be taken in accepting donations as there may be hidden costs in transport or destroying expired or inappropriate goods. If needs can be outlined for donors early on, duplication can be reduced as limited funds are used to the greatest effect. Equipment needs to be suited to the environment—climate, power sources, and skilled technicians. Emergency funds often need to be dispersed quickly, so if detailed assessments are available early, there are opportunities to invest in advanced technologies adapted to tropical climates. Furniture and administrative materials need to be sourced rapidly and locally. Beds, tables, chairs, and shelving should not be imported if local materials and labor are available. The number and types of computers, printers, and air conditioners need to be weighed against future needs and balanced with typewriters, photostat machines, and appropriate ventilation. Photocopier services are important for hospital charts and reports, but planning must include cost considerations for nonhospital use, especially if it is the only copier in the area.

Are communication networks working? Information needs to circulate within organizations, between sectors, to the local population, and back around. Forums for the exchange of information and reporting are important for keeping people informed, coordinating activities, and addressing new needs that arise. The local population needs to be seen as more than simply a target for information but as active participants in the evaluation, decisions, and monitoring.

The end to a conflict allows for attention to shift to the poor and marginalized. Services can be reestablished or extended to remote rural areas. There is no guarantee that a future administration will maintain these services, but it is an opportunity to provide them with a model and opportunity that works.

Medical organizations have sometimes been alluded to as Band Aid operations. To some extent this is a fitting title, as doctors and nurses can do very little to stop conflicts or bring political groups to a negotiating table. What they can do is deal with individual needs and stand in solidarity with people who are suffering and help make their cause known in attempts to stop the violence. Sometimes applying the Band Aid is one of the most humane acts and a first step in the longer road to recovery.

Notes

1. See Way (2000) for the 484 Australian government cables and reports from 1974 to 1976. The documents reveal that as early as July 1974, Prime Minister Edward Whitlam suggested to the Suharto regime to launch undercover operations in East Timor to ensure its incorporation into Indonesia.

2. The Portuguese pinned hopes on the discovery of oil and the expansion of tourism. Growth from 1953 to 1962 was a meager 2 percent while the three successive five-year plans brought 6 percent annual growth. See UNDP (2002c).

3. The Popular Consultation was an autonomy proposal made by the Indonesian government under the auspices of the UN and an agreement with the Portuguese government on May 5, 1999.

4. Sources include Australian diplomat James Dunn's report on *Crimes Against Humanity in East Timor, January to October 1999: Their Nature and Causes*, as well as the February 2003 UN tribunal in East Timor indictments against the former TNI chief and six generals for crimes against humanity.

5. Objectives of the CAP can be found in the UN General Assembly Resolution 46/182 (1991).

6. The cost of keeping one soldier on the ground varies from U.S.$180,000 in Sierra Leone to U.S.$500,000 in Kosovo (Guha-Sapir 2003).

7. Sergio Vieira de Mello, SRSG and transitional administrator, introduction to UNDP, *East Timor Human Development Report 2002*.

8. Examples where funds have been available include Ethiopia, Sudan, Mozambique, and Angola.

10

Protecting the Environment

Martijn Bijlsma

nvironmental concerns are generally not considered a priority in postconflict situations. Yet there are various arguments in favor of incorporating them into development efforts. When addressing these issues, however, decisionmakers may face various dilemmas, often narrowly related to conflict. In fact, success may largely depend upon the sensitivity shown toward these dilemmas and the way decisionmakers handle them.

This chapter aims to provide a general introduction to the theme of environment and postconflict development. It sets out by examining the arguments for incorporating environmental concerns in postconflict development. Some of the dilemmas decisionmakers may face are discussed, and suggestions are given for how to overcome these. This chapter draws heavily from the experience of El Salvador—a country that has not only been relatively successful in achieving a sustainable peace but where postconflict development efforts coincided with an incipient environmental policy.

Why Bother About the Environment?

When the violent stage of conflict has ended and a formal peace settlement has been concluded, most countries still present a large conflict potential. Mutual distrust and hatred often persist for years, if not decades; and only little is needed to revive overt conflict. What is more, some people may attempt to obstruct negotiated reforms and reestablish (overtly or not) former status quo relations.

There is no universal answer to the questions of how to deal with the remaining conflict potential and how to build a sustainable peace.

However, as is argued throughout this book, a crucial determinant of whether former conflictive parties resort to outright violence again is the degree of economic and social development that is achieved in the meantime and the fair distribution of its fruits over different parts of society. The more successful postconflict societies are in achieving this goal, the more people are likely to take the view that peace brings larger benefits than war, and opposition to those who intend to pick up arms again is likely to grow.

It is in this context that environmental concerns are of significance in postconflict situations. As environmental conditions could limit the prospect of broad-based economic and social development, decision-makers are well advised to take them into account, both during the stage of emergency relief and when efforts start concentrating on medium and long-term development. In this sense, environmental protection can be said to contribute to the goal of achieving a sustainable peace.

In line with this general argument, at least four specific reasons can be given for incorporating environmental concerns into postconflict development: (1) Civil conflict may have had grave environmental effects; (2) environmental conditions may have been a source of conflict; (3) postconflict development may have environmental effects and obstacles; and (4) postconflict development may provide an opportunity to incorporate environmental concerns into national policy.

The first reason to incorporate environmental concerns into post-conflict development is that conflict itself may have had serious impacts on both environmental conditions and capacity. If not addressed in an adequate manner, these could turn into a severe constraint on postconflict development. In this respect, one can distinguish between the effects of military operations, lack of priority on the political agenda, institutional demise, and refugees and displaced persons.

Military Operations

Military operations generally impose a severe toll on the civilian population: numerous deaths and wounded, refugees and displaced persons, and the destruction of productive and social infrastructure. They can also, however, inflict considerable damage on the environment and natural resources. The effects are often felt years after conflict has ended.

In most cases, environmental damage is an unintended effect of military operations. Such damage includes the physical destruction of local ecosystems due to bombardments, the movements of military vehicles and ground forces, contamination caused by scattered ammunition, or the destruction of industrial sites. A widely discussed topic in recent years has been the use of depleted uranium in ammunition, first during the 1991 Gulf War and later in various conflict hotspots throughout the Balkans. Although in most site studies no widespread significant contamination has been detected, there is still great concern about the long-term environmental impacts and health effects on soldiers and civilians who have been exposed to depleted uranium during and after conflict (UNEP 1999, 61–63; 2002, 32–35).

Another cause of concern is the widespread proliferation of antipersonnel mines. An estimated 65 million antipersonnel mines are currently threatening both population and wildlife in fifty-six countries, many of whom just revived from civil conflict.[1] Apart from posing enormous safety risks, mines also constitute a minor source of environmental contamination. What is more, the widespread existence of antipersonnel mines could provoke large-scale population movements to safe areas, which in turn could become sources of environmental stress.[2]

In addition to such collateral environmental damage, conflict parties may also deliberately pursue the destruction of the environment and natural resources as part of their military strategy. During the Vietnam War, for instance, the U.S. Air Force deployed on a massive scale potent herbicides—such as Agent Orange—in order to strip the Viet Cong of their natural protective cover. Aided by U.S. materiel and military advisers, the Salvadoran army later pursued the same counterinsurgency strategy against the Farabundo Martí National Liberation Front (FMLN) (Weinberg 1991, 58–66).[3]

Deliberately or not, the environmental effects of military operations are often far-reaching, and they could even turn into a severe constraint on postconflict development. For example, it has been estimated that it will take at least seventy years for ex–South Vietnamese forests to recover from the environmental damage inflicted during war. Moreover, many inhabitants still suffer adverse health effects—such as cancer and birth defects—due to the high toxicity of defoliants used during the war.[4]

Political Agenda

When countries are engaged in civil conflict, war efforts and their immediate social and economic effects generally dominate the political agenda of both national and international actors. As a result, other policy issues tend to suffer from a relative neglect, including environment and natural resource management. At best, this may lead to a postponement of policy interventions that are then still carried out; at worst, the relative neglect itself may generate significant adverse impacts, for instance, by magnifying the social and economic effects of military operations.

In El Salvador, civil conflict clearly had a downgrading impact on the political priority accorded to environmental issues. Although the country's environmental conditions were generally considered to be among the worst in the Western Hemisphere, it was not until the end of conflict that significant initiatives in this area took hold. National and international actors, from the governmental and the nongovernmental sector alike, all concentrated on war efforts and their immediate social and economic effect. By comparison, most other Central American nations (though by far not suffering the same degree of environmental degradation) already experienced incipient environmental initiatives during the 1980s (Barry 1994, 1–2).

However, the lack of priority on the political agenda may not be held exclusively accountable for the neglect environmental issues tend to suffer during conflict. For even if a formal environmental policy is adopted, the war effort and a climate of public insecurity often inhibit its implementation. For instance, it is unlikely that insurgent groups will allow government agencies to enter areas they control, even for environmental operations, because they fear that official activities might conceal military-strategic objectives.

Even when armed conflict has ended, environmental issues tend to have a low priority on the political agenda. Attention generally focuses on disarmament, the reconstruction of productive and social infrastructure, national reconciliation, the return of refugees and displaced persons, and the reinsertion of ex-combatants into economic and social life.

Such disregard for environmental issues is questionable. As stated above, neglect of environmental conditions can significantly limit the achievement of postconflict development goals. For example, deforestation and soil erosion tend to have an adverse impact on agrarian production, which may not only be essential to guarantee food security but is also likely to be a sector on which many ex-combatants will depend as a source of income. Similarly, lack of access to safe water and sanitation may generate adverse health effects, thereby limiting both human well-being and productivity. At any rate, it is advisable to make a country environmental profile so that critical problems can be identified and quickly addressed. In particular, such a profile is likely to be needed because large parts of the country may long have been inaccessible, so up-to-date information may be lacking.

Institutional Demise

In addition to the aforementioned effects, civil conflict may also occasion the demise of institutional capacity for environment and natural resource management, thus limiting the possibilities for policy interventions both during and after conflict. Accordingly, efforts will equally have to focus on assessing the remaining capacity and the existing needs, and—where necessary—on rebuilding capacity.

To a large extent, institutional demise may result from the lack of priority given to environmental issues during the conflict. After all, with war efforts and their immediate social and economic effects drawing most political attention, budgetary resources are also likely to be directed to these areas. At the same time, civil conflict often provokes severe economic breakdown, thus requiring general budgetary cuts. Apart from that, environmental institutions may be forced to suspend operations due to growing public insecurity. Finally, the administration may suffer from a "brain drain" as qualified staff leave the country or look for alternative employment opportunities for political or economic reasons.

In El Salvador, environmental capacity was largely lost due to conflict. Although budgetary allowances for the environmental sector were already low compared to general levels of public spending, cuts were nevertheless significant. In 1993, real central government spending on natural resource development represented just 16 percent of what it had been in 1978. For its main beneficiary, the Renewable Natural Resource General Directorate (DGRNR), a part of the Ministry of Agriculture and Livestock (MAG), the effects were severely felt. Slowly but surely, budgetary constraints called for the suspension of ever more programs and services. In some cases, this was aided by the climate of public insecurity, as with the hydro-meteorological stations of the Meteorological and Hydrological Division, the majority of which had to be abandoned because they were located in areas controlled by the FMLN.[5] In addition, with real salaries plummeting and conflict intensifying, qualified staff began to leave the institution. In the end, the institution remained largely demoralized, with no resources to carry out programs (PRISMA 1995, 27–28).

Environmental institutions may also become a direct target of sabotage acts or violent attacks by conflict parties. In El Salvador, this has particularly been the case with the installations of the national electricity company, the Río Lempa Executive Hydroelectric Commission (CEL). Between 1980 and 1992, the FMLN committed about 3,600 sabotage acts on the company's transmission and distribution system, occasioning a total damage of U.S.$245.8 million (MIPLAN 1992, 4, Appendix 1).

As a result of these sabotage acts, CEL had to direct a large share of its resources to the repair of the transmission and distribution system. Despite being relatively successful at these activities, it could not prevent the population from becoming frequently subject to interruptions and rationing of the electricity supply, in particular toward the end of the 1980s. One of the main reasons was that by focusing on the repair of its installations, the company came to neglect other important aspects of its functioning, especially in the area of administration and planning. Eventually, this resulted in large-scale production shortages (Guerra y Guerra 1993, 34–35).

Due to the frequent interruptions and rationing of the electricity supply, many inhabitants—in particular, in the San Salvador Metropolitan Area (AMSS)—turned to individual generators, mostly working on diesel. This caused a significant rise in air contamination because the emission level of individual generators is substantially higher than that of electricity plants.

As the example shows, sabotage acts and violent attacks may have effects that go well beyond their immediate objective. When making damage assessments, such unintended or second-order effects should equally be taken into account. At the same time, although reconstruction of productive infrastructure may be a priority for decisionmakers, it should not lead to a neglect of other important aspects of an institution's functioning.

Refugees and Displaced Persons

The human tragedy involved in civil conflict is often most cuttingly portrayed by people massively fleeing their homes—either because of growing public insecurity or because they become a direct target of attacks. Due to their size and intensity, such migratory movements tend to have large-scale impacts on the environment and natural resources.

In geographic terms, the demographic effect of civil conflict may follow different patterns, depending (among others) upon the focal point of conflict, the number of refugees involved, as well as the possibilities for both internal and external resettlement. In El Salvador, civil conflict had a twofold demographic effect. On the one hand, about 1 million inhabitants (some 20 percent of the population) fled the country, mainly to the United States. On the other hand, with conflict largely concentrating in rural areas, it served to greatly speed up rural-urban migration, which in preceding decades had already gained some impetus. This has been the main reason for the population of the AMSS more than doubling between 1971 and 1992, from 0.7 to 1.5 million inhabitants (DIGESTYC 1974, 1–4; 1992, 1, 7–8).

The growing concentration of inhabitants in the metropolitan area turned into a major source of social and economic problems, such as unemployment and the formation of marginal communities. It also, however, served to increase environmental stress—even more so as no adequate policy measures were taken in response to population growth. For instance, unregulated urbanization and the deforestation of the city's outskirts associated with this process largely diminished the capacity for water retention in the AMSS and surroundings, thus limiting water supply from local subterranean sources. For the same reasons, the area presents an increased risk of floods and landslides, as—like most Central American capitals—it is located in a volcanic valley. Furthermore, as the capacity for the collection and disposal of solid waste did not keep pace with population growth, an increasing share of solid waste remained uncollected, posing severe health risks to the population. Finally, rapid increase in vehicular traffic became a major source of air contamination (Lungo 1995, 2–5; PRISMA 1995, 7–20).

Obviously, environmental impacts are often not just generated by internally displaced persons but can be caused by international refugees as well. According to the Central Intelligence Agency (CIA), for instance, refugees from Burundi and Rwanda arriving in the DRC in mid-1994 were responsible for significant deforestation, soil erosion, and wildlife poaching in the eastern part of the country.[6] A similar observation was made by the United Nations Environment Program (UNEP) in relation to the influx of some 600,000 refugees from Sierra Leone and Liberia in Guinea at the outset of 2000, noting a transformation of wildlife and forest zones with grave consequences for the biodiversity and the hydrographical network in the southern part of the country.[7] The crucial point with regard to such trans-boundary environmental impacts is that they may not just have a long-term economic and social effect on the host country, but they may also—just like other refugee-related impacts—turn into a source of (renewed) regional instability and conflict.

Environmental Conditions as a Source of Conflict

In recent decades, disputes over scarce natural resources have increasingly become a source of tensions, at a local, national, and international level. In particular, access to safe water is causing growing tensions, especially in developing nations. In most cases, such disputes do not just involve a scarcity problem, that is, a (presumed) surplus in demand in relation to the supply, but also relative differences in access to the resource.

Although at a local level environmental disputes have already made people violently oppose one another more than once, there is no evidence they have ever been a direct cause of civil conflict; nor could this be said of other environmental problems, such as the contamination of soil, water, and air.

However, one will often find environmental conditions to be indirectly contributing to conflict, especially as they tend to deepen social and economic inequity. This is particularly the case in countries where differences in the distribution and the use of land are among the root causes of conflict. In many cases, a small group of large landholders is entitled to most of the arable land, using it for the cultivation of export crops, whereas the vast majority of subsistence farmers is increasingly becoming marginalized. Adding to this, subsistence farmers are often allotted marginal lands with a low fertility or located on hillsides that are highly susceptible to soil erosion. Furthermore, sanitary conditions are generally low and in order to survive, subsistence farmers tend to overexploit the environment and natural resources—even though in the long run this will only worsen their chances of survival.

Insofar as postconflict development efforts intend to deal with the fundamental causes of conflict, such mediating factors should be taken into account as well. For instance, land transfer programs may be accompanied by reforestation and soil conservation projects or the construction of sanitary latrines and improved stoves. The overall result will likely be an increase in the development potential of the beneficiary population, thus enhancing the chances of achieving a sustainable peace.

An additional problem is that conflict parties have increasingly come to dedicate themselves to the (often illegal) exploitation of profitable natural resources in order to finance war efforts. To some extent, this is due to the end of the Cold War, as a result of which material support from ideological allies has largely come to an end, and conflict parties increasingly had to look for alternative sources of funding. Examples include diamond mining and associated illegal activities in Sierra Leone, the Democratic Republic of Congo, and Angola; the production and export of cocaine in Colombia; and wood logging in Cambodia.

No doubt, such activity may adversely affect the environment, as natural resources become overexploited. For most international observers, however, the main point of concern is that by buying these goods, foreign countries become indirectly responsible for the continuation of war efforts, as it will provide conflict parties with financial means to buy arms. For this reason, the European Union has adopted a certification scheme to ban trade in so-called blood or conflict diamonds (OJEC 2002, 28-48).

Yet there is another aspect to such practices that is often essential to understanding the dynamics of conflict, as well as the threats to peace when overt fighting has ended. For in many cases, the exploitation of natural resources is not just (or no longer) a means to obtain funding for war efforts but a *reason* for conflict. Conflict, in this situation, revolves around efforts to gain or maintain control over natural resources and, in particular, to destabilize central authority, for such illegal practices generally only flourish under unstable central authority. In addition to international trade measures, the country's legal authority will have to establish firm and impartial control over these natural resources (if necessary with international support), as well as provide viable social and economic alternatives to the illegal trade in natural resources for the population.[8]

Environmental Effects of and Obstacles to Postconflict Development

Even when environmental conditions have not played a part in a conflict, they should be taken into account, for they could limit the achievement of postconflict development goals. This is not just the case for existing environmental conditions. Due to the size and often wide range of activities involved, postconflict development itself may also generate significant adverse environmental impacts, thus limiting the achievement of development goals.

To enhance the chances of achieving a sustainable peace, decision-makers—not least those outside the environmental sector—should try to control, prevent, or mitigate such adverse environmental impacts. One of the ways to do this is by using an Environmental Impact Assessment (EIA). Though definitions vary, an EIA can be defined as "an activity designed to identify and predict the impact on the bio-geophysical environment and on man's health and well-being of legislative proposals, policies, programs, projects and operational procedures, and to interpret and communicate information about the impacts" (Munn 1979, 1).

A full EIA usually entails a threefold process: (1) establishing a ground database; (2) describing a planned project and identifying

sources of change in the environment associated with that project; and
(3) predicting the likely environmental change that will be caused by
the project under design and making suggestions to avoid adverse
changes. Based on this information, project proposals might be refor-
mulated or rejected, or measures to control, prevent, or mitigate adverse
environmental impacts might be taken (Di Santo 1992, 545–550).

For instance, when constructing a rural road, a variety of environmental effects may occur. Short-term impacts include the production of
dust, noise, dragging sediments, and erosion. In terms of long-term
impacts, the project could affect land use, threatened species, natural
areas, mangroves, wetlands, floodplains, and food chains. The long-
term impacts could be a direct effect of construction activity, but it can
also indirectly be generated by the project, as with a population increase
due to the improvement of access roads, increase in vehicular traffic, or
the elimination of species due to the destruction of their natural habitat.
Likewise, adverse impacts may be generated by the use of machinery
that has oil leaks, by a bad operation of machinery, or by a spilled load
of combustibles or lubricants, producing soil contamination (Green and
Ochoa 1995, 8–14).

In El Salvador, an EIA has been applied at various stages and levels
of postconflict development. For instance, the Plan for National
Reconstruction (PNR) included a set of basic criteria and operational
procedures for EIAs carried out as part of the program (MIPLAN 1992,
Appendix 8). Although the issue initially received relatively little attention, an environmental guidelines sourcebook was later issued, providing executing agencies with practical recommendations (written in a
nonspecialist language) for mitigating measures to be taken in case of
significant adverse environmental impacts (Green and Ochoa 1995,
i–vi).[9] At the same time, a system of environmental units was created in
order to disseminate EIA procedures in public sector institutions, such
as the National Association for Waterworks and Sewage Systems, the
Salvadoran Institute for Municipal Development, CEL, and the MAG
(Barry 1994, 4–5). In 1998, the legislative assembly finally adopted
EIA legislation—as part of an environmental framework law—making
the procedure required for most types of development activity.[10]

At present, an EIA is a basic requirement in most bilateral and multilateral donor operations; and in many postconflict societies the procedure is also part of national policy, in a more or less elaborate way. If
such is not the case, however, it is still prudent to incorporate it in activities, as it is likely to improve project performance.

A negative aspect of the EIA is that it can be quite time-consuming.
A full EIA may take weeks or months, depending upon the nature and

the magnitude of the activity under examination. Given the enormous time constraints existing in most postconflict situations, and in particular the need to achieve some social and economic progress quickly, such a delay may not be desirable. In addition, there might be insufficient technical and institutional capacity to carry out such procedures, which could even cause further delays, with all consequences involved.

Of course, this problem might be solved by turning to external consultants or analysts. However, such a solution generally implies high expenditures, while at the same time it may not contribute much to strengthening national EIA capacity. For this reason, policymakers may in some cases decide initially not to put too much emphasis on an EIA—preferring the objective of achieving some social and economic progress quickly to that of improving project performance—while starting the process of strengthening national EIA capacity to carry out such procedures in the medium or the long term. Furthermore, it may be decided to perform an EIA after instead of before the execution of a project. Even though an EIA is most effective when conducted in the preparatory stages of a project, there are many environmental impacts that can equally be addressed after its execution.

Postconflict Development as an Opportunity to Incorporate Environmental Concerns

So far, the relationship between environment and postconflict development has been looked at from a structural point of view, that is, attention has focused on the environmental causes and consequences of conflict, as well as the environmental effects of and obstacles to postconflict development. The aim has been to show the relevance of environmental concerns for postconflict development, thus providing decisionmakers with an argument to incorporate them into their actions.

Yet there is another reason to take environmental concerns into account: Postconflict development itself—given the size and often wide range of activities involved—provides an outstanding opportunity to incorporate environmental concerns into national policy. Or, to put it differently, environmental concerns may not just be functional to postconflict development, but postconflict development itself may also be highly functional to environmental concerns. After all, development efforts after a conflict often entail large-scale political, social, economic, legal, and institutional reforms, which might equally be used to address environmental issues.

In El Salvador, for instance, two institutions created as part of the

1992 Chapultepec Peace Agreements—the National Civilian Police (PNC) and the Human Rights Proctor (PDDH)—were endowed with an environmental unit. Peace agreements did not include any environmental provisions, yet the occasion was seized to create an institutional basis for two environmental functions that up to then had been without such an instrument: law enforcement and human rights protection.[11] In this sense, too, environmental policy came to be linked to the process of democratization, which implied (among other things) compliance with the law and the protection of civil rights (PRISMA 1995, 31–34).

Obviously, environmental opportunities may not just arise with institutional reforms. For example, the reconstruction of social and productive infrastructure could be used to introduce "clean" technologies or environmental controls. In a similar way, educational reforms may provide an opportunity to add elements of environmental education to the primary and secondary school curriculum. In the end, much will depend upon the sensitivity decisionmakers show toward the issue, as well as their skill and ability to incorporate it into their activities.

Some Postconflict Dilemmas

As is argued throughout this book, to prevent former conflictive parties from resorting to outright violence again, some initial development will have to be achieved quickly. When making efforts to do so, however, the remaining conflict potential and the various dilemmas it creates will have to be taken into account. This involves a careful understanding of the conflict, as well as the opportunities for reconciliation and recovery presented by the respective society. On the basis of this, strategic choices may also differ, for instance, whether to take a strict or a diplomatic stance on a policy issue.

It has been a major flaw to consider (material) self-interest as the only driving force in human behavior. In many cases, human choices are equally motivated by emotion, tradition, and ideology. This is essential to understanding the dilemmas emerging in postconflict situations. Although it might be considered in people's rational interest to prefer peace instead of war and make a joint effort for reconstruction and development, there is often still a strong preference for war—or at least a refusal to cooperate with the former enemy. Besides, even for reasons of self-interest, war may be preferred to peace, for example, by those who benefit from the opportunity to pursue the illegal trade in natural resources.

Even though environmental issues are hardly ever a direct source of conflict, they might easily turn into a conflict commodity. When addressing environmental issues in a postconflict situation, decision-makers will have to be highly aware of the remaining conflict potential, as well as the general limitations posed by the situation. Among the specific dilemmas decisionmakers might be confronted with are: (1) the politicization of environmental policy, (2) the selection of beneficiaries, (3) the hostile relation between institutions involved in environmental operations, and (4) the lack of resources.

Politicization of Policy Issues

One of the main problems decisionmakers may be confronted with when addressing environmental issues in postconflict situations is that policies, programs, and projects become politicized. In particular, this may be the case when conflict involved ideological differences or the role of the state.

In the worst case, this could become a source of renewed violent conflict. More likely, however, is that the decisionmaking process will suffer delays or that persons, parties, and organizations refuse to participate in activities. Eventually, none of these scenarios will benefit the environment—all the more as resources are often limited, so cooperation with as many entities as possible is desirable.

In these circumstances, one may choose (at least temporarily) to treat environmental issues in a nonpolitical manner, that is, as technical problems. Whereas in other policy areas often difficult and potentially conflictive political choices cannot be avoided, environmental issues lend themselves relatively well to being treated in a nonpolitical way. An important advantage of this is that it can make it easier for people, parties, and organizations to participate in environmental activities and to reach decisions. As a result, more is achieved in the areas of the protection, restoration, and improvement of the environment and natural resources. In addition, the experience of former conflictive parties working successfully together on these issues might contribute to the process of national reconciliation. It could even—as a spillover effect—stimulate success in other, more sensitive policy areas.

For instance, when endowed with the task of developing an environmental policy in a postconflict situation, the 1990-created Executive Secretariat for the Environment (SEMA) in El Salvador deliberately chose to treat the issue as much as possible in a technical manner. This may also be explained by the fact that the institution was led by technocrats belonging to the moderate and reformist faction within the governing Republican Nationalist Alliance (ARENA), yet the main arguments used were that a politicization of the issue would neither benefit the environment nor the process of national reconciliation. Moreover, the institution's leadership considered that politicization could be an argument for international donors to suspend funding for environmental operations.[12]

Obviously, environmental policy, like all policy issues, involves making political choices; in this process, diverging views or even conflict cannot be excluded. They are part of the political process. For instance, one of the main political issues in the environmental sector is whether to focus on the causes or on the effects of problems—also known as the beginning-of-line and the end-of-line approaches. However, as most postconflict situations still present a large conflict potential, and swift and tangible results may be needed to consolidate peace, it is preferable not to touch too much upon the political aspect of environmental issues.

Beneficiaries

Another issue decisionmakers will have to treat with special attention involves the selection of the beneficiaries (be it persons or areas) of policies, programs, and projects. Again, this issue applies not only to the environmental sector but to all policy areas.

When deciding upon the allocation of resources, decisionmakers need to be aware that their decision may not just have a material effect upon the beneficiary population or area but is also likely to contribute to the perception within the general public. Thus, by benefiting one group or area, others may feel neglected or excluded. Obviously, this can never be entirely avoided. In making political choices, some will benefit more than others. However, in postconflict situations the issue is much more sensitive, and environmental investment may easily turn into a conflict commodity.

Accordingly, decisions should be well motivated and bear the spirit of the peace agreements. As a general rule, they should be based upon the nature and magnitude of problems—that is, they should benefit those persons or areas that most need it, and this fact should be well communicated to the public. An additional argument may be that the choice of beneficiaries helps to overcome the fundamental causes of conflict. In the environmental sector this may involve, as noted, efforts to improve the living standards of a marginalized peasant community in order to reduce the potential for a violent uprising by that community and/or its resorting to the unsustainable exploitation of natural resources.

What should be avoided at any cost is that decisions reflect political bias; even the impression that this happens could be harmful. For it will not only be contrary to the peace agreements, but it may also become a source of renewed conflict. Whenever this occurs, decisionmakers should take strict action or whatever is in their competence to halt this. In some instances international donors could play an important role in this respect.

In El Salvador, this has been the case with the Salvadoran Environmental Fund (FONAES). The institution was set up as an umbrella organization to coordinate the activities of two debt forgiveness funds—the Initiative for the Americas Fund (FIAES) and the Canadian Environmental Fund (FCMA)—and to capture new environmental funds. The advantages of this institutional arrangement were that it would contribute to the allocation of resources in priority areas, bring coherency between the operations of both funds, and avoid institutional and operational duplicity. For this reason, the U.S. and Canadian governments had also been strong supporters of the institution.

However, many held the impression that FONAES was a political organ, benefiting entities belonging to or affiliated with ARENA, the governing party. In addition, there was widespread doubt as to the professional qualities of the institution's leadership.[13] For this reason, FIAES always kept some distance from FONAES, and FCMA later decided to continue on an independent basis. In this decision, various arguments were weighted. Decisive arguments were that the practice of FONAES gave the impression of partiality in the allocation of funds. Another argument was that a lack of professional qualities in the institution could cause bad use of the debt forgiveness operations' funds.

Learning Period

In addition to the selection of beneficiaries, the relationship between the institutions involved in postconflict development efforts may also be a highly sensitive issue. In many postconflict situations, development efforts—such as the process of initial capacity building or the execution of policies, programs, and projects—involve a wide range of institutions. These efforts may, however, be significantly limited by mutual distrust and hatred between various institutions.

To overcome such hostilities, one may opt for a learning period, giving institutions the opportunity to take away mutual distrust and hatred and start building on a common purpose. An additional argument may be that postconflict development activities often involve relatively large-scale investments, as well as new policy instruments. A learning period will thus help to avoid start-up problems and ensure an optimal and efficient use of available resources.

This may be illustrated by the experience of the 1992–1994 Salvadoran small project program—a credit line for environmental projects, solicited and carried out by NGOs and coordinated by the environmental secretariat of the government, SEMA. The program constituted one of the main preparatory activities on FIAES, FCMA, and FONAES. In El Salvador, no institutional precedents existed in the area of the public financing and coordination of civil initiatives on environment and natural resource management. To avoid start-up problems and an inefficient use of the financial resources of these relatively large environmental funds, it was considered desirable to have a learning period in which both the public sector and the NGO community could become familiar with this new type of policy instrument.

For the public sector, the program provided an opportunity to gain experience in determining the investment priorities for environmental projects, financing and supporting NGOs, and evaluating the final results. In addition, an overview could be acquired of the NGOs that might participate in the country's environmental policy. The Salvadoran NGO community, though, was able to become acquainted with submitting project proposals within a determined policy framework and complying with specific administrative, organizational, and technical requirements in order to qualify for financing. Due to their modus operandi during conflict, only a few NGOs had experience in these areas.

In addition, during conflict strong polarization had arisen between the public sector and the NGO community. Both sectors accused one another of serving as a conduit for specific political interests: for the public sector those of ARENA and for the NGO community those of the FMLN. When conflict had ended, the relations between both sectors were still highly tense. In this respect, the program provided an opportunity to take away mutual distrust by jointly developing environmental activities. This could also lay the basis for eventual later contacts between the public sector and the NGO community, for instance, within the framework of FIAES, FCMA, and FONAES.[14]

Lack of Resources

Finally, decisionmakers may be confronted with a lack of technical and institutional resources to address environmental issues. As noted, part of the environmental capacity may have been lost or become fragmented, and up-to-date information may be lacking due to conflict. To be sure, this problem does not only arise in postconflict situations. However, it may be far more pressing, as conflict may have exacerbated environmental problems, and swift and tangible results may be needed to consolidate peace.

As indicated earlier, a structural solution of this problem requires an assessment of the remaining capacity, the existing needs, and rebuilding capacity. Yet such a solution may be quite time-consuming and only bring results within the medium or the long term.

In order to overcome this problem in the short term, the best available option is to exploit the possibilities of seeking cooperation with other persons, parties, and institutions—be they public, private, or NGOs. In most postconflict societies, there is still much environmental capacity to be found, but it will have to be rediscovered and reassembled, so to speak. These activities could also constitute a starting point in finding a structural solution toward the capacity bottleneck.

Within the public sector, technical and institutional capacity may not just be found in environmental institutions but also in the departments of education, public health, agriculture, public works, economic affairs, and foreign affairs. In many cases, these include small units or professional staff specifically endowed with environmental functions. Similarly, capacity may not just be found in central government institutions but also at a regional or municipal level. Furthermore, environmental capacity may be found in private sector institutions or NGOs, such as associations, foundations, professional bodies, academic organizations, universities, and churches.[15] All these entities could participate in environmental operations, though, of course, this should not lead to a neglect of other important aspects of their functioning.

A good example of how a short-term lack of resources may successfully be overcome—by careful understanding of the situation and optimal exploitation of available options—is provided by the initial experience of SEMA in El Salvador. The first mandates that the institution (which had started operations in mid-1991) received were to prepare a National Environmental Emergency Plan (PNEA) and an environmental agenda and action plan for the 1992 Earth Summit in Rio de Janeiro (Araujo 1992, 8).[16]

With respect to the PNEA, SEMA designed a working plan aimed at coming up with a first draft in October 1991. Considering the existing institutional fragmentation and the lack of coordination in environmental matters, the institution's leadership thought it important to start by organizing a series of workshops with environmental experts from various national institutions. This would not only permit a general revision of the country's environmental situation, but it would also give SEMA—which was set up as a coordinating and supervising body—insight in the different technical capacities, in both the governmental and the nongovernmental sector. Thus, in June and July 1991 five workshops were organized, where the main environmental problems, their causes, and possible solutions were analyzed (Araujo 1992, 8–9).

These workshops were decisive in motivating the experts from the various institutions in working more closely together in the process of preparing the PNEA. In this respect, a strong emphasis was laid on convincing the institutions that the creation of SEMA had opened new roads toward addressing environmental issues with a national focus. This was aided by the fact that environmental policy enjoyed political support from President Alfredo Cristiani (1989–1994), whose five-year plan explicitly addressed the issue. Another important message SEMA transmitted to the consulted institutions was that by no means would it enter their field of competence, as it would only coordinate and supervise environmental activities, thus avoiding unwillingness to cooperate due to institutional rivalry (Araujo 1992, 9).

Partly based on the positive results obtained during the workshops, SEMA decided it would be appropriate to elaborate the national document for the Rio Conference in a joint form. Apart from the fact that SEMA itself lacked sufficient capacity, it was clear that various sectors had to be consulted, in particular given the country's incipient democratization process. For this purpose, a special commission was created, consisting of thirty technicians belonging to both governmental and nongovernmental institutions. Within the commission, more than ten working groups were organized, each covering a specific environmental area in detail. These groups worked *ad honorem* intensively during August and September 1991 and produced the first version of the environmental agenda and of the PNEA in October (Araujo 1992, 10–11; SEMA 1992, Preface).

After the process of national technical consulting was completed, it was considered useful to hear the opinion of international experts. For this reason, an international environmental conference was organized in October 1991, assisted by more than thirty delegates belonging to different environmental institutions and bilateral and multilateral organizations. In addition to receiving comments and suggestions from these institutions, the conference also served as a first major step in the process of obtaining funding for environmental operations, in particular from the World Bank and the Inter-American Development Bank (Araujo 1992, 11–12).

After the conference, a second stage of national counseling started, involving various social sectors, such as syndicates, political parties, private sector entities, deputies from the legislative assembly, the media, professional bodies, and cooperatives. After these stages of preparation and counseling, the final draft of the environmental agenda was made up and eventually presented during the 1992 Rio Conference (Araujo 1992, 12–13; SEMA 1992, Preface).

As the example shows, it is possible to overcome an apparent lack of resources and develop environmental activities in postconflict situations. Key to the success are (1) political determination, (2) the rediscovery and motivation of national experts, (3) a participatory focus, and (4) the existence of an institution capable of coordinating both governmental and nongovernmental efforts in environmental matters (Araujo 1992, 38).

Notes

1. Fred Pearce, "Guerra y Medio Ambiente: Reacciones en Cadena," UNESCO, 2000. http://www.unesco.org/courier/2000_05/sp/planet.htm, August 21, 2004.

2. Sean D. Morris, "Landmines, Cleanup, and Trade," American University, Inventory of Conflict and Environment, http://www.american.edu/TED/landmine.htm, August 21, 2004.

3. Technical note: All Spanish names are translated into English. The acronyms, however, are the ones used in the respective country.

4. Pearce, "Guerra y Medio Ambiente: Reacciones en Cadena."

5. Interviews with Guillermo Navarrete Lopez, SEMA, May 20, 1996, and June 10, 1996.

6. CIA, The World Factbook 2003: Democratic Republic of the Congo, http://www.cia.gov/cia/publications/factbook/geos/cg.html, August 21, 2004.

7. Pearce, "Guerra y Medio Ambiente: Reacciones en Cadena."

8. For further discussion on this issue, see Chapter 17 in this volume.

9. Interview with Anne Levandowski, head natural resource unit, USAID/El Salvador, June 3, 1996.

10. Asamblea Legislativa, 1998, Decreto Legislativo No. 233, Ley del Medio Ambiente, March 2, 1998, San Salvador: *Diario Oficial* (CCCXXIX) No. 79, May 4, 1998, Part I, Title III, Chapter IV, http://www.marn.gob.sv/legisla/leyes/leyma.htm, August 21, 2004.

11. Interviews with Hugo Adiel Bonilla, subchief, environmental division, PNC, July 25, 1995; and Carlos Gonzalo Cañas, deputy proctor for the environment, PDDH, September 6, 1995.

12. Interviews with Miguel Eduardo Araujo Padilla, secretary-general, SEMA (1991–1994), August 16, 1995, and May 24, 1996.

13. Interviews with Francisco Alcides Molina, head, FIAES, August 19, 1995, September 2, 1995, and May 28, 1996; and Gerardo Escalón Gomez, president, FONAES, November 29, 1995.

14. Interviews with Alberto Martínez Hidalgo, head, environmental education, SEMA, August 23, 1995, and December 4, 1995.

15. An important point to bear in mind in this respect is that due to conflict, environmental experts from public sector institutions may have moved to private sector institutions or NGOs. In some cases, environmental experts from public sector institutions have created an NGO to compensate for the budgetary restraints the public sector has to cope with.

16. Interviews with Miguel Eduardo Araujo Padilla.

11

Economic Policy for Building Peace

Bertine Kamphuis

P rotracted civil war changes the economic structures of the national economy profoundly and creates a "conflict economy" that is not quickly altered by a peace agreement. Such an economy perpetuates the very structures that have given rise to the conflict and can easily lead to new violence. The people that profit from the conflict economy have a strong interest in a continuation of the conflict situation. They will strive to maintain the security problems and prolong the lack of law enforcement, which contribute to a favorable environment for the perpetration of criminal activities. They may also strive to ensure a continued presence of foreign aid organizations, NGOs, and peacekeepers because this will provide them with income opportunities.

This chapter attempts to reveal the structures of a conflict economy and its dominant actors. It illustrates how economic policy can either be a stumbling block or a stepping stone to a lasting peace in the policy areas of employment, public finance, and export strategies.

Characteristics of a Conflict Economy

Civil wars have a strong adverse effect on national incomes and government revenues. They lead to the interruption of production and trade, massive capital flight, and the destruction of physical capital. They also lead to the breakup of administrative and social institutions, the flight of human capital through migration, and the destruction of infrastructure for education and health care (Humphreys 2002, 8–11). This destruction goes hand in hand with the creation of alternative structures of power and exchange, mostly outside the formal economy. The fragile peace that results from a peace agreement does not alter these conflict-induced alternative economic structures.

In a typical postconflict situation, four different economies can be distinguished that coexist and are intertwined:

1. the *international aid economy,* related to the arrival of numerous aid organizations and their international experts who demand offices, housing, luxury consumer goods, and services (hotels, restaurants);
2. the *criminal economy,* consisting of a broad range of criminal and paracriminal activities, from organized criminal acts such as the drug trade and looting to "gray area" activities like the sale of state property, monopolized trade, and security services;
3. the *informal economy,* in which subsistence farming prevails; and
4. the remaining *formal economy,* covering only a small fraction of the total economic activity (Ehrke 2003, 150–152).

The integration of the criminal economy in trans-border networks strongly contrasts with the disintegration of the formal economy. The linkages that interconnect these economies are multifaceted, as is illustrated in Figure 11.1.

The authority of the central government often does not reach much further than the country's capital, and some areas remain under the fac-

Figure 11.1   The Four Economies of the Conflict Economy

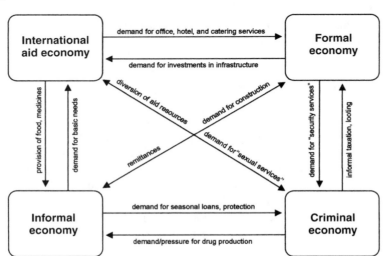

tual control of opposition forces, warlords, or foreign armies. The legitimacy and the resource base of the new government are generally weak, which limits the capacity of the government to reorganize the state, production, and trade. If the government itself benefits from the conflict economy, economic reform is unlikely to come about. Furthermore, a weak state is vulnerable to capture by groups that have an interest in the continuation of the conflict economy.

Winners and Losers in a Conflict Economy

Rebel groups, conflict exploiters, and aid agencies create new structures of access to resources and power. These alternative structures produce new "winners" and "losers." Economic winners and losers of the conflict economy can be found at both sides of the conflict, independent of who "won" or "lost" the civil war. Table 11.1 provides an overview of possible economic winners in a conflict economy and the profitable activities they practice; some of them will be discussed below.

Combatants are highly dependent on the continuation of violence to

Table 11.1   Profitable Activities and Economic Winners in the Conflict Economy

	Profitable Activities	Economic Winners
Lack of security	Privatized security, looting	Warlords, foreign security firms, violent enterprises, combatants
	Informal taxation of trade, remittances, aid	Warlords
	Weapons trade	Conflict exploiters
Lack of law enforcement	Informal protectionism	Profiteers
	Drug production and trafficking	Criminal organizations, smugglers, farmers
	Smuggling	Smugglers, customs officials
	Primary commodity extraction	Extractive industries (often multinational corporations), armed groups
	Money trade, diaspora funding	Money traders, middlemen
Presence of aid agencies	Transport and office services	Taxi drivers, couriers, translators
	Hotel and catering services	Hotel and restaurant employees
	Construction industry	Construction companies and workers
	Prostitution and human trafficking	Brothel owners, traffickers

secure their income. They are the most obvious people who benefit from continued violence, particularly those who do not receive any direct payments but earn their income from looting, protection rents, or other violent and criminal activities. Hence, the threshold for combatants to revert to open violence is low, often for economic as much as for political reasons.

The lack of security creates a market for those who can provide it. Local warlords are in the position to do that. They also control the local economy. The profits they have accumulated during protracted conflict contribute to their power. Some enjoy loyalty and high social standing because they share a part of these profits with the local population. A large number of people will directly depend upon them and, therefore, support them. Warlords can pay the salaries of (ex-)combatants and civil servants in exchange for noninterference with their illegal activities, while the new government, after the peace agreement, is often unable to mobilize enough revenue.

Not only those directly involved in violent activities have an interest in the continuation of the conflict economy but also those who benefit from the lack of law enforcement, including criminal organizations, smugglers, and profiteers. In the absence of strong law enforcement, the production of illegal goods and illegal trade will continue to be profitable and, therefore, continue to be undertaken. Informal protectionism, namely, the ability to set high prices as long as consumers are immobile,[1] will generate interesting profits that will be lost when the national market becomes more open as a result of a more secure environment.

The presence of foreign aid agencies and peacekeeping troops creates new economic incentives that are not necessarily beneficial for postconflict development. Most foreign agencies provide wages above local standards. In that way they pull qualified employees out of public employment, further reducing the human capital that can be deployed for nation building.

The interests of those linked to the contending military forces and the global criminal and aid networks sharply collide with the interests of the majority of the population because they prosper on the very conditions that make the majority suffer. Large groups in society are considered losers of the conflict economy. Having lost their former sources of employment and income, they are forced into alternative survival strategies. Many are forced to retreat into subsistence farming and become partly dependent upon remittances and support from aid agencies. They suffer not only from direct physical violence but also from the poor economic conditions (scarcity, high prices, lost savings) and the limited employment opportunities to satisfy their basic needs.

The economic winners of a conflict economy have a strong interest in the perpetuation of the conflict situation. If their newly acquired positions are threatened by specific policy measures, they will either try to prevent them, delay their implementation, or circumvent them, that way undermining their effectiveness. The longer such a situation continues, the more problematic the consequences will be. Conspicuous consumption of the winners draws additional people into their ranks. Criminal activities will increase because of a lack of alternatives, and norms for government and civil behavior deteriorate. Postconflict economic policy can contribute to the continuation of this situation by inadvertently strengthening the position of the winners.

Economic Policy: Potential for Peacebuilding?

Every economic measure is a direct intervention in the balance of power between different groups—not only between the different conflict parties but also between the economic winners and losers on either side.

Economic factors have often played a role in the outbreak of violence. Secession ambitions can be motivated by the relative welfare of a region and the reluctance to share this wealth with other regions. Unequal access of different groups to education and to the labor market and its different segments (e.g., civil service, military, different private sectors) often contributes to civil strife. Discrepancies between tax burden and public investment in different regions can also stimulate dissatisfaction and opposition (Ballentine and Sherman 2003, 260–262). Economic policy can thus not only strengthen or weaken the winners of the conflict economy, but it can also heat up or reduce the economic factors that played a role in the outbreak of the violence. When violence breaks out again, all reconstruction efforts are nullified. Therefore, economic measures may be ineffective by strengthening those who have an interest in undermining economic reforms, or they may even be counterproductive by triggering a relapse into violent conflict.

This chapter explores some of the economic policy measures in the policy fields of employment, public finance, and exports that can contribute to peacebuilding in a conflict economy; an overview of these measures is given in Table 11.2.

Table 11.2   Economic Policies That Strengthen Peacebuilding Objectives

Peacebuilding Objectives of Economic Policy	Economic Policy Measures in Conflict Economy
Employment	
Integration of ex-combatants, warlords, conflict exploiters	Linking reintegration programs to demobilization programs; providing jobs in the new professional multiparty army as well as job creation by, for example, applying labor-intensive rehabilitation techniques; freezing financial assets of warlords
Reconciliation between the different conflict parties	Taking a multistakeholder approach in development planning
Creation of sustainable livelihoods for war-affected households	Providing micro-credits
Rehabilitation of infrastructure, health care, and education	Early training of the local population for new jobs
Public finance	
Implementation of the peace agreement	Avoiding donor conditionality that conflicts with the peace agreement
Creation of inclusive, capable civil services	Level down wages in the international aid economy to local standards
Independence from international donors, foreign borrowing	Mobilizing government revenue through conflict-economy-specific methods, such as taxing remittances, applying the same tax collection techniques used by armed groups, formalizing informal trade (as part of international efforts, such as the Kimberley Process)
Capable and efficient line ministries	Avoiding the creation of parallel structures, such as aid-management agencies; and, if created, defining an explicit exit strategy that includes local capacity building
Civilian oversight of the defense sector	Avoiding donor pressure to reduce the level of military spending; promoting the inclusion of the defense sector in public expenditure work
Transparent and accountable government budget	Making money transfers from multinational corporations (working in the extractive sector) to governments public (as part of international efforts such as the Publish What You Pay campaign and the Extractive Industries Transparency Initiative)
Privatization: Diffusion/distribution of power and profit structures and mobilization of funds for an underfunded government	Settling preconflict property rights first (timing); establishing a single, multiethnic, statewide privatization agency, using a voucher system (with a strong oversight mechanism)

continues

Table 11.2   continued

Peacebuilding Objectives of Economic Policy	Economic Policy Measures in Conflict Economy
Exports	
Reduction of risk of war and competition for control of the state	Reducing the reliance on a few primary commodities; promoting diversification of exports and other economic activities that typically create economic power bases independent of the state
Government revenue (from raw materials exports) to mobilize finance for postconflict recovery and be independent from aid	Establishing law and oversight mechanisms for raw material revenues; strengthening the revenue management capacity; establishing compensation mechanisms for the social and environmental impacts; involving local actors in the planning
Reduced reliance on international criminal networks (involved in the agricultural exports of drugs)	Creating alternative income opportunities for drug producers by promoting alternative agricultural production of high-added-value crops (vegetables, flowers); providing seasonal loans/advance payment schemes based upon the production of these alternative products; using the logistical experience with the drug trade
Government revenue (from tourism)	Promoting tourism by attracting tourists to national monuments, beautiful landscapes and beaches, and interesting projects and social innovations
Increased local and international capacity to address the most pressing problems of the country/region, and overcome traditional cleavages (exposure to international norms, values, and communication flows)	Promoting large-scale social experiments that attract tourists, bring in foreign exchange, contribute to problem-solving, and give additional identity and self-consciousness to a community

Employment Policy

High levels of unemployment increase the existing social and political tensions in a postconflict society and threaten the fragile peace. The unemployment level in Bosnia and Herzegovina, for example, by mid-1997, eighteen months after the Dayton Peace Agreement, was 65 to 75 percent, and almost half a million ex-combatants had to regain civilian life. The cities were overcrowded with people, including rural workers waiting for the demining of their fields (UNHCR 1997, Box 4.4).

Violent conflicts interrupt production in many sectors of the *formal economy*. Rural and urban sectors will be affected differently. In rural areas, land mines scattered over the fields and infrastructure facilities hamper reengagement in agricultural activities (ILO 1998). In Cambodia an estimated 35 percent of the land had become unusable because of land mines (Date-Bah 2001, 2). In urban areas industrial activities can effectively be paralyzed by the destruction of industrial complexes, damage to infrastructure and the energy sector, international trade embargos, and the increased risks associated with transportation. In Serbia after the NATO air campaign in 1999, the whole fabric of industrialized society was either paralyzed or destroyed, leaving many urban workers unemployed.[2] As a result, large groups that had lost their jobs during the conflict were forced to retreat into the *informal economy,* particularly subsistence farming. In general, violent conflict forces large segments of the population into subsistence farming, barter trade, on-/off-farm wage laboring, labor migration, and small-scale (informal) production.

Violent conflict, however, also creates new jobs, mainly through expanding activities of warlords and criminal organizations. These jobs will not disappear overnight when the conflict is ended and do compete with jobs in the formal economy. The large numbers of foreign aid agencies and NGOs that operate in postconflict areas create new jobs as well.

Job Opportunities in a Conflict Economy

In a conflict economy the majority of the population is not dependent upon formal, institutionalized employer-employee relations for income. Instead, patron-client relations based upon personal, ethnic, religious, or Mafia linkages give access to jobs. Many jobs that, on the surface, seem to reflect formal structures are in fact based upon ethnic and/or conflict-party affiliation.

The *criminal economy* stimulates the production of illegal goods, such as drugs, or the illegal trade of legal goods, such as diamonds. The reach of the criminal economy can be widespread. The opium economy in Afghanistan is believed to involve 3 million people.[3] This group can be roughly divided into three categories: warlords, drug smugglers, and poppy growers. This latter, and largest, category consists mainly of farmers who have to cope with the increased costs of bringing livestock or harvest to traditional markets. Often the national market is highly fragmented due to persistent insecurity. The cultivation of opium thus becomes an attractive alternative. Drug smugglers connect the producers of poppy to the global drug market and local warlords "tax" these criminal activities (Pain and Goodhand 2002, 32–34, Table 7). Other job opportunities exist in the security sector. The absence of security provided by the state leads to the factual privatization of the security sector. But not only warlords and organized crime operate in the criminal economy. Different types of paracriminal activities increase with reduced law enforcement.

The *international aid economy* creates a demand for local drivers, administrative personnel, translators, and other staff. The large numbers of international officials that work in postconflict areas fuel a booming hotel and restaurant business, especially in the capital where international organizations and NGOs set up their presence. In Afghanistan the humanitarian aid budget exceeded the Afghan formal export revenues in 2001. NGOs "contributed an estimated US$86.6 million to the economy, employing 25,000 people" in 1998 (Pain and Goodhand 2002, 28). In post-Dayton Bosnia and Herzegovina, there were up to 240 NGOs (UNHCR 1997, Chapter 4.4).

Potential for Peacebuilding?

Most employment-generating efforts of aid agencies are targeted at the "losers" of the conflict economy: refugees, internally displaced persons, war-affected households, disabled persons, and subsistence farmers. However, providing the warlords, ex-combatants, and conflict exploiters a viable alternative to their violent and criminal activities might be an even more important contribution to peacebuilding. From a peacebuilding perspective, employment can play a crucial role in (1) the reintegration of ex-combatants, warlords, and conflict exploiters; (2) the reconciliation between different conflict parties; (3) the creation of sustainable livelihoods for war-affected households; and (4) the rehabilitation of infrastructure, health care, and education.

Demobilized combatants are a ready labor surplus to be attracted by violent enterprises involved in privatized security or plunder (Mehlum, Moene, and Torvik 2002, 1). Warlords need to be disarmed economically as much as militarily. Otherwise, they can effortlessly purchase new weapons and reequip soldiers. As much as they need to be given a position in the new political structure (or become marginalized), they also need to obtain a stake in the peace economy that is attractive enough to prompt them to stop their illegal activities (drugs trade, smuggling, taxing, etc.).

In many conflict-affected areas, opposing conflict parties live next to each other. Cooperation between these parties is essential for economic rehabilitation at the local and regional level as well as for the building of peace. The promotion of a social dialogue about priorities in the local economic development can reduce mutual distrust and stimulate reconciliation in the long term.

In war-torn areas in Croatia, interethnic "Local Development Committees" were created to identify common development objectives. "Local Economic Development Agencies" coordinated and planned regional economic development programs. By following this so-called Local Economic Development approach, the agencies promoted social dialogue, socioeconomic integration of war-affected groups, and a strengthening of the economic infrastructure of Croatia (Van Empel 2000).

Many war-affected households have lost all their income-generating activities and are highly dependent upon remittances or international aid. These less vocal groups require special protection and support to regain their previous income-generating activities or to start new ones. Female-headed households, due to existing gender roles, can have serious difficulties in reclaiming land or obtaining formal jobs (see Box 11.1 on employment opportunities for women).

The urgent need for the rehabilitation of infrastructure, health care, and education often results in the use of technology-intensive techniques and flown-in foreign construction companies. But rehabilitation can also contribute to employment creation. The following two examples show how labor-intensive techniques and early training have increased local employment in the reconstruction sector.

The "MAG's [Mines Advisory Group] programme in Cambodia started in 1992 and now employs nearly 400 Cambodian civilians, including 48 amputees and 46 women de-miners."[4] This experience shows that mine-clearance operations can contribute directly to employment creation, including for those most affected by the conflict. In northern Cambodia, the International Labor Organization (ILO) commenced training people in refugee camps for infrastructure works even before the peace agreement was signed; this was done to maximize local involvement in the labor-intensive infrastructure projects and facilitate the reintegration of refugees (ILO 1998).

Aid agencies can contribute to peacebuilding through their employment policies, but in the end, the national government is responsible for employment. Its legitimacy will partly depend on its ability to create employment for all parties involved and to provide equitable access to employment opportunities in the civil services, national army, state-owned companies (or a stake in the privatized companies), and the different segments of the private sector.

Box 11.1   Conflict Redefines Gender Roles

In societies where female participation in the labor force was historically restricted on cultural, religious, or other grounds, the protracted conflict sometimes redefines gender roles out of sheer necessity. Because mainly men are recruited to fight in the conflict, the continuation of production increasingly becomes dependent on women (CPRU 2002).

High rates of male unemployment in a postconflict society caused by demobilization and economic decline and restructuring can lead to a reversion of the above-mentioned pattern. Women are (again) denied formal employment, regardless of their qualifications. This is not a general pattern: "[I]n some countries the post-war need for human resource development is so strong that women are encouraged to take up employment even when this contradicts existing gender roles" (Sørensen 1998).

High numbers of female-headed households create a central role for women in postconflict economic recovery. Women rely heavily on petty trade and small-scale businesses when access to land and work in the formal sector is limited for them (Sørensen 1998). Then, specific projects, such as providing women with micro-credits to set up small enterprises, become crucial for their survival. Women have proved to be very reliable in the repayment of loans and have shown remarkable entrepreneurship (Date-Bah 2001, 54–55).

Public Finance

Fiscal policy can strengthen the peace agreement by bringing public-expenditure priorities in line with the peace agreement and by accommodating inclusive, multiethnic public employment.[5]

Most conflict countries already had a weak tax-administration capacity before the conflict and primarily relied on import and export duties for government revenues. With little to expect from a "peace dividend,"[6] serious efforts are needed to increase the revenues for postconflict recovery. The illegal, informal, and criminal activities that dominate the conflict economy by definition remain outside of the tax system. Although some of these activities should be firmly counteracted, others could be integrated into the tax system to increase government revenues. In addition, the presence of foreign aid agencies and NGOs may generate government revenue.

This section focuses primarily on the link between the informal, criminal, and international aid economy and revenue mobilization. Also, the privatization of state-owned companies in a conflict economy is discussed. Chapter 12 of this volume addresses the necessity for building revenue institutions or even wholesale reform of the fiscal system and for strengthening customs and excise collection to mobilize revenue for postconflict recovery.

Revenue Mobilization in a Conflict Economy

Parallel structures of taxation and the provision of public services arise with the breakdown of formal public institutions. In some areas pseudo-governments are created. In 1992 a parallel administration was established in Kosovo that provided relatively well-developed services, particularly in health and education, with funds from a "3 percent tax on Diaspora remittances and a 5 percent tax on domestic economic activity."[7] Following the Dayton Peace Agreement, which ignored the Kosovo problem, the Kosovo Liberation Army was financially supported by these funds as well (ICG 2001b, 4). Taxing these remittances can generate substantial government revenue for the postconflict recovery, especially if the conflict has resulted in a large diaspora community.

The *criminal economy* creates taxation structures in the areas no longer under government control. Not only during the conflict, but also after that, the capacity of national governments to collect revenues beyond the national capital is often limited. Hence, informal taxation in large areas of the country continues, in particular if the local population remains loyal to the opposition groups. In some cases, the government could consider applying the same techniques to collect taxes as were used for informal tax collection during the conflict. In Somalia, checkpoints were used to collect taxes. Accompanied by 150 armed men and a couple of pickup trucks mounted with antiaircraft guns, taxes were collected from the passing trucks. The transporters welcomed these official tax collectors, because before that militias ran checkpoints, randomly collecting "taxes" and providing no security in return (Crawley 2001).

Armed groups and warlords involved in the informal trade in legal goods (diamonds, coltan, hardwoods) will have limited incentives to formalize their trade. Government measures to formalize trade can form part of an international effort, such as the Kimberley Process that has put the diamond trade under an international control mechanism. The

Kimberley Process Certification Scheme was launched on January 1, 2003, and sets an international benchmark for national certification schemes.[8] In the end, the success of the Kimberley Process will depend upon future developments in the international monitoring of adherence to the scheme.

In the *international aid economy* parallel structures to the new government are established to increase the effectiveness of donor funds in postconflict public sector projects. Structures such as "social funds, post-conflict funds, multidonor trust funds, UNDP area-based schemes, and independent revenue authorities" are used to channel funds outside the central government ministries, which are considered to be cost inefficient in the use of funds (World Bank 2002, 25). To channel budget support more efficiently and effectively, the recipient government is stimulated by bilateral and multilateral donors to create an Aid Management Agency (AMA). However, using an AMA can seriously undermine capacity building in the line ministries themselves. If donors choose to channel their funds through an AMA, there should at least be an explicit exit strategy (Schiavo-Campo 2003, iii).

Also, donors generally find it unacceptable that their funds are used for military purposes. They pressure the recipient government to reduce the level of military spending. However, this narrow focus can be counterproductive. It denies potential real security needs. Furthermore, it leads to off-budget military expenditures/revenues, which have a debilitating impact on security and undermine economic development through their impact on the overall budget planning and implementation process, macroeconomic stability, and defense cost-effectiveness (Hendrickson and Ball 2002, 7–8). Moreover, they undermine civil oversight over the defense sector, which in itself can be a major source of insecurity.

Another fiscal dimension related to the international aid economy is the potential tax revenue that can be derived from the foreign agencies present. Worldwide, aid resources and activities are considered nontaxable. This regulation in some cases is disputable, especially if its implementation results in abuse. The Customs Service of Kosovo complained that international officials tried to escape duties when it came to their own goods, (ab)using the privileges of their exemptions.[9] Indirectly, international officials can be taxed by a hotel, food, and beverage service tax. This was established in Kosovo, primarily to tax foreigners, who were the main users of hotels and restaurants.[10]

When government revenue is based on taxation of oil and minerals, the postconflict fiscal recovery can be rapid, but this strong dependence on oil and mineral revenues can have serious costs from a peacebuilding perspective. Governments that depend on the extractive industry for most of their revenue do not have a good record in providing public goods.

In Angola, diverted oil revenues are estimated at U.S.$1.4 billion during the fiscal year of 2001 alone. This accounts for almost one-third of the overall government budget (Global Witness 2002, 3). The Publish What You Pay campaign,[11] launched on June 13, 2003, by George Soros and a coalition of over thirty NGOs, calls for the mandatory disclosure of all payments to governments by oil, gas, and mining companies. This way, the population will get access to information on the government's revenues. Backed with this information they can put pressure on the government to be accountable over the public budget. A similar action—which aims at voluntary, instead of mandatory disclosure—is the Extractive Industries Transparency Initiative (EITI). With the EITI, various governments, civil society organizations, multilateral organizations, and private sector actors have expressed their commitment to improving payment and revenue disclosure.[12]

Privatization

Privatization of state-owned companies is often recommended to the postconflict government for the resources it generates for an underfunded government and the opportunity for reform seen in the postconflict period. Privatization in formerly communist countries shows a poor record in putting the economy back on track, particularly in the short term. This gives little reason for optimism for countries that face a double transition: from a centrally planned to a market-led economy and from conflict to peace.

Some proponents also see benefits from a peacebuilding perspective, arguing that privatization contributes to the depoliticization of the conflict economy through the diffusion of ownership. There are two reasons why this is unlikely to happen.

First, only those who have economically prospered in the conflict economy will have the necessary funds to take over the privatized enterprises. Second, even if interested entrepreneurs manage to generate the required financial resources, they are unlikely to face a transparent and unbiased privatization procedure. The well-connected insiders of the "right" ethnicity or conflict party affiliation are the most likely to gain control of key state-owned assets. The organizational structure of the privatization agency is of major importance to the privatization process. A single, multiethnic, statewide privatization agency can reduce the practice of allocation based upon ethnic linkages.

The use of a voucher system in the privatization process is an alternative,[13] which aims to benefit all previous employees. It requires that all preconflict employees receive a privatization voucher. The neglect of the imposed voucher rules makes this process nontransparent and biased, as was the case in Bosnia and Herzegovina (see Box 11.2).

Quick fiscal measures can provide the new government with much-needed revenues to strengthen its legitimacy and the legitimacy of the peace agreement. In the long term, however, to consolidate its accountability and commitment to a lasting peace the government needs to be dependent upon the productive capacity of its population.

Box 11.2   Ethnic Privatization

International advisers opted for a rapid privatization of state-owned enterprises in postconflict Bosnia and Herzegovina. However, the internationally enforced peace agreement did not suddenly end the ethnic tensions. "What international advisors originally envisaged as an apolitical, rapid and orderly transfer of assets from public to private hands has become a corrupt, ethnicized, and protracted struggle for power, which has done little to stimulate economic growth or promote inter-ethnic reconciliation" (Donais 2002, 4). The Bosnian privatization plan was set out by the U.S. Agency for International Development (USAID) independently from the economic reform process that was coordinated by the Office of the High Representative (OHR).[14] The international community's objective to undermine the strength of hard-line nationalists as part of the broader peacebuilding agenda proved incompatible with the privatization strategy pursued by USAID.

Aluminium Mostar is a clear example. The required distribution of privatization vouchers to prewar employees was ignored and denied to non-Croat prewar employees. Aluminium Mostar continued a "Croat only" job policy, and its profits appear to have financed the Democratic Croat Union parastate in Bosnia and Herzegovina (ICG 2001a, 25–26). The decentralized privatization agencies and the voucher system were purposefully used to discriminate against ethnic minorities.

Export Strategies

Civil wars curtail most forms of export. Harvests get spoiled. Tourists stay away. Transportation becomes dangerous. Yet war also gives rise to new forms of international exchange. Import dependence increases. Raw material exports may expand to finance the war efforts. Trade in weapons intensifies. Smuggling proliferates. Pieces of art are sold. Aid deliveries are rerouted. Drug transit increases.

The concept of "civil war" underestimates the international dimension of most internal conflicts. Foreign companies that trade with rebel groups provide them with the necessary foreign exchange to buy arms. Global trafficking networks allocate their activities in areas where law enforcement is weak.

In a postconflict economy, a country has to replace these transactions by other means to earn foreign exchange. It has to find its role in the global economy. It needs export earnings to pay for necessary imports. International trade helps to catch up with international developments in creating a modern economy. But there are other reasons to increase exports and to insert the country solidly into the international division of labor that go beyond purely economic reasons:

1. Government income in postconflict countries often depends to a considerable degree on import taxes and export levies, as other types of taxes do not work effectively.
2. Foreign currency from exports is necessary to achieve independence from international donors and increase political self-determination.
3. Trade increases exposure to international norms, values, and communication flows, which can help to protect human rights.
4. Export income reduces reliance on international criminal networks to provide foreign goods.

A discussion of the three important sources of foreign exchange—raw material exports, agricultural exports, and tourism—follows next.

Raw Material Exports

Many developing countries continue to derive most of their export income from raw materials. This may just be one of the reasons why they are "developing countries." A high share of raw material exports has been identified as one of the best indicators of civil conflict. When primary commodity exports reach 32 percent of gross domestic product

(GDP), the statistical risk of war is twenty-two times higher than for a country with no such exports. Oil exports have an especially distinct effect on the risk of conflict (Collier and Hoeffler 2002, 12). Primary commodity exports substantially increase conflict risk because the availability of finance is an important factor influencing the opportunity for rebellion. The opportunities such commodities provide for extortion make "rebellion feasible and perhaps even attractive" (Collier and Hoeffler 2002, 12). Raw material deposits encourage secession movements (as in Katanga in the 1960s), because the spoils of commodity exports would then no longer have to be shared with the central government or other less prosperous regions. High-commodity exports also intensify competition for government positions because they imply a share of the rents through side payments for concessions, procurement deals, export allowances, and the like. For a government it is much easier to monopolize the income from raw material extraction (particularly oil extraction and mineral mining) than from other economic activities such as industry and services, which typically create economic power bases independent of the government. That is another reason why competition for raw material income is so intimately tied to competition for control of the state.

In spite of the fact that the struggle about income from raw material exports may have contributed to civil strife, any government in a post-conflict situation may be tempted to turn to these exports again for urgently needed resources. With much of the infrastructure destroyed or neglected during the conflict, and there being limited scope for domestic private/public investment, the government will try to attract foreign direct investment. But foreign investment in a risky environment only comes forward if expected profits are high. Rich raw material deposits are an excellent guarantee for future income. Countries that have oil or mineral deposits are, therefore, tempted to exploit these to the maximum.[15]

A country for which this is especially tempting is East Timor, where 70 percent of the population is unemployed, 40 percent lives below the poverty line of U.S.$1.50 per day, and annual government expenditures amounted to a mere $77 million in the fiscal year 2002/2003. From such a perspective, an income of about $5 billion over the next seventeen years from the Bayu-Udan oil and gas fields is very attractive (Ufen 2002, 81–82). However, the big danger could be that, as a result, East Timor becomes another "rentier state"—a state in which the elites could easily live from oil income, without taking the needs of their own population into account (Ufen 2002, 84). The access to such resources is so attractive that:

- it might be tempting for outside forces (the former occupation power Indonesia) to take the country back;
- it would be highly attractive for a small armed group to launch a coup and take power, because it would allow the disposal over such a large source of income; and
- it could encourage a small group to strive for independence of an even smaller part of the country in order to avoid sharing the oil revenues with others.

But also the direct economic impact can be problematic. The demand of oil exploitation companies could be so large in a small economy that it would drive prices up. If East Timor had not adopted the U.S. dollar as its currency, high export income would also keep the exchange rate up and in this way make other exports more difficult (the "Dutch disease"). As long as enough money can be earned with work for the raw material companies, there is no need for the government to support other activities and no incentive to start anything else.

The East Timor case is extreme but illustrates the general problem that many postwar economies have to face. Economies with abundant natural resources tend to grow less rapidly than natural-resource scarce economies.[16] This is no iron law, though. Whether they grow may ultimately depend on the quality of institutions (Mehlum, Moene, and Torvik 2002). Postconflict societies, however, do not usually have strong institutions, which could ensure a positive use of the income. This creates a dilemma for countries with rich oil or mineral deposits, such as Angola, Congo, and Sierra Leone. On the one hand, the exploitation of these deposits is necessary for a quick start of the recovery process. On the other hand, reliance on this resource may preprogram future conflicts. The Chad-Cameroon "experiment" (see Box 11.3) provides some ideas for a way out of this dilemma.

Agricultural Exports

But what could be an alternative? Most low-income countries may have little else to offer other than agricultural products. In a war environment, agriculture has typically been neglected. Livestock is slaughtered, fields are devastated, and large areas are inaccessible because of land mines.

Some of the remaining agricultural activity may have shifted into the high-value production of drugs. The most prominent examples are Colombia and Afghanistan. In Colombia, both the originally left-wing rebel groups and the paramilitary groups finance their activity with cocaine trade. In Afghanistan, where about three-quarters of the

Box 11.3   Turning the Resource Curse into a Blessing?

The collaboration effort between the World Bank, oil companies, and the governments of Chad and Cameroon in the Chad-Cameroon Petroleum Development and Pipeline Project is an innovative attempt to reduce and compensate the social and environmental impacts of oil production and to generate benefits for the poor. For this purpose, monitoring and advisory groups were set up,[17] the pipeline was rerouted from its original plan, individuals and communities affected by the pipeline and the oil field construction were compensated, and new national parks were established. World Bank engagement is focused on increasing the revenue-management capacity of the government of Chad, reflected in the "Revenue Management Law" and the establishment of a "Revenue Oversight Committee," in which civil society is also represented. The law stipulates the depositing of all direct revenue from the Doba oil fields on an offshore account opened with international banks. These oil revenues are targeted to a "Fund for Future Generations" (10 percent), five priority sectors (education, health and social services, rural development, infrastructure, and environmental and water resources) (80 percent), and the Doba oil-producing region (5 percent).

Oil revenues started to flow into Chad in 2004, a country shattered by civil war; and transit fees are paid to Cameroon, one of the most corrupt countries in the world. Critics point to specific problems with this project as well as to flaws in the applied model. The institutional capacity building in Chad through World Bank assistance is lagging behind the commercial project activities—not surprisingly because institutional capacity building is a long-term effort. Substantial oil revenues from the project (indirect revenue, such as taxes, custom duties, and signing bonuses) as well as possible future oil revenues (from other areas) fall outside the law and the oversight mechanisms that have been established. Moreover, the World Bank institutional capacity-building project does not involve Cameroon.

But even if all oil revenues were managed properly, this does not guarantee that the conditions of the poor will improve. Mismanagement in expenditure can create macroeconomic instability and can destroy the cotton and sugar sectors of the rural

continues

Box 11.3   continued

economy of southern Chad through Dutch-disease effects. Without political commitment to poverty reduction, the agreed earmarking of part of the oil revenues for social spending does not guarantee improved conditions for the poor. For example, investment in health services in state-of-the-art hospitals in the capital, instead of primary health-care clinics in rural areas, does not contribute significantly to improved conditions of the poor. Furthermore, considering the history of ethnic and regional discrimination, the absence of specified regional allocations may result in future conflicts over the distribution of oil rents. Finally, once oil revenues start to flow into Chad, the leverage of the World Bank will diminish, limiting its capacity to promote poverty reduction in case there is no political will to do so.

Source: This box draws upon information provided by the Catholic Relief Services, www.catholicrelief.org/africanoil.cfm, March 18, 2003, in particular I. Gray and T. L. Karl, 2003, pp. 60–76.

---

world's opium was harvested in the second half of the 1990s, the Taliban finally forbade its cultivation in 2000, and the harvest is said to have plunged from 3,276 metric tons of raw opium in 2000 to a mere 185 metric tons in 2001 (Parry 2001), but the victory of the Northern Alliance removed all restrictions. A study of the UN Office for Drug Control and Crime Prevention (UNODCCP) confirmed that "Afghanistan has re-emerged as the world's biggest producer of opium, accounting for almost three quarters of global production. . . . Income from opium and heroin trafficked into neighbouring countries may have doubled from 2000 levels of $720m or more." Compared to an average wage below $2 a day, "these are extraordinary revenues" (*Financial Times,* February 4, 2003).

It is extremely difficult to find ways of agricultural production that can compete with the income that can be obtained from drugs. It is only when farmers become weary with the way of life connected to drug production (competition between armed gangs, insecurity, etc.) that they may consider alternatives—if they are not forced to continue by local strongmen.[18]

In regions near international airports, alternative agricultural production of high-added-value products (vegetables, flowers) might be an

**Box 11.4   Alternatives to Poppy Production
in Afghanistan**

To simultaneously tackle the poppy production and the poor living standards of rural Afghan households, the production of horticultural crops seems a viable alternative. The horticultural sector used to be an important part of the agricultural sector in Afghanistan and once accounted for 30 to 50 percent of Afghanistan's export earnings (World Bank 2003b). Protracted conflict has destroyed the existing research centers and paralyzed the production and trade in the horticultural sector. Horticultural production can generate three to seven times more income per hectare than wheat (ICARDA 2002), while poppies are estimated to yield approximately eight times more than wheat. Although the profit potential of poppy production will be hard to meet, horticultural production provides at least a viable economic alternative and increases the capacity of the poppy growers (and their families) to fulfill their own food requirements. For these reasons the Future Harvest Consortium provides farmers with seeds, including native Afghan crop varieties lost during the conflict, and technological know-how (ICARDA 2002).

Alternative income generation will not in itself completely reduce the need for poppy production, because poppy production also plays an important role in seasonal loans and advance payment on production. This is crucial for survival of the farm households during the winter. In addition, returning refugees need credit to start farming operations. Although advance payments on other crops were provided as well, "opium was the crop on which the majority of borrowers had obtained loans" (UNODCCP 1999a). Thus, future poppy production gave households access to credits, where formal credit institutions were lacking. Furthermore, poppy harvesting provided other farmers with off-farm income, which was a necessary supplement to their on-farm income (UNODCCP 1999b).

alternative (see Box 11.4), although international competition is tough. Direct relations with migrants who have left the country may provide help in marketing the products. And some experience with the logistics of the drug trade could be helpful to ship more conventional products abroad as well.

Tourism

Tourist flows could be brought to a country by at least three types of attractions: (1) historical monuments and sites, (2) beautiful landscapes and beaches, and (3) interesting projects and experiments. A combination of these different types is even more attractive.

The temples of Angkor Wat in Cambodia are a good example of the first type. The government sees these monuments as the country's greatest economic asset, a treasure that could liberate it from its current dependence on Western and Japanese aid. But the ruins also occupy a central place in the Cambodian psyche as an undisputed symbol of national identity and pride. "With Phnom Penh gearing up to cash in, Cambodians, who now have free, unfettered access to the complex, face the prospect of increasing restrictions, a result of the need to protect the site in deference to the tastes of high spending foreign tourists" (Kazmin 2002).

In Croatia, tourism could easily become the most important source of foreign exchange again. It has accounted for 40 percent of all exports and has generated between 15 and 17 percent of the country's GDP. With a coastline of 3,720 miles and more than 1,000 unspoiled islands, at a short distance to the (wealthy) rest of Europe, it has great potential. But Croatia lost about 34 percent of its hotel capacity as a result of the war (Ostrovsky 2002).

Tourism in the northeast of Cambodia relies very much on gambling. Gambling is a flourishing industry in Cambodia near the Thai border, where former Khmer Rouge members play a powerful role. This pastime is illegal in Thailand and many Thai are drawn to the Khmer Rouge–run illegal casinos just across the border (Verkoren 2003, 125). Gambling frequently gives rise to unofficial casinos and bolsters criminal groups. It is also closely associated with prostitution. The foreign exchange generated by gambling is often more than compensated for by the negative impact of induced criminal activities.

The most attractive form of tourism, the third type, is that associated with interesting projects and social innovation. Few countries and cities have experimented with it. A good example, although not from a country torn apart by civil war, is Curitiba in Brazil. The mayor succeeded to turn the city into a famous experiment with environmentally friendly public transportation. As a result, the city attracted visitors from all over the globe to get a firsthand impression of how his system works.

Large-scale social experiments, which address some of the most pressing problems of a country or region, could in this way have a threefold benefit. Besides dealing with the problems at hand, they could bring many foreign visitors to the country. This does not only generate foreign exchange but may also contribute additional ideas about how to solve the problems tackled. Becoming famous worldwide for an ingenious approach to solve specific problems, which many other countries share, would also give an additional prominent identity and self-consciousness to a community, thus helping to overcome traditional cleavages. In such a way, a pressing problem of a society can be turned into an asset.

Conference facilities could be connected to this (with a library, research institution, and media center on the topic, which the region has become known for). On a small scale, the Inter-University Center in Dubrovnik in Croatia is a relevant example; it was started way back in the 1970s when Croatia still was part of Yugoslavia.[19]

One or more landmark buildings could further enhance the attractiveness of a city for international tourism. The Guggenheim Museum in Bilbao, Spain, is a case in point. It attracts almost 1 million visitors a year (with an average expenditure of 69 euros per tourist), has been financed largely by outside sources (so that it would not compete with the scarce local financial means), and has considerable spin-off effects for the local economy. The direct and indirect impact of the museum on the generation of wealth in the Basque Country is reflected above all in the tertiary sector, generating a total of 816 million euros between 1997 and 2002. Since it opened in 1997, the art gallery has paid 144 million euros in taxes.[20]

The exploration of other opportunities for exports is a long-term project. Probably, all societies would be well advised to diversify their exports and not rely exclusively on a few primary commodities—not only because of large fluctuations of market prices and a long-term decline of the terms of trade but also because of the internal consequences for the distribution of power in society and the risk of future conflicts. A diversified export structure in the long run is a precious asset that helps to prevent a decline into new violent internal conflicts.

Conclusion

Economic policy for peacebuilding can only be achieved if the policy is based upon a comprehensive knowledge of the conflict economy. Many aspects of this economy remain overlooked because standard economic assessments are focused on the formal economy, which covers, in a typical postconflict economy, only a small fraction of the total economic activity. A broader view is required that takes into account all the ways in which the formal economy is supplanted by criminal, informal, and aid-induced structures. The remaining formal economy becomes interconnected with a criminal, informal, and international aid economy through various linkages.

Economic measures should be analyzed from the perspective of whether they imply an undue advantage to one of the conflict parties, thereby intensifying existing tensions. Not only should economic policy avoid *increasing* conflict potential, the crucial question is whether economic policy does enough to *reduce* the conflict potential. Again, considerable background knowledge of the existing social and economic structures and political affiliations is necessary.

The implementation of economic policy to reanimate the national economy will be hampered by those who benefit from the security problems, the lack of law enforcement, and the presence of large numbers of NGOs and foreign peacekeeping troops. They are likely to accumulate more and more power and wealth in the conflict economy, further strengthening their position. The limited success of economic policy in generating growth, in this context, reveals only a fraction of the negative consequences; the bigger consequences are in terms of peacebuilding.

The impact of economic policy on the building of peace can only be revealed by analyzing its influence on the balance of power between different groups in the postconflict society—not only between the different conflict groups but also between the economic winners and losers of the conflict economy.

Employment does not only provide income; it also gives people a new identity and self-consciousness. Much depends on creating employment that integrates people into society and gives them a stake in the strengthening of peace.

Taxation and public spending mirror the distribution of political power in society. If governments' revenue predominantly relies on rents from raw material resources, governments become irresponsive to their citizens, because their power base does not depend directly on the work and the well-being of the population. This will preprogram future conflict over control of the state.

Privatization is no neutral transfer of public assets into private hands; it sheds the cards for the future. If criminal welfare and warlord control is the likely outcome of privatization, continued public ownership becomes a reasonable alternative.

To participate fully in international exchanges, comparative advantages have to be created; they do not just exist. Trade is not just an ephemeral, external aspect of the economy. It depends on practically all structures of the economy and society. To strengthen the peace, economic strategy at the individual, group, and national level needs to adopt a long-term rather than a short-term perspective. This requires a basic cultural shift, from a rent-seeking mentality to creative entrepreneurship.

Notes

The section "Export Strategies" in this chapter is coauthored by Gerd Junne.

1. Shopping in the next-door village can be a risky, time-consuming effort for those confronted with continued ethnic tensions, lack of public transport, and bumpy roads.

2. See Flounders (1999) and Chossudovsky (1999). Chossudovsky refers to Yugoslav sources: "By totally destroying business facilities across the country, 500,000 workers were left jobless, and 2 million citizens without any source of income and possibility to ensure minimum living conditions."

3. Pain and Goodhand (2002, 32) refer to M. Von der Schulenburg, "Illicit Opium Production in Afghanistan," paper presented at a conference on Afghanistan: Country Without State? June 15–18, 2000, Munich.

4. Mines Advisory Group: http://www.mag.org.uk/magtest/magwproj/projcam.htm, August 11, 2003.

5. In Chapter 12 of this volume, Tony Addison, Abdur R. Chowdhury, and S. Mansoob Murshed address some of the fiscal dimensions central to the creation of a working peace agreement and an inclusive public service.

6. Some have argued that the signing of the peace agreement will bring a peace dividend through fiscal recovery and the decline of the military burden on the government budget. The reduced need for combatants and military equipment in peacetime made them argue that the military budget would radically decline. However, the reduction in the military budget is in some cases not recommended. The need to compensate badly paid armies (if unofficial taxation is to be prevented), the costs associated with demobilization and the construction of a professional multiparty army, and continued conflict in neighboring countries will limit the scope for radical reduction in military spending. Moreover, the destructive impact of the civil war on the fiscal institutions itself partly counterweights a fiscal peace dividend.

7. World Bank Group Response to Post Conflict Reconstruction in Kosovo: General Framework for an Emergency Assistance Strategy, http://www.worldbank.org/html/extdr/kosovo/kosovo_st.htm, August 13, 2003.

8. http://www.kimberleyprocess.com/background.asp, August 12, 2003.

9. The ICG (2001b, 12) refers to an ICG interview with a UNMIK Customs Official, September 2001.

10. The ICG (2001b, 18) refers to UNMIK Regulation 2000/5, "On the Establishment of a Hotel, Food and Beverage Service Tax," February 1, 2000, http://www.kosovolawcentre.org/PDFDocuments/English/Compilation5NEW-PDF/English/5-/REG%202000-05%20E.pdf, August 20, 2003.

11. http://www.publishwhatyoupay.org/appeal, August 13, 2003. The

appeal document concludes: "[W]e propose that publicly traded resource companies be required by regulators to disclose net payments, including taxes, royalties, fees and other transactions with governments and/or public sector entities, for the products of every country in which they operate."

12. "Statement of Principles and Agreed Actions," http://www.dfid.gov.uk/News/News/files/eiti_draft_report_statement.htm, August 13, 2003.

13. A voucher-based scheme for privatization is not based on attracting new capital; it only changes ownership on paper. The transfer of state ownership to private ownership is accomplished by the free distribution of vouchers to the former employees of the company. These vouchers can then be converted into shares of privatized enterprises.

14. The 1995 Dayton Peace Agreement designated the OHR to oversee the implementation of the civilian aspects of the peace agreement on behalf of the international community. The OHR is also tasked with coordinating the activities of the civilian organizations and agencies operating in Bosnia and Herzegovina. www.ohr.int, August 13, 2003.

15. The International Financial Corporation (IFC, the private sector financing body of the World Bank Group) directly harms peacebuilding at times. "The IFC has even supported mining in war-torn countries like the Democratic Republic of the Congo by companies with bad track records: projects that have been condemned by the United Nations" (Caruso et al. 2003, 4). To "break the conflict trap," more coherent World Bank policies will be necessary. For further details, see Caruso et al. 2003, 61, box: "The UN Indicts While the IFC Invites."

16. This is the "resource curse" identified by Jeffrey D. Sachs and Andrew M. Warner (Sachs and Warner 1995).

17. http://www.worldbank.org/afr/ccproj/project/pro_monitor.htm#iag0703, August 18, 2003.

18. Alternatives are described in many publications of the UNODCCP. See the special section on alternatives on the website, http://www.unodc.org/unodc/en/publications/publications_alternative_development.html, August 29, 2003.

19. http://www.iuc.hr/, July 10, 2004.

20. http://www.bilbao-city.net/English/proyectos/guggenheim_more.asp, July 10, 2004.

12

Financing Reconstruction

Tony Addison
Abdur R. Chowdhury
S. Mansoob Murshed

T he economics of postconflict reconstruction are critical to the politics of reconstruction. Achieving economic growth contributes to peace by generating more livelihoods for demobilized fighters and returning refugees. If economic recovery reduces the grievances of disadvantaged regions and groups, then peace is more secure. Inevitably a large measure of economic reform is required to achieve these objectives, and it must be designed with care: Bad policy can undermine economic recovery, thereby damaging peace; good policy can help by raising growth.

This is not to say that there is some mechanical relationship between economics and conflict and between economic policy and peace. Complex noneconomic factors such as ideologies and belief systems also play a role, as do the effectiveness of institutions in resolving conflict by nonviolent means. But postconflict strategies that fail to address the economic dimension will certainly endanger otherwise promising political settlements. This chapter looks at one crucial dimension of the economics of postconflict recovery, namely finance.

Public Finance

Conflict has fiscal dimensions. Who gets what (via public spending) and who pays for it (via taxes) may play a role in the descent into conflict (see Ndikumana 2004 on Burundi and Rwanda, for example). In turn, violent conflict leads to further fiscal deterioration (Gupta et al. 2002). Revenues from indirect taxes fall as economic activity shrinks, the quality of tax institutions declines, and governments become ever more dependent on import duties and other trade taxes (which also decline as external trade shrinks and the quality and honesty of the customs service deteriorates). Hence, conflict has significant and negative effects on the tax/GDP ratio, and this effect increases as the *intensity* of conflict increases from localized guerrilla war up to nationwide civil war (Addison, Chowdhury, and Murshed 2003). The resulting fall in revenues reduces the ability of governments to fund development expenditures and, in raising the fiscal deficit, it contributes to macroeconomic instability. These all contribute to raising poverty.

Revenue Mobilization for Postconflict Recovery

Whatever form the political settlement takes, it will invariably have a fiscal dimension; people will expect some new and often radically different distribution of services and infrastructure. This new pattern of public spending must be financed. Therefore, tax and revenue generation, including some measure of political agreement on their incidence, are central to the creation of a working peace agreement. However, this imperative is often ignored—until it is too late.

In rare cases one party or parties to the conflict may insist that the peace deal include an *explicit* set of fiscal commitments. Guatemala's 1996 peace accords that ended the thirty-eight-year-old civil war incorporated specific fiscal measures to redress grievances; a target was set to raise the tax/GDP ratio to fund more basic services and infrastructure for the country's indigenous people who formed the core of the rebel movement. Yet opposition from the country's powerful landed elite has thwarted progress on tax reform, for instance, in property taxes, which are progressive in their incidence. This illustrates the problem that afflicts most peace deals, namely, that one or more parties to the agreement may subsequently renege on all or part of their earlier commitment.

Aid inflows can buy time for domestic political actors to reach a working agreement and time for necessary revenue institutions to rebuild. As the economy recovers, a rising tax base will provide some revenue buoyancy (using existing tax arrangements), and revenue growth will accelerate as new tax arrangements and institutions come on stream (e.g., the experience in Mozambique's postwar recovery). But aid inflows to reconstructing economies can quickly tail off, and political actors can store up trouble for the future if they neglect early attention to revenue mobilization (Addison 2000; Collier et al. 2003).

Even if all parties are genuinely committed to peace, revenue institutions may be so degraded that they are unable to meet the agreed targets for raising revenue; and state capacity, including the public expenditure system, may be so weak that it is unable to use any revenue raised to deliver improved infrastructure and services. This will also affect the ability of governments to use aid, including debt relief, to make the fiscal transfers necessary to redress grievances and achieve broad-based recovery (Addison and Murshed 2003b). Further difficulties arise from the need in most countries to undertake very necessary but wholesale reform of the fiscal system. This often involves a measure of fiscal federalism to reverse the overcentralization of political and fiscal powers (see Bevan 2003 on Ethiopia; and Fox and Wallich 1998 on Bosnia and Herzegovina). And territories that secede need to build national fiscal institutions on the often weak foundations of the local institutions that were imposed by previous central or colonial authorities (e.g., Eritrea and East Timor). This takes considerable time and investment, which inevitably constrains the effectiveness of revenue mobilization in the early years.

Because it is often easier to create public sector jobs than to create actual working services and infrastructure, revenues may simply create a postwar public employment bubble. This is in any case encouraged by the dynamics of the war-to-peace transition: Former belligerents often agree to divide up ministries and jobs between them in part to reduce everyone's incentive to go back to war—a characteristic of the immediate postwar years in Cambodia and now in Afghanistan. Although this may help secure the peace, the result is an ineffective public service, which in turn creates a governance problem for revenue mobilization; people become increasingly reluctant to pay taxes when better services are not forthcoming. Lack of revenue undermines services further, and a large and underpaid public service—tax collectors included—is a recipe for corruption and a further decline in governance (Kayizzi-Mugerwa 2003).

How to pay for all of this? For resource-rich countries, the authorities need to recover control of mineral revenues, a task that is easier said than done in the Democratic Republic of Congo (DRC) where the government has lost effective control of large areas of the country (Nzongola-Ntalaja 2002). If the revenues are under the government's control (as is the case with Angola's oil), then the task is to create a transparent budgetary structure to ensure that the ample revenues are put to best use. Unfortunately, exactly the reverse may occur; the winners of the civil war may see the country's mineral wealth as their personal prize rather than as any kind of revenue base for national development—this was largely the attitude of Laurent Kabila in the DRC. But progress is possible. In Sierra Leone the government now has some of the revenues from the country's diamond wealth under its control.

For all countries, but particularly those without mineral wealth, considerable innovation is necessary in revenue institutions, both tax authorities and customs and excise. Some success has been achieved with semiautonomous revenue authorities, notably in Uganda, where the ratio of revenue to GDP rose from a low of 5 percent in the mid-1980s to 12 percent by the end of the 1990s (Chen, Matovu, and Reinikka 2001). However, such authorities are not without their own governance problems (DFID 2000; Fjeldstad 2002). Equal attention must be given to reforming customs and excise collection; these revenue sources are especially important in the early years of reconstruction when revenues from indirect taxes and income taxes are low. Mozambique put its customs service out to tender; the UK's crown agents won the contract and proceeded to reorganize the service to improve its efficiency and meet the higher revenue targets set by the government.

Whereas conflict may originate in the grievances of a poorer group, competition over valuable natural resources may be equally or more important, and this motive can escalate once war has begun (Ballentine and Sherman 2003). Moreover, one or more belligerents may engage in extensive criminal activity (extortion, drugs, etc.), initially as a source of finance for their political and military efforts but then as a means for personal gain (e.g., Afghanistan, Colombia, and the former Yugoslavia). This has two fiscal dimensions.

First, fiscal transfers that may have been sufficient to help redress grievances and prevent war from starting—such as higher public spending focused on the aggrieved group and financed in ways that largely fall on other groups—may offer little incentive once war has begun and aggrieved groups have access to natural resource wealth and criminal activities that can yield revenues far in excess of any potential fiscal transfer. This problem increases the longer the duration of the conflict and thus the greater the amount of time and opportunity that belligerents have to develop criminal activity.

Second, criminal activity is untaxed. As formal taxed activity shrinks during conflict, so the state loses its revenue base and the resources at the disposal of criminals—including warlords—may become greater than those of any legitimate postwar authority. Criminal resources can be used to thwart government attempts to collect revenues, as with the extensive rackets run to evade excise duties on petrol, alcohol, and tobacco in the countries of the former Yugoslavia. They can also be used to corrupt and control the political process, including tax concessions for "legitimate" businesses acting as fronts for organized crime. In Afghanistan, warlords are very reluctant to cede their local tax-raising powers to the Kabul government, and some of their revenue is derived from the lucrative opium trade. However, the scale of this problem varies significantly depending on the history of each country's conflict. Countries that organize their people to achieve successful secession, as in Eritrea and East Timor, come out of conflict with high levels of social capital (and low amounts of criminality), which help postwar revenue mobilization for a perceived sense of nation building (see Hansson 2003 on Eritrea, for example).

In summary, redressing grievances is important to postconflict reconstruction and includes major fiscal dimensions. At the same time, it must be recognized that while attention to the economics of postconflict recovery is crucial, economic instruments—in this case fiscal policy—do not offer simple and mechanical levers for achieving peace and broad-based recovery in what are often deeply divided and fractured societies.

The Financial System

Economic recovery followed by sustained and fast growth will not be achieved unless the economy's financial sector—principally its commercial banking system as well as its central bank—is restored to health. The depth and quality of the financial system strongly affect the level of private investment as well as the ability of governments to finance themselves in a noninflationary manner by selling public debt. And confidence must be restored to the currency, or a new currency introduced, otherwise normal economic activity will not resume.

Different types of conflict have different financial effects. These include guerrilla insurrections that disrupt the rural financial system (e.g., Colombia today and Guatemala during its long civil war); cronyism in bank lending linked to autocratic rule (e.g., the Yugoslav Federation in the 1990s and Zimbabwe today); and temporary shutdowns in the financial system caused by military revolt (e.g., Côte d'Ivoire in 1999–2000 and Guinea-Bissau in 1998) as well as successful or attempted secessions (most recently East Timor and Kosovo).

Other types of conflict and their financial effects include the looting of banks to finance genocide and profit from it (e.g., Rwanda in 1994); civil wars that leave central banks intact but otherwise damage financial infrastructure (Angola from the 1970s onward and Mozambique during its sixteen-year civil war); and civil wars that comprehensively destroy the formal financial system (e.g., Cambodia in the 1970s and Somalia 1992–1994). Finally, there are interstate conflicts in which formal financial institutions are stressed but nevertheless continue to operate, such as the 1998–2000 war between Eritrea and Ethiopia. Consequently, national priorities for financial reconstruction vary significantly depending on the scale and character of the destruction as well as the country's institutional resources and human capital. And the political dynamics of the conflict, as well as the war-to-peace transition, also play a role.

Institution Building

Rebuilding or creating a central bank and other monetary authorities is crucial. A country's central bank may remain operational during civil war (e.g., Angola and Mozambique), it may shut down temporarily but reopen relatively quickly (e.g., Congo-Brazzaville and Rwanda), or shut down completely (Somalia's central bank remains closed after its looting in 1991, although the self-proclaimed Somaliland Republic opened a central bank in 1995). Technical assistance can sometimes improve a wartime central bank, as in the case of Mozambique, but generally the institution's ability to run a coherent monetary policy and supervise the financial system degrades, often alarmingly.

Central banks are also looted. The Taliban and Al-Qaida leaderships looted U.S.$6 million to $7 million from the central bank's reserves shortly before their departure from Kabul. Taking advantage of the *hawala* system—a comprehensive and highly active informal financial mechanism that has survived decades of conflict—they rapidly transferred much of the money abroad. International sanctions on the central bank have now been lifted allowing it to normalize relations with the international financial system, but it struggles to build the necessary institutional capacity after decades of neglect.

Creating a central bank is high on the list of priorities for institution building in countries that have seceded. Eritrea established a central bank in 1993 shortly after independence from Ethiopia. But institutional capacity may initially be too meager to create a fully operational central bank. East Timor never had a central bank; in colonial times the Portuguese currency circulated and then the rupiah after the 1975 Indonesian invasion, with a branch of the Indonesian central bank handling payments. As East Timor moved to independence, the UN Transitional Administration in East Timor created the Central Payments Office (CPO) to facilitate official payments, and the CPO now has responsibility for prudential supervision and regulation of the financial system, thereby laying the foundations for a future central bank.

A central bank's modus operandi can also be highly political in a country that has undergone civil war, and ethnic feuding can damage the institution's credibility. Central banks require independence to function properly. They need to be free of influences from various warring factions and the political party in control of the country at any point in time. At crucial moments, such as before elections, politicians may want to engineer temporary booms via loose and unsustainable monetary policies that are ultimately only inflationary. Such acts not only create crises in confidence in a new or stabilized currency but are destabilizing for a recovering postwar economy due to damaging output variations. Central bank independence can be achieved in a variety of forms. One example could include an independent head acting together with a rotating set of independent council members deciding on monetary policy, including interest rates.[1] The rotation in membership is to avoid the simultaneous capture of all members of the council by politicians. Ultimately, however, central bank independence is a *constitutional* guarantee requiring the application of the rule of law both in the letter and spirit. This in turn makes the institutions of governance and their smooth and efficient functioning central to efficient and independent central bank operations.

For example, the Dayton Peace Agreement authorized the creation of a central bank for Bosnia and Herzegovina. Another stipulation was that the bank governor cannot be a citizen of Bosnia and Herzegovina or of a neighboring country for the first six years of the bank's life. These institutional arrangements laid firm foundations for the institution, and the central bank has performed well subsequently.

Currency Reform

Europe's medieval monarchs debased the currency to finance their wars, as do many modern dictators; the resulting hyperinflation has catastrophic results for economies and societies. Examples include Zaire under Mobutu Sese Seko and the former Yugoslavia under Slobodan Milosevic (Beaugrand 1997). People seek out inflation hedges, such as foreign currencies and gold, and the national currency depreciates, often dramatically, leading to further capital flight, as has been the case in Zimbabwe since 1997. Remittances of foreign currency by migrants and asylum seekers may be one of the few means for people to survive (Sumata 2002). All of this results in a radical decline in the use of the domestic currency, as well as its value. This further undermines the government's revenue base because seigniorage revenue, that is, the net revenue from issuing notes and coins, falls.[2]

In some conflict countries the authorities may cease to be the monopoly supplier of currency, either because warlords find it profitable to do so or because separatist regions wish to assert their economic and political independence. In Afghanistan at least seven versions of the currency, the afghani, circulated throughout the 1990s, including those printed by previous Kabul governments, but also by warlords—the latter were worth less in the foreign exchange market than "official" afghanis. In Sudan, the southern rebel movement has printed a currency of its own, an action condemned by Khartoum as an attempt to undermine the peace negotiations; the rebels responded by arguing that since the central bank in Khartoum was governed by *sharia* law, which prohibits the payment of interest, the Christian south had a right to make its own monetary arrangements. After the 1991 Gulf War, Iraq had two versions of the dinar: the Saddam dinar, which was issued by the central bank in Baghdad, and the so-called Swiss dinar, foreign-printed dinar notes used in the Kurdish-controlled northern part of the country.

Restoring monetary stability is, therefore, imperative for successful postconflict recovery. After the Rwandan genocide, the new government withdrew the old currency and issued a new one. After the fall of the Taliban regime, the new Afghan authorities restored a measure of confidence by withdrawing the old notes and replacing them with new notes carrying special security devices. This was largely successful, although the difficult terrain and communications led to delays in getting the new currency to the more remote regions.

One option is to replace the national currency with a major foreign currency. This policy is known as "dollarization," for it is the U.S. dollar that is usually adopted but any major convertible currency can be used; the euro was seen as an option in early discussions of currency reform in Afghanistan. In East Timor the U.S. dollar replaced the Indonesian rupiah. Both the euro and the dollar have been raised as options for Iraq (in the 1920s the Indian rupiah was introduced by the British administration).

Dollarization must be considered with care for it has both positive and negative implications for the economy. On the positive side, dollarization can improve policy credibility, especially when political uncertainties—often very high in the first years of peace—cause destabilizing (inflationary) runs on the currency, which in turn deter private investment. The use of a foreign currency by enterprises, households, and the authorities themselves introduces an element of much-needed stability into economic life, and a foreign currency may be the main instrument for household and enterprise savings until commercial (deposit-taking) institutions rebuild. On the negative side, the authorities lose seigniorage revenue, an important consideration when income taxes and indirect taxes are difficult to collect—the case for most con-flict-affected countries. And when a country has its own currency, the authorities can devalue to offset adverse terms of trade shocks; this pol-icy tool is obviously lost when the economy is dollarized.

A currency board system is a halfway house: It improves credibility while not being as rigid as dollarization. Under a currency board the authorities commit themselves to exchanging the domestic currency for a foreign currency (often the dollar) at a fixed exchange rate (often one-for-one), holding sufficient reserves to exchange the entire domestic money supply if necessary (Williamson 1995). Provided that the public believes in this promise, an outcome economists label "credible," then no actual large-scale conversion will take place.

The first use of a currency board in a conflict-affected country was in northern Russia during the civil war that followed the Bolshevik Revolution of 1917. The board operated successfully, but for only a short time, in the area controlled by the expeditionary force sent by the Western powers. More recently, Bosnia and Herzegovina's central bank operates a currency board in which the convertible marka, intro-duced in 1997 at the bank's inception, is pegged to the euro (previously it was pegged to the deutschemark). This has kept inflation low and facilitated the resumption of normal economic activity. However, cur-rency boards do have drawbacks. It is almost impossible to introduce a currency board until the political situation stabilizes, and introducing one when the political environment is rapidly deteriorating will simply facilitate capital flight. In 1998 Indonesia's Suharto regime toyed with the idea in its dying days but stalled as political uncertainty and vio-lence rose.[3]

In summary, there are no easy answers to the issue of currency reform in conflict-affected countries, and the authorities must carefully balance a range of economic and political factors in reaching their final decision. This will include their prospects for joining regional monetary arrangements that offer stability: Guinea-Bissau is a member of the Franc Zone in West Africa, and the Balkan countries ultimately hope to join the European Union and adopt the euro.

Reviving the Commercial Financial System

Resuming normal economic activity will be severely impeded without a revival of commercial banks and insurance companies. The provision of bank finance for working capital, fixed investment, and residential reconstruction must also restart. And households and enterprises need deposit and savings accounts and effective mechanisms for transferring money; their ability to receive international monetary transfers from family members abroad is an important informal safety net.

Commercial banks can take considerable time to restore their capital base, restructure and write off bad debts, and reequip and restaff. Four of Afghanistan's six banks had virtually no assets by the time the Taliban regime fell, and only two of the six are functioning. And at least U.S.$7 million was transferred out of Rwanda's banks and into the hands of those responsible for the country's genocide. A halt in bank lending results from the loss of bank records together with the business records of borrowers as well as their collateral.

Expenditures for postwar reconstruction and poverty reduction make large demands on public funds, which typically remain low until the economy's tax base starts to recover. Little public money is left to recapitalize state banks, and infusing private capital (both domestic and foreign) by means of complete or partial bank privatization is favored by the IMF and the World Bank (and accordingly this becomes a condition on their lending). In Afghanistan a number of foreign banks are awaiting the passage of new bank laws, which will then govern the issuance of licenses to begin operations.

Although privatization and the entry of new private banks both help to recapitalize the system, the process can be highly nontransparent, especially when it begins during war. And the legal framework in which to pursue bank fraud is often grossly inadequate and corruption is often rife. Mozambique's attorney general was sacked in 2000 after allegations in parliament that his office had been slow to investigate the theft of U.S.$14 million from a former state-owned bank before it was privatized. An official of the central bank and a widely respected journalist were both murdered while investigating fraud in Mozambique's banking system (Hanlon 2002a). This is not to say that privatization is the wrong strategy, but greater attention must be given to its conduct so that the public interest is protected.

The weaknesses prevalent in the financial systems of developing countries are seen in acute form in conflict-affected countries. These include banking legislations that either omit important prudential regulations or are imprecise; shortages of supervisory skills in financial authorities; and supervisors unwilling to enforce prudential regulations. Considerable technical assistance is required. Professional staff must also be paid a salary commensurate with their responsibilities—otherwise they will leave for the private sector—and this requires significant public funds. Ensuring that key public sector workers receive a market salary has been a major issue in East Timor and Mozambique.

Political interference in bank supervision is prevalent in conflict-affected countries, especially when the oversight provided by such democratic institutions as parliamentary committees and an independent media is weak or absent. Warlords may own private banks and other financial institutions, originally capitalized with war booty (Liberia under Charles Taylor is an example). The international community's High Representative to Bosnia and Herzegovina had to impose special legislation to protect bank regulators from intimidation. But in many cases organized crime can be more powerful than any external actors, and personal threats may still be effective despite legislation. A number of Cambodia's private banks are alleged to have laundered money arising out of drug trafficking and illegal logging, and some regulators are also alleged to have received bribes connected to bank licensing.

Not surprisingly, bank crises are frequent in conflict-affected countries. Fourteen of Bosnia and Herzegovina's banks have collapsed since the end of the war in 1995, including one that held NGO and donor accounts. In 2000 two of Mozambique's largest banks reported substantial losses, possibly as high as U.S.$400 million (Hanlon 2002a, 53). The government of Mozambique, part shareholder in the country's two largest banks, experienced losses estimated to be at least U.S.$100 million (3 percent of GDP) (IMF 2002, 5).

Conclusion: Toward Broad-Based Recovery

We started this chapter by emphasizing the importance of poverty reduction to the design of postconflict recovery. East Timor is an example of what can be done rapidly and effectively for people, including society's worst off, given enough political will and generous international support. Liberia under Charles Taylor is an illustration of what happens when a warlord runs reconstruction for his own benefit: rising misery and eventually a return to civil war.

Public finance is crucial for broad-based recovery. Domestic revenues need to be mobilized to fund the recurrent costs of government administration and basic pro-poor services—primary education, basic health care, and safe water and sanitation—that foreign aid only partially covers. Revenues need to be raised while at the same time avoiding as much as possible taxes and user charges that bear disproportionately on poorer groups. Nevertheless, revenue reforms that threaten elite interests may falter. These may be traditional elites, such as a landed oligarchy, or new elites created by war and economic reform. Therefore, building a functioning democracy that represents the interests of the majority is crucial to the effectiveness of any reform that aims to achieve a broad-based recovery from war.

How does an overarching priority for the poor affect the reconstruction of the financial system? There are two ways. First, currency reform should be directed toward ensuring a rapid resumption of normal economic activity; a buoyant economy creates more employment for the poor and more demand for their micro-enterprises. As we have seen, the different options for currency reform must be carefully assessed, with economic stability being a paramount concern: Recessions inflict large costs on the poor who are least able to cope. Second, every effort must be made to ensure that banks engage in sound lending because financial problems invariably become fiscal problems, and states generally become responsible for at least part of the recapitalization that follows bank crises. Public money is then diverted away from development priorities, including poverty reduction (this is the hard lesson recently learned by Mozambique). To achieve this requires considerable capacity building in central banks and, critically, democratic oversight to ensure that regulatory authorities act in the public interest and do not become captured by powerful private interests.

When there are so many humanitarian needs and so much human misery connected to war, it might seem overly narrow to discuss taxation, currency reform, bank regulation, and all the other seemingly arcane issues of public finance and banking. But there is little prospect for a fast recovery in output, employment, and services without a well-functioning financial system. And without economic recovery, demobilized fighters will have few livelihoods other than war and crime, and economic hardship will enable demagogues to exploit ethnic rivalries and tensions, thereby undermining peace itself.

Notes

This chapter arises from research conducted under the UNU-WIDER project on "Why Some Countries Avoid Conflict While Others Fail." The views expressed in this chapter are those of the authors alone and should not be attributed to UNU-WIDER.

1. For example, members can be appointed for six years with some being replaced every two years, as with the U.S. Senate.

2. For developing countries, seigniorage revenue ranges from 5 to 25 percent of total government revenue. See Agénor and Montiel (1999, 144).

3. Moreover, a currency board cannot act as lender of last resort to distressed banks. And currency boards will eventually collapse if other economic policies, particularly fiscal policy, are not supportive, as Argentina, a nonconflict economy, showed in 2002.

13

Donor Assistance: Lessons from Palestine for Afghanistan

Rex Brynen

P alestine and Afghanistan represent, together with the postconflict reconstruction programs in Bosnia and Kosovo, two of the largest programs of peacebuilding in the post–Cold War period. In Palestine, donors have disbursed an estimated $4.8 billion since 1993, or approximately half a billion dollars per year. In the case of Afghanistan, donors met in January 2002 and pledged at least $4.5 billion in assistance over five years. Both assistance programs dwarf typical flows of official development assistance to developing countries. The levels of aid directed to Palestine and Afghanistan also stand in contrast to other war-torn and postconflict countries that are of lesser political interest to Western donors, notably in such African countries as the Democratic Republic of Congo ($3.70 per capita), Sierra Leone ($36.77), or Rwanda ($38.75).

Palestine and Afghanistan also share another important parallel: Both represent cases of peacebuilding and reconstruction amid uncertainty, tension, violence, and the danger of a return to war. In the West Bank and Gaza (WBG), the Oslo agreement and its successors established transitional arrangements, but the full resolution of the Palestinian-Israeli conflict was postponed until permanent status negotiations. Violence, confrontation, and occupation continued, ultimately engulfing and destroying the peace process and perhaps even the Palestinian Authority (PA) itself. In Afghanistan, too, peace and stability are highly contingent commodities. The central government remains weak, with many opponents; terrorism continues; warlords compete for power in the hinterland, often through military means.

Yet while both are examples of large-scale assistance to strategic, conflict-torn areas, the socioeconomic and political differences between the two cases are so substantial as to raise questions about the validity of any comparison. Life expectancy in the WBG, after all, is seventy-two years, almost five years higher than that of Russia and more similar to poorer eastern European countries than to the developing world. By contrast, life expectancy in Afghanistan is only forty-three years. Prior to the eruption of the current intifada, gross national product (GNP) per capita in the Palestinian territories stood at roughly $1,800, approximately five times greater than that of Afghanistan. The population of Palestine is urbanized, educated, and works predominately in the industrial and service sectors. Afghans are rural, predominately agricultural, and suffer from high levels of illiteracy. Indeed, before the UN stopped ranking it due to a lack of data, Afghanistan's human development index was among the very lowest in the world.

Given these vast differences between the two cases, this chapter does not intend to examine the WBG in an effort to shed light on appropriate aid priorities for Afghanistan. Rather, it focuses on the processes and dynamics of aid itself, and some of the political and developmental dilemmas of the Palestinian case that may have broader relevance to reconstruction efforts. Four issues will be explored in particular detail: pledging gaps and disbursement delays, aid coordination, host-country ownership, and the political usages of aid. First, however, overviews of each case will be offered. These will include a discussion of lessons to be learned from Palestinian experiences, as well as some of the weaknesses of peacebuilding and reconstruction assistance in Afghanistan.

Peacebuilding and Foreign Aid in Palestine

As in Afghanistan, development aid to Palestine has been fundamentally political in its origins. Following the signing of the Palestinian-Israeli Declaration of Principles (Oslo Accords) in 1993 and the establishment of the nascent PA the following year, aid to the WBG was intended to "mobilize resources to make the agreement work."[1] Donor declarations frequently spoke of the need to create benefits associated with progress toward peace or even of building the institutions necessary to eventual Palestinian statehood.[2] By almost any comparator (except, perhaps, U.S. aid to Israel), aid to the WBG has been massive, far beyond what might be expected in a fairly developed lower- to middle-income country—were it not for the strategic importance of the Palestinian issue.

At the same time, while the impetus for Palestinian aid was fundamentally political—and the levels of resources mobilized a reflection of this—the actual disbursement and allocation of aid was affected by a far broader and more complex array of variables: political and socioeconomic context, bureaucratic politics and standard operating procedures within donor agencies, donor rivalries, Israeli policies, the capacities and interests of the PA, and even idiosyncratic factors.

In exploring this, the aid effort in Palestine is best broken down into four (approximate) periods. The first was an initial start-up phase in 1993–1995. The second, in 1996–1997, saw development efforts (and the Palestinian economy) stall in the face of harsh Israeli mobility restrictions. The third period, from 1998 until the start of the intifada in late September 2000, saw Palestinian and donor efforts shift to long-term development impaired by the economic consequences of Israeli mobility restrictions. The fourth period, starting with the intifada, has been characterized by violence, reoccupation, economic collapse, and an emerging humanitarian crisis.

1993 to 1995: Establishing a Palestinian Authority

The first and most immediate challenge of international donor assistance to Palestine was to support the transition to Palestinian limited self-rule and establish the institutions of the PA. Some sectors of the Palestinian public sector—notably in health and education—already existed under the Israeli Civil Administration, albeit in distorted form. Others—including ministries of finance, planning, economy and trade, and local government—had to be constructed from nothing. At the same time, the geographic scope and functional powers of the nascent PA were slowly being negotiated and extended in a series of Palestinian-Israeli agreements.[3]

Donor assistance to Palestine started with a major high-profile donors' conference in Washington in October 1993. At this time, donors pledged around $600 million in support over the next year, with indications of approximately $2 billion in the pipeline. Over the next nine years total disbursements would be far higher than this, although annual disbursements were typically below the levels suggested by press reports and public statements, and many donors were slow to deliver on what they had promised. These twin problems of *pledge inflation* and *disbursement lag* afflict many cases of high-profile international aid.[4] Palestinian officials complained of this but also sometimes raised the issue to divert local blame for slow Palestinian performance or to increase the political pressure on donor agencies to contribute.

In any case of peacebuilding, time is not neutral: Certain challenges must be met promptly or the developmental and political costs can be high. Support for establishing the PA was one such case. At first, donors were slow to do this, for a variety of reasons. First, some of the essentials of transitional assistance—such as support for paying, equipping, and even arming the Palestinian security forces—lay outside the preferred purview of most donor agencies.[5] Contributions thus lagged, and creative institutional workarounds had to be found (notably, transferring funds via a UN agency) to establish a conduit for donor funds that was transparent, accountable, and met the legal requirements of donor agencies.

Also, in Palestine, the fiscal instruments to support PA expenditures lagged, with the PA having been established before it had gained much territorial or tax authority. The result was a large, structural, budget deficit in the first years, which necessitated budget support from donor countries. However, aid agencies do not favor recurrent budget support either, seeing this as unproductive wage expenditure rather than longer-term development investment. As with short-term support for the police, medium-term financing for start-up costs and budget support required both political pressure on donors to provide such support and the establishment of new institutional mechanisms to make it possible. In this case, the primary conduit would be the World Bank–administered Holst Fund. Donors would eventually disburse $291 million for transitional costs and budget support in 1994–1995 (around 29 percent of all aid in this period), with around $169 million of this going through the Holst mechanism (Brynen 2000, 180). Indeed, the Holst Fund would come to be recognized as a hugely important and valuable innovation,[6] shaping the development of similar instruments in other cases—including in Bosnia, Kosovo, East Timor, and the current Afghanistan Reconstruction Trust Fund (ARTF).

It was also during this first phase of donor assistance to Palestine that the architecture of donor assistance began to take shape. A high-level Ad Hoc Liaison Committee (AHLC) was established comprising leading donors. It was complemented by a more inclusive series of Consultative Group meetings held under World Bank auspices. It soon became apparent that local coordination mechanisms were needed on the ground, too, so in late 1994 an inclusive Local Aid Coordination Committee (LACC) and exclusive Joint Liaison Committee (JLC) were established, as well as a series of Sectoral Working Groups (SWGs) in key areas.[7] Over the years, this basic structure would endure, although the number, sectors, and format of SWGs would be changed several times. Also in 1994, the Office of the United Nations Special Coordinator (UNSCO) was established in lieu of the Special Representative of the Secretary-General normally appointed in war-to-peace transitions.[8]

Development priorities in this early stage were often donor driven, reflecting the weakness of Palestinian planning capacities, as well as the directions imparted by funding envelopes, prior donor engagement, and perceived needs. Overall needs assessment was provided by a six-volume World Bank study that had been fortuitously completed in 1993, as well as a later 1994 World Bank–designed emergency assistance program that outlined $1.2 billion in priority investments (World Bank 1993; 1994). However, while donors may have used these assessments for insight into conditions and immediate needs in the WBG, there is little evidence that they actually used them to determine aid priorities. As a result, sectoral disbursements tended to differ widely from those suggested in the World Bank's initial program.[9]

1996 to 1997: (Fore)Closing Development

In October–December 1995, following the signing of the Palestinian-Israeli Interim Agreement, Israeli forces withdrew from additional areas in the West Bank. In January 1996, elections were held for both the PA president and the Palestinian Legislative Council. Shortly before, another high-profile ministerial-level donors' conference met in Paris, pledging some $1.4 million in assistance to the WBG, and sending a very public signal of confidence in the PA and the peace process.[10] This second period was also intended to mark a shift in donor and Palestinian priorities from transitional and start-up assistance to longer-term development investments.

In practice, however, this did not happen. The most important reason for this was Israel's increasing imposition of closure and other mobility restrictions, which prevented Palestinians from leaving the WBG or even from moving from place to place within the West Bank. Such restrictions, justified in the name of security, predated the peace process but grew much more extensive after Oslo. Closure dramatically reduced the earnings that Palestinians had once made working in Israel, severely interrupted imports and exports, disrupted local economic activity, impacted negatively on the fiscal revenues of the PA, and deterred potential private sector investment. Unemployment rates, which had averaged 5.6 percent prior to the peace process (1990–1993), grew to an average of 18.3 percent in 1994–1998, peaking at 24 percent in 1996. In a comprehensive assessment of aid effectiveness prepared for the donor community by the World Bank in June 2000, the data was clear: Israeli restrictions had cost the Palestinian economy 15 to 20 percent of GNP in 1995–1997, more than offsetting the positive effects of aid (World Bank and Government of Japan 2000, paragraph 2.7. and figure 2.41).

Because of the devastating effects of closure, the donor program for the WBG was seriously affected in several ways. First, many projects encountered delays and other difficulties. Second, it became difficult to move ahead on projects that sought to promote private sector development, given the very poor business climate. Finally, mounting unemployment (and its potential political consequences) led donors to focus some resources on projects with substantial short-term job creation effects—although perhaps fewer resources than were needed.

Closure also exacerbated the tendency of the PA to use public sector employment as a tool of both political patronage and local job creation. The public sector payroll thus continued to expand at a rapid rate, growing from 9 percent of GDP in 1995 to 14 percent by 1997 (World Bank 1999, 22). This sapped public funds needed for investment purposes and threatened to outstrip fiscal revenues.

1998 to 2000: Palestinian Development at Last?

By 1998, Israeli use of closure had eased. With this, donors and the PA could at last make a transition from emergency stabilization into investment in sustainable development. While the Palestinian territories had yet to fully recover from the aftereffects of closure, a more normal economic climate was established. Business activity and investment in the WBG grew and unemployment began to fall. GDP grew by an estimated 3.8 percent in 1998 and 4.0 percent in 1999, while unemployment dropped to 12.4 percent by 1999, almost half its 1996 peak (World Bank and Government of Japan 2000, paragraph 2.9). By the third quarter of 2000, on the eve of the intifada, GDP growth was projected by the IMF at 5 percent, and unemployment had fallen still further, to 10 percent (Office of the United Nations Special Coordinator 2002; IMF 2001, 5).

Several development concerns preoccupied donors. The first issue was that of fiscal stability and the continued growth of the public sector payroll. Related to this were the recurrent costs of development investments and assuring the sustainability of these beyond the initial investments by donors.

A third set of issues related to the off-the-books finances of the PA, including the failure to consolidate fiscal accounts, the activities of publicly owned commercial enterprises, semiofficial monopolies (or protection rackets), and even more murky forms of economic activity. Although the day-to-day levels of public corruption in the WBG remained quite low by most objective measures,[11] frequent political patronage, financial diversion, the importance of *wasta* (connections), human rights abuses, and a lack of transparency and accountability were weakening public trust in official institutions. These abuses also inhibited effective capacity and institution building within the PA.

Finally, donors increasingly emphasized the need for policy reforms so as to foster strong institutions and create a legal, regulatory, and economic environment conducive to growth and investment. Strengthening the rule of law, reforming civil service and budgetary procedures, fiscal reform, and encouraging investment were all important parts of this. In the context of good policies and strong institutions, the World Bank noted, donor aid tends to foster economic growth and poverty reduction. However, in the absence of such policies and institutions, cross-national analysis shows that aid has little or no positive long-term effects and may even slow reform by "serv[ing] to insulate governments from the costs of their own shortcomings."[12]

For the PA, leadership in development planning was an issue of growing importance. In the initial years of the donor assistance effort, there had been little Palestinian planning capacity. Consequently, donors were faced with a choice of pressing ahead with the projects that they thought best or delaying aid until Palestinian priorities could be fully developed. The initial, rather complex, coordination structure—dominated by donors and international organizations—had reflected this. While it served many useful functions, the multiplicity of meetings and fora sometimes overtaxed the capacities of emerging Palestinian institutions. Donors also tended to pick and choose Palestinian partners, channeling more funds through already responsive counterparts (some government ministries, the larger municipalities), and shying away from weaker and hence less responsive institutions despite their evidently greater need for institutional development.

Later, Palestinian planners, in conjunction with donors, began to produce a series of public investment programs. Finally, in 1998, the first Palestinian Development Plan (PDP) was presented for 1998–2000 and later updated to 1999–2003. This set of key goals outlined sectoral needs and strategies and provided a shopping list from which donors were expected to choose projects. While a positive step, however, problems remained. Donors complained that the PDP was little more than an extended PA wish list and that priorities needed to be more rigorously set. Donors (often in conjunction with Palestinian ministries or other potential beneficiaries of specific aid projects) also exerted pressure on the PDP to have key donor-favored projects placed on the list. Palestinian planners also frequently complained that donors, having pressed the PA to set priorities, would then ignore these and work outside the PDP framework.

The PA also had other complaints about the nature of donor assistance. Not enough, it suggested, was directed to large infrastructure investments. Too much—more than $450 million by mid-1999—was being disbursed in the form of studies and technical assistance. Such expert advice, although sometimes very useful, was all too often short term, poorly attuned to local realities, politically naive, and donor driven rather than responding to the Palestinian-identified needs and priorities (World Bank and Government of Japan 2000, paragraphs 5.28–5.35).

2000 to mid-2004: Chaos, Crisis, and Collapse

In July 2000, Israel and the Palestinians met under U.S. auspices in Camp David to reach agreement on a permanent end to the Palestinian-Israeli conflict. Those negotiations were unsuccessful, although they paved the way for a series of secret negotiations inside and outside the region—the Clinton Proposals of December 2000—and finally a last round of negotiations in Taba in January 2001. At Taba the parties made striking progress, and the outlines of a permanent status agreement could readily be discerned.

However, it was not to be. In late September, a deliberately provocative visit by then–Likud opposition leader Ariel Sharon to the Temple Mount/Haram al-Sharif set off a wave of violence. Years of accumulated Palestinian frustration at occupation and illegal Israeli settlement activity, harsh responses to protests by the Israeli police and military, and a tragic miscalculation by the Palestinian leadership to use violence as a negotiating tool all set in motion a dynamic that engulfed and ultimately destroyed the peace process. The election of Sharon as Israeli prime minister in February 2001, and waves of Palestinian terrorism against civilian targets within Israel, reinforced the vicious circle of violence, anger, and counterviolence, resulting in the Israeli reoccupation of most of the West Bank in the spring of 2002 and the destruction of much of the basic administrative infrastructure of the PA. Checkpoints proliferated, mobility restrictions grew more severe than ever, and curfews became commonplace, often confining hundreds of thousands to their homes. Palestinian labor within Israel essentially ended. According to the UN, some 688,000 Palestinians in thirty-nine towns, villages, and refugee camps were under some form of curfew in September 2002 (Office for the Coordination of Humanitarian Affairs 2002, 11).

In such a context, development has become impossible. Indeed, far from promoting development, donor efforts have been increasingly focused on attempting to blunt a growing humanitarian emergency.

According to data compiled by the World Bank, the physical damages caused by Israeli military actions and other violence totaled some $930 million by the end of 2002. Between October 2000 and April 2003, Palestinian income losses due to closure and economic disruption were estimated at $5.2 billion, an amount equivalent to almost a full year's pre-intifada gross national income (World Bank 2003a). Approximately one-third of the population is unemployed. As a consequence, poverty rates are estimated to have reached 55 percent or more in the West Bank and 70 percent in Gaza (UNSCO 2002, 2). Two separate nutritional assessments have revealed signs of growing malnutrition, with 13 percent of children in Gaza showing signs of acute malnutrition and 18 percent showing signs of chronic malnourishment (Al-Quds University et al. 2002).

The intifada also resulted in a collapse of PA finances. Israel suspended all payments of Palestinian customs clearances to the PA shortly after the eruption of violence. These had averaged $60 million per month, representing around two-thirds of all PA revenue. In addition, the economic crisis in the territories severely depressed domestic tax revenues. Even with emergency austerity measures, the PA has faced a budgetary shortfall of about $72 million per month. Some of this was made up by emergency budget support from Arab donors and the European Union, worth around $40 million to $50 million per month (UNSCO 2002, 23–24).

In general, donor disbursements seem to have risen in response to the crisis: UNSCO estimates disbursements grew to $900 million in 2001, and Palestinian estimates seem to suggest $1.4 billion was disbursed over fifteen months. However, with closure, reoccupation, and violence, the donor-tracking system put in place by the Palestinian Ministry of Planning and International Cooperation has essentially stopped functioning, and actual donor expenditures are unclear.[13]

As Peter Hansen, the Commissioner-General of the Relief and Works Agency for Palestine Refugees in the Near East, has noted: "Few places have ever undergone as steep and rapid a decline in income and living standards and as rapid an increase in mass deprivation as the Palestinian population has been experiencing for the past two years."[14] Signaling the severity of the crisis, the UN issued an emergency Humanitarian Plan of Action for 2003, calling for $293 in emergency assistance, including almost $130 million in food aid for Palestinians.

It was in this context—somewhat bizarrely, in the view of many—that international attentions were increasingly focused on administrative and institutional reform of the PA. In his policy speech of June 24, 2002, U.S. president George W. Bush declared that "when the

Palestinian people have new leaders, new institutions and new security arrangements with their neighbors, the United States of America will support the creation of a Palestinian state whose borders and certain aspects of its sovereignty will be provisional until resolved as part of a final settlement in the Middle East."[15] Political, economic, and security reform of the PA has thus become a prerequisite for U.S. support for eventual Palestinian statehood. Anticipating the president's comments, the PA issued a "100 Days [Reform] Plan" of its own. This called for local, legislative, and presidential elections; the reorganization of the Palestinian security services; administrative and financial management reforms; greater controls on civil service hiring; judicial reform and strengthening the rule of law; and promulgation of several pending pieces of legislation, including the then-pending (constitutional) Basic Law.[16] The diplomatic "Quartet" (the United States, European Union, Russia, and UN) added its backing to these reform efforts and subsequently an expanded "Task Force on Palestine Reform" (TFPR) was established, consisting of the Quartet plus Norway, Japan, the World Bank, and International Monetary Fund. In turn, the TFPR established seven thematic Reform Support Groups.[17] The Quartet's "roadmap" for peace, released in May 2003, explicitly included requirements for Palestinian reform.

Few doubt the value of Palestinian reform, which is and always has been a very desirable goal. Preoccupation with the topic, however, obscures the considerable efforts that donors had been making in this area since 1993–1994, as well as the significant successes of the PA in many areas. More important, however, it is highly questionable how much reform can be undertaken at a time when PA revenues are being withheld by Israel; when legislators, officials, and technical experts are frequently unable to travel or even reach their places of work; when much of the infrastructure of the PA has been disrupted or destroyed; and when almost all of the West Bank is under Israeli—not Palestinian—control. As of mid-2004, emergency needs overwhelm local capacities and make it difficult to engage in effective medium- or long-term planning. Moreover, the notion that reform will bring progress to peace (or that an absence of reform was the cause of the collapse of the peace process in 2000–2001) is itself fundamentally flawed.[18]

There is also a deeper danger that the well-meaning and necessary efforts of the international community to alleviate growing suffering in the WBG will inhibit, rather than contribute to, efforts to build the structures of eventual Palestinian statehood. International humanitarian assistance has become vital to meeting the basic needs of a Palestinian population afflicted by very high unemployment, widespread impoverishment, and even growing childhood malnutrition. International experience, however, suggests that emergency relief often has a built-in tendency to circumvent local capacities, generate dependency, and weaken local institutions. Several general examples of this syndrome can be offered:

• Donor resources that were once allocated to capacity building and institutional development are increasingly diverted to emergency needs. Relief supplants development.
• Mobility and security considerations lead to an increasing reliance on international staff. Competencies are thus imported from (and exported to) abroad, rather than developed locally. Key decisions are increasingly shifted out of local hands.
• The perennial trade-off between acting quickly and consulting with stakeholders is increasingly tipped toward the former by the emergency. Key local actors and institutions, already weakened by declining resources and difficult work conditions, increasingly find themselves "out of the loop."
• The provision of needed resources becomes dependent on the international community and not on the performance of local institutions.
• The multiplicity of emergency donor programs, international organizations, NGOs, and others involved in the relief effort creates growing problems of coordination, circumvents local authority, and overwhelms the ability of local governmental institutions to act as effective counterparts.
• The growing importance of nongovernmental service providers (as part of the system of humanitarian relief) impedes the ability of governmental institutions to monitor needs, develop and implement policy, deliver services, and provide leadership.
• Aid delivery has become channeled through local structures and municipalities, circumventing Palestinian national structures and reinforcing the fragmentation and "cantonization" of political authority.
• The failure of governmental institutions to provide essential public services delegitimizes such institutions in the eyes of the local population. Reformers, unable to make progress, lose credibility.

Already, some of these pathologies are beginning to emerge in the Palestinian context. Certainly, donors and relief agencies are aware of the dangers that humanitarian assistance will supplant, rather than enhance, local capacities (Lister and Le More 2003).[19] However, while the damage can be minimized by careful programming, it cannot be eliminated. Indeed, the highly fluid conditions in the WBG—characterized by sudden upsurges in violence, military activities, and changes in mobility restrictions—are likely to aggravate the dysfunctional side effects of relief activities. If local mobility and other restrictions continue, the Palestinian economy will deteriorate, the humanitarian emergency will grow, and relief efforts will become more needed and more entrenched. With this, external dependency will grow, internal capacities may wither, and the prospects for institutional reform and (proto) state building could fade beneath the weight of emergency needs and procedures.

Aid, Peacebuilding, and Reconstruction in Afghanistan

Afghanistan has known decades of brutal war. The Soviet intervention of 1979 and subsequent resistance by the Afghan mujahidin resulted in between 1 million and 2 million deaths and many more injured or dislocated. The bitter civil strife that followed the Soviet withdrawal in 1989 resulted in tens of thousands more dead. Following the terrorist attacks of September 11, 2001, came the U.S.-backed campaign to unseat Afghanistan's Islamic fundamentalist Taliban government.[20]

In November 2001, Kabul fell to the forces of the U.S.-backed Northern Alliance, and with it Taliban rule over Afghanistan ended. A week after the city fell, key donors met in Washington to plan Afghan reconstruction. An Afghanistan Reconstruction Steering Group (ARSG) was formed in Washington, and the ARSG held its first meeting in Brussels the following month. This was the precursor to a major ministerial donor-pledging conference in Tokyo on January 21–22, 2002.

The preliminary needs assessment of Afghanistan presented to the Tokyo conference, prepared jointly by the Asian Development Bank (ADB), the United Nations Development Programme (UNDP), and the World Bank, highlighted the sheer magnitude of the task facing both Afghan authorities and the donor community. Life expectancy in Afghanistan is low, infant and maternal mortality very high. The education system, the report noted, "is also in a state of virtual collapse," with a minority of boys and almost no girls attending even primary education (ADB, UNDP, and World Bank 2002). Basic infrastructure, to the extent that it had existed, has been devastated by decades of war. The report estimated that less than one-quarter of Afghans had access to safe water, only one in eight had adequate sanitation, less than one in fifteen had electricity, and only two telephones existed per thousand people (ADB, UNDP, and World Bank 2002, v). The already inadequate road network was in an extremely poor state of repair. Drought has, in recent years, halved agricultural production. At the time of the Taliban's defeat, an estimated 3.8 million Afghans were refugees and 1.2 million were internally displaced (UNHCR 2002a). Afghanistan is one of the most heavily mined areas in the world, with millions of mines and items of unexploded ordnance littering the country, including at least 344 square kilometers of "high priority" populated areas (International Campaign to Ban Landmines 2001, 469–451).

The preliminary needs assessment outlined a program projected to cost $1.7 billion in its first year, $10.2 billion over five years, and $14.6 billion over ten years (ADB, UNDP, and World Bank 2002, paragraph 8.3). Particularly in the first years, a large portion of this was devoted to (re)establishing structures of security and governance in Afghanistan coupled with budgetary support for the government. An Afghanistan Interim Authority Fund (AIAF) was established in December 2001 by UNDP as a conduit for donor support for transitional costs and budget support. This has now been superseded by the ARTF, administered by the World Bank, and managed in cooperation with the ADB, the Islamic Development Bank, UNDP, and the United Nations Assistance Mission in Afghanistan. The ARTF is intended to support government recurrent costs, development investments, and the return of Afghan expatriates.[21] In order to facilitate donor support for security-related projects, UNDP established a separate Law and Order Trust Fund (LOFTA). A UN Trust Fund for Afghanistan was also established to provide a mechanism for donor contributions toward the building of a national army.

The immediate political framework for postwar Afghanistan was provided by the UN-mediated Bonn Agreement of December 5, 2001, in which representatives of the major Afghan opposition groups agreed on the establishment of the Afghanistan Interim Authority (AIA).[22] Under the terms of this agreement, an emergency Loya Jirga (consultative assembly) was held in June 2002 to select a president—Hamid Karzai—and an Afghanistan Transitional Authority (ATA). A second, constitutional Loya Jirga was held in December 2003 to approve a new Afghan constitution. National elections were scheduled for June 2004 but then postponed for three months.

To coordinate development planning and provide the official interface with donors, the ATA established an Afghan Assistance Coordination Authority (AACA). The AACA is to approve all contracts and aid agreements between government ministries and the donor community. It is also intended to play the leading role in development of the Afghan government's National Development Framework (NDF).[23] The NDF calls for aid efforts to be focused on three pillars: humanitarian and human social capital, physical reconstruction and natural resources, and private sector reform. It also emphasizes the importance of providing for good governance and the rule of law, enhancing security, and addressing gender issues.

As of mid-2004, the still ATA represents an extremely weak and ill-equipped central government, with inadequate tax revenues. The reach of the Afghan state has never extended much into the rural hinterlands, and many outlying regions are still under the control of local warlords or tribal leaders who resist the extension of central government authority. Postwar security is highly problematic in much of the country, due both to banditry and politically motivated violence. Once the home of 70 percent of global production of opium poppies, until cultivation was banned by the Taliban in 2001, the postwar period threatens a resurgent drug trade in Afghanistan due to political chaos, weak enforcement, and economic need in the countryside.[24] The drug trade in turn is likely to fuel criminality and warlordism in a potential vicious circle.

Coordination of donor assistance in Afghanistan is complicated not only by the magnitude of the challenge but also by the plethora of aid actors. One directory of NGO aid agencies and UN and other international aid offices in Afghanistan, published in February 2002, runs forty-nine pages with more than 750 separate organizational entries (UNAMA/Afghanistan Management Information System 2002).

Aid coordination is also complicated by the presence of preexisting and overlapping donor frameworks.[25] In the late 1990s, sixteen donor countries established an Afghanistan Support Group (ASG) to discuss Afghan aid policy at a headquarters level. Until April 2002, the ASG and others also participated in an Afghanistan Programming Body intended to provide more local coordination. In 1998, the UN approved a Strategic Framework for Afghanistan, accepted by many bilateral donors and NGOs. By outlining themes and priorities, and by establishing thematic and regional working groups, the framework was intended to provide a degree of common purpose among key aid actors. Coordination and leadership of the UN system on the ground in Afghanistan was vested in a series of differently named (and mandated) bodies. Since March 2002, this has taken the form of the United Nations Assistance Mission in Afghanistan (UNAMA), which has both a political role ("pillar one," to assist in the implementation of the Bonn Agreement) and a technical one ("pillar two," to coordinate UN relief and development activities). UNAMA chaired weekly coordination meetings of the "Emergency Task Force," yet another (local) coordination body consisting of UN agencies, plus bilateral donors, NGOs, and Afghan representatives, and largely focuses on humanitarian issues (AREU 2002, 31).

As noted earlier, late 2001 saw the establishment of a new high-level donor coordination body, the Afghanistan Reconstruction Steering Group. The ARSG comprises more than sixty countries plus the UN system and international financial institutions. In January 2002, a Kabul-based Implementation Group (IG) was also established, chaired by the ATA. The World Bank, the Asian Development Bank, the Islamic Development Bank, UNDP, and ASG chairs all serve as vice chairs of the IG. An IG Standing Committee meets regularly in Kabul.

Of the earlier coordination mechanisms, the ASG continues to function, although amid debate as to its appropriate size and purpose. The Afghanistan Programming Body, it has been decided, would be absorbed by the IG. There is also discussion on the establishment of a standard World Bank "Consultative Group" for strategic donor coordination on Afghanistan, which might replace some of the existing mechanisms.

In addition to all of this, at least two major NGO coordination groups exist, the Agency Coordinating Body for Afghanistan relief, formed in 1988 by local and international NGOs, and the Afghan NGOs Coordination Bureau, established in 1991 largely for smaller Afghan organizations. In addition, the UN's Afghanistan Information Management Service attempts to track programs of NGOs, donors, and international agencies throughout the country in its "Who Is Doing What, Where" database.[26]

Assessing the Effort

The effectiveness of international aid efforts in Afghanistan to date is hotly debated. On the positive side, the immediate postwar risk of starvation due to drought, famine, violence, and economic dislocation appears to have been largely averted through emergency food programs and other efforts. Emergency winterization efforts were undertaken for vulnerable populations in 2001–2002 and again in 2002–2003. As of September 2002, 1.7 million Afghans had been helped by UNHCR to return home (UNHCR 2002b). Actual repatriation levels are likely to be even higher than this. Primary schooling has been restarted in many or most areas, and some health indicators appear to be improving. The central government has successfully introduced a new Afghan currency, a critical step in reestablishing monetary stability.

By early September 2002, some $890 million of the $1.8 billion pledged for the first year of the aid effort had been disbursed, an amount that the Afghan finance minister (a former World Bank official) later admitted was "extremely good" by global standards.[27] Of this amount, some 29 percent had gone to reconstruction assistance, most of it quick-impact or emergency projects; 18 percent to trust funds; 44 percent to humanitarian relief; 6 percent to support costs for the aid effort, and 3 percent to refugees outside Afghanistan (UNAMA 2002).

Despite this, there have been frequent complaints that some types of funds have been slow to arrive. Among agencies in the field, criticism has been leveled that donors have been slow to finance urgent programs, notably those related to refugee repatriation. There have also been complaints that refugee repatriation has been taking place faster than projects to provide water, shelter, and sustenance for returnees.[28] In Kabul, the return of refugees and IDPs has swollen the population from 1.2 million to 2.3 million persons, with a corresponding strain on already limited local services, infrastructure, and housing stock (Ahmad 2002).

Among Afghan officials, "a growing thread of Afghan opinion asserts that the only people dependent on international aid for Afghanistan are the aid employees themselves" (Stockton 2002, 40). Such criticism tends to focus on the slow pace of disbursements for budget support and public infrastructure investment. In the case of the former, Afghan officials have complained about the volume of aid disbursed through NGOs rather than government channels. As of the end of October 2002, approximately $65 million had been paid into the old AIAF by donors and $100 million paid into the ARTF—less than one-quarter the level of budget support suggested at the Tokyo donors meeting.[29] In October, the ATA complained that its $460 million budget was still short by $90 million.[30]

In the case of infrastructure, the most frequent complaint concerns the lack of labor-intensive road construction. In the words of Afghan president Hamid Karzai at a meeting with the Council on Foreign Relations in September 2002:

> Building highways and repairing road networks in Afghanistan is an important undertaking with significant economic, political and social impact for the Afghan people. It creates jobs, helps with security and demobilization, provides better connectivity, strengthens national unity and assists with the reintegration of Afghanistan into the regional economy.[31]

In November 2002, work finally began on the Kabul-Kandahar-Herat highway, with the financial support of the United States, Saudi Arabia, and Japan. Indicative of the economic and strategic importance of the project, the groundbreaking was attended by Karzai and lauded by U.S. president Bush in a White House press statement.

There has been little disarmament and demobilization in Afghanistan, other than of defeated Taliban forces. On the contrary, the U.S. military continues to ally with regional warlords, and factional fighting and banditry in the countryside remain common. In October 2002, the SRSG, Lakhdar Brahimi, warned the UN Security Council that "there will be no long-term solution to the security problems in Afghanistan unless and until a well-trained, well-equipped and regularly paid National Police and National Army are in place." In the meantime, "the Government and people of Afghanistan need and ask for international support to provide security while the National Police and National Army are trained."[32] The expansion of the UN-mandated International Security Assistance Force outside Kabul has been blocked by both initial U.S. opposition and, more recently, an evident lack of troop contributions and international will. The building of a national army and police force has proceeded slowly, both due to local politics and because of the reluctance of donors to finance security-related expenditures (although this reluctance is gradually being overcome). In the meantime, periodic attacks against UN and NGO workers in outlying areas have hampered development efforts.

Finally, there are the frequent, but no less serious, negative side effects of operating a large aid program in a very small country. Rents in Kabul have skyrocketed tenfold as agencies and international staff seek offices and accommodation. Relief organizations siphon off many of the most talented local staff from potential government service, paying salaries many times higher than those in the Afghan public sector, in a process that Michael Ignatieff calls "capacity confiscation" (Ignatieff 2002).[33] A range of aid-related economic local activities have sprouted up, variously symbiotic and parasitic.

Conclusion: Learning Lessons (and Repeating Mistakes?)

Having reviewed both the experience of international assistance to Palestine since the Oslo agreement, and the current post-Taliban aid efforts in Afghanistan, what lessons can be learned from the first case that might be applicable to the latter?

As noted at the outset of this chapter, given the vast social and economic differences between the two cases, there is little point in drawing conclusions about aid priorities—other than to note the key importance of transitional budget support in building or rebuilding the necessary institutions and capacities of statehood. It also bears repeating that public order, strong institutions, good governance, appropriate policies, and the rule of law are all essential elements of postconflict recovery, and that without them aid can do little to promote social development or long-term economic growth. However, the exact form initiatives should take in these areas, as well as the investment needs of individual sectors and the optimal allocation of resources between them, are highly context specific. Yet it is possible to highlight process-related issues that both Palestine and Afghanistan have in common. In this regard, four sets of such issues will be discussed next: pledging and disbursements, coordination, local ownership, and the politics of aid.

Pledging Gaps and Disbursement Delays

As noted earlier, "pledging gaps" are a common aspect of peacebuilding assistance. They typically stem from a tendency by donors to exaggerate their intended contributions, delays (both inevitable and entirely avoidable) in project approval and disbursement, and unrealistic expectations about how quickly money can be made to flow. In Palestine these problems were only severe in the early years, when the rapid creation of tangible benefits associated with the peace process was especially important. Later, once a regular pipeline was established, funds flowed relatively smoothly, and actual disbursements proved to be higher than the initial donor pledges made in 1993.

The problems of pledge gaps appear to be much more severe in Afghanistan. According to an analysis by Nicholas Stockton:

> Universal criticism was heard from all [Afghan] officials interviewed at the slow pace of the reconstruction and recovery programme. In some cases this was accompanied by expressions of anger, accusations of corruption, and a growing rhetoric of "betrayal by the international community." (Stockton 2002, 31)

In this connection, the Afghan minister of reconstruction, Amin Farhang, has complained:

> The reconstruction process at this point is not satisfactory. Promises made in accordance to the Tokyo reconstruction conference have yet to be fulfilled. In total, the donor countries promised US $4.5 billion for the next five years for Afghanistan, including $1.8 billion for 2002. Of this $1.8 billion, $600 million were given to the United Nations, $600 million for the NGOs, and only $90 million was given to the government of Afghanistan. This is not enough for the projects we have.[34]

Farhang's comments unintentionally reveal another aspect of pledge gaps: They can be more perceived than real, rooted in poor information, misunderstanding, or efforts by local officials to increase the pressure on donors to give more, faster. The quote above, for example, somewhat underestimates the level of assistance given to the government of Afghanistan and cites clearly erroneous figures about the level of disbursement to UN agencies and NGOs. However, it is perceptions that ultimately count. As the Afghan National Development Framework warns: "Afghans have been disappointed by the international community before. Hope could then be replaced by frustration, and frustration, in a context of raised expectations, is a recipe for anger, discord, and finally conflict" (Stockton 2002, 63).

The Challenges of Coordination

Donor coordination in Palestine was, it must be said, better than in many other cases of international peacebuilding. It deliberately featured both exclusive, more political fora (the AHLC and JLC) and more inclusive, more technical ones (Consultative Group meetings, the LACC, and SWGs), as well as coordination at senior (AHLC, Consultative Group) and local (LACC, SWG) levels. Critical to the success of coordination mechanisms was the value added in participation: Stakeholders ideally walked away from meetings with information, data, analysis, political backing, an opportunity to voice grievances or address bottlenecks, and other assets that were only available in the context of participation in ongoing coordination meetings. Where and when such benefits were absent, coordination soon withered.

Nonetheless, it did encounter a number of problems. Some participants found the myriad coordination settings and meetings confusing and a burden on smaller aid programs with only limited staff resources. The PA complained of this, too. Stronger Palestinian ministries were able to extract considerable value out of coordination meetings, while weaker ones were not. This, and the natural tendency of donors to prefer easier partnerships over more difficult ones, sometimes led to a clustering of aid projects around the most efficient Palestinian ministries, agencies, and local governments—at the expense of capacity building where it might have been needed most. Aid programs in Afghanistan must be mindful of this tendency and work to offset it.

In Palestine, the collapse of the peace process and the emerging humanitarian crisis in the occupied territories has brought with it the establishment of new emergency/humanitarian coordination mechanisms. On top of this, the Quartet, the Task Force on Palestinian Reform, and the working groups established by the task force have now eclipsed the previous AHLC/LACC coordination structures—further confusing the picture.

In Afghanistan, participants in the development effort voice similar confusion. According to Stockton's assessment of coordination and strategic planning:

- There are too many coordination mechanisms and meetings, such that "coordination [is] getting in the way of implementation."
- There is widespread confusion as to the membership and mandates of the various Afghan aid coordination mechanisms.
- Tensions exist between too much inclusion (resulting in meetings that are large and unwieldy) and excessive exclusion (resulting in elite or secretive "clubs" of key donors/agencies).
- Participants often complain of poor communications and information sharing.
- Competition and rivalries sometimes exist between different agencies and donors. Relations between official agencies and the (diverse and independent) NGO community have also been problematic at times.
- There are a variety of coordination-related effects stemming from bureaucratic and institutional factors, including differences in "headquarters," "Kabul," and "provincial/regional" perspectives within agencies; and potential tensions arising from the differing political, developmental, or humanitarian priorities and procedures of different organizations and sub-agencies. (Stockton 2002, 29)

One lesson of the Palestinian experience has been that coordination is important—but that it can be time-consuming, costly, and yet never succeed in fully harmonizing the efforts of myriad, often competing, donors, agencies, and recipients. Similarly, strategic frameworks are nice to have but difficult to use, especially in dynamic and highly politicized settings. As a result, it is important to see coordination not in terms of organizational charts and meetings but rather as "putting in place the appropriate set of institutions and individuals, and forging the most productive possible interaction among them." In addition, incentives to coordinate need to be built into projects and processes (Brynen 2000, 215).[35] In Afghanistan, this suggests less complexity in coordinating structures, and greater effort at optimizing the role of UNAMA and the Afghan Assistance Coordination Authority.

Host-Country Ownership

The potential importance of the AACA in strengthening coordination and strategic planning in Afghanistan leads to a second point of parallelism between Afghanistan and Palestine: the question of host-country ownership.

In Palestine, a frequent complaint of the PA was that coordination efforts and investment priorities were too donor driven and not always responsive to Palestinian priorities. The Palestinian Development Plan and revisions in the structure of the SWGs were intended to address this but never really fully succeeded. Donors responded that it was quicker to work through other channels (and time was of the essence), or tended to have political or economic interests that led them in other directions, or were driven to do their own thing by dint of bureaucratic inertia.

In Afghanistan, there are at least as many (and perhaps more) donors, agencies, and NGOs; more pressing humanitarian needs; a greater political and geographic fragmentation of authority; and a weaker central government. All of this has compounded the problem.

Some analysts have urged a decentralized aid program, with the laudable intention of increasing responsiveness to local needs and avoiding the delays associated with a weak government in Kabul (ICG 2001, 3). Decentralization, however, also inhibits national strategic planning, weakens central ministries, and reinforces centrifugal political tendencies. Some aid officials are reluctant to endorse Afghan development plans that envisage aid as a tool of political consolidation, a carrot to be used to extend the sway of the central government and to reward loyal constituencies and clients. As Stockton notes, while the notions of conditionality and "aid-induced pacification" may be favored by the AIA, the UN Security Council, and by many within UNAMA, they are much more controversial in the aid and (especially) the humanitarian relief communities (Stockton 2002, 27). Because many ministries are controlled by warlords, some donor officials have been reluctant to work with these local counterparts for fear of sending a signal of acceptance of past human rights abuses and war crimes (Stockton 2002, 30–31). Conversely, the U.S. military continues to rely upon, and support, regional warlords as part of its military campaign against remnants of the Taliban and Al-Qaida.[36]

As a result, donor programs continue to be donor driven, and it is difficult to assess how much real effect the AACA and Afghanistan's National Development Framework actually have on donor disbursements. The NDF warns that "the development agenda must be owned domestically, and the recipient country must be in the driver's seat." It further warns that "donor-funded investment projects, unless they are anchored in coherent programs of government, are not sustainable" (Stockton 2002, 63).

Stockton's assessment on this issue is blunt:

> While there appears to be a wide measure of agreement about the strategy to transfer authority to the AIA and the primary importance of capacity-building for Afghan institutions, the daily practice of pro- gramme delivery and operational coordination seems yet to be little changed, and certainly Afghans are not yet occupying the driver's seats of most parts of the international assistance effort, Indeed, many of the more high-level inter-agency meetings are reported to take place with no Afghan involvement at all. (Stockton 2002, 32)

There are no easy answers to the paradoxes and trade-offs of host-country ownership. As concluded elsewhere with regard to the Palestinian case, however, it is important that these dilemmas are recognized for what they are, rather than simply being swept under the carpet. Moreover, it is particularly important, when doing so, to recognize the immense political importance of, and hence politicization of, aid resources (Brynen 2000, 212–213).

Politics, Patronage, and Payoffs

This final point made above suggests the need to assert—and perhaps reassess—some truisms of political economy:

• *Aid is political.* Aid is a source of power and enrichment, whether in Palestine, Afghanistan, or elsewhere. How it is disbursed, by whom, and to whom has important implications for local balances of power and the shape of bureaucratic development. The notion that aid has political consequences is almost universally accepted in the aid community today, as is the notion that negative consequences can sometimes stem from the best of intentions. However, it is not always the case that these consequences are understood by agency personnel, whose analyses may be shaped by either the universalist, nondiscriminatory, need-oriented ethos of humanitarian relief work, or by the technical parameters of their particular sectoral specializations.

• *Corruption is bad.* This is even more universally recognized in the aid community. Corruption siphons public resources into private pockets, fuels criminality, weakens institutions, erodes public confidence, subverts accountability, and undermines programs and development strategies. In Palestine, corruption has been less of a problem than commonly perceived, but perceptions of corruption have been highly corrosive of public confidence in the PA and the aid effort more generally. In an Afghanistan that is even poorer and weakly institutionalized, the dangers of corruption are even greater.

• *Patronage is dysfunctional.* This is also accepted as a truism. (Well, sort of.) It is also a lesson that requires more careful examination.

In Palestine, political patronage by the PA is rightly pointed to as a major root cause of poor financial transparency, weak institutional capacities, and the fiscal unsustainability of the pre-intifada Palestinian budget. Arafat was and is suspicious of alternate power centers, strong figures, and rules that limit his autonomy and influence. Consequently, he managed a chain of patron-client relations, partly financed by the public payroll and partly by off-the-book resources, that reached deep into the PA, the security services, Fatah (a national revolutionary movement), and local communities. Eliminating this patronage is now a central focus of U.S.-backed reform efforts, blamed for poor Palestinian performance and for sustaining the violence that has wracked the area since September 2000.

The political assessment of Fatah patronage depends heavily, however, on the strategic choices made by Arafat. The Palestinian leader chose to tolerate violence, use it as a negotiating tool, and was reluctant to spend the political capital to rein it in. Now it may be too late, with his resources sharply diminished, and having lost control of his party rank-and-file, grassroots activists, and "the street." Had Arafat instead used political patronage to control, contain, or prevent violence—had he chosen a better strategy, or more sensibly linked Palestinian goals, strategy, and tactics—all of this may well have resulted in a different political outcome.

The economic and institutional effects of patronage also depend on choices. Palestinian patronage showed scant regard for merit or institution building, thrived on a lack of transparency, and even fostered abuse and corruption. This is not unusual, as a brief survey of political development in the Palestine Liberation Organization's former Lebanese sanctuary would quickly indicate. It is not always so, however: Jordan's political system, too, depends heavily on patronage and (royal) favoritism but does so generally within the context of the stronger institutions, accountability of a sort, and the rule of law. Legislators in Western democracies spend considerable time engaged in "constituency service," pork-barrel politics, legislative log rolling, and similar activities, but in ways that fall within agreed rules and do not inhibit national development. State leaders in those same countries invariably make budget, expenditure, and other economic decisions with an eye to political constituencies and reelection.

In Afghanistan, as noted in the discussion above, there is considerable tension over the use of aid resources for political purposes. Politicians and diplomats tend to see it as an important raison d'être of the entire aid effort, which is in their view intended to consolidate a new post-Taliban, Al-Qaida–free political order. The Afghan NDF is clear about the need to utilize aid resources to "[re-establish] the national unity of the country on the basis of strong institutions and the rule of law."[37] The AACA's desire to rein in excessively independent NGO activity, shift aid resources to government channels, discipline donors to support national priorities, and raise additional funds for budget support (and security sector reform) reflects the importance of all of these in facilitating political consolidation as well as development.

Aid agencies, and especially relief agencies, are more suspicious, as also noted above. Certainly, they need to be suspicious of patronage that taxes scarce resources, fuels corruption, weakens institutions, aims at reinforcing political factions, benefits individuals, or inflates bureaucratic empires. It would be ludicrous, however, if Afghanistan were held to a level of apolitical economic planning that would be alien to most donor countries or UN member states and deprived of key policy instruments at a time of overwhelming need.

The trick in all of this, once again, is to face up to the economic choices and political imperatives, discuss them, address them. Instead of condemning the politicization of aid, or technocratically ignoring it, it is incumbent to find ways of doing things that contribute to sustainable social and economic development *as well as* political consolidation, to patronage *and* institution building, to *both* peace and prosperity. It is not clear that this was adequately done in Palestine, and as a result donors (and Palestinians) lost the opportunity to construct a proto-state that looked more like Amman and less like Beirut.

The task will be even harder in an Afghanistan afflicted by poverty, warlordism, and a weak state. It is not, however, impossible.

Notes

Research support from the United States Institute of Peace and the Social Sciences and Humanities Research Council of Canada is gratefully acknowledged.
    1. U.S. secretary of state Warren Christopher, speaking at Columbia University, September 20, 1993.

2. For a detailed examination of international assistance to Palestine prior to the collapse of the peace process, see Brynen (2000).

3. These were the Palestinian-Israeli Declaration of Principles, or "Oslo Accords" (September 1993), the (Paris) Protocol on Economic Relations (April 1994), two agreements on the Transfer of Powers and Responsibilities (August 1994, August 1995), the Palestinian-Israeli Interim Agreement (September 1995), the Protocol Concerning Redeployment in Hebron (January 1997), and the Wye Memorandum (October 1998).

4. For an extensive discussion of this, see Forman and Patrick (2000).

5. For a more detailed account, see Brynen (2000, 172–178) and Lia (1998).

6. World Bank (1998b, 36, 38); World Bank (2002b, 2).

7. For a diagram of these, see Brynen (2000, 88).

8. The aid "coordination" aspect of UNSCO was emphasized to assuage Israeli opposition to any leading UN role in the peace process. Despite this, UNSCO did play a quiet but significant political role.

9. To some extent this was attributed to changed circumstances or updated assessments. However, there were also other reasons. Donors provided more funds to education and health than first anticipated, in part because it was easy to work in these sectors due to greater PA institutional capacity. They provided much less than needed to agriculture, due to the political sensitivity of land issues, and also because of the weakness of the PA Ministry of Agriculture.

10. The figure of $1.4 billion in new aid was something of a fiction, constructed by adding together various overlapping categories of current, planned, and possible future aid. The purpose of this pledge inflation was to bolster pro–peace process forces in the territories on the eve of Palestinian elections. See Brynen (2000, 76).

11. A cross-national study of business leaders showed that there is much less bribe paying in Palestine than is typically the case in other developing areas. See Sewell (2001).

12. World Bank and the Government of Japan (2000), *Aid Effectiveness in the West Bank and Gaza*, paragraph 5.3, based on the comparative findings of World Bank (1998a).

13. Private correspondence with a World Bank official, October 8, 2002.

14. "Palestinian Refugees Face Acute Humanitarian Crisis, Head of UN Relief Agency Says," *UN News Center*, November 18, 2002, at http://www.un.org/apps/news/story.asp?NewsID=5290&Cr=unrwa&Cr1=.

15. The text of the president's remarks can be found at http://www.whitehouse.gov/news/releases/2002/06/20020624-3.html.

16. The text of the plan can be found at http://www.mopic.gov.ps/key_decuments/100day.asp.

17. These are in the areas of civil society, elections, financial accountability, judicial and rule of law reform, market economics, local government, and ministerial and civil service reform.

18. For an incisive assessment of this point, see ICG (2002).

19. There is a voluminous literature on the "relief to development" continuum, examining the disjunctures and unintended externalities of each and suggesting ways to reduce these. Usually, however, the literature assumes a general

path from humanitarian emergency to economic reconstruction and sustainable development—not the other way around.

20. The death toll from the U.S.-backed campaign appears to be relatively limited given its scope, in the low thousands.

21. For detailed information on the ARTF, see World Bank, "Afghanistan Reconstruction Trust Fund," at http://www.worldbank.org/artf.

22. For the text of the Bonn Agreement, see http://www.uno.de/frieden/afghanistan/talks/agreement.htm.

23. The text of the NDF can be found at http://www.undp.org/afghanistan/ndf.pdf.

24. United Nations Office on Drugs and Crime (2002). The report estimates that opium production in 2002 returned to its 1990s levels and that total income to farmers would be in the hundreds of millions of dollars—that is, levels equivalent to foreign aid disbursements.

25. For an excellent overview of donor coordination and related issues, upon which this chapter depends heavily, see AREU (2002). See also Duffield, Grossman, and Leader (2002); and Stockton (2002).

26. http://www.aims.org.pk.

27. Ashraf Ghani, quoted by Agence France-Presse, September 26, 2002, via AFGHANDEV listserv.

28. "UNHCR Warned Over Rapid Afghan Refugee Returns," Agence France-Presse, November 5, 2002, via AFGHANDEV listserv.

29. UNDP, "Afghanistan Fact Sheet," at http://www.undp.org/afghanistan/FactSheet-final.doc; World Bank, "(ARTF) Table of Donor Contributions as of 30 October 2002," at http://www.worldbank.org/artf. Given that not all funds received by the ARTF have been disbursed and that the ARTF supports more than just recurrent expenditures, actual levels of budget support are even lower.

30. "World Donors Praise Kabul's Budget and Development Plans," *New York Times*, October 14, 2002.

31. "Karzai Pushes for Reconstruction Projects to Begin," The United States Mission to the European Union, at http://www.useu.be/Categories/GlobalAffairs/Afghanistan%20Future/Sept1302KarzaiReconstructionPush.html.

32. Press briefing by Manoel de Almeida e Silva, UNAMA spokesman, October 31, 2002, via AFGHANDEV listserv.

33. Afghan officials complain that local Afghan staff are paid up to fifty times more by agencies and NGOs than the local public sector pay scale and that international staff are paid as much as 1,000 to 2,000 times more.

34. *IRIN News*, October 7, 2002, via AFGHANDEV listserv.

35. This might done be through building donor consortiums around specific donor-supported institutions or local areas; integrated planning that calls upon the sectoral specializations of multiple donors; project planning or management committees that involve both local stakeholders and key donors; cost-saving harmonization of procedures; shared field offices; or a variety of other approaches.

36. "US Under Fire for Backing Afghan Warlords," *Financial Times*, November 6, 2002, via AFGHANDEV listserv.

37. Statement of President Karzai on January 25, 2002, at http://wwww.reliefweb.int/w/rwb.nsf/0/dbc457336cf852d249256b4f0024ceba?Open Document.

14

Donors in War-Torn Societies: A Case Study of El Salvador

Chris van der Borgh

This chapter aims to improve our understanding of the role that foreign assistance plays in a postwar society, looking at the ways external donors and their counterparts intervene in a highly sensitive political context. The focus is on development programs that have as their objectives to alleviate poverty of the population and to strengthen local capacities by way of institution building and the strengthening of local governance. This kind of program is generally not addressed in the peace accords and, therefore, called "low priority." "High-priority" programs are directed at activities that have a direct relationship with the implementation of the peace accords. They support the agreements made in the accords or target specific groups, such as ex-combatants, a new police force, and vulnerable or politically sensitive groups in society (e.g., refugees, ex-combatants). Low-priority programs do not aim to support the implementation of specific agreements in peace accords but instead focus on the process of postwar reconstruction, development, and peacebuilding. It is regular development assistance in a postwar context that aims to support development and to combat poverty in combination with the strengthening of local institutions and organizations.

In modern development practice it has become common sense to combine these objectives, as it is generally assumed that strengthened capacities of organizations, institutions, or entire sectors are needed to make development sustainable. Most external donors nowadays claim to strengthen local capacities in some way. Some focus exclusively on the strengthening of local capacities as an end in itself; others treat it as a means to build civil society and to deepen the democratic process (Carothers 1999). But even in programs of rural development, attention paid to capacity building has increased as most external actors claim to meet local needs through the participation of target groups while simultaneously supporting processes of organization and institution building through empowerment, which is assumed to improve governance in general.

This chapter looks at rural development programs in Chalatenango, a province in El Salvador that was heavily affected by the civil war. A large number of international donors started working in this department with a view to supporting the process of reconstruction. The programs discussed in this chapter were initiated or supported by various donors, including multilateral, bilateral, and private agencies. The focus of this chapter is on the different interpretations and practices of capacity building in a postwar context. The chapter looks at the intentions and contributions to build local capacities. It also discusses the practice of intervention itself by looking at the processes in which development programs become embedded in local society as well as the mechanisms external agents create to establish contacts with and between local and national actors. As political tensions are still considerable, the decision to work with particular actors and to bypass others is crucial. Do external agents choose to work with government agents, groups from civil society, or political parties (or a combination of them)? How do external agents and local counterparts establish their agenda? Is this agenda related to broader government policies, and if so, how? And in what ways, both intended and unintended, do the programs affect local governance? Finally, the question of what can be learned from this is addressed.

I start with a brief analysis of the Salvadoran peace process, which can be regarded as a relative success story. I then sketch the social and political context of the department of Chalatenango as the specific context in which development programs had to operate. Next, I discuss the challenges that external actors saw themselves confronted with, paying attention to the role, focus, and dilemmas faced by external agents working toward strengthening local capacities. Three development programs are analyzed in detail: (1) a governmental program of social infrastructure, (2) a regional development program coordinated by the United Nations Development Program, and (3) a program of reconciliation at the community level implemented by an NGO. The chapter is based on extensive fieldwork conducted between 1994 and 2002.[1] During the research periods the interventions of a wide range of development organizations were analyzed, and attention was paid to decisionmaking processes at different points of each intervention chain, particularly the agendas and actions of local organized actors. The more general aim of the research was to assess the consequences of these development programs on political processes at both the village and the provincial levels.[2]

The Salvadoran Peace Process:
A Relative Success Story

Compared with peace processes in, say, Bosnia, Cambodia, and Angola, the case of El Salvador is commonly depicted as a success story of multidimensional peacekeeping (UN 1995). The Salvadoran peace process culminated in peace accords signed in January 1992 leading to an effective cease-fire, to the participation of the former guerrilla movement FMLN in national elections, to the military's retreat from political life, and to the building of a new civilian police force. One can argue that the situation in El Salvador was somewhat less complicated than in other societies, since by the start of the 1990s there existed a stalemate between the military and the guerrilla movement, and the end of the Cold War permitted the UN to play a more active role in the peace process, leading to negotiations between the parties.[3] Also crucial was the radical shift in U.S. foreign policy from a costly counterinsurgency strategy to active support for a negotiated compromise.[4] During the peace talks and the implementation of the peace accords, the United States put pressure on the Salvadoran military. This active involvement of both the UN and the United States, followed by wide international support for the rebuilding of the country, certainly contributed to the Salvadoran story.

The limited salience of ethnic identity in Salvadoran society in general and in political organization in particular may have contributed to the reaching of an agreement, by making it unnecessary to address issues of territorial secession and minority rights. Nevertheless, there were many extremely sensitive issues that made it difficult to reach a consensus. There still were different interpretations as to the causes of the war and how they should be addressed. The opposition and the guerrilla movement had used a socialist discourse that emphasized the need to subvert the political and economic structures that caused widespread exclusion of large sections of the population. The right-wing government of the ARENA (Alianza Republicana Nationalista, or Republican National Alliance), by contrast, had emphasized the international communist threat and highlighted the importance of maintaining the status quo.

The Salvadoran peace accords consisted of a deal between the two parties whereby the government approved further democratization and demilitarization of Salvadoran society, while the FMLN acquiesced not to discuss the economic policies during the peace talks. This resulted in peace accords that focused on reforms in both the security sector and the political system, while largely leaving out socioeconomic issues.[5] These agreements were successful in ending political violence and civil war and bolstered the process of democratization but were unable to improve human security and foster the social inclusion of the poor.[6]

One of the flaws of the Salvadoran peace process was to make political and economic transition highly separated processes. Although the political transition was at the core of the peace accords, the economic reforms were entirely defined by the government, which had been in power since 1989 and radically redefined the Salvadoran development model along orthodox neoliberal lines.[7] The ARENA party won the presidential elections in both 1994 and 1999, and so economic policy-making remained the exclusive domain of a party that represents the interests of new and old economic elites. Moreover, consensus building on social and economic issues has never really been practiced, either in the peace accords or in the proposed mechanisms to build consensus on the economic policies that were laid down in the accords (Zamora 2001). Although the economic model led to economic growth in the 1990s, and to some poverty reduction, poverty remained a structural problem and large sections of the population continued to be deprived of basic services such as health care and water (Rivera Campos 2000, 216–218).

Defenders of the model argue that in the longer-term economic growth and liberalization will lead to a reduction of poverty and increased social stability, whereas critics emphasize the need for equity in order to build a stable peace. In their view, peace, economic growth, and equity should and can be aimed at simultaneously through measures such as the redistribution of income and investment in natural, human, and physical capital (Boyce and Pastor 1997).[8] This may require a more active and prominent role of the state in the definition and implementation of sectoral policies (among them agriculture), as well as a more moderate and balanced process of economic liberalization.

The inability of the Salvadoran economic model to address the historical problem of social exclusion also partly explains the persistence of violence in Salvadoran society. Both violence and social exclusion are structural problems throughout Salvadoran history, although their manifestations have changed, along with the rest of Salvadoran society. The massive migration of Salvadorans to the United States, and the importance of remittances they have sent home, are just two examples of the profound changes in Salvadoran society since the late 1970s.[9]

The remittances have become extremely important both for individual family members and for the national economy. In fact, remittances are nowadays far more important as a source of foreign currency than earnings from coffee exports, which once were the backbone of the Salvadoran economy. These developments have led to new tensions, conflicts, and violence such as crime, youth gangs, and localized conflicts over the use of land.

One of the most worrisome features of postwar El Salvador is the increase in violence and homicides as compared with the civil war period. This violence has largely become depoliticized since the end of the war, and it has become an option for a multitude of actors. Contemporary violence is partly a legacy of the civil war. It is the result of failed social integration of ex-combatants, of a security vacuum due to problems in building the new civilian police force, and of the internalization of violence over many years of civil war. But it is also the consequence of a process of modernization that despite some economic growth and poverty alleviation has not been able to address the chronic problems associated with social exclusion.

It was under these complicated and changing conditions that external donors redirected their funding to support a process of postwar rebuilding and development from 1992 onward. Foreign assistance was extremely important during the war years, as a number of external donors supported the political agendas of either the Salvadoran government or the popular movements. For example, the principal governmental donor during the war years, the U.S. Agency for International Development, funded projects that were part of a counterinsurgency strategy. Conversely, a number of NGOs from western Europe, Scandinavia, and the United States supported popular movements that were closely allied to the FMLN (Biekart 1999). Hence, external donors were themselves political players in Salvadoran society. The contradictions between donors influenced the choices that were made in the postwar period as USAID opted to continue working with the Salvadoran government, while other donors were more reluctant to do so.[10] However, in the postwar period the political tensions between external donors rapidly diminished.

The peace accords stated that the Plan for National Reconstruction should be based on consensus. In fact, it proved difficult to reach a consensus on an agenda for postwar reconstruction.[11] The plan was drawn up by the Salvadoran government almost entirely without consulting the FMLN, which endorsed the plan for tactical reasons. In practice, many low-priority programs directed at poverty alleviation were largely uncoordinated and took place outside the sphere of the PNR. There was a multitude of initiatives that aimed to foster postwar rebuilding, all with their own agendas and rationale, and many of them based on foreign assistance.[12] Due to the interest of external donors in working in marginalized and war-torn areas such as Chalatenango, the role of foreign assistance in development efforts was considerable in these regions.

War-Torn Chalatenango: Damaged, Divided, and Externally Funded

When the peace accords were signed, Chalatenango was a heavily damaged and divided department that counted on the interest of numerous external donors to implement programs in the region.[13] Many of its inhabitants had escaped the fighting by fleeing to neighboring Honduras or to the safer southern zones of the department. Much of the physical infrastructure was damaged, and government services like health care and education were either neglected or completely absent. Many inhabitants became dependent upon food donations; increasing numbers migrated to the national capital or the United States.

One of the most striking features of postwar Chalatenango is the virtual division of the department during the war years and the consequences of it that still exist. In the northeast of the department, formerly under the control of the guerrilla movement, government structures had virtually disappeared during the war as mayors were expelled by the FMLN and fled from their municipalities. The people still living in these areas generally sympathized with the FMLN, and they were encouraged by the FMLN to form local community organizations.[14] These popular organizations formed an influential umbrella organization, the Coordination of Rural Communities (CCR),[15] which became extremely important in delivering services like education and health care independently of formal government services. This was done together with local and international NGOs and in close cooperation with the FMLN leadership. Hence, during the war years the northeastern part of the province developed its own institutions and public services, outside the influence of the government, and was funded by donations from abroad. In the other parts of the department, the government had maintained substantial influence, with the military continuing to play an important role in local politics. Although the military had formally dismantled its paramilitary structures, compulsory participation in civil patrols still existed while independent popular organizing was discouraged.

By the end of the war, civil society had become either politicized in the northeastern zone—where popular organization had been strong but controlled by the FMLN—or virtually absent in the south where it had been thwarted by the military. The challenges and opportunities to build upon local structures were, therefore, quite different in the two parts of the department. In the years following the civil war the community organizations in the northeast played a crucial role in many of the local reconstruction activities, but they faced several problems that were inherent to the transition process from war to peace. Under the harsh conditions of the war years, these community organizations had fostered a tradition of solidarity and militancy that had provided the inhabitants with some degree of support and protection. When the war ended and the external threat disappeared, it became more difficult to organize villagers in the same way as during the war years. This was mainly because community organizations now became critical in the management of a large number of projects in their villages, for which they were hardly prepared. The hierarchical structure of some of these organizations became problematic, as well as the tendency of villagers to wait and see what their representatives would do for them. Despite these problems, the community organizations in this region reflected a tradition of popular organizing that was not only unique for rural El Salvador but could also be a valuable foundation for the rebuilding of the department.

When the war ended, there was a strong increase in the number of local organizations in both parts of Chalatenango. This may point at the resilience of civil society, but it may also be the consequence of development organizations stimulating their formation. Many newly formed organizations directed their activities at the acquisition of externally funded projects. Whether these organizations will prove to be merely opportunistic organizations that try to capture funds, or whether they will become organizations with their own public agenda, is partly dependent upon the way that external development organizations will work with them. We will return to this question in the next section.

Government structures remained rather centralized in the postwar period. There was no strong provincial political structure in place, although some ministries, like the local department of the Ministry of Education, became more important in the implementation of services. The governor and a small staff are the formal link between the central government and the municipalities; but in practice their role is rather limited. The governor is appointed by the president and is often a member of the ruling party. In the case of Chalatenango, the governor had been in place since the war years and is generally seen as a conservative figure. Although a new municipal code was adopted in 1986, municipalities still received very limited state funding and had a limited capacity to make policy.[16] This situation improved somewhat in 1997 when the municipal budget was raised.[17]

In the years following the civil war, the population living in the formerly FMLN-controlled areas still distrusted the government (both local and national), and so the reestablishment of public administration in these areas was problematic. Refugees returning from Honduras, who originally did not come from this area, had repopulated many of the villages in the area during the war years. Because the mayors of these villages had been elected by the former inhabitants (of whom many had fled to other parts of the province), they were not considered to represent the new inhabitants. Therefore, transitional Municipal Councils for Reconstruction and Development were created in which mayors and members of community organizations would discuss policies. These bodies, however, often functioned poorly. The municipal elections of March 1994 (taking place two years after the peace accords were signed) only partly put an end to this situation; owing to registration problems, many were still voting in municipalities other than the ones in which they were actually living. Hence, in the postwar years, the existing structures of local administration and political representation were still insufficient to adequately address the needs of the inhabitants of the northeastern zone. For this reason, special attention was still needed for transitional measures.

Strengthening Local Governance in a War-Torn Context

Former conflict zones, like Chalatenango, are often characterized by highly contested structures of authority and legitimacy. Such a situation is a potential minefield for international donors aiming to support some kind of political, economic, or social rebuilding. The ways in which development programs become embedded in local society (which is to a large extent reflected by the actors they work with or pass by), and how policy formulation and implementation take place (which is about the communication and interactions between external and local actors), are, therefore, political processes that may affect the future balance of power.[18] The three programs that are discussed later in this chapter explicitly took into account the political polarization in the department of Chalatenango and aimed at improving relations between local actors (civil society, government, and private sector) and strengthening their capacities to give direction to the postwar process of reconstruction.

Thus, the three organizations shared the goals of supporting local organizations, of streamlining policy processes through coordination and reconciliation, and more generally of fostering local governance.

The objectives of strengthening capacities and fostering (good) governance, however, were applied in very different ways. This was not surprising given the open-ended nature of these objectives.[19] Smillie concludes in his review of how the concept of capacity building has been used throughout the years, that "because contexts differ so widely and because the intent of a capacity building effort may differ from one agency or one situation to another, writers offer general, all-inclusive and high-sounding definitions" (Smillie 2001, 17). Hewitt del Alcantara states that "the concept of governance is used by different groups of different ideological persuasions, for a number of different and often contradictory ends" (Hewitt del Alcantara 1999, 126, 131). In the present chapter, the concept of capacity building refers to the intention of and the process in which external actors aim at supporting local abilities of collective actors to discuss and define their own needs and policy agendas and to implement them in a coordinated and concerted manner. Hence, in all these interventions there is the intention to go beyond the strengthening of separate organizations in order to foster policy processes or local governance, which can take the form of coordination, consensus building, or any other form of local management.

It is important to emphasize that external donors are by no means outside actors, but that their actions and resources are part and parcel of local society. In the case of Chalatenango, foreign assistance played a very important role in reconstruction and development activities, and most projects of infrastructure (roads, latrines, buildings, water systems) as well as credit schemes were funded by external donors. This had three important consequences on local governance that are characteristic of marginalized rural areas emerging from civil war. First, foreign funding became an important resource for both local government and local organizations in Chalatenango. In fact, a number of organizations were founded to obtain external funds. This led to situations in which local government agencies were dependent on foreign assistance, while in other cases community organizations had more resources than governments. Second, foreign assistance replaced central government funding in a number of cases, due to the fact that international donors were more inclined to work in the relatively marginalized departments of the country, thus relieving the central government of this responsibility. According to Pearce this creates a danger of international donors becoming substitutes for national governments that do not assume their responsibility vis-à-vis the poorest sectors in society, thus reinforcing historic exclusions. Moreover, Pearce argues that externally funded projects have the risk of becoming "islands of hope" that are completely dependent upon the goodwill, generosity, and ultimately the political predisposition of international donors (Pearce 1999). Third, foreign assistance is, by its nature, extremely fragmented as funds are supplied and channeled by a myriad of foreign and national organizations, all using their own mechanisms and channels to reach their target groups.[20] As a result, the degree of planning and coordination between these organizations is limited, leading to a variety of ad hoc local initiatives. Whereas all intervening organizations each claim to work with local organizations and to strengthen local capacities in the process, there are also unintended consequences, like dependency and lack of coordination, that are the result of *combined* and *uncoordinated* interventions. Yet it can be argued that a diversity of local organizations trying to gain access to foreign funding represents, to some extent, a form of decentralization of foreign assistance. This may be of importance in a postwar context where the risk of politicization of aid is considerable.

We now turn to an analysis of three interventions that took into account these problems: (1) a program of municipal infrastructure that was implemented by a government agency and funded by USAID; (2) a program to strengthen municipal governance, implemented by a local NGO funded by Scandinavian donors; and (3) a UN program that paid particular attention to the building of provincial development mechanisms, funded by the Italian government.[21] All three aimed to strengthen local capacities, paying particular attention to the reconciliation of and coordination between local actors.

Municipalities in Action:
Mayors, Open Town Meetings, and Small Projects

The objective of the Municipalities in Action (MEA) program was to provide municipalities with financial and technical aid in order to strengthen the democratic process (SRN 1993). The Secretary for National Reconstruction (SRN) that implemented the program was one of the main governmental organizations that worked in the framework of the National Reconstruction Plan. It embodied the transformation of a former counterinsurgency organization that had developed the program in close association with its principal donor, USAID. This was a reason why community organizations in northeastern Chalatenango, and NGOs linked to the popular movement, distrusted the institution and its programs. However, although the SRN was widely known as a government institution with ties to the right-wing ARENA party, there was little space for the Salvadoran government to politicize the program with USAID closely monitoring it.[22] USAID also tried to secure financing for the program by lobbying the Salvadoran government to establish a local tax structure based on the taxation of local landowners. This would provide the municipalities with more funds than what the MEA program was giving. The Salvadoran government was, however, reluctant to implement this reform, although pressure from mayors and parliament eventually led to a substantial increment of the municipal budget.[23]

Within the MEA a fixed sum of money was donated to a municipality for the construction of small infrastructure works, such as school buildings, communal roads, and small water systems (SRN 1994). Disbursement of funds was made conditional upon the organization of Open Town Meetings (an institution outlined in the municipal code), to be organized four times a year, in which citizens could make requests for specific projects. The mayor and the town council prioritized these needs and presented these to the SRN, which had the final say on the basis of technical criteria. The department of Chalatenango was one of the most important regions for the MEA program, as twenty out of the thirty-three municipalities were reconstruction municipalities and received higher amounts of funding. Many of these municipalities were located in the former FMLN zones, where the SRN was generally distrusted. Many community organizations were suspicious of the government, which was perceived as having been responsible for substantial suffering in these areas. To deal with this situation, it was decided that Municipal Councils for Reconstruction and Development (in which participated mayors and representatives of the community organizations that distrusted the SRN) should decide upon the priorities that were expressed in the Open Town Meetings.

The experiences of the MEA program in the politically sensitive northeastern zone were mixed, depending on the local political context, the size of the municipality, and the attitude and behavior of the mayor and the community organizations. For example, in San Antonio los Ranchos, a very small municipality consisting of only one village, the community organization and the mayor, who did not live in the village, cooperated. The mayor had no other choice than to work with the communal leaders, who in turn were quite open to cooperation. The situation was more complicated in neighboring Guarjila, a village that was also located in the FMLN's zone of influence but belonged to the municipality of Chalatenango Town. This was one of the larger municipalities in the province, and only some of its hamlets and villages—which were among the most heavily damaged villages of the municipality—

were located in the zone that was formerly controlled by the FMLN.

The ARENA mayor and the communal leaders from Guarjila did not trust each other in the postwar years. Community leaders preferred to work with NGOs whom they already knew and continued to govern their own village without any interference from the mayor. The mayor, however, was not interested in working with these leaders, as she preferred to allocate the funds in the municipal town itself—a town that had hardly been affected by the war.[24]

The MEA program had taken into account some of the difficulties in the former war zones and, accordingly, chose to give priority to the most affected communities (calling them "reconstruction municipalities") using the Municipal Councils for Reconstruction and Development to decide upon the allocation of funds. These measures were, however, too limited and did not give rise to large-scale practices of concerted action. More attention paid to the internal problems of these councils would have made them more successful, and in places like Guarjila outside support to bring the sides together was needed. This, however, is time-consuming, and it requires specific capacities of the staff. It may be doubted whether the SRN could have played such a role, given the distrust shown toward it by a number of community organizations. Furthermore, the dominant role assigned to mayors was in some respects detrimental to a process of reconciliation and coordination. When coordination did not succeed, mayors were allowed to set the priorities. Some of them did this in a balanced way, taking into account the needs of the entire municipality, but more frequently the actions of mayors were motivated by political or personal interests.

Stricter guidelines set by the donor of the program for the allocation of resources within municipalities were also needed. Within reconstruction municipalities, there were large differences between the levels of damage of its villages and hamlets, which were not taken into account by the MEA program. The MEA program spent the largest amount of funds in the years following the civil war, when the mechanisms to allocate these funds were still rather weak. It might have been better to spread these funds over a longer period of time. Furthermore, the selection of the reconstruction municipalities was rather arbitrary. There was some ill feeling that the villages in the northeastern zone were nearly all designated as reconstruction municipalities, even though they already had more access to funds, especially from international NGOs. This was because they were well organized and also the most harmed by the war. However, the internally displaced people in the southern part of the province had also suffered from the war, and the infrastructure in their (often newly established) communities was quite deficient as well. Hence, the distribution of funds and the selection of target groups was a political process in which intermediary persons and organizations (SRN, mayors, community organizations) tried to attract funds and play a role in defining needs and creating images of who are poorest and in most need. The challenges of programs of poverty alleviation in general, and in war-torn societies in particular, lie in truly reaching the grassroots and building a concerted agenda of reconstruction.

Program for Municipal Capacity Building: Reconciliation and Concerted Action

Compared to the activities of the SRN, the Program for Municipal Capacity Building in El Salvador (PROCAP) took a different approach. PROCAP was founded in November 1992 with the support of the American Friends Service of the Quakers. It began by exploring the problems encountered by the Municipal Councils for Reconstruction and Development. PROCAP found that distrust between mayors and community organizations was still considerable. It, therefore, organized workshops and seminars to build confidence, to formulate a concerted agenda of action, and eventually to establish local development committees.[25] PROCAP was funded by a group of private and bilateral Scandinavian donors who coordinated between themselves and held a very flexible attitude toward the development of PROCAP's program.[26] PROCAP did not have funds to implement actual projects, but it did help local groups to formulate project proposals for submission to donor agencies and development organizations working in the area.

The experience of PROCAP in the northeastern zone—on which it focused its activities—was generally positive. The organization was able to enter the area easily as it had already conducted informal talks with members of the FMLN and the umbrella organization, the CCR (which represented the community organizations from this area). In its workshops, it brought together the mayor, members of the municipal board, and the representatives from all hamlets. In these workshops the main problems in the municipality were analyzed, possible solutions were discussed, and priorities for action were defined. It may be argued that the initiative of PROCAP was complementary to the MEA program, but this was true only to some extent. PROCAP started when the MEA program was already in full swing. Moreover, the initiative of PROCAP did not lead to a lasting cooperation between mayors and community organizations in all municipalities. In the municipality of San Antonio los Ranchos, PROCAP became deeply involved in a large-scale housing project. Less success was achieved in other municipalities, as the work of PROCAP was rather labor intensive, making it impossible to continue intensively in all municipalities. PROCAP also extended its activities to other sectors. Besides support for local organizing, it worked with youth and became involved in some projects concerning agricultural development. Hence, by extending its mandate, PROCAP became a "regular NGO" that aimed to support the postwar development of war-torn areas.

As PROCAP had no funds available for projects, its main asset was a capable and independent staff that, through "sensitive guidance" of local actors, tried to foster reconciliation and to build a concerted agenda of development.[27] On the one hand, it can even be argued that it was PROCAP's strength that it did not have funds for projects, as this avoided the creation of ad hoc mechanisms to channel these funds. On the other hand, it proved rather difficult to build sustainable local organizations, mainly because other organizations that funded projects did not work together with the development organizations founded by PROCAP, while some of them aimed to build similar local structures independently of PROCAP's initiative.[28] Hence, the strategies to stimulate coordination and concerted action were not coordinated among themselves. This was largely due to the fact that there was no unified donor strategy, making it extremely difficult to build lasting structures of local governance. It can be argued that the invisible hand of the donor community, with its myriad of channels of intervention and equal numbers of local counterparts implementing these interventions, restrained local coordination and the formation of a longer-term structure of governance.

Development Program for Internally Displaced, Repatriated, and Refugees

The objectives of the Development Program for Internally Displaced, Repatriated, and Refugees (PRODERE), by contrast, were ambitious, given that the program tried to coordinate the actions of both local actors and donors at a regional level, thereby building new forms of governance and concerted action more likely to be sustainable. PRODERE was one of the first UNDP initiatives to apply a human development approach to war-torn areas. It worked in several regions of Central America, including Chalatenango between 1990 and 1995. The PRODERE program in Chalatenango received a lot of attention for its innovative approach in which capacity building and reconciliation were central. The Italian government was the main donor of the program, with other donors funding parts of it.

The PRODERE program in El Salvador had some specific features that were of great importance for the way it established relations with different local actors. Most important was that although the Salvadoran government was formally the counterpart of the UNDP, its involvement in the program was limited. The relationship between the Salvadoran government and the UNDP had deteriorated in 1989 when, during the guerrilla offensive, the Salvadoran army ransacked the UNDP offices. After that, the UNDP had left the country and stayed in neighboring Guatemala until 1992. Government officials on their part distrusted the PRODERE program as it was considered an initiative of the former Christian Democrat government, together with the Italian Christian Democrats. Therefore, the Salvadoran government was not actively involved in the program.[29] This provided the staff of the program in Chalatenango with substantial autonomy to develop it according to its own view. For example, the staff successfully objected to bringing the program under the Secretary of National Reconstruction after the signing of the peace agreements because the PRODERE staff considered the SRN to be too politicized.[30]

PRODERE aimed to provide economic and social support to Chalatenango's population that had been hardest hit by the war. It developed from a program of humanitarian assistance into a program that focused on local governance, by supporting the formation of development mechanisms in which local actors would formulate and implement policies collectively. Since the program was started during the war years, staff concentrated on the problems of internally displaced people in the less conflict-ridden, government-controlled southern zone. In the course of 1991, when the peace agreements were about to be signed, PRODERE's activities in the northeastern zone were initiated.

In its first years, PRODERE actively supported the formation of new organizations, like small enterprises, cooperatives, and community organizations, in order to implement development projects with them.[31] PRODERE sought cooperation with NGOs and government agencies and was rather successful due to its capable and independent staff—most of whom had previously worked with the UN or international NGOs—and the considerable amount of funds it had at its disposal. The funding of direct needs of NGOs, local ministries, refugees, and other groups was a means to establish contacts and to inspire confidence. These contacts served as a basis for the development mechanisms or network organizations created from 1993 onward.[32] These network organizations came to be the spearhead of PRODERE.

Network organizations were formed in the fields of education, health care, human rights, economic development, and general affairs. They brought together the organized actors working in these policy areas, such as government agencies, NGOs, small enterprises, and community organizations. The main objectives were to coordinate activities, formulate policies, and establish contacts with external donors. The formation of the entities themselves was seen as an important contribution to the improvement of the interaction between state and civil society and to the transition to democracy. The network organizations functioned at several levels. For health care and education they covered the municipal, the subregional (north and south), and the provincial level. The economic network only existed at a provincial level.

The network organizations in health care and education had been important in discussions on the status of the autonomous structures of health care and education that had been created in the northeastern zone during the war years. The creation of these mechanisms together with the active involvement of PRODERE staff had a positive impact on negotiations with the central government, leading to partial solutions, mainly in the field of education. However, when PRODERE left, these negotiations became more difficult. This highlights the importance of the PRODERE staff in the negotiations about politically sensitive issues and the difficulties of these mechanisms to become autonomous (after the withdrawal of the staff).

By far the most successful of all network organizations was the Agency for Local Economic Development (ADEL), the agency that supported the economic development of Chalatenango. It consisted of approximately twenty members, among them enterprises, NGOs, and community organizations, while government agencies were represented in a Consultative Group.[33] The success of this agency was due partly to the absolute priority PRODERE accorded to it, supporting it technically and financially. The proactive role of PRODERE in the foundation of ADEL was extremely important in bringing together groups from the southern and northern parts of Chalatenango.[34] Furthermore, ADEL obtained fresh external funds to pay its technical staff, which partly came from the PRODERE program, thus sustaining the initiative.

ADEL initially gained the reputation of being extremely successful. However, by the end of the 1990s, tensions between the members of ADEL had increased and the agency was in serious crisis. The problems that ADEL faced were not related to political tensions but merely the result of the ambitious objectives of the agency, its problematic organizational structure, and of conflicts between some of its members. The ambitious objectives of ADEL included support for the economic development of Chalatenango, the coordination of activities, the development of a strategic framework, as well as external fund-raising for ADEL and its members. In practice, these objectives were extremely difficult to combine. Over time, attention paid to the political objectives of planning (and lobbying the provincial and central government) dwindled, while focus was increasingly turned to the technical expertise of the staff of ADEL and its capacity to attract external funds. This gave rise to conflicts between the salaried staff of ADEL and some of its member organizations, which claimed that ADEL had become "just another NGO."[35]

The network organization that aimed to address general affairs, the Provincial Corporation for the Development of Chalatenango (CODDICH), faced serious problems as well. It was founded in 1995 and included representatives of these four network organizations, political parties, mayors, community organizations, and NGOs.[36] It aimed to develop a fully fledged policy of integral development for the province and to represent Chalatenango toward external donors and the central government. According to the PRODERE staff, this initiative would simultaneously strengthen local capacities and spur the process of decentralization. The composition of CODDICH's leadership was appealing: A representative of a left-wing NGO together with the right-wing governor of Chalatenango headed the organization. Furthermore, the three members of parliament from Chalatenango (representing left-, center, and right-wing parties) were willing to cooperate for the benefit of Chalatenango. However, they cooperated with each other only when external donors were involved, yet hardly ever in parliament.

As in the case of the other network organizations, CODDICH weakened after the PRODERE program withdrew from Chalatenango. This was in part because the organization was still relatively new, with a very small technical staff, and its objectives were not clear and to some extent overlapped with those of ADEL. In this particular case, political tensions also played a role in the demise of the organization. In particular, the role of the governor was criticized by the director of the Foundation for Cooperation and Community Development of El Salvador (CORDES)—the most powerful NGO working in the northeastern zone—for dominating the organization and using it for its own political objectives.[37] Hence, the PRODERE program was successful in bringing together local actors, but it was far less successful in building institutions that were sustainable in the longer run. External support dwindled, partly because important providers of resources, such as external donors and central government, did not assign a central role to these organizations. ADEL, for example, never developed a working relationship with the central government, and the agency was largely bypassed in a large program of rehabilitation and development in Chalatenango (PROCHALATE).[38]

Relative Success Stories of Strengthening Local Governance

From the experiences discussed above, it appears it is possible to build organizations in which actors can come together and decide how funds are to be distributed (MEA) or to organize some kind of concerted action at a municipal or provincial level (PROCAP, PRODERE). In practice, however, we have seen that it is difficult to make the network organizations sustainable and to strengthen local governance in the longer run. In the short term, interventions that aimed to strengthen local governance helped to build network organizations in which local actors could decide upon priorities and so try to establish an agenda for concerted action. These network organizations, however, were fairly unstable, and their contribution to local governance in the longer term seems to be limited. What were the factors that were conducive to building local mechanisms of coordination and concerted action in the short and the medium-long term? What were some of the main problems in making these mechanisms sustainable?

A first factor that contributed to the successful establishment of local coordination and concerted action is that efforts to strengthen them were the core objective in the interventions and not merely added on in ad hoc fashion. A comparison of MEA and PROCAP illustrates this. In the MEA program, the funding of small infrastructural projects was combined with attention paid to local decisionmaking through Open Town Meetings. Although this breathed new life into the town meetings, the focus of the program was strongly dominated by the implementation of projects. In PROCAP's projects there were no funds available for infrastructure, and the objectives of reconciliation and concerted action at the municipal level were the core objectives of its intervention. Consequently, PROCAP gave far greater attention to local processes of planning and decisionmaking than was the case with the MEA program. This is not to say that service delivery and capacity building cannot be combined, but it shows that service delivery should be connected to more intense processes of planning, prioritization, and decisionmaking.

A second factor was the effort that took into account the political sensibilities and the will to build bridges between both sides. The MEA and PROCAP both worked through the Municipal Councils for Reconstruction and Development, while PRODERE brought together the governor and representatives of left-wing NGOs. However, the case of the MEA program shows that the formation of a Municipal Council in itself is not enough and that some kind of assistance is needed to make these councils work.

As a third factor, the cases show that it does make sense to stimulate cooperation between state agencies and civil society. The three programs all sought to work with government agencies, local organizations, and (in the case of some of PRODERE's mechanisms) also with firms and political parties. This led to new, albeit temporary, forms of cooperation. The MEA program focused on service delivery and used the Open Town Meetings to improve the allocation of funds. PROCAP and PRODERE supported local processes of decisionmaking and agenda setting, in which consensus building and longer-term planning were central. Whereas MEA had a rather limited view on local governance, by placing emphasis on service delivery and the use of these services, PRODERE and PROCAP emphasized the need for a concerted agenda of different institutions and groups.

A fourth factor is the presence of a qualified and experienced staff that were able to play the role of third party. This is needed to stimulate processes of reconciliation and concerted action. Minimal requirements are that the staff of these programs (both local and international) has, as Smillie notes, the "capacity to build capacity," which means that staff has experience or is trained by experienced persons and is independent and willing to work with local actors (Smillie 2001, 20). Both PROCAP and PRODERE played an extremely important role in creating and accompanying the newly created mechanisms while also playing an important role in the daily working of these mechanisms. In the case of the Municipalities in Action program, we saw that staff who could assist local processes of concerted action and reconciliation was the missing link. It is of particular importance that outside actors take into account their temporary presence and avoid creating dependencies. In the case of PRODERE, the withdrawal of the staff negatively affected the performance of the network organizations, revealing dependence on external capacities and resources, and the absence of a clear exit strategy for PRODERE. It is not easy to indicate how to find a balance between outside support and the need to avoid dependency, which is a major dilemma for many local development workers around the world. Dependency results from too much involvement by external actors and a possibly overly optimistic view on the involvement and primacy of local actors. The local staff of PRODERE may have been unaware that until the end of the program, they were the driving forces behind the newly created network organizations. Longer time frames of intervention may be one answer; more modest and realistic ambitions another.

A fifth factor is that some room for maneuver for the local staff vis-à-vis the external donors is needed in order to adapt intervention strategies to local agendas and to changes in the local context. Both PRODERE and PROCAP were able to adapt their frameworks of intervention, according to what in their view was necessary, after consultation with local actors. Comparatively, the format of the MEA program was less flexible.

With regard to the possibilities for longer-term success, this chapter has addressed two recurrent issues that deserve attention: the role of the central government and *local* coordination between external agents (both donors and their local counterparts). In the case of the war-torn and marginalized department of Chalatenango, the involvement of the central government has long been limited and remains so in the postwar years. Although a number of external donors formally channeled their funds via the central government, in practice they often worked with agencies that were created to channel external funds. The MEA program worked entirely on the basis of foreign assistance, whereas in the PRODERE program there was hardly any commitment of the central government. In the short run this may be a successful strategy to stimulate concerted action between local government entities and civil society groups. But in the long term, commitment from central government agencies is much needed. In the case of the MEA program, the main donor, USAID, systematically tried to convince the Salvadoran government of the need to develop mechanisms to maintain its funding. Although USAID's strategy failed, the budget for municipal governments was eventually raised. In the case of PRODERE, this commitment did not materialize. What is more, the staff of the network organizations did not prioritize the need to lobby the central government but preferred instead to raise external funds—this being a matter of survival of these organizations.

To be successful, network organizations that seek to foster local concerted action need to scale up and to lobby the provincial and central government to become involved. In contexts where the legitimacy of the government has been affected by the war, third parties (such as PROCAP and PRODERE) may, therefore, play an important role in bringing together local actors and building trust. However, not involving or lobbying the provincial and central government leads to forms of government that in the short run merely relieve the central government from the obligation of doing work with, or for, the marginalized sectors of society. Given that the Salvadoran government gave low priority to working in these regions, and given the negative consequences of neoliberal economic reform for many of the poor in El Salvador, the initiatives may appear to be merely donor driven, which in the long run is certainly unsustainable. Hence, in order to make interventions sustainable, there is a need to find a balance between donor interventions and longer-term commitments and policies by the national government.

Another issue of concern is the lack of coordination between external donors and their counterparts, which has serious consequences for local governance. By its nature, low-priority assistance is—like most foreign assistance—channeled in a fragmented and uncoordinated way, as donors decide upon their own funding channels and target groups. This leads to a myriad of ad hoc initiatives (projects) that are extremely difficult to streamline and that lead to an avalanche of project activities that are not interrelated. These initiatives do support tangible needs and do take into account the participation of local actors, but the sum of these interventions appears extremely difficult to manage, as the experiences discussed in this chapter have shown. If external donors would coordinate their programs and projects at a local level, both with each other and with local actors, while making their funding conditional upon provincial processes of planning and the involvement of government agencies, this could have positive consequences on local governance. Obviously, this is not the panacea; it does not necessarily change the adverse macro context in the country and may even create new problems and dilemmas. I agree with Pearce (1999) that peacebuilding is not primarily a dollar-driven process and that donors might find that the process is far less manageable than they envisage at present. The suggestions made above may, however, contribute to a more solid and integrated support for local governance in the long run, as well as to more realistic and modest ambitions of external donors.

Notes

I thank Jenny Pearce and Mario Fumerton for comments on an earlier draft of this chapter.

1. This included three longer periods of research: from October 1994 to March 1995, October 1995 to April 1996, and January 1997 to April 1997. Short visits were made in November 1999 and April/May 2002.

2. This chapter further elaborates on my doctoral research, which was published in Spanish in 2003.

3. Stedman (2001) argues, for example, that El Salvador was a relatively "easy case" of peace implementation because of the combination of a great willingness of international actors to commit to the effort of peacebuilding in

combination with a low "Conflict Difficulty Score," which is an indication for the problems one can expect in a process of peace implementation. For a detailed description of the Salvadoran peace process, see Acevedo (1992).

4. During the 1980s the United States supported the counterinsurgency strategy and funded both its military and nonmilitary components; see Cuenca (1992). In the period 1980–1991 military aid and economic assistance amounted to more than $4.5 billion; see Rosa (1993).

5. The peace accords contained a socioeconomic paragraph that included a land-titling program for ex-combatants of both sides, as well as a socioeconomic forum of government officials, employers, and employees. This forum would be an opportunity to discuss social and economic issues, but it would never play such a role.

6. With social inclusion, I mean what de Haan and Maxwell refer to as "the process through which individuals or groups are wholly or partially excluded from full participation in society in which they live" (1998, 2).

7. The neoliberal reforms were far-reaching, in particular the privatization of the banks and the sharp reduction in trade barriers. See Rivera Campos (2000).

8. See also Boyce (1996).

9. Approximately 1 million Salvadorans (out of 6 million) live in the United States, most of them illegally.

10. Rosa and Foley write that in the years following the civil war, the support of the United States for the Salvadoran government gave the latter the possibility to pursue its preferences on a variety of issues avoiding "unwanted conditionality on the part of other donors," while it discouraged certain of them (chiefly the Nordics, but perhaps others) from participating more fully in the PRN (2000, 147).

11. For the debate on postwar reconstruction in El Salvador, see Murray (1994); Sollis (1993).

12. This ad hoc nature of foreign assistance is among others discussed by Patrick (2000). For a discussion of the role of foreign donors in the Salvadoran reconstruction, see Rosa and Foley (2000).

13. Chalatenango is the northernmost department of El Salvador. It covers around 10 percent of the national territory and it hosts around 3 percent of its population (approximately 200,000 inhabitants).

14. See Pearce (1986) for a description of the history of Chalatenango and the development of peasant rebellion in this region. The FMLN faction in this area built on a process of popular organizing in Christian base communities and radical peasant organizations. A number of people in the northeastern zone had a past in these movements. Others had come to the northeast during the war years when refugees living in camps in Honduras were able to return. This led to a repopulation of abandoned villages in this zone and to new forms of popular organization. See, for testimonies of inhabitants from these villages, Keune (1996).

15. Until 1995, CCR was the acronym for the Coordination of Communities and Repopulated Villages in Chalatenango; after 1995 it was transformed into Coordination of Rural Communities. Many viewed the CCR as a foundation for the alternative, more participative and equalitarian, kind of society that the FMLN and popular movements advocated. See, for example, Montoya (1994).

16. See Córdova Macías and Lara (1996) on the structure of municipalities and decentralization.

17. In 1997 a law was adopted that raised the percentage of current government income available for municipal works from 1 percent to 6 percent. See Pleitez (2001, 167).

18. For example, Hanlon has stated for the case of Mozambique that it is of fundamental importance who administers foreign assistance and who benefits. "These are deeply political questions about creating structures and systems which will influence the rebuilding of Mozambique" (1991, 249). A similar point was made by Boyce referring to the case of El Salvador, stating that "external assistance has played a critical role in El Salvador's peace process. [It] has not only affected the balance of payments, but also the balance of power" (1995, 2101).

19. According to Howell and Pearce, writing about the use of the concept of civil society in donor circles, this is precisely one of the explanations for its attractiveness, stating that "its diffuseness has also been a secret of its success, enabling it to be legitimately claimed by everyone" (2001, 1).

20. This lack of coordination among external donors is among others discussed by Patrick (2000), who focuses on the national level.

21. The discussion of the SRN and PROCAP covers the period between 1992 and 1997. The Development Program for Internally Displaced, Repatriated, and Refugees also includes a discussion of the developments after the program was finished (from 1991 to 2002).

22. Rosa and Foley write that "the change in personnel that accelerated in 1994" led to a more open attitude toward these popular NGOs of the USAID mission in El Salvador (2000, 147). There have been accusations about the politicization of both the SRN and the MEA program. Despite difficulties in the MEA program to work in a war-torn context, I did not find any evidence of its politicization.

23. As already mentioned, in 1997 a law was adopted that raised the percentage of current government income available for municipal works.

24. Funds were among others spent on the surfacing of roads in the town and the renovation of a school where the mayor had been employed for years.

25. These committees were called Municipal Development Committees.

26. These donors were the bilateral donor agencies DANIDA (Denmark) and NORAD (Norway), together with the private development agency DIAKO-NIA (Sweden).

27. The term "sensitive guidance" is from Carroll. He points at the role of outside actors that aim at empowering local actors. He writes that "the secret of effective external assistance is not only permanent consultation and two-way information flows [between outside and local actors] but also a process that empowers the members of a local organization to analyse their own situation, figure out what the problems are, what options are available to resolve them, and how to choose workable options" (1992, 115).

28. Apart from the Municipalities in Action Program, there were other programs that had rather large sums of funding available, for example, the Social Investment Fund, PCI, Foster Parents Plan, World Vision, as well as other provincial development programs. One of these programs, the Development Program for Internally Displaced, Repatriated, and Refugees, tried in 1991—just before the war had ended—to set up a number of local

development initiatives that promoted the coordination between different actors at the local level in southern Chalatenango. In 1993, the development program tried to create six micro-regions in Chalatenango, in which several municipalities should work together, an experience that also largely failed. By the end of the 1990s, there were efforts by the Environmental Committee of Chalatenango to organize local actors in micro-regions (micro-basins) around both environmental issues and socioeconomic themes. Hitherto, the outcome of these experiences is rather mixed and dependent upon the particular problems at the local level and support by local NGOs, as well as foreign funding for these initiatives.

29. Interview with Mirna Lliévano de Marques, former minister of planning, December 1995.

30. Interview with Walter Urbina, former director of PRODERE, Chalatenango, March 1997.

31. The sustainability of a number of these organizations has been limited. PRODERE was rather unsuccessful in building community organizations, and the cooperative enterprises established in the western part of the province are currently either abandoned or facing financial problems.

32. As mentioned in Note 28, PRODERE had sought to establish local development initiatives in which cooperation between local actors (teachers, mayors) was encouraged at a municipal level.

33. In practice the government organizations played a marginal role in ADEL, and the organizations, therefore, mainly represented those from the private sector and civil society. This made concerted action between state and other actors within ADEL rather difficult.

34. As Graciela Colungo, director of CORDES Chalatenango stated: "If I had invited the others for the first meeting, they would have rejected. If the others would have invited me, I would have been reluctant as well" (interview, November 1995).

35. This is a general description of the main problems in ADEL and based on interviews I conducted with staff and members in April–May 2002.

36. As already mentioned, it was envisaged that PROCAP would also have local expressions; for that reason six micro-regions were created, each with its own local structure. These structures functioned rather poorly, as they were very much developed in a top-down manner.

37. Interview with Graciela Colungo, director of CORDES, Chalatenango, May 2002.

38. See Borgh (2003, especially Chapter 7).

15

Bringing It All Together: A Case Study of Mozambique

Joseph Hanlon

With a peace that has held since 1992 and GDP growth rates of more than 8 percent per year, Mozambique is often billed as the prototype success story. But there were special circumstances that predisposed Mozambique to peace—no one wanted to keep fighting, a strong government remained in place, and some UN interventions were highly effective. Unusually, Mozambique came to independence in 1975 with a single liberation movement, Frelimo, which remains united and in government after two multiparty elections. The opposition movement Renamo was created by Rhodesian security services and then taken over and expanded by apartheid South Africa (Flower 1987, 300). Although it gained local support during the war and receives more than one-third of the vote in elections, Renamo has failed to convert itself into an effective political opposition.

More than a decade after the peace accord, there are growing concerns about the stability of the country on two grounds: Growth has been sharply unequal because of the failure to permit a special postconflict development strategy, while the governance transition has become locked in what is called "democratic minimalism." Narrow donor obsessions and short-term demands have played into the hands of an increasingly corrupt elite.

Repeated War and Exhausted Peace

Mozambique was at war almost constantly from 1965 to 1992. The liberation struggles of the Portuguese colonies eventually led to a coup in Portugal, and Mozambique became independent in 1975. Frelimo was the single liberation movement, and it has obsessively maintained its unity, at all cost, since then. There have been no high-level splits, resignations, or expulsions, but the price has been to not take decisions when consensus cannot be reached, and more recently to accept a growing degree of high-level corruption.

Frelimo followed the fashion of the late 1970s and adopted a one-party state based on modernization, rapid development based on big projects, and central planning based on Marxism-Leninism. With the spillover of the liberation war in Rhodesia, Mozambique was back to war again between 1976 and 1979.

When Ronald Reagan became president of the United States in 1981, he intensified the Cold War, and southern Africa became a Cold War battlefield. Nearly all its wars ended with the end of the Cold War, and forces that had been opposed by the United States won all five multiparty elections: Namibia, Angola, South Africa, Malawi, and Mozambique. But for the decade 1982–1992, apartheid South Africa (with U.S. backing) attacked and destabilized Mozambique at a huge cost. More than 1 million people died in the war, and damage exceeded $20 billion (Hanlon 1996, 15).

The South African–backed Renamo guerrilla movement made extensive use of terror against civilian populations. Frelimo retained popular support mainly due to its major expansion of health and education, so Renamo attacked schools and health posts, even killing patients in their beds. This caused a Frelimo success to crumble by making teachers and nurses too frightened to work outside the towns, and it made peasants afraid to go to schools and health posts. And to cause maximum economic disruption, Renamo attacked roads and railways; with tactics such as burning passengers alive in buses, it made people afraid to travel. Terrorism was targeted and effective.

No movement survives for more than a decade without some local support, and Renamo built on peasant discontent with Frelimo economic and modernization policies in rural areas, particularly in central Mozambique. From 1986, Renamo began a serious effort to become an autonomous movement and started a program of targeted recruitment of better-educated people who could become political and administrative officials. It explicitly raided secondary schools and health posts and kidnapped health workers, teachers, and students. Indeed, virtually all district and senior Renamo officials at the time of the 1992 peace accord had been kidnapped, although Renamo ensured that people stayed voluntarily by creating reasonable conditions and by giving them more career prospects than they would have had otherwise, notes Carrie Manning in her study of Mozambique (Manning 2002, 91).

By the late 1980s, however, this new group saw the war as

unwinnable, while Renamo was losing the tacit support it previously had from peasants in rural areas (Manning 2002, 88). Many peasants fled the countryside to go to government-controlled zones and neighboring countries. Meanwhile, President Samora Machel was killed by South Africa when his plane was drawn off course by a false navigational beacon on October 19, 1986.[1] His successor, Joaquim Chissano, also realized the war was unwinnable. A drought in 1990 made it even harder for Renamo to keep going, and the end of the Cold War meant a reduction of political and practical support. Peace talks started in 1990 in Rome.

By this time, neither Renamo nor government soldiers felt they were fighting for anything—there was no ideological, social, or ethnic base to the war. During the 1990–1992 peace talks there were numerous local cease-fires, and the final cease-fire in 1992 was virtually unbroken. The peace accord called for 30,000 soldiers in the new army, half from each side; in the end, so tired of war were the fighters that only 12,000 volunteered, and most of those were officers. Continued opposition to war remains strong in the early twenty-first century; Mozambique has reintroduced military conscription, but in 2003 95 percent of eighteen-year-olds refused to register (Mozambique News Agency, April 3, 2003).

The peace talks were a classic success of track-two diplomacy. They were hosted in Rome by the Sant'Egidio Catholic movement, which was trusted by both sides (Armon, Hendrickson, and Vines 1998, 32). Their success came about in part because Sant'Egidio was able to keep the big players, notably the United States and Portugal, away from the negotiations. Away from Cold War and postcolonial politics, Mozambicans were eventually able to reach a settlement.

The UN had been present during the talks and was called on to oversee the implementation of the agreement. The peace accord was signed in Rome on October 4, 1992, just when the settlement in Angola was collapsing, so the UN eventually threw huge resources at Mozambique to prevent a recurrence. But the UN Operation in Mozambique (ONUMOZ) was almost stillborn because of infighting at UN headquarters in New York. James Jonah delayed the appointment of a Special Representative of the UN Secretary-General until he was sure he did not want the job himself. Aldo Ajello was a total unknown chosen as SRSG because he was the only available Italian of the right rank. The UN headquarters only dribbled out money, making it difficult for Ajello to set up a local office in Maputo (Synge 1997, 28, 37). It took six months for the ONUMOZ to begin operation. Ajello was an unorthodox wheeler-dealer who proved a lucky choice, and he eventual-

ly built up a $1 million per day operation with a large military presence
that provided important reassurance to Renamo fighters to disarm. The
large budget also gave Ajello the resources to openly buy off the
Renamo head Afonso Dhlakama with $3.9 million, simply to keep him
on board (Synge 1997, 60).

Two other factors played an important role in the relatively smooth
two-year peace process. First was an imaginative demobilization
scheme. All demobbed soldiers (and dependants) were transported anywhere in the country they wished and were then paid for two years, at
$15 to $120 per month, according to rank, using vouchers that could be
presented at the local bank branch. This provided enough money for
soldiers to return home with something and contribute to and reintegrate into their communities. In all, 78,000 fighters were demobilized.

The other important factor in the success of the peace process was
that the peace accord recognized the imbalance between the two sides.
Renamo reluctantly accepted that the Frelimo government was the legitimate government of the country and that the multiparty constitution it
had unilaterally introduced in 1990 was acceptable, with minor modifi-
cations. In exchange, the Frelimo government agreed that Renamo was
a legitimate political party with special standing, rather than simply
"armed bandits" as they had been labeled in the past. Throughout the
war Mozambique's government retained control of all cities and nearly
all towns; Renamo controlled 25 percent of the land area but only 6 percent of the population, according to the UN (Hanlon 1996, 20). Thus,
the government had an operating administration and reasonably well-
functioning health and education systems that with donor support were
quickly extended to those areas that had been cut off from the government. Government and donors worked together to smooth the return of
1 million refugees from outside the country and 2 million displaced
from within the country. The lack of institutional breakdown, the recognition of the government by Renamo in the peace accord, and the
acceptance of the legitimacy of the government by donors and the UN
all smoothed the transition.

Therefore, the peace process in Mozambique was successful
because of special circumstances:

- The roots of the war were not domestic so the insurgents were
  not fighting for a deeply felt issue.
- Both sides were exhausted by the war and did not want to con-
  tinue fighting.
- There were generous medium-term demobilization payments.
- The authority and sovereignty of the government was accepted

by the UN and the opposition, which meant that the peace process was bolted onto a functioning state administration.

- The armed opposition was given special status and felt protected by the UN.
- The UN presence was, eventually, well funded and dynamically led.

Establishing Positions

Arms-length discussions with the United States in the late 1980s in an attempt to end U.S. support for Renamo and South African destabilization led to the 1990 constitution, with its presidential system and a winner-take-all multiparty electoral system. Frelimo had wanted a national unity government, which it thought it could dominate, but the United States demanded winner take all because it believed its own propaganda that Renamo would win. Once Renamo came out of the bush and U.S. officials realized how weak it was, the United States began to press for a national unity government, but Chissano resisted, insisting that he had already given the United States what it demanded.

Renamo faced three linked problems, which have continued until the present. First, despite its relatively successful forced recruitment, Renamo had a severe shortage of skilled and experienced people. After 1992, Renamo recruited experienced people who had fallen out with Frelimo and less educated people who saw more chance for advancement in Renamo. Even now, more than a decade later, Renamo is less educated and less skilled than Frelimo. Renamo president Afonso Dhlakama does not trust many of the opportunists and the forcibly recruited and is reluctant to train them—which in turn reduces their competence. Dhlakama often changes policy and overrides decisions made by people he appointed. He frequently rotates people, or gives people power and then takes it away, in order to block any challenger. Where Frelimo goes to extreme lengths to keep its critics inside the party,[2] Renamo has expelled some of its best people, including Raul Domingos, a kidnapped railway worker who rose to become Renamo's chief negotiator at the Rome peace talks. Dhlakama does not delegate and has maintained the tightly centralized and hierarchic structure of the guerrilla movement, which means that Renamo has failed to build up a party structure with any kind of dynamism and organizing capacity and thus has only a limited mass base. By contrast, Frelimo had built up a party machine during the one-party-state years and was able to convert it effectively to the kind of party organization that would be recognizable to political parties in much of the world.

Second, perhaps not unreasonably, Renamo had a deep distrust of Frelimo. Recognizing that Frelimo people were often brighter and more experienced meant that Dhlakama and Renamo came to believe that Frelimo was tricking them, and they became even more distrustful when they could not see a trick. Dhlakama's response was often to demand larger committees with more Renamo members, for example ever-bigger National Election Commissions (CNEs), in the hope that more Renamo eyes would spot the Frelimo tricks. For its part, Frelimo, like a good magician, knows that it is easier to divert the attention of a larger group. This in turn also leads Dhlakama to distrust the formal institutions of democracy and formal solutions, such as changes to electoral procedures, because he is afraid of hidden tricks.

Third, Renamo quickly came to realize that it was not going to win power at the ballot box and that prestige, power, and a share of the spoils had to be won outside the political system. Its only power was to boycott, disrupt, and threaten to go back to war.

During the ONUMOZ period of 1993, a pattern was established that has remained constant since then. Frelimo would stand on its dignity as the governing party and would often propose formal, bureaucratic solutions. Renamo would threaten boycotts and walk out of meetings, often turning to the donors for financial and political support. This won Renamo status, money, and other resources such as houses. But it has never given Renamo real power. The ONUMOZ and then donors became increasingly important, by giving money, by putting pressure on Frelimo to make concessions, and by building up Dhlakama's status as a president, if only of the formerly armed opposition. Boycotts continued through the entire ONUMOZ period. Dhlakama even boycotted the first day of the first elections and only agreed to continue with the election when his ego was boosted through a telephone call from Zimbabwe president Robert Mugabe and an appeal from the UN Secretary-General (*Mozambique Peace Process Bulletin,* issue 14). Manning notes that "this triad of Renamo, Frelimo, and international community also permits the continued exclusion of the population from playing a central role in the political process" (Manning 2002, 8).

Elections and Politics

Elections were the focus of the peace talks and the OMUMOZ period. With much negotiation the parties agreed on a system managed by a

CNE chosen by the political parties. Inevitably, the state bureaucracy, with the CNE and the international community looking over its shoulder, would have to run the system. But once committed to the multiparty electoral process, and with supreme confidence that it would win, Frelimo and the government created a particularly transparent and effective electoral system. For example, to prevent ballot box stuffing, there are party and independent observers in all polling stations, the count is done individually in each polling station in front of observers (so there was no movement of ballot boxes),[3] and the results are immediately posted on the door of the polling station to permit parallel counts. There was a prior registration, in which all voters obtained photo ID cards. More than 80 percent of eligible adults registered, and of those 88 percent voted in the October 27–29, 1994, election. In the presidential vote, Chissano was reelected with 53 percent and Dhlakama gained 34 percent. The parliamentary election was run on a provincial party list basis; Frelimo gained 44 percent of the vote and 129 seats while Renamo gained 38 percent and 112 seats in the 250-member parliament. The election won high praise from the nearly 3,000 international observers (*Mozambique Peace Process Bulletin,* issues 12, 14; Hanlon 1994).

Renamo has never become an opposition in a European or U.S. sense, where the party out of power proposes alternative policies, suggests legislation, and tries to amend government bills in ways that would benefit its constituency. In parliamentary commissions, outside the limelight, Renamo does cooperate with Frelimo to smooth the passage of uncontroversial bills. But in full parliament sessions, which are broadcast live on the radio and have a substantial following and, therefore, provide an opportunity to make political points, Renamo makes no effort to, for example, challenge spending priorities or amend IMF-imposed policies in ways that would benefit the poorest. Renamo limits itself to speeches, often vague and confused, criticizing Frelimo, and to disruption. In some cases Renamo creates a cacophony with horns, kazoos, and whistles to disrupt proceedings; in December 2000, President Chissano's state-of-the-nation speech was simply drowned out.

Indeed, Frelimo in parliament became the de facto opposition to Frelimo in government. This was clearest in the debate on a new land law, finally approved by parliament in July 1997. Frelimo members of parliament and a committee chair held public hearings and made links with peasant associations, finally overriding objections by the Council of Ministers to give more security of tenure to peasants (*Mozambique Peace Process Bulletin,* issues 17, 19). But the struggle was between

Frelimo in government and Frelimo in parliament; Renamo, the official opposition, played no role.

The second national elections took place December 3–5, 1999. Again they were well run; this time there were thousands of local observers. Turnout was again high. Eighty-five percent of eligible adults registered, and 74 percent of them voted. Chissano was reelected with 52 percent of the vote compared to 48 percent for Dhlakama. In the parliamentary race, Frelimo won 48 percent of the vote and 133 seats, while Renamo in a coalition with smaller parties gained 39 percent of the vote and 117 seats (*Mozambique Peace Process Bulletin,* issues 23, 24). Renamo and Dhlakama declared the election fraudulent but gained no support from the international community, which considered the election relatively well run and the result accurate.

Renamo demanded the right to appoint governors in the six provinces where it won a majority of the vote. Unexpectedly, Chissano did not name governors when he named ministers, and he entered into negotiation with Renamo. In the end Frelimo offered a complex deal that would give Dhlakama a role in choosing the governors: In three provinces Dhlakama would propose a shortlist of three candidates and Chissano would choose one, and in three provinces Chissano would propose the shortlist and Dhlakama would choose. It would have meant Renamo governors in three provinces, far beyond any concession Frelimo had ever offered, and would have given Renamo officials their first real power. Dhlakama's response was all or nothing, and he rejected the proposal (*Mozambique Peace Process Bulletin,* issue 26). It appears that the offer reflected a division within Frelimo and had been promoted by a group that wanted to develop a less antagonistic relationship with Renamo. Dhlakama's rejection of this olive branch meant that Frelimo's hard-line faction regained the leading role.

Adjustment

As part of its attempt to make peace with the West, Mozambique joined the IMF and World Bank in 1984 and began economic reform. Privatization had started in a small way in 1979, well before it was fashionable with donors, and a partial shift to a market economy began in the mid-1980s. The war was having a huge economic impact, but the initial reforms were enough to lead to a 25 percent increase in per capita GDP between 1986 and 1990. Then, despite the ongoing war, the IMF imposed much harsher reforms and fiscal austerity, which included sharp cuts in civil service wages, particularly of front-line staff such as nurses and teachers, whose income fell below the poverty line. The IMF medicine did not work, and GDP per capita fell 12 percent in four years, despite the end of the war and the ONUMOZ pumping substantial amounts of money into the Mozambican economy (Hanlon 1996, 50, 161).

Paul Collier, who later became director of the World Bank Development Research Group, was then director of the Center for the Study of African Economies and had done studies on the transition from civil war to peace. He found that "the conversion of swords into ploughshares directly increases macro-insecurity and needs to be offset by a visible redistribution of ploughshares to the potential enemy." The winner is seen as partisan and must make a "public gesture of redistributive expenditure . . . in the form of compensation to the loser." Failure to do so, he argued, may have contributed to wars in Ethiopia and Uganda (Collier 1994). But the World Bank and IMF imposed a strict form of structural adjustment, with no concessions to the postconflict problems, so the government and donors could not redistribute money to Renamo and war-affected areas. Furthermore, the IMF argued that Mozambique could not be allowed to repair war damage because it would be inflationary, which meant damaged bridges and shops in rural areas were not repaired; donors were actually stopped from giving money to the government for reconstruction (Hanlon 1996, 126).

By 1995 this led to an unprecedented attack on the IMF by a group of donors in Maputo who issued an open letter on October 6, 1995, criticizing the IMF for squeezing the world's poorest country (Hanlon 1996 135; *Mozambique Peace Process Bulletin,* issue 16). The IMF and World Bank did ease off. Although adjustment policies continued to be applied, donors were allowed to give more aid, and reconstruction increased. In exchange, however, there was a further push for privatization and restrictions on government interventions.

The outcome was the growth that has led Mozambique to be billed a success story and the "poster child" of the international financial institutions (IFIs). Finance Minister Luisa Diogo told parliament on May 7, 2003, that over the previous six years the average GDP growth rate had been 8.5 percent (Mozambique News Agency, May 7, 2003).

The problem is that this growth is concentrated in the south of the country and especially in the capital, Maputo. Most of it comes from capital-intensive, mineral-energy projects, such as a $1 billion aluminum smelter. Furthermore, the independent National Statistics Institute (INE) reports that in many ways the headline figure is a statistical artifact. It shows that despite the headline growth, real GDP per capita fell by 16 percent between 1999 and 2001 and that private consumption per capita was as low as it had been at the end of the war (INE 2002, 125). The UNDP's Mozambique National Human Development Report gives provincial GDP figures, which differ slightly from those of INE. It found that in the poorest province, Zambézia, real GDP per capita had fallen from $106 in 1997 to $78 in 2000. The ratio between Maputo City and Zambézia jumped from 10:1 up to 14:1 in just four years (UNDP 2002b, Table 17). The poor are getting rapidly poorer. But in Maputo, there is cable television, fancy restaurants, a building boom of expensive houses, and traffic jams of luxury cars.

There has been a massive increase in corruption. Many of the expensive new houses and cars are owned by ministers and government officials who could not afford them on their normal salaries. Mozambique has become an important transit center for drugs, particularly hashish and heroin; some estimates are that the drug trade is now bigger than any legal trade except aluminum exports. Police and customs officials turn a blind eye, there are few seizures, and a substantial amount of money enters the Maputo economy. Indeed, so much drug money was entering the economy that the government started to issue bonds as a way of capturing some of it into the normal financial system (*Metical* [a faxed business daily newspaper], June 28, 2001).

The IFIs insisted that two Mozambican state-owned banks be privatized, even when told by honest Mozambican officials that the privatizations would be corrupt. The result was the theft of at least $400 million by people linked to the most senior figures in Frelimo. Two people who tried to investigate, journalist Carlos Cardoso and the Bank of Mozambique's head of banking supervision, António Siba-Siba Macuácua, were assassinated in 2000 and 2001 (Hanlon 2002a). International pressure, particularly from journalists, led to the conviction of some of those involved in the killing of Cardoso but apparently not those who ordered the killing. Siba-Siba's murder was simply not investigated. It seemed those who ordered the murders had high-level protection.

Mozambique remains highly aid dependent, so donors play a very influential, even controlling role. Yet the donor community has turned a blind eye to the growth of drug dealing, corruption, and murder that has taken place during more than a decade. There has, for example, been very little donor pressure to investigate the Siba-Siba murder, even though donor budget-support money was used to plug the holes in the banking system caused by the high-level thefts Siba-Siba was investigating.

Image and other priorities seem to be the two overlapping reasons. The top donor priorities have always been linked to IFI structural-adjustment policies, with their emphasis on macroeconomic indicators, notably inflation, deficit, and money supply, and with privatization and moves to the market economy. Donors also want reasonably clean elections. If the Mozambican ruling class satisfies these demands, and in particular does not consult parliament and civil society about donor-imposed controversial policies, then it can continue its drug dealing, theft, and murder. At the same time, donors need to maintain the image of Mozambique (along with Uganda) as the only postwar structural-adjustment success stories in Africa; donor officials in Maputo and their home capitals cannot afford to admit that meeting IMF benchmarks and having a high growth rate have gone hand in hand with massive high-level corruption and growing rural poverty. It is essential to maintain the pretense of success.

The result is another version of the triad of Renamo, Frelimo, and international community that excludes the population from playing a central role in the political process.

Is the Masque of Success Coming to an End?

There is a lengthening series of articles linking the political and economic and arguing that the failure to transform either creates a growing threat to peace. The link is quite explicit because of voting patterns. There are two overlapping voting patterns. One is regional, with Frelimo majorities in the south and Renamo in the center. And there is a class difference; Renamo voters are more rural and poorer than Frelimo voters (de Brito 1995, 486). But the vote remains very mixed; ten of the eleven provinces elected members of parliament from both parties (*Mozambique Peace Process Bulletin,* issue 28).

"Voters in strong Renamo areas tend to be poorer than those in Frelimo areas, and little has been done to rectify the situation since 1992," warned the U.S. academic Jeremy Weinstein. "As time passes, and little changes at the local level, it is possible that those Renamo supporters who once bore arms but grew weary of war may grow less weary and conclude that their only avenue to political change lies outside the system, in the realm of force" (Weinstein 2002, 153).

This was shown dramatically on November 9, 2000, when at least forty people were killed in Renamo-organized demonstrations. In Nampula and other cities, police shot into peaceful demonstrations. But the main death toll was in Montepuez in Cabo Delgado province in the north, where armed Renamo men attacked and captured the town center; twenty-five people were killed including seven police (*Metical,*

November 13–15, 2000; *Savana* [an independent weekly newspaper], November 10, 2000). But when the government regained control of Montepuez there was a wave of arrests, and nearly 100 of those arrested suffocated to death in an overcrowded jail cell on November 22. Montepuez is an obvious flash point and shows many of the problems of Mozambique. The city was divided during the war and voted 71 percent Frelimo and 29 percent Renamo in the 1999 election. It is under intense economic stress because the collapse of the largest local business, a cotton company owned by the British company Lonrho, caused unemployment and a drop in peasant income.

Weinstein underlines this: "Rural Mozambicans are largely left out of national debates and structures. Competing elites from Frelimo and Renamo squabble in Maputo to advance their own respective agendas, and spare little time or attention for local party administration and other matters relating to 'grassroots' politics." He notes that "even the local Renamo officials are almost totally ignored by the higher-ups who debate national politics in Maputo." Weinstein partly blames donors which "focused too squarely on the idea of national presidential elections as a way of legitimating governments" (Weinstein 2002, 155).

"Mozambique has hardly demonstrated much progress toward democratic maturity," and this creates "high levels of political instability," warns Andrea Ostheimer. She criticizes the tendency to characterize Mozambique "as a success story" and says instead that "the paralysed state of Mozambique politics" is leading "towards a permanent entrenchment of democratic minimalism." She attacks both parties. Renamo "has been constrained by a lack of political imagination, that can conceive of little other than its well-known boycott strategy," while Frelimo has not yet "shown a sufficient commitment to democracy to accept a possible loss of power" (Ostheimer 2001).

But the real difficulty is that Mozambique's elite and minimalist democracy seems unable to deal with worsening economic problems and unresolved issues of the ONUMOZ period. A study by Chris Alden of the London School of Economics reported that whereas donors' own evaluations "found unanimously that former combatants had been fully integrated into society," in practice one-third of community leaders interviewed said there were still problems with demobilized soldiers (Alden 2002, 345). These seem to arise partly from two failures of the ONUMOZ. Because of donor infighting, there was sufficient money for demobbed fighters, but very little training was offered, and what was provided was of little use, mainly because the lack of economic recovery meant there were few jobs. Mozambique's representative to the UN in New York, Carlos dos Santos, noted that "many demobilised soldiers were left without means for survival, without training and without jobs. They joined the group of the unemployed in society" (dos Santos 2000, 109). A linked problem was that the ONUMOZ admitted it failed to collect many of the weapons it was supposed to (Jett 2000, 122; *Mozambique Peace Process Bulletin,* issue 14). Dos Santos notes that "unless the combatant is given the means of returning to civilian life, he or she will resort to using a gun to attain intended goals" (dos Santos 2000, 109). And this happened. According to Alden, "the bulk of the leadership of criminal gangs operating in Mozambique today is drawn from the upper echelons of the former military" (Alden 2002, 350).

"Poverty levels that remain very high are having a serious social impact, including an increase in crime," warms Prakash Ratilal, an economist and former governor of the Bank of Mozambique. Officially, GDP may be rising, but this comes largely from capital-intensive "mega-projects" and "the majority of the people do not feel the effect of this growth." The incomes of most Mozambicans are not significantly different now than they were at the end of the war a decade ago, and in some cases people are worse off, he says. In many small cities, the industrial base has completely disappeared. Hundreds of companies, including large foreign-owned ones, have gone bankrupt. There is growth in the capital, yet there is decline in the richest agricultural province, Zambézia. Agricultural credit has collapsed to half its former level. "For a country that is essentially agricultural, the economy is showing signs of specializing in trade and services" (Ratilal 2002b, 369, 370).

Even the government has become worried. In a report on its anti-poverty program, the government notes that increased peasant production is a key to poverty reduction but that production of cereals, cotton, and cashew nuts stayed the same or fell in the period 1997–2002. One problem is limited access to markets (see also GoM 2003, Chapter 5, 6.8, Conclusion). "Nationwide coverage of transitable highways is still fragile, however, which has discouraged private-sector investment and slowed the development of rural markets." The government also admits that real spending on poverty reduction is decreasing, from 19.1 percent of GDP in 2001 to 18.4 percent in 2002. The report is posted on the IMF website, and it contains the unusual statement that Mozambique cannot afford to "channel additional resources into priority sectors [because this would] undermine performance in other sectors." This would seem a convoluted way of saying that the IMF is still restricting anti-poverty spending (GoM 2003, 31, 45).

Furthermore, the government admits it is spending money in the rich south rather than in the poor north. Per capita expenditure in 2000 in Zambézia, the poorest province, was only half that in the rich southern province of Maputo (GoM 2003, 40).[4] Finally the report underlines the way the Frelimo-Renamo-donor elite pact excludes ordinary people when it admits "there seems to be relatively limited knowledge of the [poverty-reduction] plan among technical and even senior staff with responsibilities for implementing policies" (GoM 2003, 45). This makes clear that the poverty plan only exists to satisfy donor demands and that donors have, until now at least, been satisfied.

There have been real gains. As Ratilal notes, "[T]he Rhodesian and apartheid regimes have passed into history" and Mozambique has had a decade of relative peace (Ratilal 2002b, 373). And this allowed the Maputo elites—national and international—to maintain the masque of success, a formal dance in which each plays their role. The government presents its poverty plans, satisfies IFI macroeconomic demands, presents data showing high GDP growth, runs elections, and fawns on the donors with obsequious praise. The donors then hail Mozambique as the success story that justifies all their aid, IFI policies, and strategies of postwar reconstruction. In donor capitals, each development minister can claim the success of her policies; in Maputo, diplomats and aid workers are assured of promotion for having been part of the success. And as the formal dance goes on in Maputo, corruption grows, rural areas become poorer, and discontent simmers. Diplomats silently hope they get out before the music stops; the Mozambican elite hopes its nest egg is big enough when the dance is over.

But outside this cozy masque, the worries grow. Manning says there is a real possibility of "delayed collapse" (Manning 2002, ix). Tony Addison, deputy director of the World Institute for Development Economic Research (WIDER), warns that "poorer regions [of Mozambique] could lose confidence in the ability of peaceful political processes to address their plight" unless "growth is sufficiently broad-based to close the gap in living standards between regions" (Addison 2003, 26). And Ratilal asks: "Can peace be built on poverty and inequality?" (Ratilal 2002c).

Notes

1. This has now been confirmed by a former head of South African military intelligence, General Tienie Groenewald, in an interview in the *Sowetan Sunday World*, April 6, 2003.

2. In 2002 there were sharp divisions within Frelimo over the choice of the successor to Joaquim Chissano, who had announced he would not stand in 2004. Over Chissano's objections, Armando Guebuza was selected as party

head and next presidential candidate. But even this bitter succession contest did not split the party; there were no resignations or expulsions.

3. This does have the disadvantage that a lot of mistakes are made by tired and poorly educated polling station staff doing the count by lamplight after two or three days of polling. In the 1999 elections, the CNE excluded 300,000 votes because of irreconcilable errors in the report forms. See *Mozambique Peace Process Bulletin,* issue 24.

4. Maputo province does not include the capital, Maputo City, which is treated separately. The capital's spending figures are distorted by the presence of all the ministries.

16

Bringing It All Together: A Case Study of Cambodia

Willemijn Verkoren

The case of Cambodia—which may be qualified as a relative failure in terms of postconflict development—illustrates the interactions among development issues in the various postconflict societal sectors and policy areas that have been addressed in this book. I will argue here that no development effort can be sustainable in a postconflict situation unless attention is paid to the cross-cutting themes of demobilization and the reintegration of combatants, the depoliticization of structures and institutions, reconciliation, and addressing the causes of the conflict. These issues have run throughout the book. The contribution of this chapter is to use the case of Cambodia to show just how these cross-cutting issues are central to the interactions between the policy areas covered earlier.

For the purpose of this chapter, I will take the 1991 signing of the Paris Peace Accords by the different Cambodian factions, the Party of Democratic Kampuchea (PDK); the State of Cambodia (SoC); the United National Front for an Independent, Peaceful, and Cooperative Cambodia (Royalist Party) (FUNCINPEC)[1]; and the Khmer People's National Liberation Front (KPNLF) as the point of departure for the postconflict period. Nonetheless, Cambodia is a case in point for the assertion put forward in Chapter 1 of this book that "postconflict" does not mean total peace. Warfare between the Khmer Rouge and the government continued for years after the Paris accords were signed, and although today such fighting no longer occurs, small-scale political and other violence is still an everyday occurrence in Cambodia.

This chapter does not focus on general dilemmas of relief and development but on the specific *consequences of conflict for the development effort*. What developmental strategies were adopted in Cambodia, and why did they not succeed? More specifically, what was the role of the Cambodian conflict in the failure of this effort? One of the reasons for the lack of development successes is the extremely low starting point: The country was almost completely destroyed after more than twenty years of civil war and total revolution. The Khmer Rouge regime that ruled the country from 1975 until early 1979 had all but eliminated the education system, dislocated agricultural production, and decimated human resources. War left behind severe bombing damage, a very large number of land mines scattered across the country, and the destruction of infrastructure and industrial plants.

But there is more to the Cambodian failure than the starting situation alone. The legacies (and the persisting causes) of the conflict play an important role in limiting success. The Cambodian experience proves that addressing these legacies—through reconciliation, demobilization, the reintegration of soldiers into society, and the (re)establishment of confidence in the government and the judiciary—is a prerequisite for effective development. Neither UN peacekeepers, nor the development community, nor the Cambodian government succeeded in achieving this prerequisite, making sustainable development an unobtainable goal.

Demobilization and the Reintegration of Combatants

To a large extent the failure of development in Cambodia is related to the fact that more or less open warfare between the Khmer Rouge and the government continued into the late 1990s. The demobilization effort of the UN Transitional Authority for Cambodia (UNTAC) failed due to the weakness of its mandate that led to an inability to use force. The Khmer Rouge refused to canton and disarm, and as a reaction so did the other parties. The UN placed a lot of faith in the fact that the Khmer Rouge were offered political participation in the elections as an alternative to armed battle, but in retrospect it can be said that this was never an attractive option for them. They knew well that their past record meant they would not receive many votes (at least, not without intimidating voters). However, the mandate and resources of UNTAC did not allow it to punish a party for noncompliance with the Paris accords. UNTAC repeatedly gave the PDK, as the Khmer Rouge now called themselves, an ultimatum to begin cooperating with the cantonment process, but when the PDK did not, UNTAC could not take any action. Perhaps the UN Security Council should have intervened by expanding UNTAC's mandate and resources in response to the PDK's noncompliance, but the opposition of China (which had been supporting the Khmer Rouge), along with the lack of will of the troop-supplying countries to run any risks, prevented this.

The Security Council also did not make any real effort to pressure the Thai military at the border to stop trading with the Khmer Rouge and offering them sanctuary and trade routes. The Security Council warned the PDK on September 25, 1992, that it would decide the following week whether to close Thailand's border with Cambodia to cut off their illicit export trade, but it did not reach any decision on the matter. The only sanctions against the Khmer Rouge were promulgated not by the Security Council but by the Cambodian Supreme National Council (SNC), the body that carried formal sovereignty during the period of UN government and in which the four main conflict parties were represented. In practice these sanctions affected only the trade by groups other than the Khmer Rouge. The very profitable nature of the gems and timber trade enabled the PDK to sustain their military opposition longer than might otherwise have been the case given that China had ceased to militarily support them in the run-up to the signing of the Paris accords.

That the Khmer Rouge soldiers were *able* to continue fighting because of their continued access to arms and resources does not necessarily mean that they *wanted* to. In fact, guerrilla life in the jungle near the Thai border, to which they had withdrawn and where there was never enough food and always too many mosquitoes, was not an attractive existence at all. But many saw no other option. In their home villages, they were sometimes not accepted because of their Khmer Rouge past, making clear the necessity for reconciliation that will be addressed later in this chapter. Ok Serei Sopheak of the Center for Peace and Development, a Cambodian organization that pursues small-scale local conflict-resolution projects, told me in November 2001 that he did not believe that the former Khmer Rouge soldiers were interested in any more warfare. "They want a normal existence, but they find it very difficult to achieve reconciliation with the rest of the population. They are afraid of revenge. Most of them are still hiding weapons in their houses because of that fear."[2]

Another reason why the former soldiers were often unable to settle back in their villages was that the villages simply did not have the capacity to feed them. (This was also true for the 370,000 refugees who returned as a part of the UNTAC repatriation program after having spent more than a decade in Thai refugee camps.) A more structural and widespread strategy to give soldiers an incentive to disarm by offering them employment or education may well have been successful. Many Khmer Rouge soldiers already defected as it was, tired of fighting and of the harsh conditions of life in the jungle. But they had limited opportunity to find a place in society. Targeted programs designed to give them such a place would probably have induced the guerrilla combatants to lay down their arms sooner and in larger numbers, helping to end the continuing warfare that was impeding development efforts. Yet there were no such targeted programs, even though the society desperately needed human resources, which had been decimated during the civil war and the Democratic Kampuchea (DK) period of Khmer Rouge rule.

The consequences of the failure to demobilize and reintegrate combatants on policies for development in the postconflict period were profound. Not only did the continued fighting jeopardize the sustainability of programs for rebuilding infrastructure, agriculture, and other sectors, it also resulted in the inaccessibility of Khmer Rouge–controlled areas to development workers and government officials. As a result, to the people in the northwest, no rebuilding programs were available. The hold of this area by the PDK also enabled this party to continue unabatedly their profitable gems and timber trade via the Thai border, which, because it was unchecked and, therefore, unregulated by the authorities, had a very negative impact on the environment. Unsustainable exploitation of natural resources has resulted in a decline of biodiversity and deforestation. As a result of illegal logging, the number of hectares of rain forest declined from 17 million in 1977 to 10 million in 1997 (Woods 1997, 425).

Although the PDK effectively ceased to exist in 1998, the Pailin area in northwest Cambodia is still controlled by Ieng Sary, a former Khmer Rouge leader who has made a deal with the government that gives him autonomous control over the region. His trading continues to be profitable and unregulated, and his monopoly on timber and gems trading also leads to the accumulation of great personal riches. Therefore, the overriding issue in the environmental sector today is how to achieve the sustainable utilization of natural resources in an equitable manner for the benefit of the local communities and the national economy (instead of being a means to finance the war effort of one party or the personal enrichment of a few individuals) while maintaining the integrity of the resources and the conservation of local flora and fauna.

Another flourishing industry in which former Khmer Rouge play a powerful role in the area near the Thai border is gambling. This pastime is illegal in Thailand, and many Thai are drawn to the Khmer Rouge–run illegal casinos just across the border.

An additional consequence of the continued fighting in Cambodia as a result of the failure of demobilization is that the government was forced for many years to spend a large part of its budget on military expenses rather than to invest in poverty reduction, health, or education. In this area one can see the conflicting demands of the donors, who insisted on the need for stability and for an end to the fighting with the Khmer Rouge, which constituted obstacles to the absorption of foreign aid, but at the same time criticized the government's high military spending. Prime Minister Hun Sen used this paradox for propaganda purposes during his 1997 coup, which he publicly justified by pointing to the need for stability that the donors had expressed. The latter, however, responded to his undemocratic act by withdrawing a proportion of their funds.

Even after the effective end of the civil war in 1998, the failure to demobilize after 1991 continued to have consequences for Cambodian society. Decades of war and civil strife have left Cambodia saturated with weapons, which are misused by police and military both in the line of duty and outside working hours and used by civilians to settle personal scores. The general atmosphere of impunity, to which I will return later in the chapter, encourages this behavior. A recent project by the European Union, Assistance for Curbing Small Arms and Light Weapons in Cambodia (ASAC), which started in March 2000, recognized the danger the weapons pose to the sustainability of development efforts and has achieved considerable success in collecting and melting small arms. Its strategy was to assist in the drafting of an arms law, which defined sanctions for the misuse of firearms, particularly by members of the army and police forces. The second step was to increase the security of official weapons stocks. These two measures, made public through a national awareness program, were intended primarily to make it less of a risk to civilians to hand over their weapons. Another important facet of the program is that collected weapons are destroyed straight away and for everyone to see, making it clear that they will never be employed for the abuse of power by anyone. Of course, the project is based upon people volunteering to hand over arms, as hidden weapons cannot easily be found. However, the large number of weapons received by the program staff constitutes a hopeful sign.[3]

The Depoliticization of Structures and Institutions

The unchecked control of the entire province of Pailin by an ex-DK leader illustrates that the people staffing and running administrative structures and institutions are most often appointed with an eye not on efficiency or accountability but on political motives. After the 1993 UN-organized elections that brought about a coalition government of the Cambodian People's Party (CPP), which has its origins in the Vietnamese-installed government of the 1980s, and the royalist FUNC-INPEC party, it became clear that these two parties were unwilling to share power in the sense of a coalition government in which ministerial posts are divided between the parties. Instead, all important posts were staffed by two officials, one from each party, creating two parallel power structures. All civil servants are appointed by one of the political parties, which means that their loyalty lies not with the government but with their party. According to Ok Serei Sopheak:

> This means that, if there was to be a democratic handover of power from one party to another, the entire body of civil servants would also have to be supplanted. This would obviously not benefit the efficiency of the government, giving parties an additional reason for wanting to remain in power. And the longer they are in power, the more people have come to depend on them through nepotism and client-patron relations, pressuring them to cling to power even more. The notion of public service provided by the government as a whole to the people simply does not exist here.[4]

After the 1997 coup by Prime Minister Hun Sen, and the 1998 elections—which his CPP won amid accusations of fraud—control of the administrative structures was placed more firmly into the hands of the CPP. However, the system of nonmerit political appointments remains, at the cost of efficiency and accountability. The parliament does not enjoy much real power. Elections, including the local ballot of February 2002 and the parliamentary elections of July 2003, are characterized by accusations of fraud and the intimidation of political opponents. At the provincial level, governors and other officials have traditionally enjoyed large degrees of autonomy in policymaking, and in Pailin and elsewhere it is used for the promotion of their own interests and those of their cronies.

This political influence over structures is not limited to local, regional, and national state institutions alone. The justice system is far from independent from politics: Judges are appointed by politicians, and whether someone is prosecuted often depends more on his wealth and connections than on the gravity of his crime. This situation is made worse by the fact that recent history has left behind a culture of violence where the instant reaction to an apparent crime is to kill the perpetrator, rather than waiting for a case to work its way through the politicized, weak, and often corrupt court system. The high incidence of abuses during arrests and in prisons reinforce this tendency. In Phnom Penh, at least one in every thirteen arrests during 1998 resulted in either death or injury (Adhoc and Human Rights Watch 1999, 3). The general feeling that justice depends on one's position is strengthened by the fact that political parties have been protecting their subordinates from prosecution. To prosecute civil servants, authorization of their ministry is needed, and this is in many cases not granted (Adhoc and Human Rights Watch 1999, 3).

More generally, there is a lack of neutrality and independence of the judicial and law enforcement systems. Both the courts and the police are vulnerable to intervention, pressure, and directives from high-ranking political or military figures. The rule of law is undermined to the extent that justice is carried out through orders and executive decrees. Due process is sabotaged because the focus in criminal justice is often on the extraction of confessions and convictions rather than the collection of evidence, the conduct of proper investigations, or the organization of impartial trials. There are numerous points in the criminal justice process when actions by politicians or state agents can undermine the possibility of bringing perpetrators of crimes to justice, particularly when they are members of the police or army or connected to powerful individuals in the government or private sector. There is minimal cooperation between the police and the courts, and both institutions are afraid to investigate and prosecute crimes committed by the armed forces. The level of professionalism in judicial and law enforcement bodies is low. These bodies fail to follow correct procedures because their personnel lack training, competence, and resources. The absence of legal mechanisms and professional competence means the security forces are often unable to conduct independent investigations into instances of misbehavior within their own ranks (Adhoc and Human Rights Watch 1999, 3).

The politicization of structures in Cambodia is also prevalent in the economic system, which is characterized by rent seeking and corruption. A private sector has come into existence since 1993, but the market mechanism is impeded by the fact that the most powerful companies have links to people in the government and civil service. The high level of corruption of civil servants is related to their inadequate salaries but also to tradition: Public positions have always been used for personal advantage in Cambodia. In fact, this was one of the causes of the Cambodian conflict in the first place. I will go into this complex situation in more detail below.

What emerges from the above is that development programs undertaken by the government are likely to benefit the friends of those in power. It is, therefore, important to work on changing the Cambodian political system and culture. This is difficult because as we will see in the next sections, they go back a long time, preceding the conflict itself, and the extreme suffering caused by the conflict has eradicated any trust that was left between the parties. In the meantime, donors may achieve better and more equitable results when they disburse their aid not through the government but directly through locally based NGOs. Due to the system of nonmerit appointments and because policy decisions are often motivated by a desire to benefit cronies, the infrastructure for channeling foreign aid is inefficient and benefits some groups and regions over others. This contributes to the country's limited absorptive capacity for aid and risks turning aid into a conflict commodity.

Thus, aid organizations should be careful when designing their programs. Strategies that appear sensible in "normal" developing countries can be problematic in postconflict settings such as the Cambodian one, where structures are highly politicized. Take the idea of the "Khmerization" of development programs, for example. This desire was expressed by the donors' Consultative Group, and it means that projects should be carried out as much as possible by Cambodians rather than by foreign aid workers. Such a strategy clearly makes sense from the point of view of capacity building and sustainability, but in the implementation it can be hard to find professional and unpoliticized Cambodians. This problem can result in delays of implementation at best, or the abuse of aid resources to benefit friends at worst (Peou 2000, 96).

As a result of the politicization of structures, "there is no rule of law in Cambodia but a rule of power."[5] To establish a rule of law, therefore, depoliticization is needed. It is also a prerequisite for the creation of confidence in the government and the justice system. However, the relationship between confidence and politicization is a chicken-and-egg one: Not only is depoliticization needed to establish confidence, but confidence is needed for depoliticization. The situation of parallel power structures would never have come into being if the different parties had trusted one another enough to be willing to genuinely share power and government responsibility. Because one cannot have one without the other, there is a need to work on both the establishment of confidence, through reconciliation between different groups, and depoliticization at the same time. This latter process will require the strengthening of parliament, democratic procedures, accountability, and the legal system. It will also require changes in the education curriculum, where democratic values should be emphasized. These values can be internalized by introducing democratic procedures into all kinds of institutions, including schools, where children could elect their class representatives.

What this section shows is that the idea that there can be no political development without economic development—that people have to be fed before they can worry about representation—has to be abandoned in the Cambodian case, because political development toward depoliticization is a prerequisite for sustainable and equitable economic development.

The lack of trust between parties, which is so central to this issue, underlines the necessity of reconciliation and dealing with traumas.

Reconciliation and Dealing with Traumas

For a genuine, equitable, and sustainable process of development to be established, what is needed is the creation of confidence—between groups, and of people in the government, the justice system, democracy, and foreigners. "Creation" is in this context probably a better word than "restoration" because, as the next section shows, to an extent these types of confidence never existed. Of course, the conflict did not help, and because of it trust between groups and in the government declined to an even lower point than before.

How is trust created? First and foremost, of course, by improving the trustworthiness of institutions. People will start trusting institutions only after they have given them a reason to. Strengthening accountability and fighting corruption and nepotism are, therefore, vital. In addition, people need to feel that the institutions are working to their benefit. This can be achieved by enhancing representation through strengthening parliament, elections, and other democratic mechanisms, making it clear to people that they can have a say in their own future. When doing so, however, it is important that the specifically Cambodian background is taken into account. As was pointed out earlier, confidence is not merely a result but also a prerequisite for the establishment of a democratic political culture. Trust between individuals, groups, and parties seems less attainable than ever because of the horrors that some Cambodians have put other Cambodians through in recent history. A first step, therefore, is to work toward reconciliation, forgiveness, and the healing of traumas.

In Cambodia, there has been no public debate about the conflict, its causes, and its consequences. Nearly every family has lost at least one member in the civil war and during the DK period. One problem is that all parties to the conflict have dirty hands to the extent that they have been involved in killing during the conflict and political violence afterward. The clearest target for the blame for all the misery the country has been through is the Khmer Rouge because of the magnitude of their crimes. When former DK president Khieu Samphan came to Phnom Penh in 1998 to negotiate a deal with the government, he was beaten up by an angry mob. Resentment against the Khmer Rouge is made even greater by the fact that their leaders have never been tried, except by a show trial set up by the Vietnamese invaders in 1979 that convicted Pol Pot (who died in 1997 in his jungle residence) and Ieng Sary (who has received an amnesty from the government) in absentia. This is in part a consequence of the politicization of the justice system. It has been in the interest of those in power not to try the leaders of DK because co-opting them into government with promises of amnesty and riches could bring an end to their armed resistance—and also because Cambodia's leaders have been worried that a trial will shed light on their own roles in DK. Prime Minister Hun Sen, for example, was an officer in the DK army before he defected to Vietnam in 1977 for fear of purges.

Nevertheless, pressure from an opposition party, local NGOs, and international groups led the government in 1998 to begin negotiating with the UN about the setting up of a trial for the former DK leaders. This trial would prosecute only the top leaders of the Khmer Rouge regime, those who made policy and gave orders. Of the people who are eligible for prosecution, only two have been arrested and imprisoned by the Cambodian authorities so far. One of them died of natural causes in prison in 2002, highlighting the need for quick action on the trial issue because of the old age of the Khmer Rouge leaders. Most people appear to agree that the lower Khmer Rouge cadres should not be brought to trial because more often than not they were victims as well as perpetrators. However, a plan has been proposed by a number of local NGOs that would bring them before a truth commission in return for freedom from prosecution under Cambodia's domestic legal system. The idea behind this is that such a construction would help bring out the truth about the DK period and enable Khmer Rouge members to publicly apologize for their deeds. The proponents of the plan want the commission to function parallel to a tribunal for the top leaders.[6] This idea was rejected by the government, however, and excluded from any of the draft plans that were later presented.

Negotiations were lengthy and revolved around the balance between international and Cambodian judges and prosecutors (the UN wanted a majority of international judges to ensure impartiality while the Cambodian government insisted on a Cambodian majority). After breaking down several times, in March 2003 the UN and the government parties arrived at a compromise. The trial and appeals chambers will have a majority of Cambodian judges, but under the agreement at least one international judge has to join in any judgment. It is to be hoped that this is a sufficient guarantee for an impartial trial, which could set a powerful precedent for the legal system and be a first step for the restoration of people's confidence in that system. As Youk Chhang of the Documentation Center of Cambodia said in November 2001:

> Cambodians are forgiving people, but only when they know the facts about what has happened. A tribunal will provide such facts. It will offer a legal fundament, to which people can refer later on. It will give them peace to know that it is wrong to commit a crime, not only according to their own intuition but also according to the judicial system. At present, when a person steals a bag of rice, or even commits murder, he will ask himself why he should be punished when the murderers of a million people are still walking free. This fundamental distortion can only be corrected by bringing the Khmer Rouge to trial.[7]

In addition, a tribunal could be a starting point for reconciliation and forgiveness—although it can be argued that this would be more so if the trial applied to war crimes by other groups as well, which is difficult considering the role of foreign powers in backing factions during the Cambodian war and revolution. Reconciliation and forgiveness are, after all, necessary for the creation of trust and the reintegration of former combatants into society.

To achieve these ends, education is also vital. Through the teaching of a balanced version of history, the memory of the events that scar the country can be kept alive, and lessons can be learned from it. Trust in democratic politics should also become an integral part of the curriculum of schools. The creation of confidence will require new leaders who are untainted by the events of recent history. At present, in the words of Youk Chhang, "Cambodians have no heroes. Often, they do not even have fathers anymore."[8] These new leaders are among today's youth, and for that reason it is important that this youth learns about the errors of the past and the lessons that can be drawn from them. This is not happening at present. One Cambodian NGO worker who gave a lecture at a university asked the group of students how many of them had been to the Tuol Sleng former Khmer Rouge torture center, which has been transformed into a genocide museum and is one of the few monuments that reminds the country of the horrors of DK. "Only a few students raised their hands."[9]

A tribunal and changes in education curricula could contribute to starting a national debate about the civil war and the Khmer Rouge. This is important because it would bring out the truth, make people aware of lessons that can be learned from the past, and contribute to reconciliation. The media have an important role to play in this context. It is their responsibility to emphasize the lessons learned and the need for reconciliation, for building up the country together. The debate could also make people realize that many of the lower Khmer Rouge cadres—who were often recruited at a very young age, drugged, and forced to commit crimes—are not primarily to blame for the horrors of DK and should be accepted back into society. This message will also help these former cadres themselves deal with their complex guilt issues.

A national debate should not solely focus on the Khmer Rouge, however. Other groups played their part in causing the conflict and in committing crimes both during and after the civil war. People feel resentment not only toward the Khmer Rouge but also toward the CPP, an exponent of the Vietnamese-installed PRK government of the 1980s. The Vietnamese occupation of those years, not just by the military but by large numbers of Vietnamese advisers in many areas of society, strengthened traditional anti-Vietnamese sentiments that go back more than a thousand years and are related to the continuing historic fear of being overrun by this neighbor. Because the CPP was created by the Vietnamese, people are suspicious of this party. The breaches of human rights by its governments, both in the 1980s and the post-UNTAC period, do not give this party a better name.

In Cambodia, radio is the medium that reaches the largest number of people throughout the country, and it has been used in positive and negative ways. The experience of Radio UNTAC is inspiring. In the prelude to the 1993 elections, UNTAC organized broadcasts in the form of serious news programs as well as plays to convince people of the importance of their vote. The broadcasts also emphasized that the votes cast would remain secret and that, therefore, voters should not be intimidated by the threats of the Khmer Rouge and the CPP. The broadcasts were a great success because they did convince the people, a great majority of whom defied threats and went to the polls, voting in large numbers for a party that had not been issuing threats. Unfortunately, in the years after UNTAC left, the freedom of the press was limited by the Cambodian government, making it more difficult for the media to address issues such as the need for more democracy.

Civil society can also play a vital part in the process of reconciliation in Cambodia. It is important that grassroots NGOs keep the debate about the past and the future going in their local activities for the promotion of human rights, democracy, conflict resolution, and development. Small-scale programs in the areas of human rights education or the reintegration of Khmer Rouge cadres should emphasize common ground between groups and their shared responsibility in building up the country. A lot of encouraging work is being done in this area. However, so many NGOs have been founded or opened an office in Cambodia since UNTAC that questions are being raised about their efficiency and coordination. At present, almost 2,000 NGOs operate in the country, both locally founded and international. As Youk Chhang has said: "These NGOs themselves consume large amounts of resources. They need to critically consider whether they are making an actual contribution and eliminate parallel projects. They, too, are responsible for the situation in the country—not just the government."[10]

The trouble with starting a national debate about the past is that many people would rather forget. This is also one of the arguments that have been raised against the setting up of a Khmer Rouge tribunal—that it would bring back traumas that are better left forgotten. This is a particularly complex issue, but it can be said that people cannot truly devote themselves to the future unless traumas from the past are addressed. A national debate uncovering the facts and untangling them from government propaganda—which during the 1980s laid all the blame for the DK crimes on a small number of Khmer Rouge leaders and called them agents of China in order to obscure the roles played by its own members—could help people deal with the past.

Addressing the Causes of the Conflict

The concept of sustainable development has an additional dimension in postconflict settings in that it will only be sustainable when it pays attention to the prevention of a return to armed conflict. For this reason this book has emphasized that the causes of the conflict should be taken into account in any postconflict development effort. Unless these causes are addressed, there is no guarantee that the conflict will not flare up once again.

In this section I mention some of the causes of the Cambodian conflict and explain the ways in which they condition the postconflict development effort. These causes represent structural states of affairs in Cambodia, which go back a long time. They concern a history of rural-urban antagonism, an inappropriate education system, an economic system of rent seeking, power abuse, anti-foreign sentiments related to the country's location and accessibility, the interference of global politics, and poverty.

During the colonial period an urban population group came into existence. Most of its members were either employed in the colonial administration, attached to the royal court, or engaged in trade. The group had access to the schools that were founded by the French. This urban elite continued to exist after independence and became characterized increasingly by nepotism and personal enrichment. Salaries for government personnel were traditionally low, encouraging rent seeking. The contrast between this group, educated and urban, and the rest of the overwhelmingly rural country could hardly be greater. Rural poverty always existed on a great scale. People who worked on the land did so from dusk till dawn, seven days a week. They never came into contact with literature, luxury, or Western ideas. Some of them did encounter the urban elite when the latter made visits, often official, to the countryside. They did not leave a good image there. Rural people came to resent these urban groups who were seen as lazy, self-centered people exploiting the rural workers. And in a sense they were right, as (foreign) capital was increasingly used by the elite in unproductive ways—not invested in rural development or industry but spent on luxury goods, on which particularly the elite surrounding the royal court increasingly focused.

Cambodia before 1970 had a very well-developed education system, a legacy not only of the French but also of high investment in education during the 1960s, when learning was seen as vital for the country's development and a number of universities were founded. The system, however, was unfit for the demands of the country's economy and society. Its curricula were geared not toward an agricultural society but toward an urban one. Subjects such as Western law and literature were taught. The rapidly expanding system educated growing numbers of young people, who found after they graduated that their education did not help them to find employment. Rather than contribute to the development of their country, they became unproductive members of the urban elite. Thus, heavy investment in education did not improve the economy and well-being. This fact was used by Pol Pot after 1975 as an excuse to destroy the economy, the educated, and the education sector (Duggan 1996, 361–375).

Pol Pot and his colleagues also capitalized on the urban-rural divide, which had become stronger as a result of the installation of an urban-centered education system. They responded to rural resentment of the urban educated class when they announced the founding of a completely rural utopia and emptied the cities. According to Vickery, many peasants in 1975 saw no reason why the "new" people could not adjust to the harsh rural life, and some may even have felt some schadenfreude (Vickery 1984, 5).

The postconflict rebuilding of education, then, should take into account the prewar precedent and ensure that the education system reflects the needs of the economy. This means that it will need to be geared more toward teaching practical skills in the areas of agriculture, basic manufacturing, medicine, administrative management, and the like, that are needed for the country to reach a basic stage of development. Of course, the country also needs lawyers and economists, certainly more of them than it has today, but their numbers should not exceed those of people with basic practical knowledge. What is needed to achieve this needs-responsive education system is the development of a specifically Cambodian curriculum, not one that is modeled after the French or any other foreign teaching program. When such a curriculum is designed, it can also take into account the ingredients needed for reconciliation such as the emphasis of common ground between groups.

In addition, an effort should be made to ensure access to the education system to vulnerable groups such as women, the rural poor, and, importantly, former soldiers. Education is one way to achieve their reintegration, because it will enhance the employment opportunities for the former combatants.

As we have seen, the characteristics of the Cambodian economic system, rent seeking and corruption, go back to before the conflict and actually contributed to causing it. The system of nepotism aroused the anger of rural poor, and the leaders of DK capitalized on this anger. After the Khmer Rouge government was toppled, however, it did not take long before the system was back, and what is more, former Khmer Rouge leaders are participating in it. It is important to realize that this system is a breeding ground for conflict. Programs aimed at capacity building, increasing accountability, and raising civil service salaries thus need to be continued and expanded.

A consequence of decades of power abuse is the tradition of distrusting the government. "People do not trust politics," says Youk Chhang. "In the Khmer language the word for 'politics' is the same as the word for 'cheating.' There is no political science in Cambodia; only propaganda. As a result, the information in schoolbooks about the Khmer Rouge is a mixture of facts and propaganda."[11] Here we come back to the creation of trust, underlining the importance of the reform of curricula and a national debate about the past once more.

Anti-foreign, particularly anti-Vietnamese, sentiments have been prevalent in Cambodia for a long time. They are related to the country's location and accessibility. Historically, the country has been wedged between Thailand and Vietnam. Although Cambodia is not extremely rich in mineral wealth, its small population, its rich alluvial soil, and Tonlé Sap Lake, which is the richest freshwater fishing ground in the world, have made the country susceptible to outside influences and tempting to immigrants and invaders. After the demise of the great Angkor empire, Siam (now Thailand) and Vietnam continuously fought over influence in the country. Vietnam even instigated a large-scale settlement program allowing inhabitants of the densely populated country to emigrate to Cambodia. The arrival of the French in 1863 probably saved the country from being absorbed by its two neighbors (Chandler 1991; Chanda 1986). After the withdrawal of the French, however, many Cambodians feared the reemergence of foreign ambitions. The large Vietnamese minority became the main target of these suspicions, as well as an easy scapegoat for other kinds of dissatisfaction. In DK these sentiments were taken up and there was large-scale killing and deportation of ethnic Vietnamese as well as the border raids that finally led Vietnam to invade Cambodia in 1978. In the postconflict period, the anti-Vietnamese sentiments have resurfaced, as can be seen in the language used against ethnic Vietnamese by the leaders of all political parties, including the opposition. It is important that human rights education programs pay attention to this issue, which could lead to escalation in the future.

It is also important to recognize the role played by global and regional power politics in causing and prolonging the Cambodian conflict. Although an extensive description of these factors is beyond the scope of this chapter, to an extent they still condition the success of the development effort. For one thing, they have resulted in a general distrust toward foreigners. Moreover, although the Cold War has come to an end, politics have continued to influence donor choices for the development of Cambodia. Even after the peace agreement was signed in 1991, no great power was willing to pressure Thailand to stop providing sanctuary and trading routes to the Khmer Rouge for fear of damaging economic and political relations with China and the Association of Southeast Asian Nations. Similarly, in the issue of the Khmer Rouge tribunal, pressure by powerful countries would probably have considerably speeded up negotiations, but it appears that no country wanted to upset China, which was opposed to a tribunal.

Finally, poverty was also a major cause of the conflict because it provided a breeding ground for revolution and made it easier for people to join armed groups, as they had nothing to lose. Therefore, development in itself is a way to prevent a recurrence of conflict, provided it is distributed equitably and takes into account all the conflict-related complications and sensitivities mentioned above.

Conclusion

Cambodia represents a special case in many ways, particularly because of the gravity of the situation in which the country found itself in 1979, and because during the 1980s not much assistance could be provided due to continued conflict and international isolation. The targeting of the educated by the Khmer Rouge and the exodus of educated refugees dealt a very severe blow to human resources. For example, in 1980 there were five lawyers left in the country, and in 2001 there were still only ten psychiatrists. Education is, therefore, central to the Cambodian development effort, provided that it is organized in such a way that it is responsive to the needs of the country. The civil war and the DK period had furthermore destroyed the country's infrastructure to an extent that is found hardly anywhere else. Even so, many of the society's prewar structures and characteristics prevailed or resurfaced in the postconflict period. This is not always a good thing considering the fact that many of them contributed to the conflict in the first place.

Although it is a special case in some areas, then, the Cambodian experience can still be instructive to other development efforts in postconflict settings. The cross-cutting issues of demobilization and the reintegration of combatants, the depoliticization of structures and institutions, reconciliation and dealing with traumas, and addressing the causes of the conflict are important in development efforts in all postconflict situations. What this chapter has also made clear is the need for simultaneous conflict resolution and development efforts, because without conflict resolution, the gains of development can become new conflict commodities. Similarly, without equitable development, there can be no true peace.

Notes

1. FUNCINPEC is the French acronym.
2. Interview with Ok Serei Sopheak, Center for Peace and Development, Phnom Penh, November 2001.

3. http://www.unidir.ch/pdf/articles/pdf-art81.pdf, December 1, 2002.

4. Interview with Ok Serei Sopheak, Center for Peace and Development, Phnom Penh, November 2001.

5. Interview with Ok Serei Sopheak, Center for Peace and Development, Phnom Penh, November 2001.

6. Interviews with Youk Chhang, Kek Galabru, Lao Mong Hay, and Ok Serei Sopheak.

7. Interview with Youk Chhang, Documentation Center of Cambodia, Phnom Penh, November 2001.

8. Interview with Youk Chhang, Documentation Center of Cambodia, Phnom Penh, November 2001.

9. Interview with Lao Mong Hay, Khmer Institute of Democracy, Phnom Penh, November 2001.

10. Interview with Youk Chhang, Documentation Center of Cambodia, Phnom Penh, November 2001.

11. Interview with Youk Chhang, Documentation Center of Cambodia, Phnom Penh, November 2001.

17

Seeking the Best Way Forward

Gerd Junne
Willemijn Verkoren

This concluding chapter draws together some of the major issues that arise during postconflict development efforts in the various policy areas and regions covered in this volume. One conclusion that arises from the book is that mere rebuilding is not enough, as it may reinforce structural inequalities and discrimination that gave rise to the conflict in the first place. This point is expanded on below. Next, this chapter goes into some of the loose ends this book leaves us with. A number of policy dilemmas that arise from the studies in this volume are listed, and an agenda for further research is outlined. Finally, using the rich source of information provided by the contributions to this volume, we will clarify and expand our argument laid out in Chapter 1, that development theory and practice have to be adjusted in postconflict situations—and be reconciled with the perspective of peacebuilding theory and practice. A number of suggestions are made as to how development studies can better incorporate the conflict dimension and how conflict studies can adopt a development focus.

Why Rebuilding Is Not Enough

As was mentioned in Chapter 1, adopting standard, one-size-fits-all development policies is counterproductive in postconflict contexts. Even simply rebuilding preconflict structures, which seems like the most basic and obvious (and neutral) action after a war, may contribute to prolonging the conflict—or even restarting the violence—rather than solving it. This is due to the fact that the preconflict struc-

tures were often part of the causes of the conflict because they bene-
fited some groups over others. It is up to postconflict developers to
alter the balance without estranging those who lose from it (i.e.,
offering them an alternative). Table 17.1 provides an illustration of
how postconflict development should differ from just rebuilding the
country.

Table 17.1   Rebuilding Is Not Enough

	Bias in Preconflict Structures	Desirable Difference in Postconflict Structures
Security forces	The security forces were often highly biased and more an instrument of suppression than of protection for large parts of the population.	Different groups of the population should be represented in the security forces that provide equal protection to all citizens.
State structures	Government positions were often in the hands of a specific group of the population, and government expenditures were regionally concentrated.	Access to government positions has to be open to all groups. Regional infrastructure should be more balanced.
Justice	Justice system was often underdeveloped, badly equipped, biased, and corrupt. In a climate of violence, judges are intimidated.	To establish the rule of law, independent judges must be installed and maintained.
Infrastructure	Infrastructure is often geared more to the exploitation of natural resources than to the service of people.	Infrastructure should provide roughly equal service to people in different regions and facilitate development of a modern economy that provides larger parts of the population with a chance to earn their living.
Education	Education was elite oriented with a concentration of universities and schools around capitals, neglecting most of the country.	Educational facilities must be extended to peripheral areas and geared toward the educational needs of the economy and society.
Health	Many developing country health systems (inherited from colonial rulers) favor urban-based curative care.	Future health systems should provide more equal care for all parts of the population and should have a strong emphasis on preventive care.

Policy Dilemmas

There is no blueprint for postconflict development. The situation differs too much from country to country. But there are a number of recurrent dilemmas. Decisionmakers cannot copy measures taken elsewhere, but they can get inspired by the ways in which similar dilemmas have been handled in other conflict-torn societies.[1] Such dilemmas come to the fore in every chapter of this book:

1. *How to deal with warlords:* Too much time, according to Dirk Salomons (Chapter 2), is often wasted in trying to probe for the underlying motives and ideology of spoilers who have only one thing in mind: exerting power and plundering their environment. But powerful warlords and criminals cannot be ignored either. How can they be integrated, isolated, marginalized, or expulsed?

2. *How democratic should the democratization process be?* How much authority should be granted to nonelected local officials in the immediate aftermath of conflict? Jose Luis Herrero (Chapter 3) is in favor of the Kosovar model (no authority), which is different from what is applied in Afghanistan and Iraq. Herrero writes that granting authority to nonelected locals risks alienating the population. But this certainly applies to third-party rule as well.

3. *Relationship between new and old power structures:* Traditional leaders and structures are stronger and enjoy more support than new ones, even if the new leaders are democratically elected. Who should be supported? If an integration of traditional and new institutions is the goal, how should this be done?

4. *International or local judges?* There are few judges left in a country after protracted civil conflict. Many were highly partisan, many were killed, others emigrated. The remaining judges may not meet the highest professional standards. But international judges often have little legitimacy and little knowledge of local customs and circumstances. So who should be responsible for the "rule of law" in postconflict societies?

5. *Infrastructure development:* Infrastructure projects should be prepared with a broad participation from the public. But how to prevent community participation in decisionmaking about infrastructure from paralyzing the process—in a situation of great time pressure to create the basis for renewed economic development?

6. *Impact of free media on conflict:* Free media play a crucial role in the process of democratic decisionmaking. But they depend on com-

mercial success. They have to serve their customers—and in that way can perpetuate rather than change preexisting opinions and perceptions. Are activities designed to stimulate a change of attitudes toward the conflicting parties in contradiction with the idea of independent and neutral media?

7. *Language policy:* Local languages should not be suppressed, and children should be able to get at least primary education in their mother tongue. But this can work to the detriment of national unity (if there is no common medium of communication) and can distribute life chances in an uneven way.

8. *Length of NGO presence:* International NGOs can make a tremendous effort to improve the health situation of a population in an emergency situation. But their continuous presence can have a negative influence on government efforts to build up a public health system. Should NGOs leave the country even if the population is not yet sufficiently provided with medical services?

9. *Environmental concerns:* The environment is not a priority in conflict situations and not in postconflict situations either. But environmental problems may belong to the root causes of a conflict. When will they have to be addressed and become a priority?

10. *Carriers of economic development:* Somebody has to invest in economic development. The international community will only finance basic infrastructure. Foreign investors can hardly be attracted to conflict regions. The only domestic sources of capital are often groups with a dubious past. How much of economic development can be left to such groups?

11. *Public finance:* Revenues need to be raised while at the same time avoiding as much as possible taxes and user charges that bear disproportionately on poorer groups. These are the groups that are the least mobile; others can more easily hide or transfer their income. Revenue reforms that threaten elite interests may falter. Where will taxes to finance development come from?

12. *Donor assistance:* Where should the money go? The most backward areas are often controlled by warlords. Does not dealing with these warlords mean further damaging these areas?

13. *Choice of cooperation partners:* The choice to work with particular actors and to bypass others is crucial. Should external agents choose to work with government agents, groups from civil society, or political parties (or a combination of them)? Working with government agencies may slow down and reduce the effectiveness of a program. But cooperation with civil society or individual political parties only can contribute to a further fragmentation of the country.

14. *Entrenchment of democratic minimalism:* Forms of political power sharing between conflicting parties can stop violence but may block further political development, because a quota may have to be maintained irrespective of political performance and cooperation. Democratic participation of the population thus threatens to become a farce.

15. *Dealing with undemocratic rulers:* A similar dilemma as in the case of interaction with warlords is posed when the government itself is not democratic. How to deal with a situation as in Cambodia, where the present ruler guarantees a minimum of stability but himself came to power in an undemocratic way? Support for him does not do justice to his role in the conflict, but agitation against him could make things even worse.

Research Agenda

The dilemmas implicitly formulate a research agenda. They cannot be solved on the basis of philosophical and ethical reasoning alone, but they have to be analyzed in detail. Under which circumstances did specific decisions lead to the intended results and under which conditions did they not?

From the chapters in this book, an ambitious research agenda can be distilled. It is not formulated as a series of open questions, but the statements below can be read as hypotheses. It is not an agenda for the traditional kind of academic research, either desk research or field research. It is more an agenda for action research—or an agenda for experimental action with some accompanying research to establish just how far the action really leads to the intended consequences.

The International Dimension of Internal Conflicts

Current large-scale violent conflicts are mostly internal, not international, conflicts. But that does not mean they do not have an important international dimension. Without a whole network of arms suppliers, diamond traders, drug dealers, traffickers, and money suppliers, the violence would not reach the same scale.

In some fields, international measures have been taken or are under discussion to curb this international support and stimulation of internal conflicts. The Kimberley Process (to control the export of diamonds from conflict areas) is a good example. The question is which additional measures can be taken to tackle other international links beside the diamond trade.

A lot is to be done to curb the international trade in arms. Disarmament as actually practiced often is a trade incentive for weapon dealers who are supplied with additional arms as a result of disarmament elsewhere (if the arms are sold abroad and not destroyed) and who face additional demand where disarmed belligerents try to replenish their arsenals or even to obtain additional cheap weapons to be turned in, if the incentive offered by the disarmament program is strong enough.

Another field of international activity could be the interaction with migrants. They often adhere to a "long-distance nationalism," which is more radical than the one shared by people who stayed in the country. They do not have to compromise or to suffer the consequences of hardline action, because they live far away. Their influence, therefore, often has a polarizing effect. But perhaps this influence could also be turned around. It can be easier to involve them in a positive interaction with people from the other side, rather than to apply such programs to the conflicting parties in the conflict area itself. If members of the various diasporas reach a better understanding between representatives of different groups, they might exercise a moderating influence on the fighting parties.

International associations of all kinds could make a more conscious effort to involve people from the different conflicting parties in common activities. It is often the confrontation with third parties from other countries and cultures that makes it obvious that the internal differences are relatively small after all and that there is a lot of common ground. Cooperation in international associations also helps to establish common standards that could then also be applied at home.

The Self-Perpetuation of the Aid Economy

Most postconflict societies are highly dependent on foreign aid. This is a kind of income that is similar to the income from raw material exports—in the sense that nobody (or only a tiny group of people) has to work for it. People quickly develop a kind of dependency syndrome. The very fact that many projects come to an end once the aid flow stops is a clear indication that these flows do not always stimulate local initiative but nail recipients down in a dependent role.

The impact of the large number of staff from foreign aid agencies that tend to swamp a conflict region after violence stops needs to be better understood. Actually, the focus is often on better evaluations of the projects with the objective to end and avoid projects that do not achieve their objectives. The suggested emphasis here is different. The question raised here is what the long-term consequences, side-effects, and externalities are of projects that are run well and do achieve their primary goals. Even those projects may have consequences that may give rise to second thoughts.

This impact cannot be evaluated at the project level only. It is the massive cumulative impact of a large number of projects by many different organizations that can become a problem of its own (irrespective of the useful outcome of the individual projects). The presence of large numbers of expatriates has far-reaching consequences for trade flows, employment patterns, wage structures, and exchange rates. Even excellent work of international agencies can have a negative impact on the nascent local structures, which may not unfold because of their comparative inefficiency, distrust of part of the population, and a lack of pressure to improve these services.

The large-scale presence of foreigners also has an important impact on the attitudes of people in the country itself and in the country where the expatriates come from. Devoted humanitarian work, disregarding all differences in ethnicity, class, or gender, could set a good example. Vanessa van Schoor mentions in Chapter 9 that medical assistance has endangered the lives of patients and health-care workers working in zones of the other ethnic group, but their courage and the model they present may be a first step in reconciliation. But the very consumption habits, spending patterns, expensive equipment, and the like of such workers can also have a quite different impact, where it stimulates theft, illegal taxation, and extortion.

The work of the agencies can also have an important impact back home. Personal reports to friends, family, and colleagues on the local situation and on the fighting parties can have a stronger impact on perceptions than the published news.

More research has to be done on alternatives to the present form of international help, which, in the worst case, implies that hordes of aid workers descend upon a local population like an ancient plague. Often the expatriates replace the group of well-educated local people that left the country as a reaction to the violence—if they were not killed. Programs to bring them back could create a more sustainable situation.

It would also make sense to bring in local people from neighboring countries that have gone through similar processes in their own society. Their experience could be more adequate, their manners might be less foreign, their salaries might be more in line with those of the local population, and their expenditures less conspicuous.

The Decriminalization of State and Economy

The main reason for the large-scale presence of foreigners is often that locals are regarded to be not knowledgeable enough, inefficient, partisan, or corrupt. The absorption of almost all existing structures (including churches, NGOs, etc.) into criminal networks during a long period of protracted conflict goes much further than is usually acknowledged. We still need a better understanding of how these structures work—and even more urgently how they can be dismantled, transformed, or at least sidelined.

It is also difficult to find actors that can actively pursue such a policy, for practically all institutions are affected by it. Some cooperation among international organizations (like Transparency International), local public and private organizations, and the media might be desirable. Successful examples should get much more public attention.

Strong state institutions are necessary to cope with criminal organizations. This increases the pressure to explore raw material deposits for additional government income. But such a development also makes the state more vulnerable to assault by groups that want to share in this income.

From a Rent-Seeking Economy to a Productive Economy

An enormous challenge is how to get from a rent-seeking to a productive economy, which may be a basic condition for a switch to a democratic society. A rent-seeking economy has much more far-reaching consequences than is often recognized. The general level of education is often much lower—with all the implications that that entails: a lack of emancipation, high population growth rates, the easy manipulation of information, bad sanitary conditions, and a weak civil society. The health situation of the general population is relatively irrelevant to the flows of income to the government because the income is not derived from work.

The informal economy and the criminal circuits reveal that there is a lot of creativity in the population, which, when given greater space, encouragement, and support, could provide a broad range of unexpected developments.

A good general education is the precondition for harnessing the creativity to learn about the state of the art, about experiments elsewhere, to exchange information with others, to integrate in international networks, and to fully participate in a "worldwide information society."

Establishing a Working Democracy

The World Bank has concluded that "there has been no comprehensive analysis of public sector reform and capacity building in post-conflict settings—this is urgently needed" (World Bank 2004, 33). The exit-strategy of international organizations is normally focused on the organization of free elections, after which the government is handed over to the elected officials. But a one-time democratic election does not guarantee that a democratic system takes root. Much more is necessary—from changes in the educational system and the growth of independent, critical media and a lively civil society to more participatory structures in factories and bureaucracies, different attitudes toward minorities, and less authoritarian family structures. The shift toward a real democracy implies nothing less than a cultural revolution in many countries.

Such a shift does not take place overnight. Even the most democratic societies still have some way to go. The question is how such a process can get sustained support from the outside, without imposing any specific model. In many countries, historical structures do exist that can serve as an example (Sen 1999, 232–240).

Just as specific ethnic identities and interpretations have been evoked recently to support the struggle between ethnic groups, a "rediscovery" of the other half of history is of paramount importance: of the history of good neighborhoods, of tolerance, and of common goals and challenges.

Another issue that relates to the success of establishing a working democracy is the much-publicized "resource curse." Under which conditions can the negative societal effects of large incomes from raw material exports be mitigated? How can a shift from a rent-seeking economy to a productive economy be realized? Under which circumstances is democracy compatible with an economy based on rent seeking?

Changes in Identity

Identities are regarded as something relatively constant, something that people are born with (like color) or have acquired very early (mother tongue) and will not change much thereafter. But we have seen that many identities have been profoundly redefined since the early 1990s. Ethnicity or nationality has become much more important for a number of reasons, such as reaction to globalization, decline of ideologies, and increasing social polarization. Troublesome as this shift is, it also offers some hope for the future: Ethnic identities are not a fixed given. They change over time (sometimes quite quickly); they are malleable. Everybody fulfills many different roles in life. These can all become more or less important in the perception of "self" and in the definition of identities. The question, then, is how a new shift away from ethnicity as a basic element of identity can be stimulated.

Much more research is necessary on historical redefinitions of identities and on the factors that have supported, accelerated, or obstructed such a process. People of different ages have a different susceptibility to changes in identity. Children acquire a specific identity at an early age, but this is open again at the end of adolescence. Young adults have anew to find their place in society. Some of the present troubles in many countries of the world stem from the fact that so few prospects for income, well-being, and status are afforded to the millions of adolescents and young adults. Millions of young people find themselves in a labor market where few jobs are available. This is especially frustrating for youths who sacrifice their education for the struggle for a political cause and then remain idle because of a lack of formal education. This lack of attractive perspectives for young adults is an important factor underlying many violent conflicts. This increases the chance that these groups will center their identity around ethnicity due to the lack of professional identities, class identity, identification with the team or organization in which they work, or identification with their product.

A New Role in the International Division of Labor

Individual perspectives are intimately connected to finding a role in the international division of labor. The international position of a country largely determines which kinds of jobs and professions are in demand and what kind of identities can be formed around them.

Just to copy international examples of cheap manufacturing work is probably no solution. In most cases, it would be difficult to match the conditions offered in Southeast Asia. So instead, a lot of creativity and intelligence is demanded to come up with something new. A pioneering status in well-publicized social experiments of all kinds (environmental projects, water management, micro-credits, education, transport, etc.) can provide the participants and their communities with a new identification, a social asset they can be proud of, international attention, the integration into international networks of a new kind, and sources of income.

The Slow Learning of International Organizations

International agencies are adapting to the new challenges. A good example is the Low-Income Countries Under Stress (LICUS) program of the World Bank. There is a wealth of experience in these international institutions, but most of them are still experimenting with ways to pass the knowledge and insight on within their own organization and to find ways of sharing knowledge among organizations.[2] As Dirk Salomons remarks in Chapter 2: "There is an impressive body of policy recommendations and lessons learned. Yet many practitioners in the field of postconflict recovery are concerned that these cumulative insights have not led to a more informed and harmonized international response activity." What could be done to assure that the lessons learned are really taken into account? What are the incentives to learn, and what are the obstacles that prevent learning processes?

There are strong contradictory pressures on the staff of international aid agencies. On the one hand, they have to work as efficiently as possible, which means to apply standard procedures and recipes, to concentrate on large-scale projects, and to keep in mind all kinds of environmental, gender, and other implications. On the other hand, they have to adapt to local circumstances, take political constellations into account, assure quick help and response in a flexible way, give local staff a larger role, and show a more experimental attitude.

Much of the help is still focused on the immediate tasks, without much thought for the design of a decades-long social change strategy, and on the technical aspects of a political transition, at the cost of attention for the social, economic, and psychological processes of transformation (e.g., on the logistics of separating and disarming troops versus how to address trauma, guilt, mourning, and identity and how to reintegrate them into society; and on *financing* aid and economic development versus *how* to address unemployment and development).

Here a cultural change is necessary in the agencies as well, starting from the educational background of the staff, the selection mechanism, the terms of employment and career patterns, evaluation procedures, and payment structures. How can this be changed?

Postconflict Development as Conflict Prevention

The best predictor of future conflict is conflict in the recent past. Manifest violence is not only an indicator of a strong conflict potential that remains in place, even when large-scale violence has come to a (temporary) end. Violence also creates and intensifies a conflict potential by stimulating hatred; causing trauma, feelings of revenge, and feelings of senselessness; and by destroying the means for survival and intensifying competition for the remaining scarce resources, such as access to international aid.

Without an economic development that provides a new basis for earning income, increasing welfare, reasonable progress, and life chances for the next generation relatively evenly distributed over different groups of the population, chances are high that new conflicts will break out.

Longitudinal analyses should study in detail how the conflict potential is built up, how conflicts perpetuate themselves, and which kind of development can reduce the conflict potential for the future.

For taxpayers and donor organizations, it would be much cheaper to help strengthen those structures that work in favor of peace rather than shoulder the cost of very expensive operations after a conflict has started. Everybody agrees on the importance of conflict prevention, but relatively little is done. The obstacles that stay in the way of conflict prevention need a closer analysis—combined with a thorough reflection of how the obstacles can be overcome.

Conflicts in Development Studies

So many developing countries have gone through a period of intensive civil strife that postconflict development has become the norm rather than the exception. But this is not yet sufficiently taken into account in development studies and in the programs of governmental and nongovernmental international organizations. They have often added postconflict development as an additional task but not integrated it sufficiently into their overall development strategy.

There are obvious differences between a "normal" development situation and the development challenge in a conflict-ridden society. The World Bank mentions, for example, that "social policy is relatively more important and macro policy relatively less important in post-conflict countries than in otherwise similar countries without a recent history of conflict" (World Bank 2004, 27). Some other differences are examined below. They are highly relevant for the core of many development programs.

Lack of Security

A basic difference is the lack of security in a postconflict situation. Although large-scale military operations have come to an end, there are still gangs of armed people that maintain themselves by robbery, murder, and extortion. Police forces are weak (and perhaps partisan and corrupt). This gives rise to the creation of other armed security forces. Sometimes, the people involved in both might be identical: Security guards during the day may turn into robbers or rebels during the night. Some areas may not be accessible because they are still occupied by rebel forces. Border areas see a come and go of armed men who cross into neighboring countries. This basic insecurity discourages any kind of investment, as any visible asset may invite thugs, thieves, and worse.

Stronger Role of the State

Pervasive insecurity, the need for reconstruction, and the demand for a strong arbiter who can broker agreements between different social groups create the need for a relatively strong state. This is in contrast with the trend since the early 1980s that saw a diminishing role of the state in many developing countries. But a weak state, unable to protect its citizens, has been one of the factors that have stimulated the ethnicization of politics: People fall back on their own kin groups for protection and survival (Ignatieff 1998, 7). A stronger role of the state is also necessary because private investors will be very hesitant to get engaged as long as the security dilemma is not solved.

Market Incentives Do Not Work

The market is often still in the hands of local monopolies. Efforts to engage outside actors do not work as long as the rule of law is not established; rules are still under discussion (and can easily be circumvented); protection costs are high; and the purchasing power of the population remains limited. Lawlessness also inhibits tourism.

Pervasive Criminality

Protracted conflict situations have stimulated the spread of criminal groups. Former rebel groups are used in clandestine activities. The need to finance combat action has given rise to large-scale criminal networks: to get the money in the first place (from extortion, drug deals, trafficking, protection rackets) and to buy arms, ammunition, vehicles, petrol, and other equipment through unofficial networks. The links to these networks remain open, the knowledge of how to operate in this environment is often the only comparative advantage that people have, and few alternative sources to earn a living do exist. Crime weakens all existing institutions, both private and public, and discourages all regular activities.

Returning Refugees

Violent conflicts imply large movements of people who flee the violence or the economic consequences of war. When they return, they often find their houses occupied. Property titles may conflict, and it can take years before the legal system has sorted out to whom a certain property belongs. As long as there are conflicting claims, the tenants will not invest in the estate, be it a house or a factory, nor will the holders of the competing claim. Investment elsewhere would be a signal that the original claim has been given up. This slows down investment in housing as well as in economic activities.

Brain Drain

Armed conflicts cause many people to flee the country. The more versatile and educated people are, the easier they can build up a new existence elsewhere. Already in the run-up phase, when public debate and policy become dominated by ethnicity, many intellectuals leave the country. Many refugees do not return after the violence has come to an end. They may have established themselves elsewhere. Widespread unemployment and the difficulty of employing their talents in their own country may prevent them from returning. The country thus loses many of the most knowledgeable and creative individuals, just those people who might otherwise take initiatives and act as catalysts for bottom-up projects.

Little Bottom-Up Participation

Many development organizations have come to understand the importance of a bottom-up approach that gives the beneficiaries of a program an important say in its design and implementation. The World Bank, for example, stresses the need to build social capital through community-driven projects (World Bank 2004, 29–30). A precondition for such an approach would be that the beneficiaries at least talk to each other, not shoot at each other. But in a deeply divided society, the level of mutual trust may be too low to start common projects. The alternative is to start parallel projects for different ethnic groups, but such projects may just perpetuate the divide and create additional rivalry. This may not necessarily be the case: In an optimistic scenario, people who have carried out similar projects for their own group might then be prepared to talk to each other, learn from each other, and finally cooperate with each other.

Everything Politicized

Postconflict situations are characterized by the politicization of seemingly neutral policy issues, such as who builds a new road and where to build it, which environmental issues to target and in what part of the country, or which type of tax system to adopt. People may not talk to the other side, but they will talk a lot to their constituency. Everything becomes politicized—every technical decision (where a bus stops, what the opening hours of a swimming pool are, whether a shop gets a license to open) becomes a political issue, because it may advantage one group over the other. Public offices might be filled by pairs from either side, as in Cambodia, making bureaucracy much more clumsy. Or additional layers of administration are created, as in Bosnia, with the concomitant difficulties of getting definite decisions taken. An over-politicized process gets into a permanent deadlock, with the result that decisions are taken elsewhere in a process, which is not transparent at all. More generally, every decision by a policymaker could serve to reinforce the underlying causes of the conflict or contribute toward their removal. It is important that postconflict decisionmakers take these possibilities into account. With each decision, thought should be given to which people and groups are likely to be the beneficiaries of the policy and what effect this will have on the conflict. By benefiting one group or area, others may feel neglected or excluded. Although this can never be entirely avoided, in postconflict situations the issue is much more sensitive than in normal situations. As Martijn Bijlsma writes in Chapter 10, "Accordingly, decisions should be well motivated and bear the spirit of the peace agreements. As a general rule, they should be based upon the nature and magnitude of problems—that is, they should benefit those persons or areas that most need it, and this fact should be well communicated to the public. An additional argument may be that the choice of beneficiaries helps to overcome the fundamental causes of conflict," which may partly relate to inequality.

Dominance of International Agencies

Just because domestic groups cannot get along with each other, foreign troops and international agencies are present. Because the destruction has led to emergency situations, international aid organizations try to bring relief. This means that, altogether, a large number of foreigners are in the country to give advice, help rebuild, keep order, protect minorities, supply goods, reform institutions, remove land mines, and so forth. They bring not only official aid, they also spend part of their own salaries there. They constitute an important economic sector that provides employment for translators, drivers, guards, and waiters. They do not only have a considerable influence on the economy, they take many decisions on the economic and political future of the country, often not consciously but by the combined effect of their individual action.

The Development Dimension of Conflict Studies

While development studies (and practice) have to take the conflict dimension much more into account, conflict studies show similar deficiencies. Conflict transformation and peacebuilding have to pay much more attention to the development needs of a society and its different social groups. There is a close connection between the multifaceted lack of development and the occurrence of violent civil conflicts. The high frequency and intensity of internal conflicts since the early 1990s have, furthermore, aggravated the development problem. Much of what had been achieved in the decades before has been destroyed in recent civil war. That is one of the reasons why past conflicts are the best predictor of future conflict; the level of development, however measured, declines. As a result, the chances of future violent conflict increase. A number of factors are mentioned here that show how important the development perspective is for conflict studies. Programs to attack these problems might be the best long-term contribution to peacebuilding.

Lack of Infrastructure

An underdeveloped and badly maintained infrastructure is the first obvious sign of a lack of development. It has immediate repercussions for violent conflict. It is an obvious grievance for groups, especially in neglected areas that have received a less than proportional share of the low level of infrastructure investment. The bad accessibility of remote areas makes it much easier for rebel groups to hide and maintain themselves, while it makes it difficult for the government to assert its authority, collect taxes, and provide services (and thus gain legitimacy). Badly maintained infrastructure also reduces the threshold to destroy it in military actions or actions of sabotage.

Lack of Education

A lack of education may make people more vulnerable for mobilization by ethnic groups, though history proves that higher levels of education unfortunately do not make people immune against it. More important is that low levels of education provide fewer life chances. In a global information society, a lack of education automatically implies a high degree of exclusion. A lack of good jobs available and a limited mobility mean that people have to get their identification and satisfaction from other means. A gun provides power where a lack of education bars other opportunities. Most "child soldiers" (under eighteen) are not forced to join the fighting forces. They rather do so by a lack of alternatives. It can be an act of compensation for life chances that their environment denies them.

Lack of Health Care

Another obvious denial of life chances is a lack of health care. Life expectancy is especially low in Africa south of the Sahara, where HIV/AIDS threatens a very large percentage of the economically active population. This can further derail development and increases the chance of conflicts. But it also contributes directly to the intensity of violence: With ubiquitous death around, life counts less. Where people face the likelihood of early death anyway, they may run higher risks for themselves and feel less remorse when killing others. Besides, bad and deteriorating health care adds to the grievances that contribute to revolt.

Scarce Natural Resources

Countries with a low level of education and a lack of infrastructure depend to a large extent on agriculture. With a growing population and a limited area of fertile land, competition for the scarce natural resources increases. Rwanda is an important example. Access to water can be an issue that is as crucial as access to land, where the fertility of the land depends on irrigation. Scarcity of land and the tendency to smaller holdings may increase the pressure to shift to higher-value-added crops, mainly raw materials for drugs. Rich natural resources, especially minerals and oil, can also trigger violent conflicts.

Lack of Employment Perspectives

Unemployment in most conflict areas is very high and has increased as a result of the destruction and the mining of rural areas. With a lack of employment opportunities, the demobilization of competing armies and the social reintegration of former soldiers becomes very difficult. Remaining idle, often forming gangs to earn a living, they aggravate the security situation. Very often, command structures remain intact after demobilization, because the soldiers are not absorbed into other functions. That makes a relapse into conflict very easy.

Barriers to Alternative Identity Formation

Unemployment does not only mean that people lack jobs and incomes. It has far-reaching psychological implications. People cannot identify with their professional status or their products, they have little to be proud of, and they may look for compensation for that in other fields. A lack of employment intensifies the competition for power (and access to government employment) and increases animosity against the "others" that pick jobs and have better opportunities. It leaves people idle to conspire and develop negative energies instead of contributing to societal welfare and progress.

Too Little or Too Much Aid

Foreign aid plays an important role in this context. Being poor alone is not enough to ensure aid flows to a country; donors' priorities do not only depend on the level of development. Some cynics believe that only when the shooting starts are aid flows mobilized. From that point of view, it seems to be a rational strategy for domestic groups to begin a conflict to draw international aid providers into the region. But not only too little aid can lead to conflicts. Large and generous aid flows have the same effect: They raise the value of being in government and thus being able to influence the aid flows into specific sectors, regions, ethnic groups, or clans. From an economic point of view, aid flows have some similar characteristics as income from the export of raw materials. People do not have to work for the income. If not given directly to small local projects, it strengthens the role of central government at the cost of other groups. And the macroeconomic impact on prices and exchange rates can be similar, making it more difficult for small projects to survive.

Government as a Source of Income

If other sources of income are blocked because of the low level of general development, access to government resources becomes even more important. This leads to relatively large bureaucracies and additional grievances among the population, a "winner takes all" mentality even of elected governments, the tendency of rulers to extend their rule by all means, and the inclination of the opposition to fall back on violence as the only way to trigger a shift in government.

Criminal Organizations

Protracted conflict invariably gives rise to criminal activity, such as the need to finance military activities as well as the spread of weapons that can be used for looting, extortion, spread of prostitution, and trafficking. The longer the conflict goes on, however, the more the causality may reverse: Criminality is no longer the instrument to procure the means to continue the war effort. The war has to be continued because it has become an instrument for criminal organizations to pursue their activities. Conflict studies, therefore, have also to cover the criminalization of the world economy and to include strategies how this might be reversed.

Autocratic Structures, Lack of Emancipation

Autocratic structures in society at large, in individual communities, and within families belong to root causes of conflict but are also strengthened and perpetuated by conflicts. The democratization of these structures, therefore, plays an important role in peacebuilding and in the prevention of renewed conflict. Political participation is also an integral part of the concept of development as we define it; much more than mere GNP growth, development is a qualitative rise in living standards for all members of all societies. Democratization, then, is an indispensable component both of peacebuilding and of development.

Conclusion

Because conflicts are embedded in the fabric of local societies, regional rivalries, global flows of information, trade and investment, and international high politics, conflict transformation needs a very comprehensive approach. It has to be embedded in an overall development strategy supported by many different groups. The implementation of such strategies requires a learning attitude, intensive multilevel coordination, and a long-standing commitment of the actors involved.

If this book can make a contribution to the exchange of experiences among different conflict regions, if it helps to increase the awareness of potential pitfalls and offers some positive examples that provide inspiration to others that have to cope with similar situations, it has achieved its purpose.

Notes

1. For this reason, we offer a discussion space on the website www.netuni.nl/postconflict, where these and other dilemmas can be discussed and examples of concrete responses to such situations are put forward, together with the consequences that have resulted from the actions taken.

2. The World Bank is experimenting with ways to effectively share and manage knowledge both within the Bank and with other organizations. See World Bank (2004, 37, 41–45). UNDP has also recognized the importance of this issue and is developing its own system called SURF. In addition, networks such as the OECD/DAC Network on Conflict, Peace, and Development Cooperation and the Conflict Prevention and Reconstruction Network have potentially important roles to play.

Acronyms and Abbreviations

AACA	Afghan Assistance Coordination Authority
AAK	Alliance for the Future of Kosovo
ADB	Asian Development Bank
ADEL	Agency for Local Economic Development (El Salvador)
AHLC	Ad Hoc Liaison Committee (Palestine)
AIA	Afghanistan Interim Authority
AIAF	Afghanistan Interim Authority Fund
AMA	Aid Management Agency
AMSS	San Salvador Metropolitan Area
ARENA	Republican Nationalist Alliance (El Salvador)
AREU	Afghanistan Research and Evaluation Unit
ARSG	Afghanistan Reconstruction Steering Group
ARTF	Afghanistan Reconstruction Trust Fund
ASAC	Assistance for Curbing Small Arms and Light Weapons in Cambodia
ASG	Afghanistan Support Group
ATA	Afghanistan Transitional Authority
BPK	Banking and Payments Authority (Kosovo)
CAP	Consolidated Appeal Process
CCR	Coordination of Rural Communities (El Salvador)
CEDE	Center for the Study of Democracy and Development (Mozambique)
CEL	Río Lempa Executive Hydroelectric Commission
CEP	Community Empowerment and Local Governance Project
CF	Constitutional Framework for Provisional Self-Government in Kosovo

CFA	Central Fiscal Authority
CIA	Central Intelligence Agency (United States)
CISPE	Civic Service and Public Employment Department (East Timor)
CNE	National Election Commission (Mozambique)
CNN	Cable News Network (an AOL Warner Company)
CNRT	National Council for Timorese Resistance
CODDICH	Provincial Corporation for the Development of Chalatenango
CPC	civil protection corps
CPO	Central Payments Office (East Timor)
CPP	Cambodian People's Party
CPRU	Conflict Prevention and Post-Conflict Reconstruction Unit (World Bank)
DAC	Development Assistance Committee (OECD)
DCDC	District Community Development Committee
DDR	disarmament, demobilization, and reintegration (of soldiers)
DFID	Department for International Development (United Kingdom)
DFO	district field officer
DGRNR	Renewable Natural Resource General Directorate (El Salvador)
DK	Democratic Kampuchea (1975–1979)
DRC	Democratic Republic of Congo
EIA	Environmental Impact Assessment
EITI	Extractive Industries Transparency Initiative
EPRDF	Ethiopian People's Revolutionary Democratic Front
FAO	Food and Agriculture Organization of the United Nations
FCMA	Canadian Environmental Fund
FIAES	Initiative for the Americas Fund
FMLN	Farabundo Martí National Liberation Front (El Salvador)
FONAES	Salvadoran Environmental Fund
FPI	Internal Political Front (East Timor)
FUNCINPEC	United National Front for an Independent, Peaceful, and Cooperative Cambodia (Royalist Party)
FYROM	Former Yugoslav Republic of Macedonia
GDP	gross domestic product
GFAP	General Framework Agreement for Peace (Bosnia)
GNP	gross national product

GTZ	Gesellschaft für Technische Zusammenarbeit (Society for Technical Cooperation)
HIV/AIDS	human immunodeficiency virus/acquired immune deficiency syndrome
IAC	Interim Administrative Council (Kosovo)
IASC	United Nations Interagency Standing Committee
ICARDA	International Center for Agricultural Research in the Dry Areas
ICG	International Crisis Group
ICRC	International Committee of the Red Cross
IDPs	internally displaced persons
IFC	International Finance Corporation (World Bank Group)
IFIs	international financial institutions
IG	Implementation Group (Afghanistan)
ILDES	Local Development Initiative (El Salvador)
ILO	International Labor Organization
IMF	International Monetary Fund
INE	Instituto Nacional de Estatístico (National Statistics Institute) (Mozambique)
IOM	International Organization for Migration
JAM	Joint Assessment Mission
JIAS	Joint Interim Administrative Structure (Kosovo)
JLC	Joint Liaison Committee (Palestine)
KDP	Kecamatan Development Program
KLA	Kosovo Liberation Army
KPC	Kosovo Protection Corps
KPNLF	Khmer People's National Liberation Front
KTC	Kosovo Transitional Council
LACC	Local Aid Coordination Committee (Palestine)
LBD	Lëvizja e Bashkuar Demokratike (United Democratic Movement) (Kosovo)
LDK	Democratic League of Kosovo
LICUS	Low-Income Countries Under Stress
MAG	Ministry of Agriculture and Livestock (El Salvador)
MEA	Municipalities in Action Program
NATO	North Atlantic Treaty Organization
NDF	National Development Framework (Afghanistan)
NGO	nongovernmental organization
OCHA	United Nations Office for the Coordination of Humanitarian Affairs
OECD	Organization for Economic Cooperation and Development

OHR	Office of the High Representative
ONUMOZ	United Nations Operation in Mozambique (December 1992 to December 1994)
PA	Palestinian Authority
PDDH	Human Rights Proctor (El Salvador)
PDK	Party of Democratic Kampuchea (former Khmer Rouge)
PDK	Democratic Party of Kosovo (formerly PPDK)
PDP	Palestinian Development Plan
PNC	National Civilian Police (El Salvador)
PNEA	National Environmental Emergency Plan (El Salvador)
PNR	Plan for National Reconstruction (El Salvador)
PPDK	Kosovo Democratic Progress Party
PRK	Vietnamese-installed government party in Cambodia in the 1980s
PROCAP	Program for Municipal Capacity Building in El Salvador
PRODERE	Development Program for Internally Displaced, Repatriated and Refugees (UNDP in El Salvador)
ROL	rule of law
RPAME	ROL Participatory, Assessment, Monitoring, and Evaluation
RRA	Rapid Participatory ROL Appraisal
SEMA	Executive Secretariat for the Environment (El Salvador)
SNC	Serb National Council
SNC	Cambodian Supreme National Council
SoC	State of Cambodia
SRN	Secretary for National Reconstruction (El Salvador)
SRSG	Special Representative of the Secretary-General (of the United Nations)
SWG	Sectoral Working Group (Palestine)
TFPR	Task Force on Palestinian Reform
UCK	Ushtria Çlirimtare E Kosoves (Kosovo Liberation Army)
UK	United Kingdom
UNAMA	United Nations Assistance Mission in Afghanistan
UNAMSIL	United Nations Mission in Sierra Leone
UNAVEM	United Nations Angola Verification Mission
UNDP	United Nations Development Program
UNEP	United Nations Environment Program
UNESCO	United Nations Educational, Scientific, and Cultural Organization

UNHCR	United Nations High Commissioner for Refugees
UNICEF	United Nations Children's Fund
UNITA	União Nacional para a Independência Total de Angola (Union for the Total Independence of Angola)
UNMIK	United Nations Interim Administration Mission in Kosovo
UNODCCP	United Nations Office for Drug Control and Crime Prevention
UNOPS	United Nations Office for Project Servies
UNSCO	Office of the United Nations Special Coordinator (Palestine)
UNTAC	United Nations Transitional Authority for Cambodia
UNTAET	United Nations Transitional Administration in East Timor
USAID	United States Agency for International Development
UNU	United Nations University
WBG	West Bank and Gaza
WHO	World Health Organization
WIDER	World Institute for Development Economic Research

Bibliography

Acevedo, C. 1992. "Balance global del proceso de negociación entre el gobierno y el FMLN," *Estudios Centroamericanos* 519–520 (San Salvador: UCA): 5–54.

ADB, UNDP, and World Bank. 2002. *Afghanistan: Preliminary Needs Assessment for Recovery and Reconstruction.* http://lnweb18.worldbank. org/SAR/sa.nsf/Attachments/full/$File/Complete.pdf.

Addison, Tony. 2000. "Aid and Conflict," in F. Tarp (ed.), *Foreign Aid and Development* (London: Routledge), 392–408.

Addison, Tony. 2001. "From Conflict to Reconstruction," WIDER Discussion Paper No. 16, June (Helsinki: United Nations University). http://www. wider.unu.edu/publications/dps/dp2001-16.pdf, August 13, 2003.

Addison, Tony. 2003. *From Conflict to Recovery in Africa* (Oxford: Oxford University Press).

Addison, T., and S. M. Murshed. 2001. "The Fiscal Dimensions of Conflict and Reconstruction," WIDER Discussion Paper No. 49, August (Helsinki: United Nations University). http://www.wider.unu.edu/publications/ dps/dp2001-49.pdf, August 13, 2003.

Addison, T., A. Chowdhury, and S. M. Murshed. 2003. *Raising Tax Revenues: Why Conflict and Governance Matter,* mimeo (Helsinki: UNU/WIDER).

Addison, T., and S. M. Murshed. 2003a. "Explaining Violent Conflict: Going Beyond Greed Versus Grievance," *Journal of International Development* 15, no. 4: 391–396.

Addison, T., and S. M. Murshed. 2003b. "Debt Relief and Civil War," *Journal of Peace Research* 40, no. 2: 159–176.

Adebajo, Adekeye. 2002. "Liberia: A Warlord's Peace., in S. J. Stedman, D. Rothchild, and E. Cousens (eds.), *Ending Civil Wars* (Boulder, Colo.: Lynne Rienner).

Adhoc, Licadho, and Human Rights Watch. 1999. "Impunity in Cambodia: How Human Rights Offenders Escape Justice," *Human Rights Watch* 11, no. 3 (C). http://www.hrw.org/reports/1999/cambo2/.

Afghanistan National Development Framework. http://www.undp.org/ afghanistan/ndf.pdf.

Agénor, P-R, and P. J. Montiel. 1999. *Development Macroeconomics* (Princeton, N.J.: Princeton University Press).

Ahmad, Khabir. 2002. "Regional Instability Further Slows Afghanistan's Reconstruction," *The Lancet,* September 7.

Alden, Chris. 2002. "Making Old Soldiers Fade Away: Lessons from the Reintegration of Demobilized Soldiers in Mozambique," *Security Dialogue* vol. 33, part 3 (Oslo: Sage), 341–356.

Al-Quds University, Global Management Consulting Group, CARE, and Johns Hopkins University. 2002. *Executive Summary of the Rapid Nutritional Assessment for West Bank and Gaza Strip.* http://www.reliefweb.int/library/documents/2002/care-opt-16oct.pdf.

Amer, Ramses. 1993. "The United Nations' Peacekeeping Operation, Cambodia: Overview and Assessment," *Contemporary Southeast Asia* 15, no. 2: 211–231.

Anderson, Mary. 1999. *Do No Harm: How Aid Can Support Peace—Or War* (Boulder, Colo.: Lynne Rienner).

Anderson, Mary B., and P. J. Woodrow. 1989. *Rising from the Ashes: Development Strategies in Times of Disaster* (Boulder, Colo.: Westview).

Annan, Kofi. 1998. *The causes of Conflict and the Promotion of Durable Peace and Sustainable Development in Africa,* report presented to the Security Council and the General Assembly. www.un.org/ecosocdev/geninfo/afrec/sgreport/index.html.

Araujo, Miguel E. 1992. *Environmental Action in a Post-War Period: The Case of El Salvador, Abstract for the 1992 World Park Congress* (San Salvador: Secretaría Ejecutiva del Medio Ambiente).

AREU. 2002. *The A to Z Guide to Afghanistan Assistance* (Kabul/Islamabad: AREU).

Armon, Meremy, Dylan Hendrickson, and Alex Vines. 1998. *The Mozambican Peace Process in Perspective* (London: Conciliation Resources).

Ballentine, K., and J. Sherman (eds.). 2003. *The Political Economy of Armed Conflict: Beyond Greed and Grievance* (Boulder, Colo.: Lynne Rienner).

Barakat, S. Z. 1993. "Reviving War-Damaged Settlements: Towards an International Charter for Reconstruction After War," unpublished Ph.D. thesis (York, England: University of York).

Barry, Deborah. 1994. "Organismos Financieros y Política Ambiental en El Salvador," *Boletín PRISMA* 6 (San Salvador: Programa Salvadoreño de Investigación sobre Desarrollo y Medio Ambiente): 1–8.

Bauman, Melissa, and Hannes Siebert. 2001. In Luc Reychler and Thania Paffenholz (eds.), *Peacebuilding: A Field Guide* (Boulder, Colo.: Lynne Rienner).

Beaugrand, P. 1997. "Zaire's Hyperinflation, 1990–1996," *Working Paper* WP/97/50 (Washington, D.C.: International Monetary Fund).

Beauvais, Joel. 2001. "Benevolent Despotism: A Critique of U.N. State-Building in East Timor," *New York University Journal of International Law and Politics* 33, no. 4.

Bell, Martin. 1997. "Journalism of Attachment," *The British Journalism Review* 8, no. 1.

Bennett, W. L., and D. Paletz (eds.). 1994. *Taken by Storm: The Media, Public Opinion and U.S. Foreign Policy in the Gulf War* (Chicago: University of Chicago Press).

Berdal, Mats. 1996. *Disarmament and Demobilization After Civil Wars,* Adelphi Paper 303 (New York: Oxford University Press).

Berdal, Mats, and David Malone (eds.). 2000. *Greed and Grievance: Economic Agendas in Civil Wars* (Boulder, Colo.: Lynne Rienner).

Bevan, D. 2003. "The Fiscal Dimensions of Ethiopia's Transition and Reconstruction," in T. Addison (ed.), *From Conflict to Recovery in Africa* (Oxford: Oxford University Press for WIDER), 228–239.

Biekart, K. 1999. *The Politics of Civil Society Building: European Private Aid Agencies and Democratic Transitions in Central America* (Utrecht, Netherlands: International Books).

Biggs, David. 1993. *The United Nations in Cambodia: A Vote for Peace* (New York: United Nations).

Bloor, Thomas, and Wondwosen Tamrat. 1996. "Multi-Lingualism and Education: The Case of Ethiopia," in George M. Blue and Rosamond Mitchell (eds.), *Language and Education* (Southampton: British Association for Applied Linguistics), 52–60.

Bonn Agreement. http://www.uno.de/frieden/afghanistan/talks/agreement.htm.

Borgh, Chris van der. 1997. "Decision-making and Participation in Poverty Alleviation Programmes in Post-War Chalatenango, El Salvador," *European Review of Latin American and Caribbean Studies* 63 (December) (Amsterdam: CEDLA), 49–66.

Borgh, Chris van der. 2003. *Gobernabilidad, Cooperación Externa & Reconstrucción Pos-Guerra. La Experiencia de Chalatenango, El Salvador* (Amsterdam: Rozenberg Publishers), forthcoming.

Botes, Jannie. 2000. "Media in the New South Africa," in *Regional Media in Conflict* (London: The Institute for War and Peace Reporting).

Botes, Johannes. 1994. "Journalism and Conflict Resolution," in *Frameworks for Interpreting Conflict: A Handbook for Journalists* (Fairfax, Va.: Institute for Conflict Analysis and Resolution, George Mason University).

Boua, Chanthou. 1993. "Development Aid and Democracy in Cambodia," in Ben Kiernan (ed.), *Genocide and Democracy in Cambodia: The Khmer Rouge, the United Nations and the International Community* (New Haven, Conn.: Yale University Law School), 273–284.

Boyce, J. 1995. "External Assistance and the Peace Process in El Salvador," *World Development* 23, no. 12: 2101–2116.

Boyce, J. (ed.). 1996. *Economic Policy for Building Peace: The Lessons of El Salvador* (Boulder, Colo.: Lynne Rienner).

Boyce, J., and M. Pastor. 1997. "Macroeconomic Policy and Peace Building in El Salvador," in Krishna Kumar (ed.), *Rebuilding Societies After Civil War* (Boulder, Colo.: Lynne Rienner), 287–314.

Brock-Utne, Birgit. 2002. *Language, Democracy, and Education in Africa* (Uppsala: Nordiska Afrikaninstitutet).

Brown, Kenneth. 1986. "Criminal Law and Custom in Solomon Islands," *Queensland Institute of Technology Law Journal* 2: 133–139.

Brown, Kenneth. 1999. "Customary Law in the Pacific: An Endangered Species?" *Journal of South Pacific Law* 3.

Brück, T., V. FitzGerald, and A. Grigsby. 2000. "Enhancing the Private Sector Contribution to Post-War Recovery in Poor Countries," *Queen Elizabeth House Working Paper Series* 45, no. 3 (Oxford: University of Oxford, International Development Center). http://www2.qeh.ox.ac.uk/pdf/qehwp/qehwps45_3.pdf, August 12, 2003.

Brynen, Rex. 2000. *A Very Political Economy: Peacebuilding and Foreign Aid in the West Bank and Gaza* (Washington, D.C.: United States Institute of Peace Press).

Carnegie Commission on Preventing Deadly Conflict. 1999. *Journalists Covering Conflict*, conference report. http://www.wilsoncenter.org/subsites/ccpdc/events/journ/journ.htm.

Carothers, T. 1999. *Aiding Democracy Abroad: The Learning Curve* (Washington, D.C.: Carnegie Endowment for International Peace).

Carroll, T. 1992. *Intermediary NGOs: The Supporting Link in Grassroots Development* (West Hartford, Conn.: Kumarian Press).

Carton, Michael. 1984. *Education and the World of Work* (Paris: UNESCO).

Caruso, E., et al. 2003. *Extracting Promises: Indigenous Peoples, Extractive Industries, and the World Bank,* synthesis report, May. http://www.eireview.org/eir/eirhome.nsf/(DocLibrary)/272EBA7B8C40541A85256D4000 26441F/$FILE/wbeirfinaltextasentout.doc, August 18, 2003.

Catenacci, Luciano, and David O'Brien. 1996. "Towards a Framework for Local Democracy in a War-Torn Society: The Lessons of Selected Foreign Assistance Programmes in El Salvador," *Democratization* 3, no. 4 (winter): 435–458.

Chanda, Nayan. 1986. *Brother Enemy: The War After the War. A History of Indochina Since the Fall of Saigon* (San Diego, Calif.: Harcourt, Brace, Jovanovich).

Chandler, David. 1991. *The Tragedy of Cambodian History: Politics, War and Revolution Since 1945* (New Haven, Conn.: Yale University Press).

Chen, D., J. Matovu, and R. Reinikka. 2001. "A Quest for Revenue and Tax Incidence in Uganda," *Working Paper,* January 24 (Washington, D.C.: IMF Institute).

Chopra, Jarat. 2000. "The UN's Kingdom in East Timor," *Survival* 42, no. 3: 27–39.

Chopra, Jarat. 2002. "Building State Failure in East Timor," *Development and Change* 33, no. 5.

Chopra, Jarat, and Tanja Hohe. 2004. "Participatory Intervention," *Global Governance* 10, no. 3 (August): 289–305.

Chossudovsky, M. 1999. *Impact of NATO's "Humanitarian" Bombings of Yugoslavia,* special for Northstar Compass. http://www.northstarcompass. org/nsc9905/chossud.htm, April 5, 2003.

Chumbow, Beban Sammy. 1980. "Language and Language Policy in Cameroon," in Ndiva Kofele-Kale (ed.), *An African Experiment in Nation Building: The Bilingual Cameroon Republic Since Reunification* (Boulder, Colo.: Westview), 281–312.

Cliffe, Sarah, Scott Guggenheim, and Markus Kostner. 2003. "Community-Driven Reconstruction as an Instrument in War-to-Peace Transitions," CPR Working Paper Series (Social Development Department, World Bank). http://lnweb18.worldbank.org/ESSD/sdvext.nsf/67ByDocName/ PublicationsWorkingPapers.

Cockell, J. G. 2000. "Conceptualising Peacebuilding: Human Security and Sustainable Peace," in J. Whitman (ed.), *Regeneration of War-Torn Societies: Global Issues* (Basingstoke: Macmillan), 15–34.

Colletta, Nat J., Markus Kostner, and Ingo Wiederhofer. 1996. *The Transition from War to Peace in Sub-Saharan Africa* (Washington, D.C.: World Bank).

Collier, Paul. 1994. "Some Economic Consequences of the Transition from Civil War to Peace: An Introduction" (Oxford: Center for the Study of African Economies).

Collier, Paul, et al. 2003. *Breaking the Conflict Trap: Civil War and Development Policy* (Washington, D.C: World Bank).

Collier, Paul, and Anke Hoeffler. 1998. "On Economic Causes of Civil War," *Oxford Economic Papers* 50, no. 4: 563–573.

Collier, Paul, and Anke Hoeffler. 2002. *Greed and Grievance in Civil War* (Washington, D.C.: World Bank).

Conflict, Security, and Development Group. 2003. *A Review of Peace Operations: A Case for Change. East Timor Study* (London: King's College).

Córdova Macías, R., and C. Lara M. 1996. *Centroamérica: Gobierno Local y Participación Ciudadana* (San Salvador: FUNDAUNGO & FLACSO).

CPRU. 2002. "Conflict and Labor Markets in Manufacturing: The Case of Eritrea," Dissemination Notes No. 7, December (Washington, D.C.: World Bank, Social Development Department). http://lnweb18.worldbank.org/ESSD/sdvext.nsf/67ByDocName/ConflictandLaborMarketsinManufacturing-TheCaseofEritrea/$FILE/EritreaNote7.pdf, August 13, 2003.

Crawley, M. 2001. "A Taxing Time to Rule Somalia," special to the *Christian Science Monitor.* http://www.csmonitor.com/2001/1213/p6s1-woaf.html, August 29, 2003.

Cuenca, B. 1992. *El Poder Intangible, La AID y el Estado Salvadoreño en los Años Ochtenta* (San Salvador/Managua: CRIES/PREIS).

Curtis, Devon. 2000. "Broadcasting Peace: An Analysis of Local Media Post-Conflict Peacebuilding Projects in Rwanda and Bosnia," *Canadian Journal of Development Studies* 21, no. 1: 141–155.

DAC Guidelines on Conflict, Peace and Development Co-operation. 1997. (Paris: OECD).

Date-Bah, E. 2001. *Crises and Decent Work: A Collection of Essays,* August (Geneva: International Labor Organization, InFocus Program on Crisis Response and Reconstruction, Recovery, and Reconstruction Department). http://www.ilo.org/public/english/employment/recon/crisis/download/crises.pdf, August 14, 2003.

Davis, Alan (ed.). 2002. *Regional Media in Conflict* (London: The Institute for War and Peace Reporting).

De Brito, Luis. 1995. "O comportamento eleitoral nas primeiras eleições multi-partidárias em Moçambique," in Brazão Mazula (ed.), *Moçambique: Eleições, Democracia e Desenvolvimento* (Maputo: A Embaixada).

Degu, Wondem Asres. 2002. *The State, the Crisis of State Institutions, and Refugee Migration in the Horn of Africa: The Cases of Ethiopia, Sudan, and Somalia* (Amsterdam: University of Amsterdam).

De Haan, A., and S. Maxwell (eds.). 1998. "Poverty and Social Exclusion in North and South," *IDS Bulletin* 29, no. 1: 1–31.

DFID. 2000. *Evaluation of Revenue Projects: Synthesis Report* (London: Department for International Development, Evaluation Department).

DIGESTYC. 1974. *Cuarto Censo Nacional de Poblacion 1971: Volumen I— Características Generales, Características Educacionales, Fecundidad* (San Salvador: Dirección General de Estadística y Censos).

DIGESTYC. 1992. *Resultados Definitivos del Censo de Población 1992* (San Salvador: Dirección General de Estadística y Censos).

Di Santo, Joseph E. 1992. "Environmental Impact Assessment," in Edgar F. Borgatta and Marie L. Borgatta (eds.), *Encyclopedia of Sociology,* vol. 2 (New York: Macmillan), 545–550.

Donais, T. 2002. "The Politics of Privatization in Post-Dayton Bosnia," *Southeast European Politics* 3, no. 1: 3–19.

Dos Santos, Carlos. 2000. "Background Paper: Mozambique," in Chang Li Lin and Nassrine Azimi (eds.), *Peacekeeping: The Nexus Between Peacekeeping and Peace-Building—Debriefing and Lessons* (London: Kluwer Law International), 105–118.

Doyle, Michael W. 1995. *UN Peacekeeping in Cambodia: UNTAC's Civil Mandate* (Boulder, Colo.: Lynne Rienner).

Duffield, Mark. 2001. *Global Governance and the New Wars: The Merging of Development and Security* (London: Zed).

Duffield, Mark, Patricia Grossman, and Nicholas Leader. 2002. *Review of the Strategic Framework for Afghanistan* (Kabul/Islamabad: AREU).

Duggan, Stephen J. 1996. "Education, Teacher Training and Prospects for Economic Recovery in Cambodia," *Comparative Education* 32, no. 3: 361–375.

Dunn, James. 1999. *Crimes Against Humanity in East Timor, January to October 1999: Their Nature and Causes,* East Timor Action Network. http://www.etan.org/etanpdf/pdf1/dunn.pdf.

Dursch, J. William. 2000. *Discussion of the Report of the Panel on UN Peace Operations* (Washington, D.C.: Stimson Center).

Ehrke, M. 2003. "Von der Raubökonomie zur Rentenökonomie: Mafia, Bürokratie und internationals Mandat in Bosnien." *Internationale Politik und Gesellschaft,* February. http://fesportal.fes.de/pls/portal30/docs/FOLDER/IPG/IPG2_2003/ARTEHRKE.HTM, August 11, 2003.

European Center for Conflict Prevention. 2003. *The Power of Media. A Handbook for Peacebuilders* (Utrecht: European Center for Conflict Prevention).

Fassil G. Kiros. 1990. *Implementing Educational Policies in Ethiopia* (Washington, D.C.: World Bank).

Findlay, Trevor. 1995. *Cambodia: The Legacy and Lessons of UNTAC,* SIPRI Research Report No. 9 (Oxford: Oxford University Press).

Fjeldstad, O-H. 2002. *Fighting Fiscal Corruption: What Went Wrong in the Tanzanian Revenue Authority?* mimeo (Bergen, Norway: Chr. Michelsen Institute).

Flounders, S. 1999. "Report from the War Zone: Yugoslavs Resist in Ingenious Ways," *Workers World,* June 3. http://www.globalexchange.org/balkans/news/flounders.html, April 5, 2003.

Flower, Ken. 1987. *Serving Secretly* (London: John Murray).

Forman, Shepard, and Stewart Patrick (eds.). 2000. *Good Intentions: Pledges of Aid for Postconflict Recovery* (Boulder, Colo.: Lynne Rienner).

Forman, Shepard, Stewart Patrick, and Dirk Salomons. 2000. *Recovering from Conflict: Strategy for an International Response* (New York: Center on International Cooperation, New York University).

Fox, W., and C. Wallich. 1998. "Bosnia-Herzegovina: Fiscal Federalism—The Dayton Challenge," in R. M. Bird and F. Vaillancourt (eds.), *Fiscal*

Decentralization in Developing Countries (Cambridge: Cambridge University Press), 1–48.

Fraser, Ian. 1999. "Legal Theory in Melanesia: Pluralism? Dualism? Pluralism Long Dualism?" *Journal of South Pacific Law* 3.

Freire, Paulo. 1973. *Pedagogy of the Oppressed* (New York: Seabury).

Gall, Carlotta. 2003. "Letter from Asia," *New York Times,* June 11.

General Peace Agreement of Mozambique. 1995. Translation from the Portuguese contained as Document 12 in the United Nations Blue Book Series, vol. 5, *The United Nations and Mozambique, 1992–1995* (New York: United Nations Publications).

Global Witness. 2002. *All the Presidents' Men: The Devastating Story of Oil and Banking in Angola's Privatised War,* March (London: Global Witness). http://www.globalwitness.org/reports/show.php/en.00002.html, August 13, 2003.

GoM (Government of Mozambique). 2003. *Republic of Mozambique: Poverty Reduction Strategy Paper Progress Report* (Washington, D.C.: IMF).

Goulet, D. 1995. *Development Ethics: A Guide to Theory and Practice* (London: Zed).

Gray, I., and T. L. Karl. 2003. *Bottom of the Barrel: Africa's Oil Boom and the Poor* (Baltimore: Catholic Relief Services). http://www.catholicrelief.org/get_involved/advocacy/policy_and_strategic_issues/oil_report_full.pdf, July 26, 2003.

Gray-Cowan, L. 1966. *Education and Nation-Building in Africa* (New York: Praeger).

Green, Kenneth M., and Carlos Roberto Ochoa. 1995. *Environmental Assessment for the Infrastructure Subactivities of the National Reconstruction Plan El Salvador, Submitted to USAID/El Salvador* (Arlington, Va.: Datex, Inc.).

Guerra y Guerra, Rodrigo. 1993. "Breve Análisis del Sector Eléctrico Nacional," CINAS, *El Salvador: Medio Ambiente y Desarrollo Energético* (San Salvador: Centro de Investigación y Acción Social), 33–40.

Guha-Sapir, Debarati. 2003. "We Need to Apply Somalia Lessons in Afghanistan," *AlertNet,* February 14, 2003.

Guide to Supporting Media in Conflict and Other Emergencies. 2001. (London: DFID, HM Government).

Gupta, S., B. Clements, R. Bhattacharya, and S. Chakravarti. 2002. *Fiscal Dimensions of Armed Conflict in Low- and Middle-Income Countries* (Washington, D.C.: IMF, Fiscal Affairs Department).

Hanlon, Joseph. 1991. *Mozambique: Who Calls the Shots?* (London: James Currey).

Hanlon, Joseph. 1994. *Report of AWEPA's Observation of the Mozambique Electoral Process* (Amsterdam: AWEPA).

Hanlon, Joseph. 1996. *Peace Without Profit: How the IMF Blocks Rebuilding in Mozambique* (Oxford: James Currey).

Hanlon, Joseph. 2002a. "Bank Corruption Becomes Site of Struggle in Mozambique," *Review of African Political Economy* 91: 53–72.

Hanlon, Joseph. 2002b. "Are Donors to Mozambique Promoting Corruption?" paper presented at conference, "Towards a New Political Economy of Development," July 3–4, Sheffield, England.

Hansson, G. 2003. "Building New States: Lessons from Eritrea," in T. Addison (ed.), *From Conflict to Recovery in Africa* (Oxford: Oxford University Press for WIDER), 190–205.

Havermans, Jos. 1998. "Better Media, Less Conflict," *Conflict Prevention Newsletter* 1, no. 1 (June).

Heder, Steven, and Judy Ledgerwood (eds.). 1996. *Propaganda, Politics, and Violence in Cambodia: Democratic Transition Under United Nations Peace-Keeping* (Armonk, N.Y.: Sharpe).

Heininger, Janet Elaine. 1994. *Peacekeeping in Transition: The United Nations in Cambodia* (New York: Twentieth Century Fund).

Hendrickson, D., and N. Ball. 2002. "Off-Budget Military Expenditure and Revenue: Issues and Policy Perspectives for Donors," Occasional Papers No. 1 (London: Department for International Development/King's College, Conflict, Security, and Development Group).

Hewitt del Alcantara, Cynthia. 1999. "Uses and Abuses of the Concept of Governance in the International Development Community," in P. P. J. Nas and P. Silva (eds.), *Modernization, Leadership, and Participation: Essays in Honour of Benno Galjart* (Leiden: Leiden University Press), 125–137.

Hoffmann, Bernd, and Colin Gleichmann. 1999. "Programmes for the Demobilization and Reintegration of Ex-Combatants: Changing Perspectives in Development and Security," paper for the International Conference and Expert-Group Meeting on the Contribution of Disarmament and Conversion to Conflict Prevention and Its Relevance for Development Cooperation, August 30–31 (Bonn: Bonn International Center for Conversion).

Hoffmann, Bernd, and Colin Gleichmann. 2000. *Programmes for the Demobilization and Reintegration of Ex-Combatants: Changing Perspectives in Development and Security* (Eschborn: Deutsche Gesellschaft fuer Technische Zusammenarbeit).

Hohe, Tanja. 2002. "The Clash of Paradigms: International Administration and Local Political Legitimacy in East Timor," *Contemporary Southeast Asia* 24, no. 3.

Howard, J., and J. Pearce. 2001. *Civil Society and Development: A Critical Exploration* (Boulder, Colo.: Lynne Rienner).

Howard, Ross. 2002. *An Operational Framework for Media and Peacebuilding* (IMPACS). www.impacs.org.

Howard, Ross. 2003. *Media Assistance in Democratic Transitions in Post-Conflict Societies* (The Hague: Netherlands Institute of International Relations Clingendael Conflict Research Unit).

Howell, Jude, and Jenny Pearce. 2001. *Civil Society and Development. A Critical Exploration* (Boulder, Colo.: Lynne Rienner).

Humphreys, M. 2002. *Economics and Violent Conflict,* August (Boston: Harvard University). http://www.preventconflict.org/portal/economics/Essay.pdf, January 25, 2003.

Huntington, Samuel P. 1991. *The Third Wave: Democratization in the Late Twentieth Century* (Norman: University of Oklahoma Press).

ICARDA. 2002. *Discussion on Key Issues on Horticultural Crops,* future harvest consortium to rebuild agriculture in Afghanistan, Restoring Food Security and Rebuilding the Agricultural Sector in Afghanistan, First

Stakeholders Meeting, January 20–21 (ICARDA). http://www.icarda. cgiar.org/Afghanistan/annex3_4_1.htm, April 23, 2003.

ICG. 2001. "Afghanistan and Central Asia: Priorities for Reconstruction and Development," *Asia Report* No. 26, November 27 (Osh/Brussels: ICG).

ICG. 2001a. "Bosnia's Precarious Economy: Still Not Open for Business," *Balkan Report* No. 115, August 7 (Sarajevo/Brussels: ICG). http://www. crisisweb.org/projects/showreport.cfm?reportid=375, August 13, 2003.

ICG. 2001b. "Kosovo: A Strategy for Economic Development," *Balkans Report* No. 123 (Pristina/Brussels: ICG). http://www.crisisweb.org/projects/showreport.cfm?reportid=514, August 20, 2003.

ICG. 2002. *The Meanings of Palestinian Reform,* November 12 (Washington/Amman: ICG). http://www.crisisweb.org/projects/showreport.cfm?reportid=815.

Ignatieff, Michael. 1998. *The Warrior's Honour: Ethnic War and the Modern Conscience* (London: Chatto & Windus).

Ignatieff, Michael. 2002. "Nation-Building Lite," *New York Times Magazine,* July 28.

ILO. 1998. *Guidelines for Employment and Skilltraining in Conflict-Affected Countries* (Geneva: ILO, InFocus Program on Crisis Response and Reconstruction). http://www.ilo.org/public/english/employment/recon/crisis/papers/guide.htm, April 4, 2003.

IMF. 2001. *West Bank and Gaza: Economic Performance, Prospects, and Policies* (Washington, D.C.: IMF).

IMF. 2002. Republic of Mozambique: Letter of Intent, Memorandum of Economic and Financial Policies, and Technical Memorandum of Understanding, June 3 (Washington, D.C.: IMF).

INE (Instituto Nacional de Estatístico). 2002. *Anuário Estatístico 2001* (Maputo: INE).

International Campaign to Ban Landmines. 2001. "Afghanistan," *Landmine Monitor Report,* 469–516. http://www.icbl.org/lm/2001/print/report/Asia.zip.

International Development Research Center. 2001. *The Responsibility to Protect,* Report of the International Commission on Intervention and State Sovereignty (Ottawa).

Jackson, David H. 2002. "Local Governance Approach to Social Reintegration and Economic Recovery in Post-Conflict Countries: The View from Mozambique," discussion paper for workshop, "A Local Governance Approach to Post-Conflict Recovery," October 8, New York.

Jett, Dennis. 2000. "Background Paper: Mozambique," in Chang Li Lin and Nassrine Azimi (eds.), *Peacekeeping: The Nexus Between Peacekeeping and Peace-Building—Debriefing and Lessons* (London: Kluwer Law International), 119–128.

Joint Assessment Mission. 1999a. "East Timor: Building a Nation. A Framework for Reconstruction and Development: Governance Background Paper (Including Civil Service, Justice, and Community Empowerment)," November. http://wbln0018.worldbank.org/eap/eap.nsf/0/a67abe6406537dcb85256847007dff36?OpenDocument.

Joint Assessment Mission. 1999b. *Report of the Joint Assessment Mission to*

East Timor. http://wbln0018.worldbank.org/eap/eap.nsf/0/a67abe6406537/ dcb85256847007dff36?OpenDocument.

Kaufman, Marc. 2003. "Karzai's Taxing Problem," *Washington Post,* March 19.

Kayizzi-Mugerwa, S. (ed.). 2003. *Reforming Africa's Institutions: Ownership, Incentives, and Capabilities* (Tokyo: United Nations University Press for WIDER).

Kazmin, A. 2002. "Loss of Magical Mystery Could Spell the Ruin of Angkor," *Financial Times,* November 9.

Keune, L. 1996. *Sobrevivimos la Guerra: La Historia de los Pobladores de Arcatao y San José las Flores* (San Salvador: Adelina Editores).

Kiernan, Ben. 1993. "The Inclusion of the Khmer Rouge in the Cambodian Peace Process: Causes and Consequences," in Ben Kiernan (ed.), *Genocide and Democracy in Cambodia: The Khmer Rouge, the United Nations and the International Community* (New Haven, Conn.: Yale University Law School), 191–272.

Kreimer, A., J. Eriksson, R. Muscat, M. Arnold, and C. Scott. 1998. *The World Bank's Experience with Post-Conflict Reconstruction* (Washington, D.C.: World Bank). http://wbln0018.worldbank.org/oed/oeddoclib.nsf/ 0/f753e43e728a27b38525681700503796/$FILE/PostCon.pdf, August 13, 2003.

Krug, Peter, and Monroe Price. 2002. "The Legal Environment for News Media," in *The Right to Tell: The Role of Mass Media in Economic Development* (Washington, D.C.: World Bank).

La'o Hamutuk Bulletin. 2000. The East Timor Institute for Reconstruction Monitoring and Analysis, Dili.

Lia, Brynjar. 1998. *Implementing Peace: The Oslo Peace Accord and International Assistance to the Enhancement of Security,* Forsvarets Forskningsinstitutt FFI/RAPPORT-98/01711 (Kjellar, Norway: Norwegian Defense Research Establishment).

Lister, Stephen, and Anne Le More. 2003. *Aid Management and Coordination During the Intifada,* draft of April (Oxford: Mokoro Limited).

Lizée, Pierre. 2000. *Peace, Power, and Resistance in Cambodia: Global Governance and the Failure of International Conflict Resolution* (Basingstoke: Macmillan).

Lowe, John, Nigel Grant, and David T. Williams. 1971. *Education and Nation-Building in the Third World* (London: Scottish Academic Press).

Lungo, Mario. 1995. "Problemas Ambientales, Gestión Urbana y Sustentabilidad del AMSS," *Boletín PRISMA* 12 (San Salvador: Programa Salvadoreño de Investigación sobre Desarrollo y Medio Ambiente): 1–11.

Lynch, Jake, and Annabel McGoldrick. 2001. *Reporting the World: Conflict and Peace Forums* (London). www.transcend.org.

Malaquias, A. 2001. "Making War and Lots of Money: The Political Economy of Protracted Conflict in Angola," *Review of African Political Economy* 90: 521–536.

Manning, Carrie. 2002. *The Politics of Peace in Mozambique* (London: Praeger).

Manoff, Robert. 1998. "Role Plays," in *Track Two* 7, December.

Media and Conflict: Special Edition. 1998. *Track Two,* December (Center for Conflict Resolution).

Mehlum, H., K. O. Moene, and R. Torvik. 2002. "Plunder and Protection Inc." Memorandum No. 10/2002 (Oslo: University of Oslo, Department of Economics). http://www.oekonomi.uio.no/memo/memopdf/memo1002. pdf, August 13, 2003.

Miall, Hugh. 2001. "Conflict Transformation: A Multi-Dimensional Task," in *Berghof Handbook for Conflict Transformation* (Berlin: Berghof Research Center for Constructive Conflict Management).

MIPLAN. 1992. *Plan de Reconstrucción Nacional: Volumen I* (San Salvador: Ministerio de Planificación y Coordinación del Desarrollo Económico y Social).

Montoya, A. 1994. *La Nueva Economía Popular, una Aproximación Empírica* (San Salvador: UCA Editores).

Moore, David. 2000. "Levelling the Playing Fields and Embedding Illusions: 'Post-Conflict' Discourse and Neo-Liberal 'Development' in War-Torn Africa," *Review of African Political Economy* 83: 11–28.

Munn, R. E. 1979. *Environmental Impact Assessment: Principles and Procedures* (Chichester, England: John Wiley).

Munro, W. 2001. "Conflicting Ideological Agendas and Institutional Imperatives: Post-Conflict Development Within the Aid Industry" (Durban: School of Development Studies, University of Natal).

Murray, K. (ed.). 1994. *Rescuing Reconstruction: The Debate on the Post-War Economic Recovery in El Salvador* (Cambridge, Mass.: Hemisphere Initiatives).

Ndikumana, L. 2001. *Fiscal Policy, Conflict, and Reconstruction in Burundi and Rwanda,* WIDER Discussion Paper No. 2001/62 (Helsinki: United Nations University).

Ndikumana, L. 2004. "Fiscal Policy, Conflict, and Reconstruction in Burundi and Rwanda," in T. Addison and A. Roe (eds.), *Fiscal Policy for Development* (Basingstoke: Palgrave).

Negash, Tekeste. 1990. *The Crises in Ethiopian Education* (Uppsala: Nordiska Afrikainstitutet).

Negash, Tekeste. 1996. *Rethinking Education in Ethiopia* (Uppsala: Nordiska Afrikainstitutet).

Nzongola-Ntalaja, G. 2002. *The Congo: From Leopold to Kabila* (London: Zed).

OECD. 1997. *DAC Guidelines on Conflict, Peace, and Development Co-operation* (Paris).

Office for the Coordination of Humanitarian Affairs. 2002. *Humanitarian Plan of Action 2003* (Geneva: United Nations).

Office of the United Nations Special Coordinator. 2002. *The Impact of Closure and Other Mobility Restrictions on Palestinian Productive Activities, 1 January 2002–30 June 2002* (Gaza: UNSCO).

OJEC. 2002. "Council Regulation (EC) No 2368/2002 of 20 December 2002 Implementing the Kimberley Process Certification Scheme for the International Trade in Rough Diamonds," *Official Journal of the European Communities* L358, 28–48.

Öjendal, Joakim. 1996. "Democracy Lost? The Fate of the UN-implanted

Democracy in Cambodia," *Contemporary Southeast Asia* 18: 193–218.

OSCE. 1990. *Document of the Copenhagen Meeting of the Conference on Human Dimension of the SCCE, Copenhagen 5–9 June 1990* (Copenhagen: OSCE).

Ospina, Sofi, and Tanja Hohe. 2002. "Traditional Power Structures and Local Governance in East Timor: A Case Study of the Community Empowerment Project," *Etudes Courtes,* no. 5 (Geneva: Graduate Institute of Development Studies).

Ostheimer, Andrea. 2001. "Mozambique: The Permanent Entrenchment of Democratic Minimalism?" *African Security Review* 10, no. 1 (Pretoria: Institute for Security Studies). http://www.iss.co.za/Pubs/ASR/10No1/Ostheimer.html.

Ostrovsky, A. 2002. "Croatia: Unlocking a Vast Potential," *Financial Times,* June 24.

Oxfam. 1999. *East Timor: One Chance to Get It Right,* donor conference preparatory document (Oxford: Oxfam).

Özerdem, A. 1998. "An Approach to Sustainable Recovery of Urban Water Supplies in War-Affected Areas with Specific Reference to the Tuzla Region of Bosnia and Herzegovina," unpublished Ph.D. thesis (York, England: University of York).

Pain, A., and J. Goodhand. 2002. "Afghanistan: Current Employment and Socio-economic Situation and Prospects," Working Paper No. 8, March (Geneva: ILO, InFocus Program on Crisis Response and Reconstruction, Recovery, and Reconstruction Department). http://www.ilo.org/public/english/employment/recon/crisis/download/wp8.pdf, 14/08/03.

Parry, R. L. 2001. "Opium Farmers Rejoice at Defeat of the Taliban," *Independent* 21, November. www.hartford-hwp.com/archives/51/125.html, August 13, 2003.

Patrick, S. 2000. "The Donor Community and the Challenge of Postconflict Recovery," in Shepard Forman and Stewart Patrick (eds.), *Good Intentions: Pledges of Aid for Postconflict Recovery* (Boulder, Colo.: Lynne Rienner), 35–65.

"Peacebuilding in Postconflict Angola." 2003. Address by Professor Ibrahim Gambari, Undersecretary General and Special Adviser on Africa, United Nations, International Peace Academy Forum on Angola, June 6, New York.

Pearce, J. 1986. *Promised Land: Peasant Rebellion in Chalatenango, El Salvador* (London: LAB).

Pearce, J. 1999. "Peace-building in the Periphery: Lessons from Central America," *Third World Quarterly* 20, no. 1.

Peou, Sorpong. 2000. "Cambodia," in Shepard Forman and Stewart Patrick (eds.), *Good Intentions: Pledges of Aid for Postconflict Recovery* (Boulder, Colo.: Lynne Rienner).

Pinto, David. 2000a. *Intercultural Communication: A Three-Step Method for Dealing with Differences* (Louvain/Apeldoorn: Garant).

Pinto, David. 2000b. *Een nieuw perspectief. Herziening van beleid, onderwijs, communicatie, maslowpiramide dringend nodig* (Amsterdam: Vossiuspers AUP).

Pleitez Rodríguez, W. 2001. *Informe sobre el Desarrollo Humano* (San Salvador: UNDP).

Plunkett, Mark. 1998. "Reestablishing Law and Order in Peace Maintenance," in Jarat Chopra (ed.), *The Politics of Peace-Maintenance* (Boulder, Colo.: Lynne Rienner).

Praxis Group, Ltd. 2002. "Willing to Listen: An Evaluation of the Mine Action Programme in Kosovo," report commissioned by the United Nations Mine Action Service, December. www.mineaction.org/misc/resultdisplay.cfm? doc_ID=848.

Price, Monroe. 2000. *Restructuring the Media in Post-Conflict Societies*, background paper for UNESCO World Press Day.

PRISMA. 1995. *El Salvador: Dinámica de la Degradación Ambiental* (San Salvador: Programa Salvadoreño de Investigación sobre Desarrollo y Medio Ambiente).

Putnam, Robert D. 1993. *Making Democracy Work: Civic Traditions in Modern Italy* (Princeton, N.J.: Princeton University Press).

Ratilal, Prakash. 2002a. "Aumento da Riqueza Nacional, Distribuição Equitativa, Coesão Nacional," in Brazão Mazula (ed.), *Moçambique: 10 Anos de Paz* (Maputo: CEDE), 253–297.

Ratilal, Prakash. 2002b. no title, in Brazão Mazula (ed.), *Moçambique: 10 Anos de Paz* (Maputo: CEDE), 367–380.

Ratilal, Prakash. 2002c. "A pobreza e a desigualidade podem sustentar a paz?" in Brazão Mazula (ed.), *Moçambique: 10 Anos de Paz* (Maputo: CEDE).

Raz, Joseph. 1979. *The Authority of the Law: Essays in Law and Morality* (Oxford: Larendon).

Rehn, Elisabeth, and Ellen Johnson Sirleaf. 2002. *Women, War, Peace: The Independent Experts' Assessment on the Impact of Armed Conflict on Women and Women's Role in Peace-Building* (New York: UNIFEM).

Reljik, Dusan. 2002. "News Media and Transformation of Ethnopolitical Conflicts," in *Berghof Handbook for Conflict Transformation* (Berlin: Berghof Research Center for Constructive Conflict Management).

Renner, Michael. 2002. "The Anatomy of Resource Wars," Worldwatch Paper 162.

Rieff, David. 2002. *A Bed for the Night: Humanitarianism in Crisis* (New York: Simon & Schuster).

Rivera Campos, Roberto. 2000. *La Economía Salvadoreña al Final del Siglo: Desafíos para el Futuro* (San Salvador: FLACSO).

Rosa, Herman. 1993. *AID y las Transformaciones Globales en El Salvador* (Managua: CRIES).

Rosa, Herman, and Michael Foley. 2000. "El Salvador," in Shepard Forman and Stewart Patrick (eds.), *Good Intentions: Pledges of Aid for Postconflict Recovery* (Boulder, Colo.: Lynne Rienner), 113–157.

Rosen, Jay. 1999. *Journalists Covering Conflict* (Carnegie Commission on Preventing Deadly Conflict). http://www.wilsoncenter.org/subsites/ccpdc/ events/journ/journ.htm.

Rubanza, Y. I. 1996. "Can a Three-Tier Language Policy Model Work in Tanzania? A New Perspective," *UFAHAMU* 14, no. 1: 82–97.

Sachs, J. D., and A. M. Warner. 1995. *Natural Resource Abundance and*

Economic Growth, mimeo (Cambridge, Mass.: Harvard Institute for International Development).

Salomons, Dirk. 2003. "Probing the Successful Application of Leverage in Support of Mozambique's Quest for Peace," in Jean Krasno, Donald Daniel, and Bradd Hayes (eds.), *Leveraging for Success in United Nations Peace Operations* (Westport, Conn.: Greenwood Publishing Group, Inc.).

Salomons, Dirk, and Dennis Dijkzeul. 2001. *The Conjurer's Hat: Financing United Nations Peace-Building Operations Directed by Special Representatives of the Secretary-General,* Chapter 4 (Oslo: Fafo Institute for Applied Social Science).

Schiavo-Campo, S. 2003. "Financing and Aid Management Arrangements in Post-Conflict Situations," CPR Working Paper No. 6 (Washington, D.C.: World Bank). http://lnweb18.worldbank.org/essd/essd.nsf/CPR/WP6, June 14, 2003.

Selassie, Tekle-Haimanot Haile. 1983. "Regional Disparity of Education: The Case Pre- and Post-Revolution Ethiopia," M.A. thesis (Ethiopia: Addis Ababa University).

SEMA. 1992. *Agenda Ambiental y Plan de Acción* (San Salvador: Secretaría Ejecutiva del Medio Ambiente).

Sen, Amartya. 1999. *Development as Freedom* (New York: Anchor).

Sewell, David. 2001. *Governance and the Business Environment in the West Bank/Gaza* (Washington, D.C.: World Bank).

Shawcross, William. 2000. *Deliver Us from Evil: Peacekeepers, Warlords and a World of Endless Conflict* (New York: Simon & Schuster).

Shebeshi, Ayalew. 1989. "Some Trends in Regional Disparities in Primary School Participation in Ethiopia," *The Ethiopian Journal of Education* 11, no. 1.

Sissons, Miranda E. 1997. *From One Day to Another: Violations of Women's Reproductive and Sexual Rights in East Timor* (Melbourne: East Timor Human Rights Center).

Smillie, Ian. 2002. *Dirty Diamonds: Armed Conflict and the Trade in Rough Diamonds* (Oslo: Fafo Institue for Applied Social Science).

Smillie, Ian (ed.). 2001. *Patronage or Partnership: Local Capacity Building in Humanitarian Crises* (Bloomfield, Conn.: IDRC/Kumarian Press).

Snyder, Jack. 2000. *From Voting to Violence: Democratization and Nationalist Conflict* (New York: Norton).

Sollis, P. 1993. *Reluctant Reforms: The Cristiani Government and the International Community in the Process of Salvadoran Post-War Reconstruction* (Washington, D.C.: WOLA).

Sørensen, B. 1998. "Women and Post-Conflict Reconstruction: Issues and Sources," WSP Occasional Paper No. 3, June. http://www.wsp-international.org/op3/toc.htm, August 11, 2003.

Soviet Constitution: A Dictionary, The. 1986. (Moscow: Progress).

Spurk, Christopher. 2002. *Media and Peacebuilding, Concepts, Actors, and Challenges* (KOFF, SwissPeace).

SRN. 1993. *Manual Operativo Alcaldías Municipales para el Programa MEA* (San Salvador).

SRN. 1994. *Memoria de Labores 1989–1993* (San Salvador).

St. John, Robert Bruce. 1995. "The Political Economy of the Royal Government of Thailand," *Contemporary Southeast Asia* 17, no. 3: 265–285.

Stalnaker, Jessica. 2001. *International Media Assistance and Bosnian Civil Society: Localization as the Missing Link* (Washington, D.C.: American University, School of International Service).

Stedman, S. 2001. "International Implementation of Peace Agreements in Civil Wars: Findings from a Study of Sixteen Cases," in C. Crocker (ed.), *Turbulent Peace: The Challenges of Managing International Conflict* (Washington, D.C.: USIP).

Stewart, F. 2001. "Horizontal Inequalities: A Neglected Dimension of Development," *WIDER Annual Lecture* 5 (Helsinki: UNU/WIDER).

Stockton, Nicholas. 2002. *Strategic Coordination in Afghanistan* (Kabul/Islamabad: AREU).

Stroebel, Warren. 1998. *Late-Breaking News: The Media's Influence on Foreign Policy* (Washington, D.C.: U.S. Institute for Peace).

Suhrke, A., A. Ofstad, and A. Knudsen. 2002. *A Decade of Peacebuilding: Lessons for Afghanistan,* report prepared for the Norwegian Ministry of Foreign Affairs, April 2. http://www.cmi.no/pdf/Peacebuilding% 20Afghanistan2.pdf, August 13, 2003.

Sumata, C. 2002. "Migradollars and Poverty Alleviation Strategy Issues in Congo," *Review of African Political Economy* 29, no. 93/94: 619–628.

Support Group to the Ethiopian Human Rights Council. 2000. *The Impact of Federalism on Education in Ethiopia 1991–1998,* seminar report (Amsterdam).

Synge, Richard. 1997. *Mozambique: UN Peacekeeping in Action, 1992–1994* (Washington, D.C.: United States Institute of Peace Press).

Tadadjeu, Maurice. 1975. "Language Planning in Cameroon: Towards a Trilingual Education System," in Robert K. Herbert (ed.), *Patterns in Language, Culture, and Society: Sub-Saharan Africa* (Columbus: Ohio State University), 53–75.

Taylor, Maureen. 1999. *Evaluation of USAID/OTI Media Transition Grants in Bosnia* (USAID).

Terzis, George, and Sandra Melone. 2002. "Using the Media for Conflict Transformation," in *Berghof Handbook for Conflict Transformation* (Berlin: Berghof Research Center for Constructive Conflict Management).

Traube, Elizabeth G. 1986. *Cosmology and Social Life: Ritual Exchange Among the Mambai of East Timor* (Chicago: University of Chicago Press).

Tuso, Hamdesa. 1982. "Minority Education in Ethiopia, Africa," in *Rivisla Trimestrde di Studies Documentzions Dell Instituto Italo* 37, no. 3.

Ufen, Andreas. 2002. *Timor Lorosa' e—Die schwierige Geburt eines neuen Staates.* Konrad-Adenauer-Stiftung/Auslandsinformationen, nr. 6, 68–84.

UN. 1995. *The United Nations and El Salvador 1990–1995* (New York: United Nations).

UNAMA. 2002. *UNAMA Fact Sheet,* September (Kabul).

UNAMA/Afghanistan Management Information System. 2002. *AIMS Directory of Organizations Working in Afghanistan.* http://www.aims.org.pk/country_profile/directory_of_organizations_working_in_afg.pdf.

UNDP. 2002a. *Human Development Report.*

UNDP. 2002b. *Mozambique National Human Development Report* (Maputo: UNDP).

UNDP. 2002c. *Ukun Rasik A'an: The Way Ahead. East Timor Human Development Report 2002* (Dili: UNDP).

UNDP. "Afghanistan Fact Sheet." http://www.undp.org/afghanistan/FactSheet-final.doc.

UNEP. 1999. *The Kosovo Conflict—Consequences for the Environment and Human Settlements* (Geneva: UNEP).

UNEP. 2002. *Depleted Uranium in Serbia and Montenegro—Post-Conflict Environmental Assessment in the Federal Republic of Yugoslavia* (Geneva: UNEP).

UNESCO. 1984. *Prospect* (Quarterly Review of Education) 24, no. 1.

UNHCR. 1997. *The State of the World's Refugees 1997: A Humanitarian Agenda* (Geneva: UNHCR). http://www.unhcr.ch/cgibin/texis/vtx/home?page=PUBL&id=3eef1d896&ID=3eef1d896&PUBLISHER=TWO, August 11, 2003.

UNHCR. 2002a. "Refugees by Numbers 2002 Edition." http://www.unhcr.ch/cgibin/texis/vtx/home/opendoc.htm?tbl=STATISTICS&id=3d075d374&page=statistics.

UNHCR. 2002b. "Summary of Cumulative Assisted Voluntary Repatriation Data from 1 March (Pakistan) and 9 April (Iran) to 4 September 2002." http://www.aims.org.pk/assistance_sectors/refugee/summary_of_cumulative_assisted_voluntary_repatriation_data.pdf.

United Nations. 2000a. *Common Country Assessment for East Timor: Building Blocks for a Nation* (New York: United Nations).

United Nations. 2000b. *Report of the Panel on United Nations Peace Operations* (New York: United Nations). www.un.org/peace/report/peace_operations.

United Nations. 2000c. *The Role of United Nations Peacekeeping in Disarmament, Demobilization, and Reintegration,* Report of the Secretary-General, S/2000/11 (New York: United Nations).

United Nations. 2002. Report of the Secretary-General on Women, Peace, and Security, S/2002/11154, October 16.

United Nations. 2003. Press Release OSRSG/PR03/11, February 28.

United Nations Office on Drugs and Crime. 2002. *Afghanistan Opium Survey 2002.* http://www.odccp.org/pdf/afg/afg_opium_survey_2002.pdf.

UNODCCP. 1999a. "The Role of Opium as a Source of Informal Credit." Strategic Study No. 3, January (Vienna: UNODCCP). http://www.odccp.org/unodc/en/alternative_development_studies_3.html, August 13, 2003.

UNODCCP. 1999b. "Access to Labour: The Role of Opium in the Livelihood Strategies of Itinerant Harvesters Working in Helmand Province, Afghanistan," Strategic Study No. 4, June (Vienna: UNODCCP). http://www.odccp.org/unodc/en/alternative_development_studies_4.html, August 13, 2003.

UNSCO. 2002. *The Impact of Closure and Other Mobility Restrictions on Palestinian Productive Activities, 1 January 2002–30 June 2002* (Gaza: UNSCO).

Van Empel, C. 2000. *Local Economic Development Agencies: Instruments for Reconciliation and Reintegration in Post-Conflict Croatia,* paper prepared by ILO for the Special Event on Development Cooperation, Geneva, June 27. www.ilo.org/public/english/employment/led/publ/croatia1.htm, August 14, 2003.

Verkoren, Willemijn. 2003. "Installing Democracy . . . and Making It Work," M.A. thesis, University of Amsterdam.

Vickery, Michael. 1984. *Cambodia 1975–1982* (Boston: South End).

Wagaw, Teshome G. 1979. *Education in Ethiopia: Prospect and Retrospect.* Ann Arbor: University of Michigan Press.

Way, Wendy (ed.). 2000. *Australia and the Indonesian Incorporation of Portuguese East Timor, 1974–1976* (Carlton, Victoria: Melbourne University Press).

Weinberg, William J. 1991. *War on the Land: Ecology and Politics in Central America* (London: Zed).

Weinstein, Jeremy. 2002. "Mozambique: A Fading UN Success Story," in *Journal of Democracy* 13, no. 1: 141–156.

Williamson, John. 1995. *What Role for Currency Boards?* Policy Analyses in International Economics, no. 40 (Washington, D.C.: Institute for International Economics).

Wolde-Mariam, Mesfin. 1991. *An Ethiopian Peace Initiative,* paper presented at the XL International Conference of Ethiopian Studies, April 1–6, Addis Ababa, Ethiopia.

Wolfsfeld, Gadi. 2001a. *The News Media and Peace Processes: The Middle East and Northern Ireland* (Washington, D.C.: U.S. Institute of Peace).

Wolfsfeld, Gadi. 2001b. "The Varying Role of the News Media," paper given at the 2001 Annual Meeting of the American Political Science Association (San Francisco, Calif.).

Wood, Bernard. 2001. *Development Dimensions of Conflict Prevention and Peace-Building: An Independent Study Prepared for the Bureau for Crisis Prevention and Recovery, UNDP* (New York: UNDP).

Woods, L. Shelton, 1997. "The Myth of Cambodia's Recovery," *Contemporary Southeast Asia* 18, no. 4 (March).

World Bank. 1993. *Developing the Occupied Territories: An Investment in Peace,* 6 volumes (Washington, D.C.: World Bank).

World Bank. 1994. *Emergency Assistance Program* (Washington, D.C.: World Bank).

World Bank. 1998a. *Aid Effectiveness: What Works? What Doesn't?* (Oxford: Oxford University Press).

World Bank. 1998b. *Post-Conflict Reconstruction: The Role of the World Bank* (Washington, D.C.: World Bank).

World Bank. 1999. *West Bank and Gaza: Strengthening Public Sector Management* (Washington, D.C.: World Bank).

World Bank. 2002. "Community Empowerment and Local Governance Project. Draft Aide Memoires from the Supervision Mission," November (Dili: World Bank).

World Bank. 2002a. *World Bank Group Work in Low-Income Countries Under Stress: A Task Force Report,* September (Washington, D.C.: World Bank).

http://www1.worldbank.org/operations/licus/documents/licus.pdf, June 16, 2003.

World Bank. 2002b. *Holst Peace Fund: Supporting Peace in the West Bank and Gaza* (Washington, D.C.: World Bank).

World Bank. 2003a. *Twenty-Seven Months: Intifada, Closures, and Palestinian Economic Crisis*, draft report, April.

World Bank. 2003b. *Alternatives to Poppy in Afghanistan*, February 10. http://web.worldbank.org/WBSITE/EXTERNAL/NEWS/0,,contentMDK: 20090590~menuPK:34457~pagePK:34370~piPK:34424~theSitePK:4607, 00. html, April 23, 2003.

World Bank. 2004. *The Role of the World Bank in Conflict and Development: An Evolving Agenda* (Washington, D.C.: World Bank).

World Bank and Government of Japan. 2000. *Aid Effectiveness in the West Bank and Gaza* (Washington, D.C.: World Bank).

World Health Organization. 2002. *Health System Inputs (HSI) Index 2002.* http://www.who.int.

Zamora, Ruben. 2001. *La Encrucijada de la Economía Salvadoreña*, Collección Aportes, No. 11 (San Salvador: FLACSO).

Zeeuw, J. de. 2001. *Building Peace in War-Torn Societies from Concept to Strategy: A Review of Selected Literature on Rehabilitation, Sustainable Peace, and Development* (The Hague: Clingendael Conflict Research Unit).

The Contributors

Tony Addison is deputy director of the World Institute for Development Economics Research of the United Nations University, located in Helsinki. He was previously director of the program in Quantitative Development Economics at the University of Warwick, UK, and has acted as a consultant for DFID, ILO, UNICEF, and the World Bank. His recent publications include *From Conflict to Recovery in Africa*.

Martijn Bijlsma studied international relations, philosophy, and Spanish language and literature at the University of Amsterdam. He spent a year doing fieldwork research in postconflict El Salvador, analyzing some of the main institutional developments in the area and their relation to the political and economic reforms experienced since the end of civil conflict.

Chris van der Borgh is a lecturer at the Center for Conflict Studies, Utrecht University. He wrote his Ph.D. on the role of foreign assistance in the Salvadoran process of postsettlement reconstruction.

Richard H. Brown is a civil engineer with some thirty years of experience. He is also a reservist with the British Army and volunteered for posting to Bosnia and Herzegovina as a civil affairs officer, assessing major civil infrastructure and initiating reconstruction projects. In his work with UNMIK as general manager of the Kosovo Rail System, he was responsible for restarting civilian railway operations. His research work has taken him to East Timor and North Maluku. He is currently an associate director with international consulting engineers ARUP.

Rex Brynen is an associate professor of political science at McGill University in Montreal, Canada. His research interests relate to peacebuilding, postconflict reconstruction, and Middle East politics. In this last area of interest he focuses on Palestine, Jordan, and the Arab-Israeli conflict and peace process (with special emphasis on development assistance and refugees), security and development in the Middle East, and authoritarianism and democratization in the Arab world.

Abdur R. Chowdhury is a professor of economics at Marquette University. He began his professional career as an economist at the World Bank Resident Mission in Bangladesh and later joined the Ministry of Planning of the Government of Bangladesh. He has also been a visiting researcher at WIDER and worked as a consultant for the FAO and USAID. His current research interests include financial reform in transition economies and macropolicy issues in developing countries.

Wondem Asres Degu graduated from Addis Ababa University, Ethiopia, with a B.A. in political science and international relations and a minor in public administration. He received his M.A. and Ph.D. in international relations from the University of Amsterdam. His research interests focus on the different aspects of state (re)construction, state collapse, postconflict development, refugee migration in Africa, and the politics of education.

Joseph Hanlon is a senior lecturer at the Open University, Milton Keynes, England. His research deals with the roots of civil wars, and he is the author of the course "War, Intervention, and Development." He is editor of the *Mozambique Political Process Bulletin* and author of five books on Mozambique, including *Mozambique and the Great Flood of 2000*. He also writes on developing-country debt and international financial institutions.

Jose Luis Herrero has held various positions within the United Nations in Haiti, Rwanda, Geneva, and Kosovo since 1994. He was a political affairs officer in the Office of the Special Representative of the UN Secretary-General in Kosovo, responsible for setting up and maintaining central institutions. He was a policy adviser in the Office of the Deputy Special Representative for Civil Administration, with responsibilities in the design and implementation of municipal administrative structures. He has published several articles on peace support operations and conflict-related issues. He is currently the director of the Fundacion para las Relaciones Internacionales y el Dialogo Exterior in Spain.

Tanja Hohe is a political anthropologist and is presently a visiting fellow at the Thomas J. Watson Jr. Institute for International Studies, Brown University. She worked for several years in East Timor as a political affairs officer for the United Nations, and with the World Bank's Community Empowerment Project as team coordinator for the preparation of a report assessing the Traditional Power Structures and the Community Empowerment and Local Governance Project. She is currently writing a book on the conflict between the international intervention and the local paradigms of societies in East Timor.

Ross Howard is a journalism trainer and consultant specializing in the role of media in conflict environments and media in elections. He is an associate of the Institute for Media, Policy, and Civil Society (Canada) and a faculty member at Langara College (Vancouver). He recently produced An Operational Framework for Media and Peacebuilding for the Institute for Media, Policy and Civil Society, the Canadian Development Agency (IMPACS/CIDA), conducted assessment and training missions in Cambodia, Sri Lanka, Nepal, and Rwanda, and is author of a conflict-sensitive journalism handbook for International Media Support (Denmark).

Gerd Junne is a professor of international relations at the University of Amsterdam. His research focuses on the interaction between international political and economic relations, changes in the international division of labor, the role of multinational corporations, development problems, and the development potential of new technologies. He has carried out projects for the United Nations, FAO, ILO, the European Union, the VW Foundation, the Rathenau Institute, the German Parliament, as well as the Dutch Ministry of Foreign Affairs, Dutch Ministry of Transport, and Dutch National Research Program on Air Pollution and Climate Research. He teaches courses on peacekeeping and postconflict development. He is also one of the initiators of the Network University, which offers online courses on transforming civil conflict, gender and conflict transformation, youth transforming conflict, and postconflict development.

Bertine Kamphuis studied international relations and international economics at the University of Amsterdam. She has worked for the Dutch Ministry of Foreign Affairs and for the European Center for Conflict Prevention. Her research focuses on the politics of economic crisis and postconflict development.

S. Mansoob Murshed is an associate professor of development economics at the Institute of Social Studies, The Hague. Previously he worked with UNU/WIDER and the Universities of Bradford, Surrey, and Birmingham. He has published extensively on subjects relating to the economics of conflict, aid conditionality, political economy, macroeconomics, and international economics.

Mark Plunkett is a barrister-at-law in Brisbane, Australia, specializing in administrative law litigation. He has worked for the UN as a human rights officer in the Cambodia peacekeeping mission in the Khmer Rouge guerrilla zone and was appointed the first UN special prosecutor investigating war crimes, crimes of genocide, and major human rights violations in Cambodia. In 1995 he returned to Cambodia for AusAID to undertake a feasibility study for Australian aid to the Cambodian legal system. He has presented numerous papers and evidence to the Australian Parliament's Joint Standing Committee on Foreign Affairs and Defense on the reestablishment of the rule of law in postconflict peacekeeping.

Dirk Salomons is a managing partner of the Praxis Group, Ltd., an international management consulting firm that works mainly with public service entities, applying its expertise in humanitarian assistance, peacekeeping, and postconflict recovery as well as in human resources management. He also teaches international affairs at Columbia University's School of International and Public Affairs, as well as New York University's Wagner Graduate School of Public Service. He has served in many capacities with the United Nations system, including FAO, UNDP, UNAIDS, UNOPS, and the UN Secretariat, most notably executive director of ONUMOZ.

Vanessa van Schoor has worked with Médecins Sans Frontières since 1992 as a communications coordinator in Canada and the international office in Brussels, as well as on field assignments in Burundi, Liberia/Côte d'Ivoire, Mozambique, the Thai-Burma border, and most recently in East Timor, where she worked with the local administration and security services to prepare them for independence. She is currently working on an M.S. in medical anthropology at the University of Amsterdam.

Willemijn Verkoren conducts research on conflict resolution and management at the University of Amsterdam International School for Humanities and Social Sciences, where she is involved in setting up conflict studies programs.

Index

Acquired Immune Deficiency
  Syndrome (AIDS). *See* Human
  Immunodeficiency Virus
Ad Hoc Liaison Committee (AHLC),
  226, 241–242
Afghan Assistance Coordination
  Authority (AACA), 235, 242–243,
  246
Afghanistan: aid coordination, 236,
  242; bloat in public sector, 213;
  creation of national army, 32;
  criminal economy in, 21, 192,
  214–215; DDR in, 33, 239; development aid as political, 246; donor
  assistance to, 40, 223; donor control of aid programs, 243–244;
  education in, 234, 237; effectiveness of aid to, 237–239; elections,
  235; financial system, 216, 218,
  220; human development index
  rating, 224; infrastructure in,
  234–235, 238; land mines, 235;
  life expectancy in, 224, 234;
  National Development
  Framework, 235, 241, 243, 246;
  opiate production in, 192, 202,
  204, 205*box,* 236, 248*n24;* pledge
  gaps, 240–241; preliminary needs
  assessment for, 234–235; refugees
  in, 235, 237–238; weaponry's role
  in, 29
Afghanistan Interim Authority (AIA),
  235, 243–244

Afghanistan Interim Authority Fund
  (AIAF), 235, 238
Afghanistan Programming Body,
  236–237
Afghanistan Reconstruction Steering
  Group (ARSG), 234, 237
Afghanistan Reconstruction Trust
  Fund (ARTF), 226, 238
Afghanistan Support Group (ASG),
  236–237
Afghanistan Transitional Authority
  (ATA), 235–236, 238
Afghan NGOs Coordination Bureau,
  237
Agency Coordinating Body, 237
Agency for International
  Development (USAID), 18*n2,*
  199*box,* 253, 258–259, 268,
  271*n22*
Agency for Local Economic
  Development (ADEL), 264–266,
  272*n33*
Agent Orange, 167
Agricultural exports, 202, 204–
  205
Aid economies, 312–313
Aid-induced pacification, 243
Aid Management Agency (AMA),
  197
Ajello, Aldo, 275–276
Alden, Chris, 284
Al-Qaida, 21, 216, 243
Aluminum Mostar, 199*box*

355

About the Book

With the proliferation of civil wars since the end of the Cold War, many developing countries now exist in a "postconflict" environment, posing enormous development challenges for the societies affected, as well as for international actors. *Postconflict Development* addresses these challenges in a range of vital sectors—security, justice, economic policy, education, the media, agriculture, health, and the environment—in countries around the globe.

The authors focus on the need to move beyond emergency relief to create new social and economic structures that can serve as the foundations for a lasting peace. Prosperity, they acknowledge, does not guarantee peace; but a lack of economic development will almost certainly lead to renewed violence. This conviction informs their thorough discussion of the policy dilemmas confronted in postconflict situations and a range of concrete, successful approaches to resolving them.

Gerd Junne is professor of international relations at the University of Amsterdam and also director of The Network University (TNU). **Willemijn Verkoren** conducts research in the area of conflict resolution and management at the University of Amsterdam International School for Humanities and Social Sciences.